Contents

PAPERS RELATING TO ASPECTS OF PIAGETIAN STAGE
THEORY AND THE DEVELOPMENT OF LOGICAL ABILITIES

METHODOLOGICAL ISSUES IN INVESTIGATING MEANINGFUL
LEARNING

THE NATURE OF MATHEMATICAL LEARNING

STUDIES OF CONCEPTUAL DEVELOPMENT IN MATHEMATICS

STUDIES OF CONCEPTUAL DEVELOPMENT IN SCIENCE

Cognitive Development Research in SCIENCE and MATHEMATICS

Edited by   W. F. Archenhold
                R. H. Driver
                A. Orton
                C. Wood-Robinson

Proceedings of an International Seminar held in the
Centre for Studies in Science Education, School of Education,
University of Leeds

17–21 September 1979

Published   1980   The University of Leeds
Reprinted   1982

The Centre for Studies in Science Education,
School of Education,
The University of Leeds,
LEEDS LS2 9JT,
U.K.

Printed in the U.K. by the University of Leeds Printing Service

*Cover illustration 'Bond of Union' by M.C. Escher reproduced by
kind permission of the Escher Foundation, Haags Gemeentemuseum,
The Hague, Netherlands.*

ISBN   0   904421 07 4

STUDIES OF DESCRIPTIONS OF COGNITIVE STRUCTURES
THROUGH SEMANTIC NETWORKS

Introduction

During the last decade we have witnessed a growth in the literature concerning cognitive development and its relation to the learning
of science and mathematics. Much of the research has been prompted
following the period of curriculum innovation in science and mathematics which began in the 1960s.

There are now some important and fundamental questions to be
raised in relation to such research. For example, are there theoretical models of learning which can give some insight and guidance to
curriculum developers and teachers of science and mathematics? Is it
possible to isolate and define the problems for research such that the
progressively more sophisticated methodology being adopted by many
researchers may indeed lead to a clearer understanding of the complexity of the learning process?

The Editors of this publication have experience of research in
the field of cognitive development and like many others have faced
these questions individually. It seemed to us that the time was right
to provide an opportunity for researchers from various institutions in
the United Kingdom and overseas to meet together, exchange ideas and
so establish links between individuals and institutions working in
this field.

These were some of the underlying concerns in organising the
Seminar, which took place at the University of Leeds from 17-21 September 1979 and which was attended by seventy-two participants from
nineteen countries. This publication includes the papers presented
at the Seminar with reports of the discussions which took place over
a period of four days.

The programme was arranged around several main themes which moved
from the consideration of theoretical and methodological issues to
those relating to practical classroom concerns. For each main theme
a review paper was presented by an invited speaker and circulated to
participants prior to the Seminar. This was followed by a prepared
response and general discussion. Twenty-four short papers on current

research were also distributed and presented. Participants were able to display and discuss materials, test items, video recordings, etc. at 'poster sessions'.

Although there has been some regrouping of papers, the structure of this report follows the main themes of the Seminar. An informal meeting was held to consider cognitive development research in developing countries and a report of this meeting is included, together with a list of all the Seminar participants and their addresses. A composite list of references has been prepared and appears at the end of the report.

We gratefully acknowledge generous financial support from a number of organisations. We are particularly indebted to UNESCO for a substantial grant which not only helped to finance this publication but which also paid for a number of participants to travel to the Seminar. In this context we would particularly like to thank Mrs. Sheila Haggis for facilitating the grant and for her encouragement throughout our planning. We would also like to thank the British Council for generously contributing to the expenses of a number of participants from outside the United Kingdom.

We are appreciative of a donation from Unilever Education which paid for secretarial help during the Seminar and enabled us to provide the participants with copies of all the fifty or so papers being presented during the week.

The School of Education, University of Leeds, has helped by releasing funds which made it possible for us to go ahead with the publication of the proceedings. We would also like to thank the University itself for providing a venue for the Seminar and for its hospitality to the participants.

Many individuals contributed to the organisation of the Seminar and to the production of this publication. We are indebted to the participants themselves, many of whom wrote papers especially for the Seminar and some of whom took the chair during the working sessions. All of them contributed to both the formal and informal discussions and made our task an enjoyable one. In addition we appreciate the help of the following who acted as editors of the discussions which followed the papers: Philip Adey, Sally Brown, Dave Carter, John Head, Richard Hull, Cam McRobbie, Charles Reynolds, Terry Russell, Ken Tait, Geoff Wain and Patrick Whittle.

Mrs. Jennifer Ellison, Mrs. Kaye Hill, Mr. Geoffrey Mattock, Mrs. Maureen Pedder and Miss Dawn Squires helped in various ways with administration arrangements before and during the Seminar. Mr. Harry Tolson and his staff of the University of Leeds Printing Service saw the publication through the press. We are most grateful to all of them.

Lastly, we owe a special debt to two of our colleagues. Mrs. Angela Terry not only ran the Seminar office so efficiently and cheerfully, but also helped us and many of the participants in innumerable ways. Mrs. Kaye Hill took on the onerous task of preparing the typescript for publication. We thank them both very sincerely.

The University of Leeds

Fred Archenhold

Rosalind Driver

Tony Orton

March 1980

Colin Wood-Robinson

The Relevance of Cognitive Psychology to Science and Mathematics Education

KENNETH LOVELL

Introduction

In this paper I attempt to consider some of the work that has been accomplished in cognitive developmental psychology which bears on science and mathematics education, and then suggest that in the future we shall have to be concerned more with the details of the ways in which humans process data. It will be appreciated that only a limited amount of the relevant literature can be discussed.

But I begin by making three points. First, I confess to a general view I hold of humans in respect of their thinking. In short, human beings appear to me to be active, self-directing and self-monitoring agents who assign meanings to the tasks they encounter. These meanings will be influenced by the situations in which the tasks are met, while the meanings themselves will be crucial in determining how they respond (cf. Harré, Secord, 1972). True there is much argument over whether or not learning can occur without awareness and hence dispute over the laws of learning. But I believe that in respect of a good deal of human thinking, learning, and problem solving, the individual is as I have suggested. Indeed, early on the infant seems to vary his actions intentionally in order to see similarities and differences in the consequences that result. As the infant experiments with his world he distinguishes causes from correlations, and he shows clear evidence of goal directed behaviour from an early age.

Second, we shall be dealing largely with theories of cognitive development and not theories of instruction. While these two types of theory may be related they are not coincident. Moreover, it is important that when we are discussing developmental theories we remember their differing bases and the possible practical outcomes. This is especially true when dealing with teachers.

Third, I point out that the NIE-SRCD Conference (1978) concerned itself with future research on adolescent reasoning. That conference dealt with two major issues: first, theoretical frameworks to guide research programmes; second, the methodological tools to fit these

1

theories. In respect of the first issue it pointed out that Piagetian theory that had guided most preliminary research presents educators with such problems as transfer, task specific variance and instruction. While no real alternative theory has yet emerged, conference thought well of using neo-Piagetian theories, and an aptitude-treatment interaction approach. The present paper attempts to look at some of the cognitive developmental issues of concern to mathematics and science educators but from a somewhat wider perspective.

A comment on cognitive developmental theory

In cognitive developmental theory today there are two broad viewpoints. On the one hand there are those who work within the Piagetian or neo-Piagetian paradigms, and on the other those who may be broadly described as skill integrationists. The latter hold that the acquisition of a particular piece of knowledge is dependent on learning a set of skills which are then practised and coordinated to yield new combinations. More precisely we can say that skills are procedures used in specific situations. The integration of these skills involves the development of schemes to unite the various skill elements, an increasing generalisation to new situations, and at the same time a move to automation. Among this group of workers we find such names as Klahr and Wallace, Bruner, Gagné, to name but a few. True there are epistemological and other differences between the skill integrationists themselves, but not as great as or important as those between the skill integrationists and the orthodox Piagetians (cf. Easley, 1978; Rowell, Dawson, 1979). The differing outlook between the two groups can have important practical consequences in the classroom. For example, Piagetians would put far more emphasis on internal age-related restrictions on the pupils' ability to coordinate their thinking than the skill integrationist would. Indeed this question provides one of the major themes touched on in this paper. Attempts have, of course, been made to build bridges between these two viewpoints.

Many present at this Seminar will have been interested in the Piagetian paradigm. It must, of course, be appreciated that Genevan views on some issues have changed over the decades. For example, Piaget (1976) and Easley (1978) have outlined how the Genevans are now working out a theory relating children's ideas of conservation to category theory rather than as earlier to the structural ideas of the mathematicians Klein and Bourbaki. Likewise Piaget is increasingly interested in process rather than structure (cf. Piaget, 1977). It is necessary to say this for ofttimes it is forgotten that Piaget himself says that he is his own chief revisionist (Piaget, 1970). Elsewhere I have indicated (Lovell, 1979) those features of his system that may be long lasting. Here I will merely make two such points. First, it puts the focus on pupils thinking as shown by their explanations and justifications; second it gives recognition to the active construction of knowledge by each pupil (cf. De Vries, 1978; Karplus, 1978). The future of the stage concept is less certain.

2

The Genevans themselves realise some of the limitations of the concept for Karmiloff-Smith and Inhelder (1975) when indicating the value of operational structures point out that they do not suffice to explain all facets of cognitive behaviour. Further, Pascual-Leone (1978) makes a useful point when it is suggested that Piaget's model of stages and equilibration might be regarded as approximately descriptive structural models of the psychological system. However Pascual-Leone maintains that psychological theories must be process structural and the processes of equilibration must contain a clear representation of the step by step working of the developing system.

To be fair it must be said that Piaget (1975) has indicated that some of his earlier views on equilibration, or restructuring, were quite inadequate. He is now concerned to give an account of what he calls 'équilibration majorante' or the process whereby an 'upgraded' scheme is constructed as in the movements from preoperational to concrete operational thought, or from concrete to formal operational thought. Noelting (1978) made use of Piaget's phases of 'upgrading equilibration' and added to them. He tentatively claims that he may have produced a model for the passage from one stage to the next, and which holds across a number of concepts, namely, ratio, fraction, chance, and geometrical proportion. Research which bears on how humans process information, and the processes of development, are likely to come to the fore in the future. It should also be noted in the light of what follows in this paper, that the kind of experiment which Noelting used (cf. Noelting, 1976), held content constant so that perceptual variations in the tasks, or difficulties which arise from variations in familiarity with the problem, were eliminated.

Some aspects of cognitive developmental theories which bear on practical outcomes

I now wish to raise a number of issues that ultimately bear on classroom practice.

First, the advantage of the clinical approach, so ably developed by the Genevans, is that it enables us to explore the framework of ideas which children hold. Driver and Easley point out (quoted by Anderson et al., 1977) that whenever we attempt to introduce a topic to our pupils they come to it with a framework of ideas relating to it which they have derived from past experience. When they are faced with the statements of teachers or textbooks, or the result of their own investigations, not in keeping with the conceptual framework they hold, they either have to modify their own view or keep two separate systems. Alas, the two systems are sometimes never reconciled; some pupils using one to pass school examinations and one they use in everyday life. Likewise Karmiloff-Smith and Inhelder (op.cit.) provide developmental corroboration that a child does not easily relinquish a theory. And when they do they first prefer to create a new theory, quite independent of the first, before attempting to unify all events under a single, broader theory. However, if the framework held by the

3

pupil is consonant with the teaching to be incorporated we can immediately and more easily make use of the advice of Ausubel et al. (1978); namely, 'The most important single factor influencing learning is what the learner knows already; ascertain this and teach him accordingly.' But if the framework held is not consonant with the framework to be imbibed, teaching is a more difficult task although we must still 'teach him accordingly'. Both Case (1975) and Karmiloff-Smith and Inhelder (op.cit.) recommend in effect the use of critical alternatives, in the sense that pupils should be helped to discriminate the correct and incorrect responses and see the relationship between them.

Second, if we accept the Piagetian stage concept there is the question of whether the structural properties that define a given stage do indeed form an integrated whole as theory suggests (cf. Brown, Desforges, 1977). The completed elaboration of such structures could not, of course, be expected before the end of the developmental period. While there is some evidence that classificatory abilities sometimes lag behind relational abilities in the 5-7½ year age range (cf. Hooper, Sipple, 1975) the position remains unclear in the 9-12 age range. Hooper and Dihoff (1975) made both a review of the relevant literature and a thorough study of synchrony using Piaget-type tests in this age range and employed a number of statistical techniques to avoid possible criticism in respect of their methodology. They conclude that at present the notion of developmental synchrony cannot be abandoned even if the future reveals otherwise. Some support for a structural position at the concrete operational stage has, I understand, also been supplied by Tomlinson - Keasey et al. who found, in a longitudinal study, that the emerging skills of seriation, classification and conservation are related. However, the demonstrated relationships still require much interpretation.

At the level of formal operational thought, argument has certainly existed over the notion of structure d'ensemble. Lunzer (1978) was very critical of Piagetian theory at this point. More recently, however, Shayer (1978a, 1979) has indicated that there is at least some unity of the intellectual skills involved in formal operational thought using class versions of Inhelder's tasks - at least as far as the context of Physical Science is concerned. Indeed he asserts (Shayer, 1978a, p.194) that of those pupils assessed at Piagetian stage 3B on any one of five tasks,an average of less than 4% were assessed as non-formal on any one other task.

If synchrony does not obtain, at least over limited areas of the curriculum, then the pupil brings to the classroom a set of relatively independent and differentially developed set of intellectual skills at both the concrete operational stage (e.g. classification) and at the formal operational stage (e.g. proportional reasoning). These are used by the pupil when he is appropriately motivated by the task and appropriately cued into it. The last sentence, of course, holds true even if synchrony does obtain, but in this latter case there is a far

4

greater chance that the several skills comprising the <u>structure</u> <u>d'ensemble</u> will be activated if required.

Third, there is the problem of whether or not young children do have some capacity for using skills regarded as formal operational. It should, perhaps, be pointed out that some workers hold that it has not yet been definitively established what is meant by formal operations (cf. Kuhn, 1979). However, I agree with Kuhn that the reasoning strategies that fall under this heading are important for they have the potential for tackling the question of cognitive processes, for investigating real-world problems, and for providing a construct that enables us to look at individual differences in cognition. But until an acceptable definition is forthcoming it is rather difficult to ask if a 7 year-old or a middle-aged industrial worker has formal operations. However, sixty years ago Burt (1919) wrote, 'All the elementary mechanisms essential to formal reasoning are present before the child leaves the infants' department.'

Ennis (1976) too asks questions about children's ability to use logic, and proposed a three-dimensional model of logical competence embracing principles, content and complexity. He pointed out from his own evidence involving conditional logic that many pupils in the first three grades could handle transitivity, contraposition and inversion although performance on inversion was poorer than on the other two. There have, of course, been a number of studies such as those of Matalon (1962) and O'Brien (1972) which suggests limited progress in the use of inversion and conversion at least until adolescence. Kuhn (1977), however, found that conditional reasoning was within the competence of children in the first three grades when using simple concrete conversational situations, although conversion was the most difficult form. It looks then as if content and context affect the use of conditional logic as Luria found in his studies in Central Asia in the 1930s. But Kuhn did give evidence suggesting that non-formal-operational pupils have difficulty in interpreting empirical evidence so as to select an appropriate inductive inference from a set of logically possible alternatives. The topic of implication is an important one for science or other aspects of the curriculum when evidence has to be evaluated (cf. Kuhn, Brannock, 1977, in the context of science).

There are now many studies that have shown that ordinary pupils find metric proportionality difficult before adolescence, while Lovell and Shields (1967), also Webb (1974), showed that high I.Q. children (e.g. I.Q.140 or more) generally failed to solve problems involving formal operational thought at 10 years of age but were superior at solving concrete operational tasks found difficult by pupils of average I.Q. The work of Halford (1978a) - and especially so the work in respect of mathematics (Halford, 1978b) - certainly does suggest an age-related constraint on pupils' thinking. He has been concerned with showing how systems can be defined which produce the kinds of thought observed at the stages of cognitive development proposed by Piaget. Indeed, for Halford, information processing limitations determine, in effect, the upper limit of the complexity of thought systems which an individual can construct.

Of course the Genevans themselves have changed their views somewhat in respect of hypothesis making - another characteristic of formal operational thought. Inhelder and Piaget (1958) wrote, 'at the concrete level, the child does not formulate any hypotheses'. However, Karmiloff-Smith and Inhelder (op.cit.) now state that the above statement has to be reconsidered. In their work on the balancing of blocks they found that children in the age range 4½ to 9½ years do act under the guidance of a powerful theory-in-action, and this involves much more than mere observation of the data in front of them. But these same children cannot think up hypothetical situations which might confirm or refute a theory. So, argue these writers, we should not take a child's theory-in-action which is implicit in his behaviour as indicating that he can explicitly conceptualise what he is doing and why. This is in line with the findings of Piaget (1977) that there is a gap in time between being successful in action and being able to explain it.

Fourth, we know that the thinking a pupil displays is affected by the content and context of the task presented, the meaning it has for him, and his perception of the goal. This is not new. More than 50 years ago Wilkins (1928) suggested some of the content variables that appeared to influence conclusions in reasoning. Thus the problem of whether there are internal age-related limitations on thinking is confounded by the effect of content and so on as indicated above. Piaget's theory is not alone in being unable to handle these variables in a satisfactory manner. Halford's theory does not in itself get over the problem of the differential difficulty of varied tasks at each of his three levels of thought complexity although he suggests that task difficulty can be studied within the paradigm. For example it is suggested (Halford, 1978a, p.215) that varying the number of items to be learned should affect learning rate.

A short paper by Linn (1978) suggests a research line that needs following. She found that performance on two tasks ostensibly involving the separation of variables scheme (two balls rolling down a shute and being required to hit a target ball) varied according to the mode of presentation. In one presentation the subject must release the two balls provided from the same position; in the second the pupil is asked if he has enough information when the two balls are released from different positions but the actual release is concealed behind a screen. Field independent subjects were able to perform equally well under both presentations. Field dependent subjects did as well as the others in the first presentation but were poor at using the control of variables scheme when they had to analyse the results of an uncontrolled experiment. Thus Linn suggests that what is called cognitive style could be one influence affecting low correlations between formal reasoning tasks, for the use of the scheme seems only independent of cognitive style in certain contexts. While this line of research may be profitable this particular experiment is somewhat marred by having only one measurement of field dependence/independence for each subject.

In the theory of Pascual-Leone (1970), which defines developmental level in terms of capacity and not in terms of structures, it is again impossible to say exactly when and how the individual will use the M capacity he has. True, if a person is to use his M capacity to the full much will depend not only on his repertoire of schemes, including affective and cognitive style schemes, but also on the features of the particular situation or task being considered. In principle the theory of Pascual-Leone can provide a basis for making predictions in respect of a task, for it provides a way of accounting for the lag between the ability to construct the necessary cognitive system and the ability to apply it to the task. But in practice this is not as feasible as it first appears. I am not alone in suggesting that while the theory might add to our understanding it does not explain everything. Scardamalia (1977) working within Pascual-Leone's theory, points out that information processing load may vary among tasks that have the same logical structure. This load is represented by M capacity quantified as the maximum number of schemes that the individual must activate simultaneously through an attentional process in executing a task. Scardamalia experimentally produced décalages on combinational reasoning tasks in which the logical and perceptual task characteristics remained constant while the demands made by a number of variables (colour, shape, four different patterns) changed. She claimed that her evidence suggests that a task must be presented in a form that has the lowest possible M demand consistent with the logical structure of the task. Combinational tasks of increasing M demand could be executed to a certain point of demand. But with a task of more than one variable, most children failed when the M demand exceeded their M capacity. So here we have the passing of some tasks and the failing of others which have the same logical structure. But Scardamalia is careful to point out that other factors could contribute to asynchronous performances such as stimulus saliency or previous experience. At the same time she claims that the M construct does reduce the amount of unaccountable behaviour.

The problem of the differential meaning of tasks which demand the same logical structure is also one of great importance. Donaldson (1978) draws attention to the fact that the pre-school child can often reason within a supportive context of meaningful events. Thinking not so supported is often termed 'formal' although she coins the word 'disembedded' for this. The tasks set by Piaget, like many of the tasks set in school, are often disembedded since they are divorced from expectations, purposes and feelings. We should, of course, have been more aware of these matters since Luria's studies in Soviet Central Asia in the 1930s revealed them. To reinforce this I refer to the study of Markman and Siebert (1976). In essence this uses the distinction between classes and collections. These differ in a number of ways: for example, in the way in which membership is determined, and the nature of the whole part relationship involved. Most classification studies have involved the class model in which the concepts are defined in terms of the intensional aspect which involves the defining criteria of class, and in terms of the extensional aspect involving the instances that meet the criteria. Against this the relationship between objects is the general determining characteristic of collections. A grape is only a member of a bunch of grapes if there is a close spatial proximity between the grapes, whereas an object quite on its own is still regarded as a member of a class. Markman and Siebert showed that, using the same materials, children aged 5 and 6 years solved the class inclusion problem posed in a collection condition ('whether the one who owned the blue blocks, or the one who owned the pile of blocks would have more to play with') more easily than when the problem was posed in the class condition ('whether the one who owned the blue blocks or the one who owned the blocks would have more blocks to play with'). Collections are the meaningful psychological units for children, whereas classes are organised in the mind of the adult who imposes on the elements certain abstract categories.

It is these kinds of findings that led Johnson-Laird and Wason (1976) to question age-related restrictions on children's thinking. It may not be that pupils' thinking necessarily develops in logical power but rather that there may be a progressive extension of the kinds of content to which processes can be applied (Johnson-Laird, Wason, 1976, p.179). Likewise Rozin (1976) argues, from different evidence, for the evolution of general purpose intelligence. The basic computational systems required to perform certain feats of reasoning may be at work at first in restricted domains - presumably because these systems were evolved for specific purposes. Later there must be a more general access to these computational systems that originally served specific purposes.

But it must be said that there is now much evidence suggesting that the verbal and cognitive processing of the home and the demands of the culture pattern make it easier or harder to use reasoning in formal 'disembedded' situations as compared with 'embedded' situations (cf. Glick, 1969; Cole, Scribner, 1974; Luria, 1976; Goodnow, 1976; Lovell, 1977). It is difficult otherwise to explain how Kalahari Bushmen can use hypothetic-deductive thinking in relation to animal tracking (Tulkin, Konner, 1973) and yet be unable to use the same skill in solving a simple physics problem in the laboratory until there had been much experience of formal physics.

Finally in this section of my paper I refer to the work of Siegler (1978). Using the Piagetian balance experiment he wrote particular rule models as characterisations of children's knowledge about the balance scale. These rule models were successful in predicting both children's (5 to 17 years of age) spontaneous performance on the balance and their performance after instruction. His results are close to those of a number of other workers who have found that while some pupils in their mid and late teens cannot solve formal scientific problems spontaneously, much younger children can often _learn_ to solve them. But Siegler is clear that this does not mean that ability to learn is independent of chronological age, since various treatments benefit different aged pupils to different degrees. Moreover, in the same paper he describes, from his further experimental evidence, the move from the tendency to use a non-rule governed approach to scientific thinking in the 3-5 age range, to the increasing sophisticated rules from 5 years to adulthood. Improved encoding in the sense of greater accuracy and completeness seems to be an important factor influencing this move.

A comment on the skill-integrationist position

The skill-integrationist would presumably accept that content-free mental structures do not exist and that it would be more useful to find cognitive structures within particular areas of content.

Gagné's (1970) theory of learning, at least till 1970, is perhaps the best known example of the skill-integrationist approach. The teacher judges which subskills the pupil must possess before he can proceed to more complex ones. These subskills can be organised into a hierarchy of skills, so that the learner moves from where he is at present to the end objective through a number of steps which were determined by the task analysis. Unfortunately as Case (1975) points out, Gagné's theory takes no account of the intellectual growth of children. It might well work with individuals who possess the cognitive skills indicated by Piaget's stage of formal operational thought, for although Gagné's model takes account of the logical analysis of the task it does not take account of the intellectual demands of the subskills.

Schaeffer et al. (1974), in the context of number conservation, looked at the order in which certain tasks were successfully completed by pupils, and found that the tasks could be organised into a skill hierarchy. Indeed, three major subskills were claimed which when integrated yielded number conservation. These major skills could, in turn, be defined in terms of more simple subskills. Schaeffer made no claim that this particular skill hierarchy described behaviour outside of number conservation, but it was claimed that the skill hierarchy arose out of specific experiences. While we are not concerned here to comment on how useful Schaeffer's work is in the context of number conservation, it must be acknowledged that it is an attempt to substitute a pupil analysis for a teacher analysis. Moreover, Case (1975) also suggests that the structure of a task to be learned should always be analysed from the learner's viewpoint. The natural units into which the pupil analyses the task should be considered along with the units into which the teacher might analyse it. If there is a mismatch then the teaching sequence may have to be changed.

It seems then that the question of age-related restrictions on thinking is not a serious one for Gagné to 1970. Schaeffer, also Klahr and Wallace (1976) support this view implicitly. Case looks upon the theory of Pascual-Leone as building a bridge between Gagné and Piaget in the sense that it combines a task analysis with the notion of stages in terms of age-related changes in information processing capacity.

To this point I have raised a number of issues which have outcomes in the classroom. These are: the value of the clinical approach; the question of developmental synchrony in Piaget's theory; whether or not there are age-related restrictions on the organisation of thinking; and the problem of the effect on the pupils' thinking of the content of a task, its context, its meaning for them and their perception of the goal; and the fact that pupils can sometimes learn to solve scientific problems at an earlier age than was thought. My own interpretation of the relevant evidence, of which only a selection could be given here, is that there remains some degree of age-related constraint on the organisation of thinking after 2 years of age when the individual begins to act intelligently with respect to inner symbolised activity, but that the problem is confounded both by the content/context/meaning-dependency of thought and by the knowledge already held by the pupil. Whether this dependency on content and meaning is better thought of in terms of general cognitive limitations or in terms of factors more specific to the problem remains to be determined.

The processing of data

I have already suggested that the future is likely to be increasingly concerned with the precise details as to how humans process data rather than concentrating on the structure of thinking as such. Indeed, it is hoped that through studies of processing a better idea of how cognitive structures develop and function will be obtained.

It is not my intention, however, to discuss what are known as information processing models that have been elaborated to date. These can be roughly and imperfectly divided into those that try to mimic - as far as the experimenter can - the step by step process through which the individual goes, or simulation models, and those whose purpose it is to perform a complete task independently of how humans do it (Artificial Intelligence models). All information processing approaches are concerned with a detailing of the processes involved in reasoning and concept formation, a detailing that a theory such as that of Piaget lacks. At present these models are of limited value to the educator, for the micro-processes are difficult and time consuming to tease out and we have very little experience of teaching these processes. But it is an important and growing area of research and those interested should consult Klahr and Siegler (1978) or Siegler (1978).

Instead we shall be looking at important issues that affect
processing: for example, how memory functions, how knowledge is
represented in the memory store, the importance of the depth of
processing, and the question of age-related restrictions on processing capacity.

Memory

I begin with a few general words about memory. Today I believe
we are becoming more concerned with the function of memory rather than
with types, so I shall only mention but not stress the latter. Thinking, remembering, perceiving are all very much intertwined with one
another in real time cognitive functioning, so memory cannot now be
thought of as a distinct and autonomous cognitive process as it sometimes was.

Thinking requires the individual to construct a system of intern-
nal symbolic processes, and in the view of Piaget and Inhelder (1973),
memories are integrally tied to the child's operative schemes. Group
analyses are generally compatible with the Genevan operative theory of
memory in the sense that the ways in which children remember stimuli
parallel age changes in operative schemes. Within-subject data also
give limited support for the Genevan view but a detailed examination
of the memorial performance of particular individuals over time reveals
inconsistencies (Lieben, 1977).   While the situation is more complex
than Piaget and Inhelder suggest, it does appear that knowledge which
is retained in memory and time undergoes progressive and continuous
change from the moment it is first apprehended. So we should regard
memory as part of a continuously changing representation of the individual's world. The current notions of long and short term memory
are, of course, hypothetical constructs that share the primary res-
ponsbility for the representation and storage of information.

Thus there is now increasing interest in the cognitive activities
that generate the outcomes of our memory. We have already mentioned
the Genevan operative theory of memory in which memory in the strict
sense is distinguished from memory in the wider sense where the individual 'conserves' in memory his previously acquired cognitive schemes.
This is a distinction somewhat similar to that of Tulving's episodic
and semantic memory or more or less permanent and temporal-contextual
memory. It is increasingly becoming evident, however, that even the
development of memory in a narrow or episodic sense cannot be grasped
without considering a person's entire knowledge structure. Indeed,
memory in the wider sense greatly influences what he stores - or in
what sense he assimilates - and what he retrieves from storage or
memory in the stricter sense. This is now well illustrated by the
differing abilities of master and amateur chess players. If pieces
are arranged randomly on the board the latter do as well as the former
players in remembering the positions of the pieces. But if the pieces
are arranged in positions which could properly occur in a game the
ability of the masters to remember the positions is far greater (Chase,

Simon, 1973). That sheer knowledge is important in relation to memory development is also illustrated by Chi (1978). She showed that 10 year-olds who were knowledgeable about chess outperformed, memorially, mildly knowledgeable adults when dealing with chess configurations, although the adults showed the usual superiority on digit span tests.

Another line of research has dealt with constructive and reconstructive memory (cf. Paris, Lindauer, 1977). There is a parallel here with the Genevan views in the sense that the former memory reflects what is stored and the latter what is retrieved. This work argues that what we remember are the meaningful and organised events and information. In other words what we remember is an organised representation of the gist of the matter. Similarly retrieval is thought of as an active process of reconstruction rather than an exact copy of what is stored in memory. Hence in reconstruction there is much putting together of ideas, logical inference, and sometimes plain guessing. Indeed in storing, processing and retrieving information there is much interpretation and inference making. Children, too, construct and reconstruct memory in this fashion and there is now evidence of developmental changes with age in this connection.

However, in connection with the inference making and guessing in retrieval, mention must be made of the work of Frederiksen (1975). He pointed out, as is well known, that responses to semantic information acquired through discourse, contain errors. But his study suggests that these reflect processes of adjustment during the acquisition or storage stage, and not in processes occurring during retrieval although the errors are made explicit at retrieval. If these results are confirmed across many and varied texts, it would suggest that a large part of the semantic structure which individuals build from a presented text is derived from, but is not a true reflection of, the text. Furthermore, repeated exposures to the text do not eliminate the derived structure; rather it becomes an integral part of the understanding of the text.

Finally in this section on memory, mention must be made of the strategies, or the potentially conscious activities, that the individual may employ for various mnemonic ends. Much work has now been done on these storage strategies. There are the many varieties of rehearsal strategies: the data to be stored can be organised or categorised; and closely related to categorisation is elaboration where there is the recognition of a shared meaning between a number of things to be remembered. It would also be broadly true to say that the older the pupil the less prompting or outside help is needed to employ these strategies. Much less is known about retrieval strategies than about storage strategies but we do know that during the early years at school pupils do acquire the skills to perform a systematic memory search, and in addition the ability to judge the acceptability of the recovered information (Kobasigawa, 1977). Unfortunately, however, much strategy research has involved relatively meaningless isolated items and studies using meaningful organised bodies of information are greatly needed. Strategy research will grow and educators must take note of this. Brown and De Loach (1978), after reviewing much current research on memory development, conclude that the pupil's increasing sensitivity to the interface between task and strategy is largely due to the thinker's increasing knowledge, control, and coordination of his own cognitions, that is, his metacognitive insights.

The representation of knowledge in memory

The brief discussion on memory was necessary to see this section in better perspective. Let us now consider how knowledge of the everyday world or specialised knowledge is organised. We are thus concerned more directly with the representation of meaning, and with how knowledge is stored, cross-referenced and indexed, and we need to know how knowledge is represented whether it be presented verbally, visually or symbolically. In one sense this semantic memory is personal since the knowledge and experience of each individual is different, although at the same time there must be a common core of culturally shared experience. But the semantic organisation is important since it is both a powerful and pervasive determinant of performance on mental tasks. The way we arrange knowledge determines how we speak and understand, how we remember and how we solve problems; for example, whether we tend to elaborate functionally related concepts or categorical ones. At the same time there are great methodological problems in studying semantic memory.

Many studies have shown that individuals have strong spontaneous tendencies to organise verbal items into categories and sub-categories and to use these imposed groupings to improve recall. Here we have a strategy, already referred to,which is used spontaneously. A number of models of semantic memory (cf. Cohen, 1977) have been proposed, e.g. a network model, although it is not our purpose to pursue these here. The intention is to emphasise the importance of how knowledge is represented in memory. None of the models proposed at present are adequate and far more complex models will be required. Mathematics and science educators will have to follow developments here.

We must also mention briefly the possible role of visual imagery in relation to the representation of knowledge although it is not my intention to discuss its nature. Visual imagery seems to provide a useful means of representing one's knowledge, and as a way of maintaining information in memory. Many experiments have purported to show that visual imagery facilitates recall as, for example, when instructions are given to subjects to try to form images as they attempt to memorise. The paper by Erdelyi and Finkelstein (1976) presents strong evidence that when, as a result of instructions, words are recoded into images, recall increases over time and resembles in other respects the recall of pictures. This is of relevance for the teacher in that it suggests that whenever information can be encoded as a visual image it should be.

The literature on the role of visual imagery in representing the conditions in problem solving is fascinating, even if much is anecdotal. Nor has all the experimental work been rigorous. Shepard (1978) has reviewed some of the anecdotal literature: for example, the role of visual imagery in the origins of the theory and applications of electromagnetic fields; in the work of Faraday, Maxwell, Einstein. Indeed Einstein is said to have stated explicitly that he very rarely thought in words, nor did his particular ability lie in mathematical calculation, but rather in visualising effects, consequences and possibilities. Likewise visual imagery according to Shepard may well have been demanded in the development of the theory and biological applications of molecular structures. As for experimental work there seems to be some confirmation of Huttenlocher's (1968) study that visual imagery is used in the solution of logical problems such as linear syllogisms. Yet, whether the data are experimental or anecdotal, some people claim that they use no visual imagery. This suggests that only some people use such imagery, or that those who do use it only as an optional extra and not as a medium of thought. Nevertheless, until we have more information, mathematics and science educators run the risk of missing something of importance for some pupils, if they assume that visual imagery is of no importance in problem solving.

The value of visual imagery in recognition is better established. For example, visual patterns too complex to verbalise can be recognised after a delay, suggesting that recognition can be a process of matching a represented stimulus to a stored image. Even if we accept Pylyshyn's view that patterns are stored as abstract descriptions, the fact that humans have an almost unlimited recognition memory for pictures would suggest visual stimuli stored as abstract representations have special characteristics not shared by memory representations stored by verbal inputs. Here again is a research area that will demand the educator's attention.

I conclude this section with a reference to the work of Simon and Simon (1978) as it reflects the importance of representation in memory. They had two students solve problems in kinematics. One subject had a good mathematical background and much experience of solving these kinds of problems; the other had done a single course in Physics early on, and had an adequate but not particularly strong background in algebra. The problems were worked under 'thinking aloud' instructions, but paper and pencil were freely used, and reference could be made to a text for formulae. From an analysis of the student behaviours and performances, the experience of the one showed up as both difference in the variety of skills used and in difference in confidence. But the authors suggest that what engineers and physicists sometimes call 'physical intuition' seems an even more important difference. By this term they mean the ability to construct a clear representation of the situation in memory, that is, one that represents explicitly the main connections of the components of the situation. The more experienced student first translated the English prose of the problem statements into physical representations which were then used to select and render concrete the appropriate equations.

The depth of processing

We are also concerned with the depth of level of processing, that is, the degree of meaningfulness extracted from the data. Eysenck (1978) points out that there is now a vital distinction between the stimulus as presented and the stimulus as encoded. In his paper he reviews much of the literature germane to this topic, and one can see the shift from situational stimuli to internal events and processes. According to Craig (1973) it is the extent of the meaningfulness extracted that defines depth. He required his subjects to answer questions involving a shallow level of processing (e.g. Is the word in capital letters?) or at a deeper level (e.g. Is the word a member of the following category - ?). Deeply encoded words were better remembered than shallowly encoded ones, while the common result that semantic encodings are better remembered than phonemic encodings is consistent with this general view. Depth then refers not to more of the same, not to trace strength, but to qualitatively different encodings.

Kleine and Saltz (1976) demonstrated the importance of spread and elaboration of encoding. Their subjects were required to rate nouns in terms of semantic attribute dimensions. Recall was superior when words were rated on two semantic dimensions (e.g. hot/cold and big/ little) than when rated on a single dimension. Moreover, recall was even higher when the two dimensions were independent as in the example given than when the dimensions were related. Note, however, that the terms spread or elaboration lack operational definitions. Again, although psychologists have used several techniques for ascertaining the nature of the encoding process of individuals, according to Eysenck (1978) there is, with the exception of the coarse dichotomy between physical and semantic analyses, no operational definition of processing depth available. But research will, no doubt, attempt to establish if, for example, verbally presented material is encoded along such dimensions as mere verbal rule, semantic reconstruction, relational processing. Nevertheless there is reasonable evidence that deep levels of processing produce greater retentivity than shallow levels. Deeper levels of processing presumably enable the individual to make more use of past knowledge and learned rules. Further, there is now evidence that the effectiveness of a given retrieval cue depends on the depth of processing. But we must take note that it is not only depth of processing that affects memory performance, but the amount of processing at any given level as well.

The problem of processing capacity

The third issue is that of processing capacity. One viewpoint is that there is no such thing as a fixed processing capacity and that it is naive to suggest that a pupil can only handle a fixed number of chunks or units at a given age. As we have already seen, memory is influenced by the growth of various strategies such as various forms of rehearsal, organisation or clustering, and other mnemonic devices.

Trabasso (1977) gives one position held by cognitive psychologists in respect of information processing using Burt's now famous item:-

> Edith is fairer than Susan
> Edith is darker than Lily
> Who is the darkest?

Brushing aside the psychometric interpretation and the Piagetian view, Trabasso points out that the psychologist interested in information processing is concerned with the way the pupil encoded the information, how he interpreted the premises semantically, and how he represented the interpretation internally. Of central concern is the fact that the pupil constructed a representation of the task and operated on the representation to draw an inference.

Reviewing his own work and that of others on transitive problems, Trabasso argues that one finds elements of logic, memory, and language in making transitive inferences. Memory is certainly involved since such tasks demand the coding of relationships, holding them in working memory, integrating the members from the end inwards, and coming up with a representation of the information in the task that contained the original premises. But language is also involved in interpreting the premises semantically and in coding, while the decision rules are logical in nature. He concluded that the median age at which pupils may pass the item which he discusses may range from 4 to 11 years of age depending on how we structure the task.

Such studies and viewpoints have been criticised especially from the Piagetian viewpoint. But Trabasso defends his views against these attacks and concludes in the paper quoted that the age performance correlation disappears if one makes sure the child understands what is expected of him, and he can remember the information critical to making inferences.

Turning to a contrary viewpoint, we note that there is now much evidence that short term memory has a limited representational capacity even in the most proficient of learners, with its working limits more severe in younger children. Thus, unless circumvented, these limits can prevent successful performance on any intellectual task that demands more momentary representation than short term memory can sustain. A great deal of information given orally can overtax short term memory, as can some problem solving tasks where the pupil has to hold in store some information while simultaneously processing other data. Rohwer and Dempster (1978) indicate examples of the tailoring of instructional presentation to the learner's capabilities. They also suggest a second approach which 'attempts to prompt or modify the learner' in some way 'so that his functional representational capacity, relative to nominal units, increases to match the more strenuous task demands.

The methods used in the second approach include improved grouping, in which the form of the presentation arranges for the data to be chunked, and encouraging pupils to use a particular grouping strategy. In both instances we are back to organisation of data so that the teacher might arrange and present data which encourages the use of organisational processes or enable the pupil to discover and use particular organisational strategies.

Halford (1978a) is clearly one of those who tends to the view that there are clear limits to what a pupil can learn at a particular point in time independent of the amount of experience or training given. While admitting that recall may be a function of strategy and of capacity he is doubtful if recall can be wholly reduced to strategy. Indeed he quotes Huttenlocher and Burke (1976) who have concluded that growth in memory span with age cannot be explained by strategies since the latter are lacking in digit span performance. While considering that at a given point in development there is an upper limit to the number of chunks that can be stored, he admits that in some instances the chunk size can be changed.

Conclusion

In this paper I have ranged far and wide. From the first part I concluded that there is a degree of age-related constraint on children's thinking but that the problem is compounded by the content of a task, its context, its meaning for the child and his perception of the goal. Kuhn once commented something as follows: 'It would be remarkable if when told, "Those who live in China eat rice", 10 year-olds believed that those who did not live in China never ate rice.' Their own experience would tell them otherwise. Yet these same pupils may well be incorrect on the corresponding form in Matalon's Green-light, Red-light problem. The latter problem may be less embedded, to use Donaldson's term, or one in which extralogical factors operate such as the two lights being connected in circuit.

In the second part I have tried to show a little of what we know about the ways in which individuals process data and to reflect the way that related research is likely to go in the future. There will be continuing studies which bear on the functioning of memory, the representation of knowledge in memory, depth of processing and processing capacity. Human information processing is, as Lindsay and Norman (1976) remind us, both data driven and conceptually driven. The data driven processing starts with signals or sensory input data and ends with interpretation and meaning structures. Here we have so to speak a 'bottom up' analysis. But some phenomena require information about the items involved before recognition and interpretation can take place. Our memory system supplies just the kind of information needed for it contains records of past experiences, general knowledge about the organisation of ongoing experiences, knowledge of language

17

structure and so forth. These expectations and conceptualisations from memory play an important role for they combine with the information from the sensory analysis. So data processing also involves 'top down' or conceptually driven processing. As I said at the beginning of this paper these expectations and conceptualisations in memory may be incorrect or partially correct and they may confound the conceptual framework which current teaching is attempting to get the pupil to develop. This is very frequently found in science and indeed in all other areas of the curriculum.

Finally let me say again that the studies discussed in the second part of the paper will, it is hoped, throw light on how cognitive structures develop, and how they function in different contents and contexts.

Discussion

The general point was made, and accepted by the speaker, that the thrust of the paper had been from the Piagetian view of process, and that other perspectives of knowledge representation had been largely neglected. It was pointed out that the summary term for a new qualitative subject/object relationship in the process of intellectual development, 'stage', may equally be applied to language, mental imagery, or moral judgement, as well as knowledge. The speaker suggested that any attack on, or defence of, the Piagetian model should focus on its epistemological basis, rather than at the more surface level of the 'stage' theory.

This issue was not taken up at length, but one view advocating an alternative approach was presented, in which the development of knowledge throughout the history of civilisation is seen as the formulation of a number of disciplines each with its own framework of unique concepts, overlapping at some points. From this epistemological viewpoint, these disciplines are transmitted to children in schools (influenced in the west by television, and elsewhere by the impact of cross-cultural translation), and as the child becomes older, his mental models approach more closely those of the discipline. The reason children think like Aristotle was not that Aristotle had not reached the formal stage, but that Aristotle did not have the 2000 years of conceptual evolution that we have.

A number of questions emerged from the discussion of Noelting's work. Firstly, to what extent can one make generalisable statements about the phases children pass through on the basis of observations of only one task? Secondly, have responses similar to those of the ratio task been obtained when other tasks relating to division, geometry and fractions were undertaken? Thirdly, to what extent can Noelting's descriptions of functioning at different levels be used to make inferences about how pupils progress from one level to the next? Fourthly, is Noelting's description too unsophisticated to represent development in general ways of thinking? Fifthly, how will Piagetians respond to evidence of 10 or 12 steps (each strategy embedded in the later one) in acquisition of the ratio concept? Sixthly, what are the logical structures identifiable in understanding the ratio problem?

With regard to the last of these questions, it was pointed out that the logical structures postulated by the logician to explain the relationships he observes may differ markedly from the actual logical structures of the child. We can only speculate on individuals' thought structures at present, and there is no evidence yet to support the Piagetian viewpoint that an understanding of ratio implies propositional logic, nor that proportionality implies the application of second order relations.

The distinction between, on the one hand, the Genevan school, and on the other hand, Gagné and Bruner's approach to epistemology were discussed in relation to age-related constraints. It was asked to what extent the Piagetian and skill-integrationist strands of the paper were complementary or contradictory, and to what extent there was differing evidence for one, or the other.

Among the problems encountered in observing stages of pupil development in real classrooms were mentioned: the context of the study, the perception of goals, and the social atmosphere. The speaker drew attention to the ambiguous way in which the word 'stage' is sometimes loosely used to cover two interpretations, i.e. (i) Piagetian stages, and (ii) the stages a child goes through in comprehending and mastering a particular concept.

The possibility of predicting the likely difficulty of a given topic for a particular pupil was raised, with reference to either the Pascual-Leone short-term memory model (increasing capacity with age) or the Case model (improved processing with time), but it was suggested that no such estimate could be made without pretesting, or even the prior history of the child. The Pascual-Leone approach seems to make some advance on Piaget in the application of cognitive research to practical problems, with more potential for inference of levels of difficulty, and acceleration studies. The view was expressed that recent work using this approach had foundered on attempts to identify individuals' schemes in solving tasks; children learn different metacognitive skills, and the analysis of their concept of the tasks has always been approached from the expert's conception rather than that of the child.

A discussion of the kind of mode of representation to be used suggested that 'support' for the child's thinking could be provided in a non-verbal graphic mode, or a symbolic mode; any mode might be expected to help 'squeeze' some children, but not others.

Questions were then asked about the value of the Piagetian approach to research in science education, the appropriate work to be done in this area, and justifications for the explanations of learning and the restrictions imposed on learning by followers of Piaget. The speaker re-emphasised Piaget's contribution to clinical methods, alternative conceptual frameworks and innumerable insights into pupils' thinking; he felt that newer alternative approaches could, at present, only be applied to science education by trained psychologists rather than classroom teachers. Nevertheless work such as that of the C.S.M.S. group is valuable in revealing the complexity of the issues and group performance levels, even if it provides no insights into the thinking of the individual child.

The final discussion centred on alternative approaches to the study of pupils' learning in science, making use of information theory and modes of learning which cannot be described at all in Piaget's theoretical framework. It was, however, pointed out that information processing models cannot achieve what a Piagetian approach can in some areas (e.g. examination of the history of the growth of science) because the two types of theory do not set out to ask the same questions. Despite the difficulty of describing complex knowledge systems, it was felt that this is what is needed at the present time; a case-study approach was advocated, in which the focus is on fine detail, in order to identify growth features in the evolution of cognitive schemes. Cognitive psychology will be of practical value to the science teacher once coherent educational research is mounted with clearly identified aims, an unambiguous vocabulary, and a clearly formulated method of representation.

This opening presentation, with its emphasis on the Piagetian approach, set the scene for the papers and discussions of the early part of the week. There emerged, however, a wide variety of questions that opened up issues to be explored during the following days and that promised support for alternative theoretical models relevant to science and mathematics education.

A Report of the Concepts
in Secondary Mathematics and Science Project

INTRODUCTION TO C.S.M.S.

P.J. Black

Introduction

The purpose of this paper is to give a brief introduction to the project on Concepts in Secondary Mathematics and Science (C.S.M.S.) which has been in progress at Chelsea since 1974. The main papers by Drs. Hart and Shayer, will be preceded by short papers concerned with the test materials. My purpose is to give a brief introduction to their papers and to emphasise a few points which should be borne in mind when appraising the test materials.

It is best to consider the science and mathematics parts of the work separately, because there are sharp differences, in approach, rationale and methodology, between them. There is a third part, concerned with personality development, which also requires separate discussion.

Science

The research in science had its origins in work by Michael Shayer, who, by applying to science teaching schemes an analysis based on Piagetian stages, established a prima facie case for further investigation. The essence of this case was that at many points these curricula might be making demands which would be beyond the powers of many of the target age groups.

In order to investigate he had first to set up test instruments. These are called class tasks. Each is derived by copying very closely tasks described by Piaget, but adapting these so they can be given to a group who respond on paper. The test administrator, often the group's normal teacher, is given detailed briefing; he presents experimental demonstrations to the group and asks them to answer questions about them. The questions are conveyed verbally, but are repeated on the sheet provided for the answers, which are all written. Many of the questions start with a fixed response, but pupils are then asked to explain their reasons for their choices and the marking depends on the reasons offered. Pupils are encouraged to ask questions to make sure they understand what they are being asked to do and administrators are encouraged to repeat or vary the explanations until pupils are satisfied. Only in this limited sense are the tests interactive. The tests have been validated by various means, including individual interviews with children to check interview results against class-task results. Dr. Adey's paper gives a detailed account of one of the tasks.

The critical question about these tasks is not whether they are ideal, or as effective as individual interviewing, which they cannot be for all purposes, but whether they are adequate to the purposes for which they have been used.

The first use has been to obtain information on a large sample of the school population in England between the ages of 10 and 15. The second use has been to assess the learning of selected school classes to see whether their success or failure with particular teaching material can confirm predictions made by combining task results on stages of cognitive development with a priori analysis of the demands of the material to be learnt. The third use has been for detailed analysis of inter-task correlations using six separate tasks. The fourth could be for teachers to assess the general level and spread amongst their own teaching groups. In all of these uses, it has been neither required nor proposed that the tasks be used for making individual decisions about pupils.

The possibility that performance on tasks is dependent on prior experience of their particular content needs attention. Piaget chose his tasks to be independent of teaching experience for his subject and any for which this did not appear equally likely for English pupils were not considered.

The science results do not of themselves lead directly to a theory or practice of instruction. They provide a constraint on any practice and the issue to be debated here is whether they are to be a strong constraint (anything demanding a stage beyond that of the population at the given age automatically excluded) or a light one (here is some of the evidence we need about where pupils are and what they might find hard to achieve).

Mathematics

The guiding idea for this work has been rather different from that of the science. The aim was to draw up a scheme of elements of the understanding of mathematics which would be recognisable to and acceptable to practising teachers, then to test the various components of this in order that intercorrelations, facilities and changes with age in the 11-16 year old range could be determined empirically. The tests were aimed at understanding, giving emphasis to problem solving for simple (usually single-stage) problems involving transfer of learning and simple translation skills; mechanical manipulation of symbols was avoided and in general, the ability to use special mathematical rules or conventions was not tested. A short account of one of these tasks is given in the paper by Dietmar Küchemann.

The tests were thus structured according to perceptions of the structure of mathematics teaching shared between teachers, not (directly) by any model of cognitive development or any theory of instruction. This is both a strength and a weakness of the work: the empirical results indicate a map of performance of the school samples which raises questions both for theory (what models of learning can account for this?) and for practice (what shall we do given these results?). At the same time the tests, with the analysed results, form research tools which are already being used by other research groups.

The mathematics results thus raise different issues from those of the science work. They could assist more directly to restructure teaching by indicating sequences to follow or topics that might be promoted or deferred at a given age. Here again, there is room for debate about how strong a constraint any results on what pupils achieve at present, and on an average over many schools, ought to be. However, it must be commented here that, hitherto, the expectations of teachers and others on what pupils should be able to achieve at various ages have been based on hardly any systematic evidence about their success or failure.

The results also raise questions about theoretical models which are of a quite different kind - for example, the relationship of the empirical levels found within the various areas of mathematics to data on Piagetian stages remains to be explored.

There is also need to link the results to work on the practice of science teaching: science teachers often make assumptions about the mathematical understanding that children can achieve, and these could well be checked against evidence. Whether the link has to be made at an empirical level or by way of a single model of development appropriate to both areas is a matter for discussion.

Personality development

From the outset of the C.S.M.S. programme it was held that it would be unsatisfactory, even dangerous, to investigate learning and provide results useful for curriculum design on the basis of work limited to cognitive development alone. A limited research could not of course study all other factors. Adolescent personality seemed to be the most rewarding and important field for an exploratory and parallel study. If a developmental model could be found here then a combination of its methods with those on the cognitive could be a significant step towards a broader approach to the understanding of how children learn. In addition, much work on 'attitudes' to science seemed both to lack adequate reference to adolescent development as a whole, and yet to be yielding results which needed to be understood. The first results of the work in this area is described in the short paper by John Head.

THE DEVELOPMENT OF A SCIENCE REASONING TASK

Philip Adey

In this paper I intend to cover only some of the technical aspects of the process of developing C.S.M.S. Science Reasoning Tasks (SRTs). A fuller account, including many of the uses of the tasks, is given in Shayer, Adey and Wylam (1979).

Our aim was to produce reliable, valid, instruments which could be used to assess the levels of cognitive development, in Piagetian terms, of thirty or more pupils at the same time. Furthermore, it was intended that the tasks (a word preferred to 'tests' for these instruments) should

- yield a Piagetian level directly, not via a raw score of number of correct items;

- be usable by science teachers who are not specialists in test administration;

- keep demands on verbal fluency (written or oral) to a minimum;

- not make unreasonable demands on laboratory or apparatus provision.

Previously, attempts at writing group tasks of cognitive develop- ment have relied either on each pupil having his own apparatus (which violates the last of our criteria above) or on paper-and-pencil tests. Now an essential part of the assessment of a child's level of thinking is observation of his interaction with apparatus. A test in which the

subject receives no feedback from experimental evidence seems most unlikely to provide a valid group parallel to the clinical interview
developed by Inhelder and Piaget. For this reason, the demonstration
of apparatus in action plays an essential part in the administration
of a Science Reasoning Task.

SRTs are derived from tasks described by Piaget and Inhelder
(1956, 1974) and by Inhelder and Piaget (1958, 1964). The process of
development involves:

1. selecting from the tasks devised by Piaget et al. those which
   cover the range of stages to be studied, and which seem most
   likely to be transposable to a group situation;

2. writing test items from questions reported by Piaget and Inhelder
   in their interview tasks, together with appropriate instructions
   for administration;

3. ascribing developmental stages to each possible reply to each
   item, following Piagetian protocols. In practice, almost all
   items test the attainment of just one level or sub-level and a
   complete task must include items covering a suitable range of
   stages. Four to six items are generally prepared for each of
   the levels in the range that the task is to cover;

4. devising an overall marking scheme by which a level may be
   ascribed to a pupil on the basis of his replies to a series of
   items. In general a two-thirds rule is followed: if there are
   six items at a given stage then four must be correct to indicate
   achievement of that stage.

A few items from a task, with administration instructions and
levels added, are shown in figure 1.

The first draft of a task is given to one or two classes, to
check on problems of apparatus or administration, or on any gross
misunderstanding of items by pupils. When such problems have been
sorted out, the new draft is administered to some 200 pupils in different schools. The task and its items are then subjected to a thorough
review, which may lead to changes in the administration of the task,
item wording, pupils' strategies in reaching solutions, scoring
rules and changes in the task itself. One or more of these may be
modified for a new trial.

Apparatus: a metre rule pivoted at its centre, with regularly spaced holes to take hanging weights

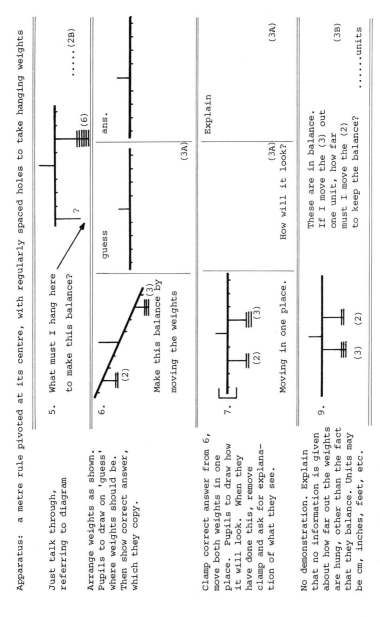

Figure 1: Some items from a science reasoning task

Facility:

A check is made whether higher level items have lower facilities than lower level items.

Discrimination:

Each item in a task is supposed to discriminate between pupils at different cognitive levels. Conventional discrimination indices do not test sharpness of discrimination between levels adequately for our purpose, and so we assess this function of each item by plotting the percentage of pupils at each level (as measured by the task) who succeed at each item. An ideal '2B' item, for instance, would be passed by 100% of 2B, 2B/3A, and 3A pupils, and passed by no 2A/B, 2A or 1B pupils. No real item is as perfect as this, but from the item discrimination diagrams we can check both the sharpness of discrimination between levels and also whether the item is discriminating at the level expected. Figure 2a is an example of such a diagram which indicates an acceptably sharp discrimination at the 2B level. The item represented in figure 2b generally discriminates between higher level and lower level pupils, but its level of discrimination is not sharp enough to be acceptable in an SRT.

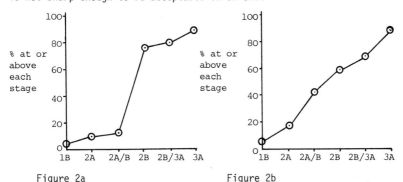

Figure 2a   Figure 2b

Examples of item discrimination diagrams

Reliability:

Reliability is determined in a number of ways. Internal consistency is measured using the Kuder Richardson formula 20, both for the whole task, and for groups of items (say, the 2B/3A and 3A items) within the task. Test-retest reliability is checked with one or two classes of pupils doing the same task twice, with a 4-6 week interval.

Thus test development proceeds through a series of small changes in item administration, scoring criteria, and assessment rules, with

27

the aim of maximising item discriminations and reliability, while
maintaining the essential features of the ideal group task outlined
above.

A final check is made on the correlation of assessments by the
SRTs with those made by interview of some of the same subjects. Such
correlations indicate (Shayer, 1979) that the SRTs do assess essentially the same thing as Piagetian interviews. What is more they do
it more reliably.

The question of validity of the tasks is considered in more
detail in Shayer's paper presented at this Seminar.

THE MEANINGS CHILDREN GIVE TO THE LETTERS IN GENERALISED ARITHMETIC

Dietmar Küchemann

This is a brief report of a class-test of generalised arithmetic
(Algebra 1) given to a representative sample of 3000 2nd, 3rd and 4th
year children in English secondary schools. The results quoted are
for the 3rd year children (n=981), who were about 14 years old.

It was found that the children interpreted the letters in a number
of different ways, which are summarised below.

LETTER EVALUATED. This describes responses where the letter is given
a numerical value instead of being treated as an unknown, as when
children write 12 instead of 8+g in item 5iii (e+f=8, e+f+g=...). It
also applies to items where children are asked to find a numerical
value, and where this can be done without having to manipulate the
letters as unknowns,as in 'find a if a+5=8'.

LETTER NOT USED. Here the letter is ignored, or at best acknowledged
(but without being given a meaning) as when children write 7 or 7n
instead of 3n+4 in 'add 4 onto 3n'.

LETTER AS OBJECT. The letter is regarded as a name for an object, or
as an object in its own right, as when '2a+5a' is thought of as
'2 apples and 5 apples', or simply '2a's and 5a's, which makes 7a's
altogether'. Some items can be solved successfully (and easily)
when the letters are used in this way, but in other cases this is
quite inappropriate, for example when a statement like '1 Pound equals
4 D-Mark' is translated as P=4M (which does not hold if P and M are
numbers).

28

LETTER AS SPECIFIC UNKNOWN. Here the letter is thought of as a particular but unknown number and the child is willing to operate on the letter viewed in this way, despite the resulting lack of closure (as in the answers 8+g and 3n+4).

LETTER AS GENERALISED NUMBER. The letter is seen as representing or being able to take several values rather than a specific value, as in 'what can you say about c if c+d=10 and c is less than d?'.

LETTER AS VARIABLE. The letter represents a range of values and the child is able to describe the degree to which changes in one set are determined by changes in another (which means establishing at least a 2nd order relationship). A minimal example is 'a=b+3; what happens to a if b is increased by 2?', where the child needs to find a relationship like 'a is always 3 more than b', rather than 'this a is 3 more than this b', which says nothing about their relationship when b changes.

The items on the test were classified into 4 levels. In the first of these (Level 1 and Level 2) the items could all be solved without having to operate on unknowns; instead the letters could be EVALUATED, NOT USED or regarded as OBJECTS. In Levels 3 and 4 the letters had to be treated as SPECIFIC UNKNOWNS, GENERALISED NUMBERS or VARIABLES.

The difference between Levels 1 and 2 and between Levels 3 and 4 was essentially a matter of item-complexity. For example, in the Level 1 item 'find a if a+5=8', a can be evaluated by recalling a familiar number-bond, whereas in the Level 2 item 'find u if u=v+3 and v=1' the child needs (temporarily) to cope with an ambiguous statement. And whereas in item 9i (Level 1) the objects to be collected together are all of the same type (p=3e), in item 9ii (Level 2) the objects differ, which means the answer (p=4h+t) can not be closed.

9i

9ii

A similar distinction holds between Levels 3 and 4. For example, 'add 4 onto 3n' (Level 3) essentially involves only a single operation (the 4 is simply 'attached' to what is given), whereas in 'multiply n+5 by 4' (Level 4) this approach would lead to an ambiguous answer (e.g. n+5x4), so that it becomes necessary to co-ordinate the two operations involved.

Levels 1 and 2 are very much tied to concrete reality so that in Piagetian terms they can be described as requiring concrete operations. On the other hand Levels 3 and 4 are concerned with abstract or hypothetical entities and with 2nd order operations and relations, which require formal thought.

Items at each of these Levels are listed in the following tables.

3rd year facility and item number		LEVEL 1 items	Other responses	%	
97	8	*[trapezium: 10 (top), 2 (left), 9 (bottom), 1 (right)]* p=			no letters involved
97	5i	If a + b = 43 a + b + 2 = ...			NOT USED
94	9i	*[triangle with sides labelled e, e and base e]* p=			OBJECT
92	6i	What can you say about a if a + 5 = 8 ?			EVALUATED
89	7ii	*[rectangle: 6 (left side), 10 (bottom)]* A=			no letters involved
86	13i	2a + 5a =			OBJECT

LEVEL 2 items

68	7iii	*[rectangle: n (left side), m (bottom)]* A=			OBJECT
68	9ii	*[figure with sides h, h, h, h and base t]* p=	4ht or hhhht	20	OBJECT, but need to avoid temptation to close (4ht)
64	9iii	*[house-shape: u, u (roof), 5, 5 (sides), 6 (base)]* p=	2u16 or uu556	16	OBJECT, but need to avoid temptation to close (2u16)

30

Level 2 (continued)

62	11ii	What can you say about m if m = 3n + 1 and n = 4			EVALUATED, but need to cope with (temporary) ambiguity of m=3n+1
61	11i	What can you say about u if u = v + 3 and v = 1	u=2	14	EVALUATED, but need to cope with ambiguity of u=v+3 (one unknown is 3 more than another unknown), and not re- duce this ambiguity to 'u and v together equal 3' which leads to u=2
60	13iv	2a + 5b + a =	8ab	20	OBJECT, but need to avoid temptation to close (8ab, which is also ambiguous)

LEVEL 3 items

41	5iii	If e + f = 8 e + f + g = ...	12 9 15	26 6 2	SPECIFIC UNKNOWN. Though e and f can be ignored by matching (as in 5i) g can not; nor can g be evaluated (4+4+4=12, etc.)
41	14	What can you say about r if r=s+t and r + s + t=30	r=10	21	SPECIFIC UNKNOWN. r can not be evaluated directly (as in 10+ 10+10=30)
38	9iv	Part of this figure is not drawn... n sides altogether. p=	p=32, 34, etc.	18	SPECIFIC UNKNOWN. n can not be used as an object (as in 9i,9ii, 9iii), nor can n be evaluated (by liter- ally closing the figure:p=32 etc.)
36	4ii	4 added to n can be written as n + 4. Add 4 onto 3n	7n 7	31 16	SPECIFIC UNKNOWN. n has to be operated upon, not avoided (4+3n → 7n) or ignored entirely (4+3n → 7)

30	16	What can you say about c if c + d = 10 and c is less than d	only one value, usually c = 4	39	GENERALISED NUMBER

LEVEL 4 items

25	18ii	Is the following always, never or sometimes (when) true? L + M + N = L + P + N	Never	51	GENERALISED NUMBER. M and P can represent a range of values, which may coincide
23	13v	(a − b) + b =			SPECIFIC UNKNOWN. The use of letters as objects is no longer plausible (an apple take away a banana..)
22	20	Cakes cost c pence each and buns b pence each. If I buy 4 cakes and 3 buns, what does 4c + 3b stand for?	4 cakes and 3 buns	39	SPECIFIC UNKNOWN (or generalised number). The temptation to use the letter as objects is particularly strong since the item involves objects
17	4iii	Multiply n+5 by 4	4xn+5 n+20 20	17 31 15	SPECIFIC UNKNOWN. Here it is necessary to coordinate two operations, and to recognise the ambiguity of an answer like 4xn+20
12	7iv	A=	5xe+2 e+10 10	18 28 13	SPECIFIC UNKNOWN
12	21	If $(x+1)^3 + x = 349$ is true when x=6, what value of x makes $(5x+1)^3 + 5x = 349$ true?			GENERALISED NUMBER or variable. x can be represented by 5x, which results in the transformation ÷5
11	22	b blue pencils (5 pence each), r red pencils (6 pence each), cost 90 pence altogether... (i.e. 5b + 6r = 90)	b+r=90 6b+10r=90 or 12b+5r=90	17 6	SPECIFIC UNKNOWN or generalised number. Not letter as object (blue and red pencils cost 90 pence, etc.)

Level 4 (continued)

| 6 | 3 | Which is larger, 2n or n+2 ? Explain | 2n (because it's multiply, etc.) | 71 | VARIABLE(2nd order relationship).Intuitively it is reasonable to assume 2n > n+2 (e.g. for n=10, 20>12). But as n changes the difference between 2n and n+2 changes, so for some (smaller) value of n, 2n may be less than 'n+2' |

PERSONALITY AND COGNITIVE DEVELOPMENT

John Head

Introduction

The division between cognitive and affective is largely one of convenience and it would be highly unlikely that cognitive development could occur in an individual without some interaction with the affective aspects of that person. The nature of such interactions is largely an unexplored area but we might want to seek answers to at least three questions:

1. Can the cognitive model be extended into the affective area? To what extent is affective development limited by the cognitive resources the individual has at his disposal?

2. To what extent do affective factors determine cognitive development, e.g. what is the nature and role of motivation?

3. Can the study of affective development give us any feedback which allows us to modify and refine our models of cognitive development?

The literature has little to offer in response to such questions. The work of Kohlberg on moral development and of Elkind on egocentrism in adolescence take up the first question, but only in a limited context. Inhelder and Piaget's (1958) The Growth of Logical Thinking has a chapter entitled Adolescent Thinking which touches on these issues but without providing any precise information or explanation.

As its title suggests, the Concepts in Secondary Mathematics and Science (C.S.M.S.) Project has been primarily concerned with cognitive issues, but from the beginning it was envisaged that the interface with affective aspects might merit examination. In the event one person (the author) was appointed for two years from September 1977 to conduct an exploratory study.

It was decided to investigate two main areas: the link between some personality measures and cognitive development; and the possibility of identifying a model of affective development to parallel the Piagetian model of cognitive development.

Some personality factors linked to cognitive development

As the Project team had a mass of cognitive data to hand it seemed appropriate to do a simple study of seeing how a number of personality and allied measures correlated with the scores obtained from cognitive tasks. It was decided to look at three such factors which we thought to be relevant and testable: popularity with peers, self-esteem, and attitudes to authority. We had the cooperation of Dr. John Coleman of the Psychiatry Department, London Hospital Medical College in developing these tests.

Popularity with peers. A simple sociometric scale was developed, each pupil was asked to name three members of his or her class that he or she would most like to sit with in class, to work with in a practical lesson, and to spend spare time with in the evening, giving a total of nine preferences. Although no restriction was placed on the choice the vast majority named persons of the same sex as themselves, hence the measure is in reality that of popularity with peers of the same sex. A point was given for each mention by another member of the class, and a total score obtained for each individual.

Self-esteem. Self-esteem was measured using a method developed by Rosenberg (1965), and used subsequently in a wide range of research (e.g. Simmons, Rosenberg, Rosenberg, 1973). Essentially this method involves the presentation to pupils of a series of statements such as 'I feel I am a person who does not have much to be proud of'. The individual is then asked to rank the statement according to whether he or she agrees, disagrees, or is not sure about it.

Attitudes to authority. This was measured using a sentence completion test very similar to that developed by Coleman (1970), and subsequently used in a large scale research project involving approximately 800 young people between the ages of 11 and 17 (Coleman, 1974).

Teacher ratings of pupil behaviour

In addition all class teachers were asked to give a rating on a five point scale for each pupil on the following five characteristics: the ease with which they can be controlled and disciplined; their level of activity in class; their independence from others, particularly to praise and blame; their willingness to participate in class activities; and finally, their originality.

Measures of formal operational thought

Group tests developed by the Concepts in Secondary Mathematics and Science Project Team were administered to the classes. The twelve year old pupils did Task II on Volume and Density, and the fourteen year olds did Task III with the Pendulum. In addition six of the fourteen year old classes were taking part in a décalage experiment, details of which are reported by Shayer (1979), in which the pupils were given five separate group tasks developed from Inhelder and Piaget (1958). These were the Pendulum, Equilibrium in the Balance, Inclined Plane, Flexible Rods and Chemical Combinations.

Subjects

A total of 602 pupils aged 12 and 14 were taken from 24 classes in seven schools. The schools were situated in both rural and urban areas in Gloucestershire, Bedfordshire, Hertfordshire, Leicestershire, Yorkshire and Essex. All had a comprehensive co-educational intake of about average ability with school means on the Calvert Non-verbal Reasoning Test (Calvert, 1958), being in the range 96-104. The Piagetian scores confirmed that the pupils gave a representative cross-section of the British school population. Approximately equal numbers of boys and girls were included at each of the two age levels.

The Pearson product moment correlations of each of these personality ratings with Piagetian cognitive level are given in Table 1.

Table 1: Correlations between personality variables and Piagetian concept levels

From pupils' questionnaires	12 year olds		14 year olds	
	boys	girls	boys	girls
Attitudes to authority	0.05	0.01	-0.06	0.14
Peer popularity	0.36*	0.34*	-0.34*	0.05
Self Esteem	0.26*	0.32*	-0.05	0.36*
Teachers'ratings				
Discipline	0.0	0.28*	0.12	0.22
Activity	0.30*	0.40*	0.16	0.34*
Independence	0.34*	0.38*	0.29*	0.14
Participation	0.34*	0.20*	0.42*	0.40*
Originality	0.34*	0.33*	0.24*	0.23*
Total (N)	171	165	143	123
Mean age	12.4	12.4	14.3	14.4

N.B. all values are positive, unless otherwise indicated.
*significant at the 0.01 level.

In general the results for the twelve year old pupils are those which might have been anticipated, and are also in accordance with the Cloutier and Goldschmid (1976) study with Canadian pupils aged between ten and twelve. The differences between the pupils of twelve and those of fourteen, and between the two sexes at fourteen are evident. The shift from +0.36 to -0.34 for boys of 12 and 14 in the correlation between popularity with peers and cognitive levels raises some questions. Not least it tends to deny the model implicit in Inhelder and Piaget (1958) that a high level of social interaction with peers would tend to assist decentring, and in time, cognitive development.

Personality measures and subject choice

With the fourteen year old population we also took note of the subject preferences and career intentions of the pupils. Two significant differences were found (see table 2). Boys opting for science were significantly more pro-authority than those opting for the humanities. Girls opting for science had a lower self-esteem than those opting for the humanities. Both findings are in accordance with the literature, see Head (1979a), although most other studies have been with older students.

Table 2: Correlations between personality variables and subject choice

		boys		girls	
		science	humanities	science	humanities
attitudes to	mean	4.06 ← ** → 3.59		4.59	4.26
authority	s.d.	1.14	1.97	1.17	1.17
self esteem	mean	13.23	13.63	12.09 ← * → 13.12	
	s.d.	2.56	2.69	2.65	2.96
N		35	27	29	27

** significant at 1% level   * significant at 5% level

Application of Loevinger's ego development model

From our point of view the most useful information would most likely come from the application of a stage developmental model of personality development in adolescence. We could then directly compare progress measured by such a model with the cognitive development. Although the general shift among psychologists studying adolescence has been away from the 'storm and stress' crisis description towards a stage model, see Coleman (1978) for the arguments, the concepts have not been fully developed nor appropriate test procedures generated.

Loevinger's work seemed to offer an exception as she has devised a detailed, comprehensive theory of personality development (Loevinger,

1976) and also a test procedure for following that development (Loevinger et al., 1970).

Loevinger's model is too complex to be outlined simply. It has some resemblances to the Piagetian work: 'Our conception of ego development is that of a transformation of structures' (Loevinger, 1976, p.431) but also draws on the long tradition of ego psychology. Ego development tasks in adolescence would include the acquisition of an appropriate self-identity, decentring and integrating the various aspects of one's developing personality. The model treats development as occurring in four conceptually separate areas: physical, cognitive, ego and psychosexual, although obviously they interact.

This work seems to be scarcely known in Britain but Hauser's (1976) survey both provides a good introduction to the work and describes its use in the U.S.A.

The sentence completion test of 36 items was administered to pupils aged 12, 14 and 17 on whom we had cognitive data. Test scoring is the rate-determining step in the process and to date we have scores for about 300 persons. From that data we can see that the tests provide data independent of the Piagetian levels ($r = +0.15$ for 84 boys and $+0.10$ for 79 girls aged 14). Furthermore there was no evidence of a 'cut off' effect. A number of pupils, who were still only at the late concrete stage, achieved the highest level on the ego development test. This finding seems to be contrary to the model of Kohlberg on moral development, but is in accordance with the findings reported by Loevinger (1976). From our point of view the low correlation was welcomed as it confirmed that we had another source of information about the subjects - too high a correlation would suggest that one measure was redundant.

There is a clear sex difference at 12 and 14, with the girls being more mature, but by 17 that has disappeared. With boys at 14 those expressing an interest in the humanities are apparently more mature than those opting for science (significant at the 5% level).

However, the limitations of this model for our work became apparent at this stage. By reducing all the information contained in the test responses to a simple numerical score for each person we are losing useful detail and, secondly, it does not incorporate any concepts about psycho-sexual development even though these are likely to be relevant. (With respect to subject choice the fact that scientists tend to be male with strong 'masculine' interests, emotionally reticent and somewhat authoritarian would suggest that psycho-sexual influences are involved.)

Item analysis of the sentence completion test

Item analysis of the test responses (which is not part of the
Loevinger procedures) has allowed us to build up a picture of what
boys and girls of 12 and 14 are like, and how those opting for science
differ from those choosing the humanities. For example, girls at the
age of 12 and 14 seem to take a more mature attitude to personal
relationships, seeing their complexity and reciprocal nature, while
boys are more exploitive. Responses of girls to the stem 'A girl and
her mother...' often produces responses like 'often go through a bad
patch for a year but once they learn to understand each other become
the best of friends' or 'can help each other with their problems'.
Similar questions asked of boys tend to produce banal responses or
exploitive ones, e.g. the parent is seen as the source of money. In
contrast boys seem to have a firmer self-identity and a clearer ambi-
tion showing more insight in response to sentence stems such as
'My main problem is...' and 'He/she felt proud that...' This difference corresponds closely to the description of Douvan and Adelson
(1976).

If we compare boys of 14 opting for science with other boys we
find that the former have very cut-and-dried views on many issues,
e.g. criminals should be severely punished; anyone who is unpopular
deserves their fate. To the stem 'When a child will not join in group
activities...' these boys give responses like 'he is selfish',
'he must be stupid', 'he deserves to be unpopular'. In contrast
other boys, and most girls, pondered the possible causes and ways of
integrating the child into the group. The science boys seemed to
possess few doubts or uncertainties, they offered clear cut answers.

No such characteristics were found with girls opting for science.
The accumulation of this evidence from the sentence completion tests,
plus what is known about the personality of scientists (Head 1979a),
suggested that subject choice in our contemporary schools could be
described in terms of Marcia's (1966, 1976) description of ego identity development. This suggestion is developed in Head (1979b).

Clearly there are many loose ends needing further study but we
have hopefully taken the first tentative steps to answering the three
questions posed at the beginning of this article.

A Hierarchy of Understanding in Mathematics

K. HART

For the last five years the project 'Concepts in Secondary Mathematics and Science' (C.S.M.S.) has been investigating secondary school children's understanding of mathematics. The aim of the research was to develop a hierarchy of understanding which would provide information for teachers and developers of curriculum. Mathematics is usually presented to children in the order dictated by the needs of mathematics, e.g. addition of two digit whole numbers comes before addition of three digit numbers. Since the one skill involved is certainly a pre-requisite for the other, the order is correct but the needs of mathematics give no clue to the relative degrees of difficulty of the two operations. As Suppes (1966) says:

> My present view, based partly on our experiments and partly on conjecture, is that the psychological stratification of math. concepts will seldom if ever, do violence to the logical structure of these concepts; but it will markedly deviate from the mathematical analysis of the same concepts with respect to the amount of detail that must be considered (p.145).

Although sequencing mathematical experiences on a skill related basis, mathematics teachers have been loth to change the traditional order of presentation. The topics introduced under the name of modern mathematics in the 1960s were rewritten and moved from the 'advanced maths' category to a very much earlier presentation (sometimes in the primary school). The traditionally taught topics seemed to appear at exactly the same time in the textbooks, however. The firmly held belief 'all children by the age of eleven should be able to do...' was never contradicted without the accusation that standards were being lowered. The teacher is in a dilemma, certainly she has presented the four operations on whole numbers but is the next step fractions? How big a jump is it from working within the set of whole numbers to working with fractions?

The idea of 'readiness' and the gradual development of the child's ability to deal with abstractions, follows from the theory of Piaget.

Collis (1975), in expanding Piagetian theory with special reference
to mathematics learning, postulated that both the elements used and
the settings in which they were used could be ordered in terms of
their cognitive demand. Neither theory provided an overall picture
of a child's developing mathematical ability in those areas which
might be called 'school mathematics'. The C.S.M.S. mathematics team
endeavoured to provide a guide to the development of understanding in
a number of topics in the secondary mathematics curriculum. To this
end problems were written which appeared to embody key aspects of a
number of topics. In order to obtain a picture of the general English
child population written tests had to be used but each was used as an
interview instrument first in order to obtain detailed information on
the methods used by children.

The topics covered were:

1. Number Operations (testing the meaning of the operations on
   whole numbers) for 11-12 year olds;

2. Ratio and Proportion, for 13-15 year olds;

3. Algebra (Generalised Arithmetic), for 13-15 year olds;

4. Graphs, for 13-15 year olds;

5. Measurement (Length, Area and Volume), for 12-14 year olds;

6. Decimals and Place Value, for 12-15 year olds;

7. Rotation and Reflection, for 13-15 year olds;

8. Fractions I & II (Fractional notation, addition and substrac-
   tion), for 12-13 year olds;

9. Fractions III & IV (as above with multiplication and division),
   for 14-15 year olds;

10. Matrices A (no multiplication), for 14-15 year olds;

11. Matrices B (including multiplication), for 14-15 year olds;

12. Positive and Negative Numbers (notation, addition and subtraction),
    for 13-15 year olds;

13. Vectors for 14-15 year olds.

This selection of topics did not cover the whole range of mathematics which appears in the secondary school syllabus but these topics
were considered important.

All secondary school children have attended mathematics lessons for some years and their past experience is varied. Even within a single secondary school class the children are from a number of different primary schools and have been taught by a number of teachers. Although realising that the influence of particular teachers is an important variable, the C.S.M.S. team decided there was no way they could control for it. However, by testing a large sample of children from many schools, the researchers hoped that the results could be said to be representative of the English child population in its present setting.

In the writing of items for each topic the writer of the test followed the following procedure.

1. Analyse the topic as it appears in commonly used mathematics textbooks and where relevant (e.g. ratio) as it appears in the science curriculum.

2. Investigate the results and examples used by other researchers with a view to using some of their findings.

3. Write a series of problems in the topic so that they span a wide difficulty range, are free of technical terms and are thought to be testing understanding rather than the repetition of a skill.

4. After team discussion, interview some thirty secondary school children using the written items as a basis for the interview.

5. Rewrite test items, adapting them in the light of the interviews.

6. Using a class test, try out the items in London secondary schools, using the resultant data to test for the discrimination of the items.

7. Carry out large sample testing.

The interviews took place in different schools and with children of different abilities. They lasted about an hour during which the child was asked to talk his way through the problems, explaining what he was doing at each stage. Not all children completed all the questions within the hour but it was thought preferable to have information in depth on a few topics rather than superficial ideas on many. The interviews were tape-recorded and later transcribed. The purpose of the interviews was twofold: i) to find the terms and expressions in the questions which were difficult and could be replaced and to find whether the question being asked could be understood; ii) to find the methods (leading to both correct and incorrect answers) used by the children. The latter was very important, since on a written test little information on methods used would be apparent. Answers which resulted from a specific incorrect method were noted and then coded; in the testing of the large sample the frequency of their occurrence was noted.

Each test paper was to be given in a normal mathematics lesson by the normal mathematics teacher so could not require more than an hour for completion. Obviously, although the items were of different difficulty, one could not hope to cover the entire secondary school syllabus. The schools in the sample for testing were all volunteered by either the Head of Mathematics or the Headteacher. They were recruited by members of the team at in-service courses or meetings at Teacher Centres or sometimes from letters written to the team in response to reading an article about the research. The sample therefore came from schools where the teachers were sufficiently enthusiastic to attend courses and where they were fairly confident. The C.S.M.S. tests were used in June-July of 1976 and 1977; the procedure for sampling was slightly different each time. The general criteria for the selection of a sample were as below.

1. Each topic paper should be attempted by more than one age group (usually three age groups).

2. The sample for each age group on each topic should be representative of the normal distribution of IQ i.e. it should not be significantly non-normal when tested with the Kolmogorov-Smirnov one sample test of goodness-of-fit. (All second years in the schools from which the sample was drawn were given the NFER Test DH [non-verbal reasoning]. Since the team could not find a suitable test of IQ for children over the age of 13, the other year groups in the school were assumed to have the same spread of IQ if the teachers stated that the criteria for admission, the status of the school and the catchment area had not changed.)

3. Entire year groups in 1976 and a quarter of each entire year group in 1977 (a quarter of each class chosen by using random numbers) were tested.

4. Six schools for each year tested in each topic were used; the schools were from both urban and rural areas outside London.

5. Each child did two test papers.

The size of the sample varied; in 1976, for example, three thousand children took the Algebra test, but that summer only four papers were being tested. In 1977, with twelve papers being used, the samples for each topic tended to be smaller (the lowest number of children was 500). In all, fifty schools were used. A longitudinal survey in Algebra, Ratio and Graphs was carried out over three years, with two hundred children for each topic (diminished to 100 by 1978) selected in their second year on the basis of IQ and tested in 1976, '77 and '78.

About ten thousand children were tested and their scripts marked according to the codes assigned to specific wrong answers as well as to the correct ones. Frequencies were found and incidence of errors (some of which occurred in as much as 50 per cent of the population) were identified (see Hart, 1978). To formulate a hierarchy in each topic the data from the testing were used and all the hierarchies are therefore dependent on the items which appeared in the tests. Each topic was analysed separately and groups of items were found. Items had to satisfy the following criteria before they were considered to form a group:

a)   they should be of approximately the same level of difficulty, i.e. same facility;

b)   the values of the homogeneity coefficient Ø(Appendix 1) item/item should be at an acceptable level;

c)   the items should be linked(Ø or Hij) with the items in both easier and harder groups;

d)   there should be some measure of mathematical coherence to the items;

e)   the groups should be scalable in the sense that a child's success (assessed as 2/3 correct) on a group entailed success on all easier groups (error responses were not to exceed 7 per cent of the sample in any one test);

f)   there should be no gross discrepancies when each age group's results were analysed in the same way.

In some topics there was a large facility gap between clusters of items, which provided an obvious cut-off between groups. In other topics there was no obvious cut-off between groups and a decision was made on the basis of criteria d) and e) above. An acceptable level of Ø depended on the test paper being considered; in some cases the easiest items were not highly correlated but were formed into a group in order that there should be some starting point to the hierarchy. The use of the criteria meant that several items on each test paper were rejected, usually because the correlation of a specific item with others of the same facility was noticeably lower than that between the other items. The values of Ø were usually around .4 (1.00 showed perfect homogeneity), for example the Ø values on Ratio and Fractions were as in table 1.

The children were stated to be at the level of understanding which corresponded to a two-thirds success rate on a particular group of items. Thus a child would be at level 2 if he had correctly answered two-thirds of the items in group 1 and two-thirds of the items in group 2 but not two-thirds of those in group 3.

Table 1: ∅ values for ratio and fractions

	Facility range (total sample)			Mean ∅	Median ∅	No. of items
RATIO						
Group 1	79	-	95%	.31	.17	5
Group 2	39	-	51%	.39	.35	5
Group 3	27	-	33%	.41	.37	5
Group 4	12.5	-	21%	.41	.38	4
FRACTIONS 3 & 4						
Group 1	72	-	85%	.492	.457	10
Group 2	52	-	66%	.436	.427	8
Group 3	31	-	40%	.441	.472	3
Group 4	6	-	15.5%	.337	.333	5

Very often a group of items could be described in terms of the methods that children interviewed had used. It soon became apparent in the interviews that the teacher-taught algorithm was neither remembered nor utilised (if remembered) until other 'child-methods' had failed. Some topics in mathematics are based on an interpretation and application of whole numbers (e.g. Ratio and Proportion) but others require the use of conventions and notation different from those used with whole numbers (e.g. fractions). Thus very often the easiest group of items might show a simple application, such as 2 : 1 in ratio, or a simple knowledge of the conventions e.g. (in fractions) shade two-thirds, the two groups being very comparable in facility.

The ratio hierarchy

		Percentage of children		
	1976	2nd yr.	3rd yr.	4th yr.
		n = 800	n = 767	n = 690
Level 0	Unable to solve 3/5 of level 1 items.	7	7	3
Level 1	Doubling, trebling or taking one half, no rate needed; e.g. *if a recipe for 8 people uses 2 pints water, how much is needed for 4 people?*	53	49	41
Level 2	Answers can be found by repetition and taking half; e.g. *eels are fed sprats, the number depending on their length, if a 10cm eel has 12 sprats, how many sprats should a 15cm eel be fed to match?*	26	23	27
Level 3	Fraction operation and repetition method cumbersome, needs a rate to be found; e.g. *if a 25cm eel is fed a fishfinger 10cm long, how long should the fishfinger given to an eel 10cm in length be?*	9	12	14
Level 4	Ratio must be recognised as needed, questions complex in either numbers or setting.	5	9	15

The graphs hierarchy

		Percentage of children 1976		
		2nd yr. n=381	3rd yr. n=589	4th yr. n=408
Level 0	Unable to solve 5/7 of level 1 items	6.5	9	4
Level 1	Easy plotting of points. Given scattergram or block graph, specific points to be read off. Recognition that a straight line corresponds to constant rate.	33	32.5	22.5

e.g.

How many children come by car?
How many children cycle to school?

Level 2	Interpretation of points shown on graph. Simple interpolation e.g. *John leaves home to go to a disco in Cambridge 3 miles away. He walks one way and takes the bus the other way. This is a graph of his journey.*	55	48.5	57

Time →

At what time did he get to the disco?
What do you think he was doing between 7.00 and 8.45?

Level 3	Relation between algebraic expression and graph e.g. *what are the equations of*	5.5	10	16.5
	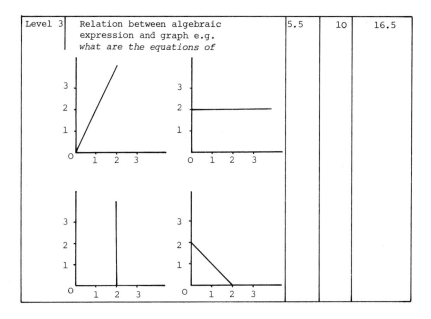			

The fractions hierarchy (age 14 and 15)

		1976	Percentage of children	
			3rd yr. n=308	4th yr. n=215
Level 0	Unable to make a coherent attempt at level 1 problems.		23.4	16.7
Level 1	The meaning of a fraction, seen as part of a whole, no equivalence needed. Equivalent fractions obtained by doubling. Addition of two fractions with the same denominator e.g. *What fraction is shaded?* or $1/3 = 2/?$		18.8	19.1

47

Level 2	Equivalent fractions not obtained by doubling. Using equivalence to name parts, with familiar fractions or when diagram provided e.g. $2/3 = ?/15$	23.4	24.7
Level 3	Questions where more than one operation is required, for example equivalence followed by addition or subtraction; e.g. *I am putting tiles on the floor. They are shown shaded. What fraction of the floor has been shaded?*	27.6	29.8
Level 4	Division and multiplication of fractions. e.g. Area = 1/3 square centimetre Length = ...	6.8	9.8

A cross-matching between the three topics is difficult because a facility gap in one topic may correspond to a group of items in another, see figure 1.

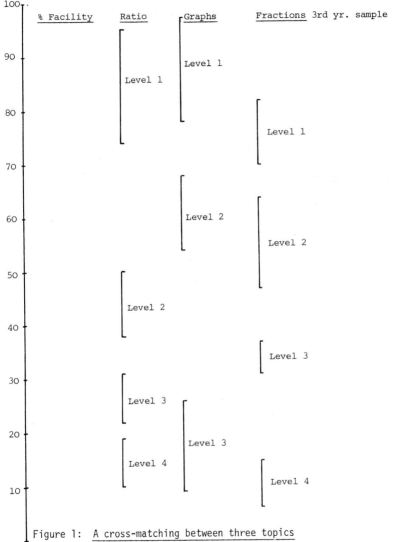

Figure 1: A cross-matching between three topics

A rough guide to the comparable difficulty of levels in each topic can be obtained by simply taking sections of the facility range 0 - 100%. For convenience we call these Stages, the lower limit of each varies according to the age group under consideration but the stages for each age level contain the same groups of items. Thus for the three topics Ratio, Graphs and Fractions (14 and 15 years only) the lower limits of the stages are as follows:

	Ratio	Graphs	Fractions	
	Level 1	Level 1	Level 1	Stage 1
80%	....			15 yrs.
70%				14 yrs.
		Level 2	Level 2	Stage 2
58%	....			15 yrs.
50%				14 yrs.
	Level 2			
	Level 3	Level 3		Stage 3
30%	....			15 yrs.
22%				14 yrs.
	Level 4	Level 3	Level 4	Stage 4

Every child in the sample tested completed two papers, so information on comparable performance by the same children was available for pairs of tests. The number of children in a subsample who did two papers was sometimes small however. The cross tabulation of performance on the Ratio and Graphs tests in 1976 (n=439) is shown in table 2 (this sample was composed of 13, 14 and 15 year olds). Although it can be seen that a clear matching of levels is not apparent (there is no Graphs level of the same facility as level 2 Ratio), nevertheless it is obvious that children below level 2 on Ratio do not perform at level 3 on Graphs and vice versa.

Cross-tabulation of performance on the Ratio and Graphs tests

		Graphs				Row Total
		0	1	2	3	
Ratio	0	13	13	2	0	28
	1	29	105	73	2	209
	2	3	21	78	12	114
	3	0	4	37	11	52
	4	0	0	20	16	36
Column Total		45	**143**	210	41	439

The gamma coefficient (γ), which quantifies the probability that if child A is better than child B on one test he is also better than child B on another test, was computed:

Ratio/Graphs (n=439)	γ = .790
Ratio/Fractions 3, 4 (n=68)	γ = .853
Graphs/Fractions 3, 4 (n=148)	γ = .739

The gamma coefficients of pairs of tests across the whole range varied from .85 to .591, the lowest being between Rotations and Reflections/ Ratio.

As mentioned earlier, the methods used by the child are not necessarily those presented by the teacher in class. For example in Ratio, the children appear to prefer methods which involve the operation of addition e.g. the repetition method (take it once, take it again, take half and add). This is sensible but limited and causes considerable difficulty when the ratio is other than a : 2. For the successful completion of all ratio problems some form of multiplication by a fraction has to be used. On interview the brightest children who used a fractional multiplier for an enlargement 5:3, did not use that method for easier items. For these children it was however still available whilst for the vast majority it appears not to be in their repertoire and some thirty per cent of the sample (n=2257) used an incorrect addition strategy when faced with harder ratios. This strategy identified by both Karplus et al. (1974) and Piaget and Inhelder (1967) utilises the difference a - b rather than a : b. So in the enlargement of (see p.52)

```
|
|
2
|
|_____        _____
     3                   5
```

where the new base is 5cm the child using the addition strategy would reason, 'the base lines differ by 2cm so the uprights must differ by 2cm, the new upright is 4cm'. Level 4 fraction questions also involved multiplication and division of fractions in the context of area. Stage 1 ratio questions can be successfully completed without recourse to multiplication. Stage 1 and 2 fraction questions deal with conventions and not the application of fractions. Stage 1 and 2 graph questions involve interpolation of given diagrams but require no knowledge of relationships. Since the lower limit for stage 2 is about 50 per cent this means very nearly half our child population cannot apply what we, as teachers, teach in mathematics lessons. The introduction of any complexity or distractor does not make the question slightly harder but very much harder.

An interesting phenomenon is the child's ability to deal with 'half'. It appears to be almost as accessible to the child as whole numbers. The plotting of the point $(1\frac{1}{2},4)$ is a level 1 Graphs question, recognising $\frac{1}{2}$ of a diagram is a level 1 Fractions question and finding one half in the recipe is a level 1 Ratio question. In describing items in different levels there is a continual distinction between $\frac{1}{2}$ and other fractions.

At the other extreme the Stage 4 levels invariably have built in to them some aspect of recognition and application. The line delineating Stage 4 is at 30% for 15 yr. olds, 20% for 14 yr. olds, 18% for 13 yr. olds, showing a steady increase of performance with age, the percentages themselves display the fact that the vast majority of children even at age 15+ are not able to deal with the application of mathematics. This application factor can be best illustrated by considering the type of item which occurs at Stage 4 across a number of tests (see figures 2a and 2b).

Applications or generalisations can be illustrated by the items in Fractions, Algebra and Decimals which require the child to think in terms of the nature of numbers, and cannot be solved by the application of a rule or taught algorithm. The two questions on volume require the use of a formula where the values are fractions or where the formula must be halved. Children on interview often counted layers and did not use a formula; the triangular prism, of course, requires the knowledge of the area of the base triangle which is not shown drawn on squared paper. The first question in Decimals and the last question in Fractions, shown in the Stage 4 items, are very often difficult because the child is fixed within the set of whole numbers and feels that the impossible is being asked of him.

52

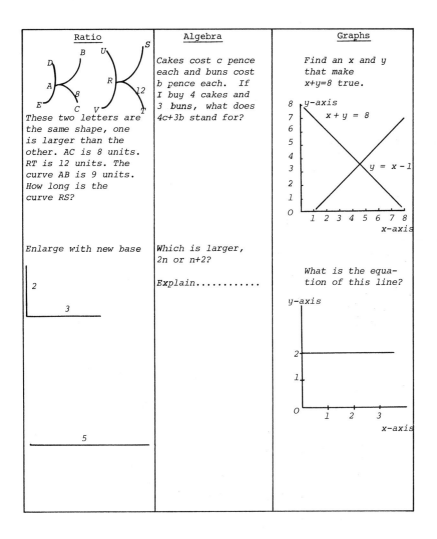

Ratio	Algebra	Graphs
These two letters are the same shape, one is larger than the other. AC is 8 units. RT is 12 units. The curve AB is 9 units. How long is the curve RS?	Cakes cost c pence each and buns cost b pence each. If I buy 4 cakes and 3 buns, what does 4c+3b stand for?	Find an x and y that make x+y=8 true.
Enlarge with new base	Which is larger, 2n or n+2? Explain...........	What is the equation of this line?

Figure 2a: Stage 4 items

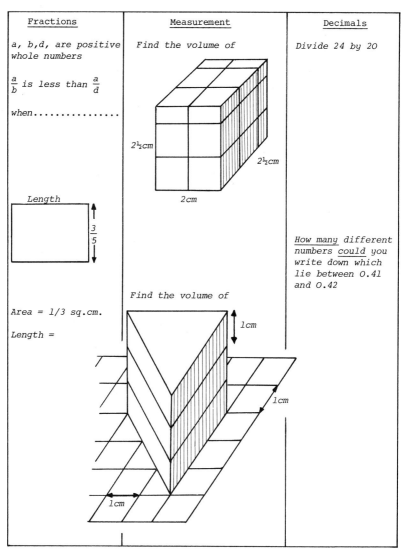

Fractions	Measurement	Decimals

Fractions

a, b, d, are positive whole numbers

$\frac{a}{b}$ *is less than* $\frac{a}{d}$

when...............

Length

$\frac{3}{5}$

Area = 1/3 sq.cm.

Length =

Measurement

Find the volume of

$2\frac{1}{2}cm$

$2\frac{1}{2}cm$

2cm

Find the volume of

1cm

1cm

1cm

Decimals

Divide 24 by 20

How many different numbers could you write down which lie between 0.41 and 0.42

Figure 2b: Stage 4 items

Powerful distractors are present in the Ratio questions (the addition
strategy) and in the first Algebra item where 'cost' or 'number'
seem equally likely. The two graphs questions are interesting in that
we would normally teach these early in the secondary school. Indeed
they are regarded as some of the easiest examples of graphs from
algebraic expressions. Incidentally few children gave the answer
$x = 2$ for the graph of $y = 2$.

In general the stage 4 items go beyond the simple application of
a rule, and they require the child to be both aware of numbers other
than integers and the need for these numbers.

Links with Piagetian theory

It was hoped that the stages and indeed the levels in each topic
could be described in terms of their demand re Piagetian levels of
cognition. To this end, items taken from the books of the Geneva
school were incorporated in as many tests as possible (in written form
of course). In addition five tasks which seemed to require mathematical thinking (Geometry, Combinations (2 tasks), Enlargement and Numbers)
were adapted to give a class test format. Children were interviewed
using the written form as an interview schedule and after revisions
the written paper was given to five hundred children. The papers were
presented by members of the research team who talked the children
through the questions and answered queries. Each of the 500 children
also did one of the C.S.M.S. mathematics tests. It was hoped that
a child could be designated as being at a particular Piagetian level
and by looking at his performance on a maths test, the mathematical
levels could also be described in Piagetian terms. When marked according to the descriptions of typical replies to the problems posed by
Piaget, we found however that the child's performance varied considerably task to task and that we could not label a child as being overall
at a certain Piagetian level. This type of result was also obtained
by Winkelmann (1975) and has been suggested by Davis (1979). The
values of the coefficient γ when the items on the Piagetian task paper
were compared in pairs were considerably lower than those between
each of the five tasks and performance on the mathematics papers.
These in turn were lower than those obtained between pairs of mathematics tests.

		Range
γ	Between pairs of Piaget tasks	.269 - .474
γ	Between a Piaget task and a maths test	.230 - .684
γ	Between pairs of maths tests	.591 - .85

The children in the sample were of course dealing with written
versions of the Piagetian tasks and were on the whole rather older
than those interviewed in Geneva. The purpose of the C.S.M.S. research
was not to validate Piagetian theory, we simply found that the test

did not successfully fulfil the objective for which it was written.

Taking those items which had been adapted from Piaget and used on the mathematics tests as pointers to the demand of Stage 4 items we find that the idea of infinity (late formal) interpreted as the number of points on a line was harder than the level 3 Graphs. The enlargement of an open figure in the ratio 5:3 was the hardest item in level 4 Ratio. This matches the description by Karplus et al. (1975) who demanded success both on the Mr. Short and Mr. Tall item (level 3 Ratio) and success on a task involving control of variables, as a requirement for late formal operational thought. The provision of a square double in area of a square side 2cm (Piaget et al., 1960) was successfully made by fewer children than those who completed level 4 Measurement questions. The understanding of a variable (stated by Collis to be at the late formal level) was the hardest aspect of the level 4 Algebra items. All of these point to the description of the hardest Stage 4 items as being at the beginning of the late formal stage. This means that less than 15 per cent of even the 15+ sample is performing at this level.

Implications for the teaching of mathematics

Mathematics teachers know that many children find the subject difficult; they do however often regard the children who fail at the level expected of them as being a small group requiring remedial teaching. Our results show that the opposite situation prevails; there is a small group who succeed on the mathematics we present and these are the exceptional ones, not those who fail to meet our criteria of success. Children appear to succeed on items which require whole numbers only and indeed on much of the 'concrete' based work done in the secondary school. Once new conventions, new language and a demand for applications is made, however, the topic becomes very difficult. In keeping with the approach to spiral development many mathematical topics such as fractions are introduced at an early age. The subsequent teaching of these topics is supposedly to further develop the expertise in the topic but in practice the spiral becomes two-dimensional and the teaching becomes re-teaching rather than development. Because the teacher expects to develop the topic she does not fully re-teach but assumes certain knowledge. Most teachers also expect that the methods of solution presented in class are those used by children for the successful completion of mathematics problems. They introduce algorithms and justify them by very simple illustrations. The child, however, because he has other methods, ignores the algorithm and still gets the answers correct. The algorithms are not needed until the questions (or numbers) become complex; it is surely then that they should be introduced. Scientists very often demand a level of mathematical competence far in excess of the capability of the child. Many scientists have in fact stated that in the setting of an experiment children can deal with ratio, but often they mean 2:1 ratio and no more.

The picture presented is true not only of British children but also of children in other countries,viz.Karplus et al. (1975). Mathematics teachers often forget that they themselves are the exceptions - the stage 4 pupils - and base their expectations on 'children should ...because I did'.

Appendix 1

The homogeneity coefficients $\emptyset$, H_{ij} use the entries in the four-cell matrix:

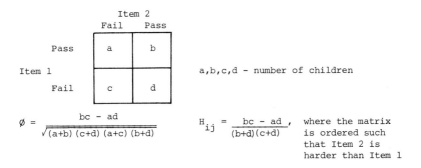

Item 2

	Fail	Pass
Pass	a	b
Fail	c	d

Item 1

a,b,c,d - number of children

$$\emptyset = \frac{bc - ad}{\sqrt{(a+b)(c+d)(a+c)(b+d)}}$$

$$H_{ij} = \frac{bc - ad}{(b+d)(c+d)},$$ where the matrix is ordered such that Item 2 is harder than Item 1

RESPONSE by W.M. Brookes

The paper represents an interesting venture into the largely uncharted seas of the development of mathematical activity (ability?) in adolescence and in particular what is termed 'school mathematics'. The aim was very general, 'to develop a hierarchy of understanding which would provide information for teachers and developers of curriculum'. The chief result for teachers is behavioural and seems to be that 'there is only a small group (of children) who succeed on the mathematics we present...'. Another implication for teaching is that it is observed that when solving problems children do not always use the methods (algorithms) that the teacher has given them.

The major part of the paper is given over to the construction of diagnostic tests and though the two conclusions above are given in the paper it is not made clear whether the team considers that the tests it has constructed are of sufficient generality for them to be used diagnostically by teachers. It is stated that 'all the hierarchies are...dependent on the items which appeared in the tests'. There is one point of clear importance, however, and that is the acceptance by the research team of the positive significance of children's mistakes in coming to understand the genesis of mathematical understanding. However, the work has a Piagetian theoretical underpinning which is to some extent responsible for limiting the possible scope of such an investigation. This became apparent when attempts were made more deliberately to associate a child's state with the sequence of Piagetian stages.

It seems to me important to discuss this work in the light of the relation between a) intentions to investigate for generally applicable characteristics, b) expectations as a consequence and c) the limited outcomes given the procedures adopted. To do this I want to use the notion of context as governing actions taken. This could be to do with choice of subjects for study (sampling), choice of material, choice of mathematical items, choice of theory, that is, explanation, choice of method, even choice of context. This last possibility indicates that there are different levels of abstraction, for example, choice of items will vary with the different contexts implied by different methods.

Cutting across this complex of context and content is a distinction I wish to draw between arbitrary context and necessary context. This distinction exists in any attempt to characterise aspects of the interpretative framework which any investigator must develop either consciously or unconsciously when he wishes to communicate with others.

The reductive methods employed in much academic work on the learning of mathematics tend to make the researcher develop an arbitrary context for his work. That is, arbitrary with respect to any given reader's understanding of mathematical learning. This does not devalue the work done but serves to remind us of that subtlety of interpretation which is needed to show the consequential limit to the work, in particular with respect to its generalisability. For example, the commonality of the phrase 'a mathematical concept' is often sufficient for researchers and readers (teachers?) to feel they know what each other is talking about. This can be disastrously false. It is not uncommon to find that 'standardised tests in mathematics' are accepted by users without considering what is in fact the commonality of the meaning of 'mathematics' they assume and the meaning accepted by the test constructor.

On the other hand where the enquirer accepts a necessary context he can continually challenge and be challenged on the relevance of his choices. In the instance of the present work a distinction is drawn between other work on the genesis of mathematical thinking and the work in 'school mathematics' undertaken by the project team. This becomes a necessary context.

Arbitrariness pervades the study of human activity in the sense that when the diverse idiosyncrasies of human behaviour are classified, the classification will be arbitrary at some level, even where at a subsidiary level the classification can be shown to be appropriate for a necessary context. Reduction in the arbitrariness of description (Thom, 1974) has been suggested as an effective way of describing scientific activity. The movement from arbitrary to necessary can only be effected when the change is acceptable to the community with whom there is communication. Such a theoretically necessary context will, of course, appear arbitrary to those not involved.

The acceptance of the necessary context of 'school mathematics' makes it much more difficult for the researcher, for he is continually exposed to the criticism 'but that's not what I mean by school mathematics'.

One can find hints of the team's actions in constructing an instrument which they felt would in some way allow them to probe understanding in the age range being studied. But only hints. Phrases like 'endeavoured to provide a guide', 'problems...which appeared to embody', 'written tests had to be used', 'but they were considered important', 'they are regarded', all conceal hypotheses, which are never discussed. Though the instrument was being constructed in the context of 'school mathematics' there was little to indicate how the team justified these acts of reduction. It is important for credibility that this discipline is attempted, otherwise the researcher builds up his own locus of activity, partly well defined, to some extent simply assumed but to a large extent 'not noticed'.* It would be <u>arbitrary</u> with respect to any generalisation that might be consequential.

A major instance is reported when, like so many enquirers before them, the mathematics team realised that the influence of teachers was important, but 'decided there was no way they could control for it'. They hoped that by testing a large sample of children from many schools that their 'results could be said to be representative'. The effect of this reduction could be assessed by asking the following questions. What information is lost by ignoring differential teacher functioning even if we achieve distinctive patternings in children's test behaviour on a large scale? How does that loss of information affect what might be said about results to teachers whose diverse idiosyncrasies have been removed from the study? On what terms will the tests be made available to teachers? There are clear limitations expressed in the report but will the implicit arbitrariness be left undiscovered? Further than that there is no doubt that there are important findings which need the discipline of further appropriate enquiry and interpretation; enquiry in which

---

* 'The aspects of things that are most important for us are hidden because of their simplicity and familiarity. (One is unable to notice something - because it is always before one's eyes.) The real foundations of his enquiry do not strike a man at all. Unless that fact has at sometime struck him - and this means : we fail to be struck by what, once seen, is most striking and most powerful.' (Wittgenstein, 1973)

teachers could cooperate. 'It soon became apparent in the interviews that the teacher-taught algorithm was neither remembered nor utilised (if remembered) until other "child-methods" had failed.' 'The introduction of any complexity or distractor (to a straightforward calculation) does not make the question slightly harder but very much harder.' Together with the failure to designate children to particular Piagetian levels because 'the children's performance varied considerably task to task', these reports hint at a complexity greater than that for which the researchers were prepared.

These spin-off developments which hint at a vastly different state of affairs to the one originally assumed to exist leads to a dilemma for a researcher. In effect, does one push on with the developed instrument, enter all the necessary caveats, and leave it at that, or does one throw over the programme and from what one has learned begin a different form of study? There is only a hint of this dilemma in the paper.

It is to their credit that they continue to make clear the limitations of the work done but the failure to meet the dilemma has, in fact, left them between two stools. It could, for instance, be argued that they have shown the Piagetian framework to be inadequate for the purpose.

They cannot claim the generality that the research set out to establish nor have they been able to tackle the task that opened up before them of establishing the complex and ramified interpretative framework necessary to study children's mistakes. The notion of 'mistake' as being a differentiable indicator of either a failure of expectation (by the perpetrator), or a signal of a non-expected (by the teacher) form of action is vital. The consequential corresponding adaptation of assimilation in the first case and accommodation in the second needs attention. Semiotic analysis is likely to be of assistance in a general framework of a phenomenological approach to enquiry (Vandenberg, 1974).

Discussion

Inevitably much of both the formal and informal discussion centred on the empirical hierarchy as suggested by the facility levels, homogeneity coefficients and scalability of the test items. In particular the possibility of matching this hierarchy to Piagetian stages was discussed. Members of the team made it clear that although it had been their original intention to aim at some matching to Piagetian stages such a framework had been abandoned. This decision had been taken in the light of the poor correlation of test results with the results of certain Piagetian tasks set on the mathematics tests, together with the low intercorrelations between the results from the Piagetian tasks. It was suggested from the floor that this might be explained by the fact that the tests provided measures of achievement which did not take into account the processes used by the pupils. Whilst the C.S.M.S. mathematics tests are primarily tests of achievement, some evidence had been obtained as regards pupils' understanding and the processes they used through the use of interviews at the pretest stage. There was evidence that the range in performance across pupils in a particular age group is likely to be greater than the change in performance of any particular pupil from one year to the next. This would seem to agree with evidence obtained by those who have used Piagetian tasks in the group situation. This evidence does suggest that our mathematics teaching must undergo a change in emphasis from what must be taught to what the pupils are capable of understanding.

The most encouraging feature of this research is that it has something relevant to say to the practitioner in the classroom. Evidence has been gathered as to the misconceptions held by pupils and the errors and mistakes they commonly make. The hierarchy of facility levels developed by the team can assist those teachers who are in the process of constructing a mathematics curriculum. One piece of evidence which should make teachers feel somewhat uncomfortable is that in many instances pupils prefer to use their own algorithms to solve simple problems and only use teacher-taught algorithms as a last resort.

From the point of view of the practitioner it was good to hear about the amount of effort put in by the team in disseminating the results and findings - not only to those teachers who had volunteered to participate in the testing but also to other groups, for example, those on in-service courses. How will teachers react to this evidence? It was suggested that groups of teachers in the U.K. are presently drawing up guidelines in which school mathematics is sequenced on the basis of no empirical evidence. This research does afford some evidence. A little testing has been conducted outside the U.K. and it is possible that this evidence may have relevance there also as to the universality of the ordering.

Although the work of the C.S.M.S. mathematics team has come to an end, one has to say that the investigation has only just begun. Those items rejected as a result of the pretesting should form the basis of a more detailed investigation into the reasons for this. More importantly the problem of pupils' understanding of the use of mathematical language needs investigation. Do pupils experience difficulty in solving apparently simple mathematical problems because of a failure to understand the context in which the problem is put? What issues does the evidence obtained so far raise for those teachers whose disciplines use mathematics, e.g. teachers of science? How can these be resolved? Is it too much to expect that the individual teacher will be encouraged by this evidence to look more closely at the interaction between his teaching and his pupils' learning?

The Match of Science Curriculum to the Learner in the Middle and Secondary School

MICHAEL SHAYER

Overview

This paper presents the work of one team in applied research in science education. It also contains a discussion of some of the problems involved in the development of research which can be of use to the teacher, and which may influence school practice.

It may be said that the curriculum development of the sixties lacked a research model. Likewise, research funding bodies distinguish rigorously between research and curriculum development. Yet which modern industry would risk going into full-scale production with a process which has not been adequately tested on a pilot-plant scale, and which is not seen through its teething stages with research aid? With hindsight it is possible to see that a closer relationship between curriculum development and practice, and research, is desirable.

It may be objected that, with adequate provision of trials in schools, a curriculum development team has no need of a research model. They need merely to get the best teacher-practitioners and set them to invent, or modify. But, as with agriculture, the answer to this is that it is unlikely that non-random trials, or trials unstructured by theory, would serve the purpose of generalising to the school population as a whole. Part of the C.S.M.S. work was initiated from an invitation to provide an explanatory theory for the revision of the Nuffield O-level Chemistry materials (Ingle, Shayer, 1971). Questionnaires had shown that between a half and three-quarters of pupils were having difficulty with the backbone of integrating concepts by which the course was structured from the third year onwards. In this case the feedback from school trials had allowed the course to be adapted to the cognitive development of the top quarter of the selective school population.[1]

(1) Selective schools - that is, Grammar and Public Schools - in England and Wales have, since 1945, educated only the top 20% of secondary school pupils, selected by intelligence and achievement tests. Before 1945, the proportion educated in such schools was even less.

In fairness to the curriculum developers it must be said that no one at the time (including the writer) realised that differentials in cognitive development were such a major variable to be controlled in trials.[2] Yet this is in itself an argument for the utilisation of research at the formative stage of new curricula.[3] As comprehensive education developed in the sixties, in England and Wales, many of us realised that the problem of cognitive differentials was much greater than we had anticipated. Was previous practice in science teaching, developed by adaptation to the top 15 to 20% of the school population[1], a satisfactory model for the other 80% of pupils? Was it possible to keep our existing models of science education, while modifying them suitably for the less able pupil? Thus a major part of the research to be described has to do with establishing a developmental description of the whole of the middle and secondary school population, and relating this model to the intellectual demands of existing science curricula.

It must be conceded that research in science education is so relatively young that the various useful roles it may play have still to be clarified, and perhaps part of the work of this Seminar may be to discuss these. The C.S.M.S. team have had to face the paradox that, while aiming at a close identification with the problems of classroom and laboratory, much of their time and imagination has been taken up with questions of pure research methodology which psychologists themselves had not answered. This will be discussed in more detail later.

It is also necessary to discuss cognitive development and to set it in the context of the development of the whole person. Although most of the published C.S.M.S.[4] work is cognitive, the research was from the outset designed to produce a general model of adolescent development from which curriculum developers could make profitable theories about

---

(2) But this could have been discovered at the time by proper randomisation in the selection of a sample of trial schools and classes, or by informed stratification.

(3) Such research would have forced the writing teams to realise that poor teaching and poor pupil-motivation were not the only explanations of differential performance on the course materials.

(4) Concepts in Secondary Mathematics and Science, is a 5 year research programme funded from 1974-79 (with an extension for one year on the science side) by the S.S.R.C. at Chelsea College. It was also the subject of a feasibility study in the year 1973/74 by two mathematicians and a scientist.

the kind of science teaching that would match pupils of different ages, sex and personality. It was only on grounds of research strategy - taking on the merely difficult - that the cognitive work was done first. Thus some mention will be made of the feasibility study on ego-development and personality variables by John Head in his paper. This raises another paradox, which again might be a theme for discussion, that whereas most of us in research on science education were trained as physicists, chemists or biologists, we find ourselves using the rules and methods of social science which, although still science, and arguably the kind of science which might be more suitable for some of our adolescents than the physical sciences, does provide fresh input to our notions of scientific method and compels humility in face of the universal tendency to generalise on the basis of ones own expertise. These remarks are not made as an aside, but are occasioned by what I take to be a most important event and indicator in the development of science education: the publication by the A.S.E. of a consultative document, Alternatives for Science Education (A.S.E., 1979). Here a representative committee of science teachers and educators have based the whole of their discussion on the premise that the developing person and not the science subject should be the focus of attention. They have, moreover, recommended that a substantial shift to social and environmental science teaching take place. What is the appropriate response and strategy which research in science education should produce?

C.S.M.S. work on cognitive development

At this point it will merely be asserted that, in the early seventies, for the purposes of describing in detail the cognitive match between pupil and curricula, the Piagetian was the obvious and only paradigm to use. On the one hand it offered the possibility of analysing the demands of science curricula, on the other it provided a method of estimating the cognitive level of pupils. Although a taxonomical method had been used for analysing the Piagetian level of thinking required by science curricula (Shayer, 1972), no workers had tested representative samples of pupils so as to be able to estimate Piagetian developmental norms. Indeed, in the original Genevan work (Inhelder, Piaget, 1958) it was assumed that all adolescents developed formal operational thinking. The estimation of these norms, and hence a Piagetian description of the developing spectrum of thinking in pupils of secondary age, was the first task.

The dilemma of the applied researcher appears immediately. An obvious piece of fundamental psychological research following the Genevan work, would have been to produce group-test versions of the Inhelder problems in order to determine developmental norms on a sample large enough to permit generalisation. For various reasons, this had never been done (Tuddenham, 1970), and thus applied researchers had to do it themselves, or leave the task. The assumption had to be made that any level of thinking, from pre-operational to late formal operational, might be shown by different pupils. Thus, during 1973/74,

64

three group-tests were developed.[5] The first, on spatial relations, spanned from pre-operational (stage 1) to late concrete operational (2B). The second, involving various conservations, volume and heaviness, estimated from early concrete (2A) to early formal (3A), and the third, the pendulum problem, covered the range of behaviours late concrete (2B) to late formal (3B). During the years 1974/75, and 75/76, these tests were given to representative samples of over 11,000 children between the ages of 9 and 16 (Shayer, Küchemann, Wylam, 1976; Shayer, Wylam, 1978).[6] These numbers were large enough to get the confidence limits for the estimation of the population mean down to the order of ± 3 around a value of about 30% of 15 year olds showing at least early formal thinking.

The results of these surveys are shown in figures 1, 2 and 3. Figure 1 shows how far from reality was the original Genevan assumption that all adolescents develop formal operational thinking. Figure 2 and figure 3 show how different, cognitively, is the population in selective and super-selective schools from the average and below-average. If early formal (3A) thinking is taken as the characteristic level for traditional O-level science courses, it can be seen how well-matched is the cognitive demand of those courses to the population of the schools they were taught in. Equally it can be seen how misleading empirical experience gained in selective schools will be for generalising to what is desirable or practical in schools with a comprehensive intake.

The immediate purpose of this work was to characterise the problem of matching, and, incidentally, to develop a research tool, the class-task, for further use. Another way of quantifying the data is to say that the correlation of Piagetian level with chronological age is only 0.35; very low as developmental variables go. For any given year-group the spread in cognitive ability is very wide indeed. The 13/14 year old pupil at the 50th percentile has only just achieved the level of thinking which his selective school counterpart at the 85th percentile has had available since 9/10. Pupils who would be selected for grammar school education at 11+ have been using for the whole of their junior school period the structured thinking (late concrete) which the average pupil only attains at nearly 11 years of age.

---

(5) Background information on item-analysis, reliability and validity of these tests are given in Shayer (1978a) and in the Test Handbook (N.F.E.R., 1979).

(6) Details of the sampling and research methods are given in the two papers cited, together with full tables of the survey results.

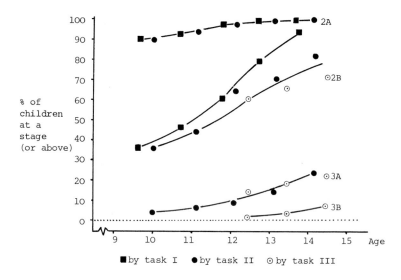

Figure 1: Proportion of children at different Piagetian stages in a representative British child population.

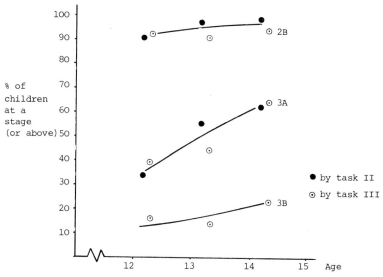

Figure 2: Selective school population (top 20%)

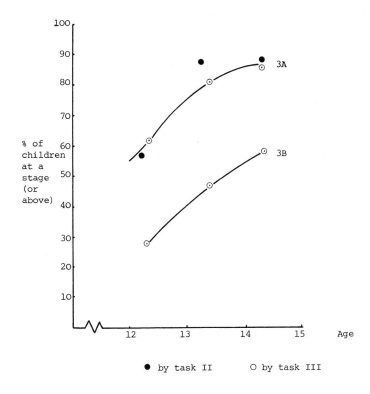

Figure 3: <u>Superselective school population (top 8%)</u>

Yet the tacit assumption behind the development of science teaching and the creation of C.S.E. examinations in the sixties was that the average and a little below average pupil was probably only a year or two behind those in selective schools. This evidence suggests that different kinds of science-teaching games altogether need developing.

Analysis of science curricula

An obvious complement to the research on developmental norms
would be to determine the extent to which science curricula can be
validly analysed for the Piagetian level of thinking required for
their understanding. At the same time fresh evidence could be
gathered on the detail of matching particular science courses to a
wide range of pupils. It would be necessary to show that the performance of pupils on particular parts of a science curriculum could be
predicted to a degree large enough to be useful from their estimated
Piagetian levels as independently assessed by class-tasks.

This work was done using Nuffield Combined Science course lessons
with British first and second year comprehensive school pupils. This
course, although constructed from the first two years of the single
subject O-level courses, designed originally for the selective school,
has in fact been offered as suitable for the bulk of pupils. It was
obviously interesting to check on this assumption. Teachers were
asked to teach a section - about two months work - 'by the book' or
Teachers' Guide. At the end of this period the pupils were given a
40-50 item structured-question type of examination to test their understanding of the various objectives of the course. This work has been
reported both in specialist and teachers' journals (Shayer, 1978b,
1978c). The essence of the research case can be seen in figure 4
based on the item-facilities of 90 pupils in an examination of one
section tabulated in table 1. The pupils are classified by their
class-task estimate of Piagetian level. The exam-items were classified
beforehand for supposed Piagetian level of thinking demanded for their
comprehension, and corresponded to named lesson objectives. It can be
seen that a reasonable degree of validity was obtained.

Table 1:   Comparison of schools on CS6 examinations

Item-levels		School A 2A	2B	3A	3B	School B 2A	2B	3A	3B	School C 2A	2B	3A	3B
Class-	3A	-	-	-	-	100	75.1	46.1	22.9	81.7	79.1	47.1	4.9
task	2B/3A	64.3	68.8	34.6	7.7	72.4	59.1	26.1	8.2	64.3	65.6	21.1	1.9
level of	2B	42.9	34.1	11.8	2.6	77.1	37.5	13.9	4.6	50.0	32.5	10.0	O
pupils	2B-	34.7	15.0	2.7	O	71.3	19.1	O	O	31.4	12.5	6.1	O

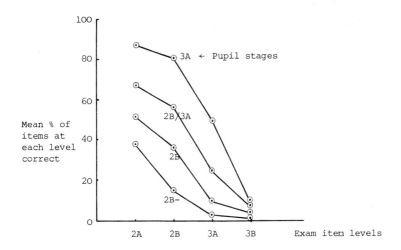

Figure 4: Pupil stage/item level

But the use of overall percentages obscures somewhat the meaning of
the differentials. Only in one of the schools was there a sufficiently
large number of pupils estimated as capable of early formal (3A) thinking, so these 8 pupils are compared with their 10 late concrete (2B)
classmates below in their performance on 12 early formal exam items.

Facilities of pupils on different 3A items

(Nuffield Combined Science Section 6 exam)

Item nos.	1b	1d	1f	1h	1i	2h	3e	3f	3h	5d	6i	6j
3A pupils	63	38	63	63	25	0	83	75	13	25	38	63
2B pupils	0	0	20	20	0	10	20	20	10	0	0	30

If the 12 items are regarded as a sample of activities to be tested
for suitability it can be seen that 8 of them are understood by enough
of the 3A pupils for most teachers to feel that the choice of curriculum material was well made. With only one item even near borderline,
it can be seen that this set of figures defines almost complete unsuit-
ability of the course for the 2B pupils. This degree of constrast
illustrates the kind of gross mismatch which this approach can pinpoint.

Is Piaget's model of operational thinking powerful enough?

It is obvious that no applied research can be sound that is based on an unsound theory. By 1977 enough doubt had been cast on the validity of Piaget's work (Lunzer, 1973; Brown, Desforges, 1977) to make one question the paradigm one was using. The problem was that the research literature was equivocal. The existing body of published work, based on small samples and clinical interviews appeared to offer no crucial experimental test. The length and number of discussion articles was in inverse proportion to the amount of hard evidence. One reason for this was that the problem of 'psychometrising Piaget' (Tuddenham, 1970) had not been solved.

Thus the decision was made to produce fresh evidence, in the first instance as a guide to the C.S.M.S. team as to how much use could be got from the Piagetian model. A very hard-nosed empirical view was taken. It was assumed that Piaget was a genius as an experimentalist, and that his experimental intuition might be better trusted than his ability to construct theoretical models. If there were a good model implicitly guiding the choice of experiments in The growth of logical thinking (Inhelder, Piaget, 1958), then the presence of the model would be shown by the consistency of the behaviours from task to task which exemplify it. Pupils should show the same Piagetian level from task to task if the assumption is to be maintained that their performance depends on the same mental structures. This was tested experimentally by devising 5 formal tasks exhibiting the three different types of problem - equilibrium of physical systems, control of variables, and combinatorial thinking - comprising the content of GLT. These were then administered to over 600 above-average 14 year old boys and girls.

This was rather an exacting piece of work (Shayer, 1978a, 1979). The spin-off was a great deal of technical expertise in Piagetian group-test methodology and the production of new tests (N.F.E.R., 1979), together with much fresh data more of interest to the pure psychologist. In passing, a quantitative check was made on a challenge thrown out by Novak (1978), and is given in the Appendix.

The correlation between the tasks was of the order of 0.6. The reliability of the tasks themselves was about 0.8, and factor-analytical studies both of the battery of tasks scored separately, and on eleven variables taken from clusters of items defining specific schemas within the tests showed that one factor was sufficient to explain the common variance (Shayer, 1978a, 1979). The quantitative evidence is conveniently summarised on the following page.

Estimates of specific and common variance
for five tasks

Task	Communality	Test retest R	Specific variance
Pendulum	.52	.78	.26
Equilibrium in the balance	.56	.77	.21
Inclined plane	.61	.81	.20
Chemical combinations	.53	.65	.12
Flexible rods	.74	.85	.11

Thus there is considerable redundancy, as there should be if Piaget's model is to have some validity, and some task specificity. In fact the predictive validity of two Piaget class-tasks, used in the curriculum analysis study, was 0.77 and 0.78 for two of the sections of Combined Science, which suggests that even some of the specific variance is involved in the understanding of science in general.

This may be summarised by saying that the empirical evidence is favourable to Piaget's account of formal operational thinking, and has shown also that it has enough predictive validity for the understanding of science to be of use. But the elucidation of the model is another matter.[7] In the case of formal operational thinking almost everyone who has looked into the symbolic logic and group-theory account has found inconsistency (Parsons, 1960; Shayer, 1972; Ennis, 1975; Brainerd, 1978). There is, however, another account, used both by Piaget in GLT, and many of those who have worked in educational research. This is to define concrete and formal operational thinking in terms of a list of general and abstract descriptions characteristic of each. Thus 1 : 1 matching of two series is a concrete schema, and proportional relationships an important formal characteristic. In a very nice study, Lawson, Karplus and Adi (1978) showed that thinking involving purely verbal logic was almost totally non-correlated with important formal operational schemas, and that if the same problems were reformulated in correlational terms they factored with the formal tasks. Thus it seems likely

_____

(7) May I remark that chemists got on for decades with a theory of acidity defined mainly in terms of the behavioural characteristics of acids, and even today have two somewhat incompatible models? This does not seem to make them prefer to do without the economy of an idea of acids as opposed to an empirical list of every known reaction.

that redefinition of the admittedly unsatisfactory theoretical model,
or meta-theory, is essentially a task for philosophers of science.

American work in the Piagetian paradigm

Later some attempt will be made to define the difference between
the pre-suppositions behind British and North American work. Quite
early Raven (1967, 1972) contributed valuable fresh evidence to the
existing Genevan work on velocity and momentum. Later he turned to
studies in which the logical model used by Piaget both for concrete
and formal operational thinking was operationalised into group-test
form (Raven, 1973; Raven, Guerin, 1975). He has used both logical
models (Raven, 1974) and operational schemas (Hammond, Raven, 1973)
in attempts to accelerate the development of primary and secondary
school children. This work is scrupulously done and these and many
other papers originating around him at Buffalo obviously repay attention. It will be clear from the earlier discussion that the author
feels that concentration on the logical model may have been unlucky;
nevertheless, there is good evidence there.

Two closely related (in the person of Lawson) schools of studies
are around Renner at Oklahoma, and Karplus at Lawrence Hall of Science,
Berkeley. Lawson and Renner (1974, 1975) published a survey of 588
pupils between the ages of 12 and 18 on Piagetian developmental norms,
producing figures not incompatible, given the sampling error, with the
British large-scale survey described earlier. Likewise, they showed
multiple-correlation coefficients of 0.59, 0.53 and 0.54 between a
battery of Piagetian interviews and pupils understanding of formal
concepts in biology, chemistry and physics respectively. Much of the
work of Renner and his associates, both at the university and the
school level is summarised conveniently in Renner et al. (1976).
The productivity, in terms of numbers of papers published, of Lawrence
Hall of Science is phenomenal. One line of work, following the development of SCIS materials, has been the production of convenient neo-
Piagetian group-tests. For example, there is the well-known test
on ratio, Mr. Short and Mr. Tall (Karplus, Karplus, Wollman, 1973),
and another demonstrated test on control of variables (Wollman, 1977).
Another line is acceleration studies, the attempt to increase the rate
of intellectual development, as understood in Piagetian terms, in
children, or to supply some kind of remedial treatment at the tertiary
level (Lawson, Nordland, de Vito, 1974; Lawson, Blake, Nordland,
1975; Lawson, Wollman, 1976).(8) Many of the papers (e.g. Nordland,
Lawson, Kahle, 1974) deal with the equivalent American problem to that
of matching discussed in this paper. Given the fact that large

---

(8) Perhaps the most elegant acceleration study is that of Kuhn and
Angelev (1976), from Harvard, for in this case there was no specific
training given, only the opportunity to explore problems.

proportions of adolescents do not seem to exhibit formal operational thinking, what, as science educators, do we do about it?

The foregoing is only a superficial mention of American work: readers interested in exploring further will find most of it in the pages of the Journal of Research in Science Teaching, and Science Education.

C.S.M.S. work on personality variables

In conceiving the necessity of a descriptive model of the developing adolescent which would have predictive power for the match of curriculum to learner it was assumed that the whole person, and not just the science-trainable mind should be the object of attention. A description both of the development of the personality and the intellect was needed. Much of the psychological work on attitudinal variables is reported in global correlational studies which obscure the aetiology of the attitudes. Only by finding a developmental model would it be possible to generate testable predictions, for example about the differences between boys and girls of 12 toward science subject-matter, or to the changing attitude of boys between the ages of 11 and 16 toward the social implications of science. Certainly it is not possible for someone to be well-motivated toward work which defeats their present understanding, and it is claimed that the C.S.M.S. cognitive work has gone far to framing the cognitive limits within which choice of science activity should be confined. But one has only dealt with a necessary, though partial aspect of the problem of science teaching, when cognitive match is assured. The science activities chosen must also be assimilable to the personal world which each boy and girl is constructing at each point in their development from childhood to adulthood.(9)

Cognitive work in progress

Earlier it was mentioned that there were severe problems about Piaget's meta-theory, even though the stage-theory construct seems to be valid.(10) It can perhaps be seen, then, why the final part of the C.S.M.S. work, for which a year's extension has been granted, was deferred until after the validity study was completed. Both British work (Shayer, 1972; Shayer, 1978b) and American work (Lawson, Renner, 1975) have shown that the lesson content of science curricula can be analysed for the Piagetian level of thinking required

---

(9) The assumption is made here that the problem of science-teaching is not one of forcing pupils into a Procrustean fit with routines of science teaching with which we are familiar, but of selecting, from the very wide range of activities which are part of science those which best give pupils access to the world of science.
(10) next page.

by experts familiar with Piaget's work (in the American study the estimates were made independently by six established workers in the field). But this leaves as a major task the development of a curriculum-analysing process which can be used by the science teacher and curriculum developer without a Piaget expert conveniently on hand. The only way to replace a process of assessment which relies on one's own trained judgement is to make one's own processes of judgement explicit so that others can use them. If this involved succeeding where Piaget had failed the enterprise would certainly be doomed! Fortunately an altogether lower level of success would be adequate, and this will now be described.

There are two ways in which the task might be done. Firstly, for each of the three science subjects, physics, chemistry and biology, about 10 areas should be chosen for each such that all the main activities within each subject are covered by one or more of them. This was the method adopted by my C.S.M.S. colleagues for the subject of mathematics. In physics, examples might be heat, volume and density, energy, momentum, speed and acceleration, and so on. For the main Piagetian sub-levels, 2A, 2B, 3A and 3B, behavioural descriptions would be given of the degree of definition attainable by pupils in the hierarchy of concepts involved in each area. For example, conservation of mass is a 2A concept, intuitive 'heaviness' and conservation of weight 2B concepts, and analytical density a 3A concept. In this way a taxonomy could be produced which would work, even if a full theory was not available of why it worked. The method chosen to develop and validate this taxonomy in 1979/80 is through a series of meetings with a consultative committee of six experienced Heads of Science, and three UDE lecturers, and three members of the C.S.M.S. team. The first phase, in which there has been one meeting to date, involves collecting the feedback from successive attempts by the committee to apply different versions of the taxonomy. In the second phase, agreed predictions made possible by the taxonomy will be validated by use of pupils in schools in which Nuffield Combined Science is being taught. In this way more light can also be shone on the ways in which its teaching routines are interpreted by the complete spectrum of early secondary pupils.

A more ambitious attempt, of which the hope of success is correspondingly less, will also be made, using the same consultative committee process. This would make use of some of the conclusions of the formal thinking validity study, which were that formal operational thinking might be definable by a set of related intellectual operations involved in designing, interpreting and weighing experimental evidence

---

(10) Readers may like to see the exchange between Jenkins and Shayer in the May and September issues of Education in Chemistry, 1978. Such formal challenges and responses tend to generate more heat than light, regrettably.

in the sciences. This would not be a complete meta-theory, but would be a sub-set relating to scientific thinking. The possibility is not ruled out that The growth of logical thinking (Inhelder, Piaget, 1958) may turn out to have been a good empirical description of the growth of scientific thinking, merely. Such an approach might be more powerful, but more tricky to apply. The example of Bloom's taxonomy is cautionary: the difficulty is to avoid leaving the levels of one's taxonomy so abstract that the inter-rater reliability is low (i.e. different people assess the same task differently). Yet to provide sharp definition in a taxonomy really requires a coherent under-lying theory covering the field of application of the taxonomy. This was what the Bloom taxonomy lacked: but it is also what may be beyond the resources of the applicable researcher to provide.

Finally, some of the methods of formative evaluation which this line of research is aimed towards will be put into practice in a study already in hand in which a sample of the Science 5-13 materials will be complemented by a hierarchical developmental study designed to guide the teacher in his or her choice of activities for children of differ-ent ages and abilities in the middle and early secondary school.

What is the role of the researcher in science education?

In a recent paper (Belbin, 1979) a distinction was made between applicable and applied psychological research. The former is problem-orientated, the latter is technique-orientated, and differs only in emphasis from pure research. From a wide experience of industrial research the author answered the question, 'Does...the applicable psy-chologist have to live off a static supply of fundamental knowledge?' in the negative, and asserted: 'It is our experience that innovative development is a great stimulator of research.' Clearly in Belbin's terms, all of us are offering applicable research. That is, we start with existing school problems, and look for ways of solving them, or ways of describing them which help their solution. But I am inclined to alter Gilbert and Sullivan's phrase to 'An applicable researcher's lot is not a happy one'. However stimulating one's work happens to be, it will frequently happen that one cannot wait for the pure re-searcher to respond to the stimulus, or for the applied researcher to develop the techniques one needs. In this paper all three roles have already been exhibited within one research programme. It certainly does seem that in this type of research no simple Rothschild customer-contractor principle could apply. To contribute to school-practice, it will often be the case that the research allows school-practice to be seen from a different viewpoint, or in more powerful definition. Such research is almost by definition not definable in customer's terms since the customer can only assimilate it after it has been done.

While it is true that in the case of the C.S.M.S. programme, both on the mathematics and the science side, the research workers have come out of schools, with the problem to be investigated imprinted on their nerves and bodies, this cannot be taken as a way of defining entry to the profession. There is a real nettle to be grasped here. One is familiar with the problem of how the school copes with educational research conceived and carried out by the psychologist who is contributing primarily to his own discipline. Yet research in all the university sciences depends upon a steady supply of able first-degree students taking higher degrees. Likewise the teaching, in a university science department, is part of the process by which the lecturers assimilate the world's work in their field and pass it on to the next generation of potential researchers. But what is the equivalent in the university department of education? Most of the teaching effort goes into the preparation of teachers for school practice. I believe very firmly in the value of research, indeed am inclined to view the curriculum development of the sixties as in principle a research activity, but am very worried about the institutionalising of the process, and of ensuring its continuity. There is a very delicate balance involving the relationship of the teacher in the school, and the researcher. One might envisage a process whereby certain teachers, with three or four years teaching experience, could transfer to research as a recognised part of their career structure, but this still leaves the problem of how the activity of teaching educational research, as distinguished from, say, first degree physics, could be structured within existing UDEs. Likewise, one would like to see a closer involvement of UDEs with the development of science teaching.

How does the C.S.M.S. work relate to other work in the field?

It seems to me that there are three issues to discuss in relating the work which has been described both to other work, and to the future. To what extent has the practice of formative evaluation been added to? What is the relation between this work and other approaches to the cognitive field? And what can be said about the nature of research in science education, and of the conditions which make for its applicability and usefulness for school practice?

It has been quite puzzling to watch the pages of Science Education in the States as the battle rages between the Ausubelians and the many American Piagetians. From here it looks like one of those family squabbles which is opaque to the outsider precisely because the background to the issue is so well known to the participants that they never have to spell it out. Our own approach to the issue is very pragmatic. Our major concern is with secondary and middle school education, whereas in the States much of the focus of attention has been senior high school pupils of 16 to 18, and first and second year college students. In the States the concern would be on how to get the intellectual most from students who have already completed most of their basic intellectual development, and who probably lie in the upper 50 percentile range.

But when it is a question of planning science activity for the whole school population between the ages of, say, 9 and 16, the very breadth of the cognitive differences causes stress to be laid on the limits to understanding consequent on the individual's present level of intellectual development. When it is a question of alerting a whole educational system to the reason why it is folly to base a curriculum model for all on what has been found suitable for the top 20%, then a comparatively coarse-definition theory may not merely be adequate but may actually be better than one focussed on the fine details, for the purpose. I would view research from a Piagetian model in this light: that it is a valuable, even essential tool for getting right the broad limits of the framing of the cognitive scope of science curricula in relation to the present and future cognitive abilities of pupils. But it is not a learning model in itself, and I view it as no more than one among several other approaches which may contribute to the structuring of curricular experiences better to facilitate the education of each individual. Among the others of immediate value is the Ausubelian stress upon the contrast between formal relationships of developed science concepts and the intuitive set of concepts which the learner is apt to impose on the same experimental evidence which is related by us to the formal system we are trying to teach, and the work of Gordon Pask on the differences in learning strategies of different individuals.

Robert Karplus and Robert Fuller have derived a learning model from Piaget's account of equilibration of cognitive structures, and the SCIS learning cycle looks, from here, very like a formalisation of some of the approaches labelled by us as the spirit of the Nuffield approach to science teaching. But when it comes to research strategy, then the assumption of some Americans that it is profitable to model the problem of learning science in terms of accelerating intellectual development as described in specifically Piagetian terms does not seem as immediately attractive as an approach based on a detailed study of the developmental hierarchy in particular areas of science. Indeed, as can be seen by the use made of Piagetian theory in the revision of Nuffield O-level Chemistry, it was precisely because the existing body of Piaget's work did appear to describe more adequately the present structure of concepts of the individual, and relate it to their future likely structure, that it was taken as the most immediately profitable source of theory. But in general it seems to me that one has to strike a balance between decisions to 'adapt to the cognitive capacity of the pupil' and decisions to 'expedite the pupil's training'. For the former the Piagetian model is often accurate enough - certainly, it is claimed, for the recommendation that for most adolescents concrete operational thinking is the correct frame - for the latter there is no substitute for detailed empirical study.[11]

(11) The idea that 'one should not teach a topic until the pupil is ready' seems to me a pure straw man. Even a genius would not long persist in trying to teach Newton's laws to an average 12 year old. Only a fool would fail to make use of an average 12 year old's intuitive concept of force. Perhaps both would find useful the information that the differentiation of the concept of force/unit area from force is an early formal accomplishment.

The use of concurrent Piagetian group-tests together with tests of understanding and attainment of new curricular objectives does seem to be an invaluable tool in the formative evaluation of curricula. In this way the design of trials can be structured so as to give immediate feedback to the curriculum development team of some of the reasons for the failure or success of course materials. Moreover, it largely gets over the problem of the representativeness of the sample of trial schools. By mapping the attainment of course objectives, where relevant, onto Piagetian level of pupils it affords a mechanism for the generalisation of the results to other pupils having the same or different ranges of cognitive levels. In effect one is arguing that curriculum development should be set up on an industrial research and development model. Other inputs to the formative evaluation should certainly, when developed sufficiently, be added. These might include both personality measures related to motivation, and what has been labelled the sociology of the classroom.[12]

As argued in the previous section, there are problems about the institutionalising of applicable research in science teaching. It is part of the present received wisdom that the D.E.S[*]., for example, will fund only on the Rothschild principle, on a fairly narrowly defined field promising immediate payoff. Yet in the A.S.E. discussion document (A.S.E., 1979, p.53) with whose drift and reasons I largely agree, it is stated:

'we recommend that substantial resources be allocated to a major programme of research and development that seeks to evaluate alternative definitions of school science; that develops and effectively evaluates curricula proposals in the areas of applied science, earth sciences and the history and philosophy of science; and which develops a series of small-scale and intensive studies of the nature of young people's conceptualisations of science and scientific processes.'

What divisions of labour and funding beteen UDEs, the D.E.S., Schools Council and LEAs would be needed to carry out that recommendation on behalf of the young people who are the final causes of our work?

*D.E.S. = Department of Education and Science

---

(12) As illustrated in Fraser (1977), it is by no means obvious that one could predict all the outcomes, beforehand, of setting up 'ASEP classrooms', or laboratories. Who other than the sociologist, or social psychologist, to monitor the process?

Appendix

Individual variation on tasks compared with variation between individuals

It has been argued by Novak (1978), in a comparison between the relevance of Piaget's and Ausubel's work to problems of cognitive learning, that:

> 'We believe the growing body of evidence obtained from the more generalised Piagetian tasks also shows approximately the same variability among age groups and for individuals tested across a variety of tasks.'

Clearly this is an assertion which can be tested on the data gathered on 5 formal tasks. The sample used only spans the upper 40% of 14 year olds and so, if the assertion is unsupported on this sample it would be even further from the truth if the whole range of 14 year olds were tested.

The components of variance to be differentiated are the variation of each subject's mean on the 5 tasks around the grand mean, and the variation which all the subjects show around their own means. If Novak's assertion is correct then the two variations will be the same, and there will be no 'between subjects' variance - that is, a component of variance due to the individual variability being less than the variability of the sample of individuals.

The analysis of variance assumed a random effects model (Armitage, 1971, p.198) in which the k tasks are assumed to be randomly selected from a population of such tasks. For the sample of 461 boys and girls who had done all 5 tasks the analysis of variance is as follows:

	df	SS	MS
Between subjects	460	1795	3.9022
Within subjects	1844	1113.6	0.6039
	2304	2908.6	

The mean square ratio then tests the hypothesis that the between-subjects variance is zero, in which case the between subjects mean square and the within subjects mean square will be the same. For this table, $F = 6.46$. Thus there is no doubt that the hypothesis is disproved, and the components of variance can be calculated as follows:

$$\text{Estimated between subjects variance} = \frac{3.9022 - 0.6039}{5} = 0.6597$$

Thus, between subjects variance ($\hat{\sigma}_B^2$)   0.6597   52.2%

within subjects variance (S_W^2)   0.6039   47.8%

Note: This Appendix is taken from Shayer (1978a). The Piagetian tasks were pendulum, equilibrium in the balance. inclined plane, chemical combinations and flexible rods.

RESPONSE by Rosalind Driver

It is not without some misgivings that I find myself in the position of discussant to this paper. The reasons are varied. First, I am aware that what is in this paper is the essence of many years' focussed work, first on Michael Shayer's own part and then with the C.S.M.S. team. Research undertaken with such consistency over this kind of time span is not common in education. For this reason it merits respect. It also makes it hard to respond to adequately in the time available, and I have to be selective in my comments.

Secondly, we know that the theoretical framework underpinning Piagetian stage studies is currently under criticism from various quarters, and as Michael Shayer stated in his paper much of this has generated more heat than light.

My final misgiving is that this is a most substantial report and it is impossible to comment at the length required to do justice to it. Therefore in the short time available it may be more helpful to focus on a restricted number of issues rather than covering more at a superficial level, and this is what I propose to do.

The beginning of the paper raises important issues for our consideration in comparing curriculum development to industrial production. It returns at the end again to the role and state of educational research. Although I do not under-rate the significance of these remarks, I shall not comment on them. I hope however they will be taken up in discussion later in the Seminar when we consider issues such as the research-practitioner interface.

The aspect of the paper which I shall focus my comment on is the cognitive matching model. The paper argues to begin with that the curriculum development movement in this country, for reasons he specifies, has produced a mismatch between the reasoning abilities of the learners and the demands of the science curriculum.

In a well-known passage David Ausubel states:

'If I had to reduce all of educational psychology to just one principle, I would say this: The most important single factor influencing learning is what the learner already knows. Ascertain this and teach him accordingly.' (Ausubel, 1968)

This is surely a statement of a matching strategy, but how differently it can be interpreted. I cite three ways:

First, there are those who Professor Lovell referred to in his paper as skill integrationists. For them matching might require first an assessment of the subordinate skills the pupil has available to him. The learning sequence is then entered at the appropriate point. For example, can the pupil use ideas of mass and volume before starting a learning sequence on density. The work of Gagné and those concerned with validating hierarchies is relevant here.

Secondly, there are those who accept that pupils may have built up ideas or conceptual frameworks about topics they meet in science which may differ from the accepted view. Such studies suggest a different problem of 'matching' exists. It is the problem of how to present material to pupils in such a way as to encourage them to reconsider and modify their existing frameworks.

Thirdly, there is the broadly based Piagetian stage model: find out what logical structures of thought the pupil is capable of and match the logical demands of the curriculum to them. Referring to the earlier example of density, the key element which would be pertinent is that it is a concept involving proportionality, and therefore demands formal level thought. To use linguists'jargon, it is the syntax as opposed to the semantic element of the concept which is of import.

The paper states that in the early 1970s the Piagetian paradigm was the only one to use; I list the above matching strategies as a reminder to us all that there are alternatives. It is the last of the three cases which Michael Shayer and his team in the C.S.M.S. project have investigated empirically. Parallel research to this has been undertaken over a period of several years in North America, notably by Renner and Karplus. The model of matching curricula to pupils' levels of logical skills has also been adopted as a basis for course design, as for example in Science 5/13, the Australian Science Education Project and the American course Science: A Process Approach.

The research reported in this paper summarises one of the most thorough investigations undertaken into the utility and validity of this approach. Because of the breadth of interest that exists in the model internationally, it is timely to evaluate carefully the results that are presented here.

Matching the science curriculum to the learner

Any matching model must have two components. One is a method of analysis of the curriculum and the other is a method for assessing the pupils' levels of thinking.

Starting with the first, Michael Shayer's work on the analysis of science curricula for the Piagetian level of demand is well known, certainly in this country. Although the principle behind the exercise is clear and I would argue, useful, the allocation of specific lesson objectives to Piagetian levels may be open to some dispute. Certain topics particularly in biology are dependent for the demand they make on the pupil not on the inherent complexity of the logic of the concepts involved, but on the pedagogical approach adopted. For example,

does the teacher pose the problem as an hypothesis to be tested placing the burden on the class to design appropriate experiments, or
are they led through the problem in a didactic way? The way the
lessons are presented will make a difference as to the level to which
they should be ascribed. This makes the curriculum analysis quite
fragile with respect to teacher interpretation.

While indicating there may be problems of this kind in assessing
the level of demand of the curriculum, I will not dwell on this side
of the work. It is the ability to assess the level of thinking of
pupils which warrants more careful scrutiny. Michael Shayer has given
a section of his paper the title 'Is Piaget's model of operational
thinking powerful enough?' Powerful enough for what? Powerful enough
to match teaching material to individual learners? Or powerful enough
to act as a general guide in design and sequencing of science teaching
material?

The method of assessing pupils' level of thinking required the
development of group tests, of necessity to collect data from a large
enough population. Of course the results from those group administered
tests were checked against those obtained from clinical interviews,
and apparently were equivalent. However, other research does indicate
there may be cause for caution. For example, Blake (1978) reports
that performance on written tests of Piagetian level are influenced by
level of reading comprehension and degree of field independence.

When I was teaching in a comprehensive school, I used to give the
11 year olds a class test based on Piaget's conservation tasks. I
found it useful diagnostically before teaching a unit on mass, volume
and density. On one occasion I had shown the class the two balls of
plasticine; we had agreed that they contained equal amounts. I
rolled one out and asked the usual question 'Does the one I have
rolled into a sausage contain more, less, or the same amount of plasticine as the other one?' and 'Say why you think so'. Walking around
the class I noticed one lad had written Less, but not being enamoured
with writing had not explained his reason. I called him up afterwards
and he said 'Of course it would be less. Look, if I roll out a lump
of plasticine like this some is left on the surface of the table.'
Well, it is dangerous to argue from one anecdote, but it serves as
a cautionary note.

Returning to the issue of establishing national norms, of the
group tasks used only two enable an assessment of early or late formal
thinking to be made; the task on volume and heaviness, and the
pendulum task. In the light of later data given in the paper on intercorrelations between tasks one wonders how sensitive such national
norms are to the criterion tasks chosen.

Despite these cautionary notes the results of the national surveys
do warrant attention. As with similar surveys undertaken by others
those results indicate a discrepancy between the British results and
the ages at which different stages are attained in the Genevan studies.

Perhaps a word should be put in for Piaget here. Piaget is not a developmental psychologist, he is not interested in establishing developmental norms. He is an epistemologist interested in the epistemic man: the development of knowledge. For him random or representative sampling is simply not an issue of importance.

The validity of the stage of formal operations

I now turn to what is the most important issue underlying this whole work. Implicit in the survey work is the assumption that the tasks used are dependent on an underlying skill or competence; that if a pupil is assessed as operating at level say 3A on the pendulum and volume tasks, this will be a predictor for performance on other tasks. We might expect the pupil for example, to understand pressure in terms of force on a unit area, or interpret experiments where controls are set up; there is an underlying assumption of the unity of the stage. This is of course the key question underlying the whole matching model, and was quite properly investigated in depth by Michael Shayer, using the five tasks listed in his paper. As the paper states, the correlations between the scores on the five tasks used is of the order of 0.6. This gives us an indication of the tasks as predictors of pupils' success in learning tasks with similar structures. The question I ask is: is this an adequate predictor to use in a matching exercise? It goes some way, but accounts for less than 50% of the variance of the scores. On this basis alone I question its utility to classroom teachers to undertake any tight matching of the curriculum to the learner. I leave on one side the variability between pupils in a class.

The next process in the analysis of the data was to look for factors to account for the common variance, i.e. to assess the validity of the stage model itself. Various people have suggested that the stage of formal operations is not a unity but a collection of separate skills. With this in mind, the results reported are interesting, in that the sub-scores on parts of the tasks which on inspection appear to make the same logical demand, for example, using proportional thinking or control of variables, are closely associated, but no more so than scores on other sub-items. One major factor appears to account for the common variance.

Establishing the existence of a common factor here is an interesting outcome. What that commonality can be ascribed to is of course open to conjecture. Michael Shayer argues that the results suggest a 'single reality processing mechanism'. There may however be other interpretations. It could be that it is the common conceptual base of the tasks, all of which are set in the physical sciences,which underlies the commonality.

A similar study by Lawson, Karplus and Adi (1978) has recently been reported. They used tasks spanning a wider concept base, and apart from those tasks involving propositional logic, they too found

all the common variance could be accounted for by a single factor.
Could it be that we are rediscovering Spearman's 'g'?

We should not however overlook the results from other sources
showing that content is important. Studies have been made of human
reasoning on tasks with identical structures but set in different
contexts, such as those reported by Wason (1977). In one case two
tasks are used, one is Wason's four card problem, the other was a
logically equivalent task in a thematic context devised by Johnson-
Laird, Legrenzi and Legrenzi. Results showed that subjects had a much
greater success in solving the thematic as opposed to the abstract
form of the task. Other relevant studies are reported by Donaldson
(1978).
In a report on a series of experiments on adult strategies in problem solving Wason and Johnson-Laird (1972) conclude:

'Content is crucial, and this suggests that any general theory
of human reasoning must include an important semantic component'

Also '...the individual tends naturally to think in a causal fashion
and that if this tendency is set into opposition with the logical
requirements of an inference, it is extremely difficult for the
correct deductions to be made.'

I understand that Professor Jungwirth's paper to be presented later in
this Seminar is relevant to this issue.

I have suggested that content as well as structure may be of
importance and on these two alternative interpretations, structure
versus content, much pedagogy depends. Adopting the position that it
is the underlying logical structure of the tasks that is of prime
importance in determining its difficulties, and that the required
logical skills arise developmentally, then the outcome from an educators point of view is wait till the pupils are ready. The alternative
interpretation suggests that if it is conceptual understanding which
is important then increased exposure to the ideas will help learning.

Of course we could view these not as opposed factors but complementary. Certain logical operations may tend to develop at certain
ages but when they appear depends on familiarity with the context.
So although I am sceptical of the value of tight matching levels of
pupils' thinking to specific topics in the curriculum, some loose
matching can be very helpful, especially when planning a programme for
pupils over several years. It would be a waste of effort to attempt
to teach say velocity to eight year olds, with the underlying problem
of proportionality to handle, when if you wait till age 13 or 14 they
may understand and use the idea without great difficulty.

Final comments

1. First let us consider the utility of the matching model. I
    suggest that the data indicates that this may have value as
    a component in the planning of curriculum development projects,
    i.e. in a loose matching exercise; as a guide in planning
    children's work in science over several years. But I ask
    whether we need sophisticated diagnostic tests for this
    purpose?

2. I am very sceptical about the use of the matching model to
    practising teachers on a topic by topic, class by class basis.
    There is too much variance unaccounted for, and too much un-
    certainty in the assessment of the demands of the curriculum
    to make it useful at this level.

3. I argue that the content as well as the structure of a task
    may be important. If it has as important an influence on
    thinking as some studies suggest then the development of
    pupils' understanding of specific concepts or topics must
    be as much the focus of our attention for matching as pupils'
    logical development.

Discussion

Discussion opened with a challenge to Shayer's assumption of
a model of stages of cognitive development comprising an equal interval scale, rather than e.g. an ordinal and curvilinear one with
differences in the upper limits greater than in the lower limits.
Shayer's response was that he had no evidence of curvilinearity in
the C.S.M.S. data. It was also suggested from the audience that
the inter-task correlation could be a correlation with a common
factor of familiarity or shared experience across the five class tasks.
Shayer's experience was that school experience did not affect performance on the tasks. His position in relation to Piaget's 'meta-
theory' was also clarified. He rejected Piaget's competence model in
favour of what he referred to as the developmental construct model,
and assumed the class tasks to have no connection with tests of logic.
Extrapolation from the tasks to subject content was done 'by establishing intermediate levels of abstractions', such as, for instance,
the ability to use a model, investigatory style, etc.

The question of achievement testing and the correlation of performance with the class task measures was raised in view of the
claim that performance on the tasks is independent of prior school
experience. With a two month Nuffield unit between the administration
of class tasks and achievement tests, two units gave correlations of
.77 and .78. As the best predictors of pupil achievement still
appeared to be previous achievement test performance, one participant
suggested that another form of assessment might be considered

redundant. The C.S.M.S. team pointed out that correlations between achievement levels for the same student could sometimes be very low, but that anyway a basic target was to predict the suitability of material rather than the achievement of pupils.

On the question of analysing the difficulties a given curriculum presented, a suggestion was posed that one of the factors causing pupils difficulty was not simply a lack of requisite intellectual skills, but the result of the inappropriate preconceptions which they brought to the material. Furthermore it was inferred that the model assumed that there was only one way of learning the material available to the pupil. Shayer strenuously denied that he was in any way adopting a learning model, stressing that his main objective was the development of a method of overcoming what he described as the appalling mismatch of curricular materials to pupils, particularly where efforts were made to teach science to the whole ability range. He went on to suggest that when this was done, the utility of the Piagetian model would be at an end. Some participants were disquieted that the class tasks would be available to possible misinterpretation through teacher usage, and since the survey work was now done, questioned their publication. Shayer's response was that the tasks could still be valuable as a research tool and to local groups of teachers engaged in developing new curricula. He suggested that the measures they provided gave a co-measure or framework for interpretation.

Papers relating to Aspects of Piagetian Stage Theory and the Development of Logical Abilities

SHOULD WE CHECK CHILDREN?

E. Rothwell Hughes

This paper stems from research promoted by the Schools Council and published in the form of two books: Conceptual Powers of Children: an Approach through Mathematics and Science, Hughes, (1979) and a guidebook for teachers Area, Weight and Volume: Monitoring and encouraging children's conceptual development, Bell, Hughes and Rogers (1975). The study analysed the responses of 1000 children between the ages of seven and eleven to a battery of practical tests designed by the project to assess conceptual development in area, weight and volume. Time and space does not allow one to summarise the results of this work but for discussion purposes I would like to highlight some of the results and findings in the area of conservation studies.

First, however, I ought to sketch the framework of the research project as it differed in a number of respects from previous work in the field. The study attempted to incorporate the following design features:

(i) Some 48 practical test items (13 for weight, 18 for area, 17 for volume) were designed over an 18 month pilot period to cover the range of thinking operations from the stage where the children rely heavily on the real, observable situation and where their powers of reasoning depend almost entirely on the immediate appearance of things, through the concrete operational stage to the stage where the children begin to display the ability to work out possible procedures and situations in their minds before handling the material.

(ii) All the test items involved a fixed presentation of the problems, questions and material but allowed the subjects to respond freely in oral and practical terms to the problems. The subjects were not involved in pencil and paper type concept tests.

(iii) As many researchers rely on evidence for particular modes of thinking (the word 'stage' is deliberately avoided here) from one or two practical test items the research team decided to follow Uzgiris' (1964) belief that a number of practical items should be devised all exploring the same conceptual level in a topic (e.g. weight). It was argued that the responses to all these situations taken together were likely to afford stronger indications of the child's level of thinking than was the case in the single practical situation.

(iv) If we examine the best known of the Piagetian researchers (see Modgil 1974 for example) we rarely read of researchers who have asked the same children questions about the same level of thinking e.g. the idea of conservation but in different topics such as weight, area and volume, and also used different practical situations and different materials. In the present research, therefore, an attempt was made to incorporate into the testing procedures, practical items in each of the concepts of area, weight and volume that could be termed 'parallel' items. The final versions of the assessment materials tried to incorporate a number of these parallel items and to include tests concerned with categorisation ability, perception, measurement and the use of concrete-logic as well as those concerned with conservation.

(v) 150 children were selected from each of the age groups 7y5m; 7y11m; 8y5m; 8y11m; 9y5m; 9y11m; (children were within one month of the selected age at the time of testing). In the light of indications obtained from the pilot survey (involving some 350 children) it was also decided to select equal numbers of children from each of the four bands of ability as indicated by a non-verbal intelligence test (N.F.E.R. Picture Test A and N.F.E.R. Non-verbal reasoning test BD). This non-random technique was used as we wished to discover how high ability children at a given age fared on the concept tests by comparison with lower ability children.

(vi) The problem of communication between the test operator and subject was studied at both design of test and interpretation of result stage. (Further details of test design and implementation may be obtained from the publications previously mentioned.)

The study developed as a result of the trend in the late sixties and early seventies for modes of teaching to be loosely based on beliefs about the conceptual development of children. It was felt by the present writer that this confidence in our knowledge about such development was not entirely warranted by the research evidence especially as the latter was usually carried out on small samples of children using limited test material. Whilst recognising the importance and value of Piaget's work in this field it was felt that practitioners of the 'new' curricula were jumping too far ahead of both theory and research evidence.

During the recent past rational criticism of Piagetian theory by Smedslund (1977); Brown, Desforges (1977); Ennis (1975) and others has caused us all to re-examine aspects of the theory. Indeed Professor Novak argues that 'David Ausubel's theory of cognitive learning is more relevant and more powerful for science and mathematics education than the developmental psychology of Jean Piaget' (Novak, 1977b) and has suggested that we may be at the point of time in the field of cognitive development equivalent to the period in the sixteenth century when the epicycle concept of planetary motion gave way to the Copernican heliocentric model (Novak, 1977a). Bearing in mind this debate and also recent research in the secondary school field for example in the U.S.A.: Lawson, Wollman (1976); Lawson, Renner (1974); in the U.K.: Shayer et al. (1976); in Australia: Rowell, Dawson (1977); Robertson, Richardson (1975). I would like to comment on one or two of the results in our research (with particular reference to the notion of conservation).

Table 1 presents the results (as percentages) of all the test items in the three concepts which required the understanding of conservation for their correct solution. Nineteen tests - five for weight, nine for area and five for volume - fell into this category. For each age group the percentage of correct responses as indicated by correct answers and correct verbal explanations is given alongside the number of incorrect responses of the type indicating that the children were basing their conclusions on simple perception or appearances (the remaining wide variety of incorrect responses are not analysed here but their percentage may be formed by subtraction in table 1). The figures in this table relate to the total number of children in the sample, i.e. all the ability ranges are included. (Details of the tests are to be found in both publications on the research by Schools Council.)

A number of general points emerge from an examination of this table.

a.   With the exception of one or two items the results follow the same general trend and also agree, in general terms, with other researchers, e.g. Elkind (1961); Lovell, Ogilvie (1960, 1961a, 1961b); Beard (1962, 1963, 1964); Smedslund (1961-62, 1963); Uzgiris (1964). However the variations in the results of these other researches (see Fogelman, 1969) occur all together in our study. It is difficult to conclude that the understanding of conservation in any one topic is more difficult for the children than any of the others.

The numbers of full correct responses range more or less between the same figures from topic to topic. The only clearly observable group trend is that fewer children seem to be dominated by visual appearances in the weight tests than in the other two topics.

Table 1: Conservation in weight, area and volume

	7y 5m		7y 11m		8y 5m		8y 11m		9y 5m		9y 11m	
	Cor-rect %	Incor-rect* %	Cor-rect %	Incor-rect* %	Cor-rect %	Incor-rect* %	Cor-rect %	Incor-rect* %	Cor-rect %	Incor-rect* %	Cor-rect %	Incor-rect* %
Weight												
Item 4a	52	28	63	24	66	26	71	19	83	8	80	14
Item 4b	39	37	57	32	60	31	63	25	80	11	77	16
Item 5	41	27	50	19	59	15	75	6	70	6	74	5
Item 6a	59	25	68	17	80	14	88	7	90	7	84	11
Item 6b	68	17	71	17	82	12	87	6	93	6	91	5
Area												
Item 6a	25	47	29	41	43	31	49	29	63	21	55	25
Item 6b	67	19	71	18	85	9	90	7	87	6	87	8
Item 7a	49	38	54	34	71	19	76	21	78	16	83	15
Item 7b	58	29	62	27	75	17	81	14	85	10	86	9
Item 8	8	69	11	70	18	68	20	64	21	66	26	66
Item 9a	58	34	68	24	81	15	83	14	90	7	88	9
Item 9b	70	15	72	18	90	6	89	7	93	2	93	2
Item 9c	61	25	68	17	84	10	83	8	90	4	90	5
Item 10	43	37	43	24	64	18	61	15	69	13	73	9
Volume												
Item 7	51	38	56	28	68	24	71	18	75	20	79	13
Item 8a	43	38	46	32	57	25	62	16	74	11	72	10
Item 8b	35	34	45	29	54	25	63	16	72	15	72	17
Item 9a	51	39	57	33	69	24	70	24	73	24	71	22
Item 9b	52	40	58	28	72	18	75	16	81	12	77	15
Sample size, N (=100%)	146		150		150		155		155		149	

*'Incorrect' refers to incorrect responses due to centring; other incorrect responses are not shown.

(b) There is more variation in the number of correct responses between similar items in any one topic than can be generally detected between items in different topics. It should be remembered that, with the exception of the one or two items referred to below, all were carefully designed to be presented in similar fashion. In all these cases the children remained in a passive situation, observing the tester handling the materials. In all these items too, the children first saw and agreed that the property in question (weight, area or volume) was equal in the two objects. One object was then deformed or rearranged to accentuate a dimension and the children were asked questions of a similar nature to determine whether they understood the concept of conservation. Incidentally, test items using discontinuous objects (weight item 6b; area items 9b and 9c) broken up into separate pieces, rather than objects rearranged into continuous, elongated shapes, produce more correct responses than any other (see Smedslund, 1961, for example).

(c) The concept of conservation of solid and occupied (space) volume is only marginally more difficult than that of conservation of weight. Indeed, one can perhaps detect that conservation of area is generally better understood than conservation of either weight or volume. This slight difference is perhaps to be expected as 'area' is commonly taught at this age. Indeed the conservation of volume compared at the same level of test item as the other topics is surprisingly well understood even at $7\frac{1}{2}$ years of age, considering that it is rarely taught directly in the classroom. At this point I should comment that I am unhappy at previous interpretations made on the problem of conservation of volume. Invariably these interpretations are based on test items using the same material for other test items, e.g. conservation of weight (usually that trademark of the Piagetian researcher - plasticine) or on complicated test items involving an understanding of displacement. (This is studied by further test items in our research but is not discussed here.)

Returning to our results; in general it would seem that there is very little basis for the supposition that the concept of volume is harder to understand than, say, that of area. From the present results, there is much to be said for the introduction of the concept of conservation in all these topics at about the same time.

On the whole then, our pupils gave answers which fitted into the typical categories by Piaget (although the remaining unlisted incorrect answers could not be categorised). The pupils, considered as a group, appeared to demonstrate the thought structures he describes. In general, too, performance does improve with age, although our figures vary slightly from those quoted by other researchers. At this level of analysis the variation in the responses within the group lead us to suspect that a group result may not reflect individual performances.

The first question that follows seems to be: 'Are the children who are correct in one test item, the same children in the correct category in another test item?'. This question was actually referred to: 'Of those children who were correct in volume tests, how many of those same children were correct in the weight tests and, in turn, in area?'. For the purpose of this paper only the age range 7y5m is considered to illustrate the point.

Comparisons are shown as follows in table 2:

Volume 7 with weight 4a   :   Volume 7 with weight 6a
Volume 8a with weight 4a   :   Volume 8a with weight 6a
Volume 7 with area 7b   :   Volume 7 with area 9a
Volume 8a with area 7b   :   Volume 8a with area 9a
Area 7b with weight 4a   :   Volume 9a with weight 6a

As an example of this particular method of display we can examine the number of $7\frac{1}{2}$ year old children who gave correct answers to volume item 7 and see how many of them also gave correct responses in weight item 4a. Reading left to right: 75 children (23+52) out of 146 gave the correct answer to the volume item, of those 23 (31%) gave the correct answers to this item but did not give the correct answer to weight item 4a. The remaining 52 (61%) also gave the correct answer to weight item 4a. Alternatively reading right to left, 76 children (52+24) gave the correct answer to weight item 4a. Of these 24 (32%) gave the correct answer to this item but did not give the right answer to the volume item.

It is argued that only such an analysis will show whether there is an order in the understanding of conservation in weight, area and volume. Without analysing these results in further detail (see research report for details) this example demonstrates the complexity of the pattern of concept development in children. Some children, at all ages, grasp one conservation concept in one test situation before grasping it in another; this is true from topic to topic and also between apparently fairly similar tasks in any one topic (say weight). From our research it is not possible to determine for certain which they will grasp first. Unfortunately, of these children who showed that they understood the concept of conservation in both a weight (say) and a volume task (say) it is impossible to determine which they grasped first.

Table 2: Comparative study of the order of acquisition
(Age 7y5m, N = 146)

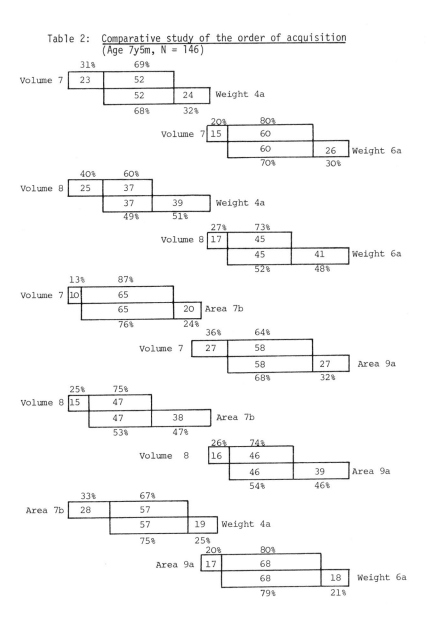

The conclusions from this more detailed analysis confirm the doubts one has for the resolving power of Piagetian type tests. It seems clear that even though we have tried to reduce communication problems (not discussed in this paper), increased the number of 'parallel' test items and used the same children over a short period of time the results display a variation in responses. This suggests that either our tests were not sufficiently refined to measure children at particular stages or else the children are constantly changing their views and forms of conclusion dependent on their perception of each task but within a conceptual range dependent on their experiences. The limits of these ranges could vary from individual to individual and could be constantly changing with different experiences. In short, to think of children as being at a particular 'stage' of development seems to be too simplistic a view. Even the test is an experience and moves the child to grapple with the problem. Whilst agreeing in general with Piagetian notions of assimilation and accommodation it would appear that Piaget's process of equilibration is mental perpetual motion and the resulting zigzag development of the child's thinking powers present the research worker with a situation similar to the atomic physicist's Uncertainty Principle. As soon as the researcher attempts to measure the stage of development reached by a child by using any communication and practical technique he causes the child to grapple with the problem and, in effect, encourages the equilibration process. This continual dynamic state of the learning process seems to be evident in the results of the exercise carried out by Lawson, Nordland, Devito (1974) when they witnessed the variation in responses to 'pre-tests and post-tests following a one week period in which the subjects received no training and simply pursued their normal daily activities'.

All in all I am forced to one of two conclusions: either the form, number and grouping of tests used (which I maintain were at least an improvement on the majority of the reported researches which tend to use a limited number of unmatched test items - sometimes of the more abstract paper and pencil variety) did not have the resolving power to indicate clearly the developmental stages reached by the children and so Piaget once more remains unproven in detail. Alternatively it can be hypothesised that any given concept is never "acquired" but is in the process of being differentiated' (Novak, 1977b). In this latter article (Alternative to Piagetian Psychology) Novak wrote 'If cognitive operations are acquired with maturation spontaneously and influenced only in a general way by experience, then we should see definite patterns in the nature and use of concepts as we observe children from early years to adulthood. If on the other hand, specific concepts are acquired as a function of specific learning experiences, we should expect to see wide individual variability in concept attainment both between individuals of a given age and for any one individual across subject matter areas...Piaget's views lead to the former interpretation and Ausubel's views favour the latter interpretation.' Having briefly looked at variation of performances across 'subject matter' (topic and test item) let us now glance at the attainment of conservation of individuals according to age and ability as measured by the intelligence tests.

Table 3 refers to items 4a, 5 and 6a (weight) and items 7, 8a and 9a (volume).

Table 4 refers to items 6b, 7b, 9a and 10 (area).

Observation shows the wide variability from the high ability 7y5m child to the low ability 9y11m child and vice versa. Once again a general group pattern is seen in all test items but individual variation is the dominant feature. Clearly it appears that the ability to conserve is a gradual development throughout the age range under study and this picture reinforces the conclusion that age provides little guidance as measure for the ability to conserve. Furthermore this presentation of the results compared with the overall impression of gradual improvement with age demonstrated by table 1 forces us to examine the Novak statement (1977b) that 'we could interpret the relatively uniform increase in percentage of children acquiring competence in each task as the result of a composite of stagewise advantages by individuals that add to an appearance of a continuous development pattern for the sample groups' with the feeling that it contains more than a grain of truth.

To conclude this analysis I would like to return to table 1 and examine in more detail those results which differ from the pattern of the rest. These are the results for test item 6a, and area test item 8. In these items the number of correct results are lower than in the other area items.

Item 6a

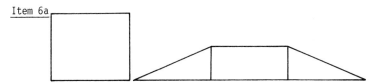

6a   Assemble the blue shapes on the table.
       'Does this square have the same amount of surface as that shape (indicate) or does it have a different amount of surface? You can move the shapes if you want to.'
If S answers *'the same'*,
       'Why do you say that?'

If S answers *'the same because one is longer but the other is fatter'* or similar compensatory reason,
       'Is there any other reason why they have the same amount of surface as each other?'
If S answers *'different'*,
       'Which shape has more surface?'
       'Why do you say that?'

Table 3: Tests of conservation of weight

		Ability band				χ^2	Signif.
		≤89	90-99	100-109	≥110		
Item 4a							
7y 5m	P	9	19	21	27	16.62	0.01
	F	25	21	14	10		
7y 11m	P	16	23	23	33	13.72	0.01
	F	22	13	13	7		
8y 5m	P	17	22	27	33	10.85	0.02
	F	14	20	10	7		
8y 11m	P	19	27	29	34	15.37	0.01
	F	19	15	7	5		
9y 5m	P	25	35	35	35	9.64	0.05
	F	12	4	5	4		
9y 11m	P	22	28	36	33	-	-
	F	15	7	5	3		
Item 5							
7y 5m	P	7	16	17	20	9.29	0.05
	F	27	24	18	17		
7y 11m	P	17	15	15	28	8.82	0.05
	F	21	21	21	12		
8y 5m	P	17	21	23	27	2.96	-
	F	14	21	14	13		
8y 11m	P	24	35	28	30	4.66	-
	F	14	7	8	9		
9y 5m	P	18	32	30	28	11.19	0.02
	F	19	7	10	11		
9y 11m	P	22	27	29	32	8.59	0.05
	F	15	8	12	4		
Item 6a							
7y 5m	P	12	21	26	27	14.96	0.01
	F	22	19	9	10		
7y 11m	P	21	22	24	35	10.64	0.02
	F	17	14	12	5		
8y 5m	P	19	32	33	35	10.23	0.02
	F	12	10	4	5		
8y 11m	P	26	40	31	39	-	-
	F	12	2	5	0		
9y 5m	P	30	36	37	36	-	-
	F	7	3	3	3		
9y 11m	P	26	27	37	35	-	-
	F	11	8	4	1		

Table 3 (cont): <u>Tests of conservation of volume</u>

Item 7		Ability band				χ^2	Signif.
		<89	90-99	100-109	≥110		
7y 5m	P	9	12	24	30	33.0	0.01
	F	25	28	11	7		
7y 11m	P	15	20	20	30	10.08	0.02
	F	23	16	16	10		
8y 5m	P	15	26	26	34	11.44	0.01
	F	16	16	11	6		
8y 11m	P	23	29	27	31	4.34	-
	F	15	13	9	8		
9y 5m	P	20	30	35	33	14.34	0.01
	F	17	9	5	6		
9y 11m	P	23	26	34	34	-	-
	F	14	9	7	2		
Item 8a							
7y 5m	P	2	13	19	28	38.97	0.01
	F	32	27	16	9		
7y 11m	P	2	16	16	27	15.15	0.01
	F	29	20	20	13		
8y 5m	P	9	21	28	28	13.97	0.01
	F	22	21	9	12		
8y 11m	P	18	24	24	30	7.89	0.05
	F	20	18	12	9		
9y 5m	P	17	31	33	34	20.85	0.01
	F	20	8	7	5		
9y 11m	P	14	27	35	32	-	-
	F	23	8	6	4		
Item 9a							
7y 5m	P	6	20	21	27	23.41	0.01
	F	28	20	14	10		
7y 11m	P	16	16	21	33	16.40	0.01
	F	22	20	15	7		
8y 5m	P	15	29	27	33	9.88	0.02
	F	16	13	10	7		
8y 11m	P	21	28	25	34	9.56	0.05
	F	17	14	11	5		
9y 5m	P	16	28	35	34	-	-
	F	21	11	5	5		
9y 11m	P	18	24	32	32	-	-
	F	19	11	9	4		

97

Table 4: <u>Tests of conservation of area</u>

		Ability band				χ^2	Signif.
		≤89	90-99	100-109	≥110		
Item 6b							
7y 5m	P	18	26	23	31	7.86	0.05
	F	16	14	12	6		
7y 11m	P	24	22	26	35	8.22	0.05
	F	14	14	10	5		
8y 5m	P	25	35	31	36	1.34	-
	F	6	7	6	4		
8y 11m	P	29	39	34	37	-	-
	F	9	3	2	2		
9y 5m	P	29	32	36	38	-	-
	F	8	7	4	1		
9y 11m	P	30	31	37	32	-	-
	F	7	4	4	4		
Item 7b							
7y 5m	P	11	22	23	29	14.4	0.01
	F	23	18	12	10		
7y 11m	P	18	18	21	35	16.7	0.01
	F	20	18	15	5		
8y 5m	P	13	29	34	37	-	-
	F	18	13	3	3		
8y 11m	P	25	33	30	37	-	-
	F	13	9	6	2		
9y 5m	P	25	34	35	38	-	-
	F	12	5	5	1		
9y 11m	P	24	32	37	35	-	-
	F	13	3	4	1		

Table 4 (cont): Tests of conservation of area

		Ability band				χ^2	Signif.
		≤89	90-99	100-109	≥110		
Item 9a							
7y 5m	P	13	23	23	26	8.59	0.05
	F	21	17	12	11		
7y 11m	P	20	24	24	34	9.49	0.05
	F	18	12	12	6		
8y 5m	P	20	32	33	37	12.21	0.01
	F	11	10	4	3		
8y 11m	P	23	36	32	37	–	–
	F	15	6	4	2		
9y 5m	P	27	35	38	39	–	–
	F	10	4	2	0		
9y 11m	P	25	31	39	36	–	–
	F	12	4	2	0		
Item 10							
7y 5m	P	8	20	15	20	7.9	0.05
	F	26	20	20	17		
7y 11m	P	12	17	9	26	14.97	0.01
	F	26	19	27	30		
8y 5m	P	12	27	27	30	11.98	0.01
	F	19	15	10	10		
8y 11m	P	20	26	19	30	7.86	0.05
	F	18	16	17	9		
9y 5m	P	18	29	30	29	8.76	0.05
	F	19	10	10	10		
9y 11m	P	18	27	35	30	16.84	0.01
	F	19	8	6	6		

In area item 6a the children did not first see and agree that the
two shapes had similar areas. In fact the two shapes were clearly
seen to be different in shape at the beginning of the test and the
children were asked if they thought they had equal areas (using first
the abstract term 'amount of surface' and secondly the concrete term
'fields'). In contrast to all the other items, they were not encouraged to use the mental operation of reversbility by any practical
procedure on the part of the tester. The children, could, however,
manoeuvre shapes in order to arrive at an answer, this proved to be
difficult for the younger children.

Item 8

Area of the two shapes
is the same

Give S a shape to hold in each hand.
>   *'I want you to imagine that these are biscuits and you are very*
>   *very hungry, which would you prefer to have?'*
>   *'Why do you say that?'*

If S gives a reason which is unmathematical,
>   *'Has this shape the same amount of biscuit as that one, or*
>   *does it have a different amount of biscuit?'*

If S answers *'the same'*,
>   *'Why do you say that?'*

If S answers *'the same because one is longer but the other is
fatter'* or similar compensatory reason,
>   *'Is there any other reason why they have the same amount of*
>   *biscuit.'*

If S answers *'different'*,
>   *'Which has more biscuit?'*
>   *'Why do you say that?'*

In area item 8 the children were shown two shapes and asked in
effect 'which biscuit would you prefer? - Why do you say that?' and
further supplementary questions to ascertain these views on their
relative areas. One would have expected that the majority of the
children who had used concrete-logical arguments in the previous
examples to do so again. However there is a dramatic increase in the
number of answers depending on the immediately observable. Although
many of these pupils had clearly demonstrated that they were capable
of using a concrete-logical argument they did not choose to use such
thinking to solve this problem. We see, therefore, that variables
such as expressions used, nature of task material and method of presentation of the problem will influence the way the child responds in a
dramatic way. One wonders if those children who demonstrated reliance
on perception in the majority of the tasks did so simply because those

features dominated in the task. In other words, we have not really demonstrated that those particular children are incapable of using concrete-logical thought but only that they prefer to use reasons based on perception in those particular tasks. From the results it is clear that arguments based on perception do dominate some children's thinking but it would appear that the key to conceptual development seems to be more related to the ability of the child to select correctly between arguments based on appearances and those based on more and more concrete-logical reasons.

Separate analysis of each item results demonstrate that children in our age range do carry out this selection procedure but often incorrectly and vary their reasons according to the test situation.

I finally include another area test item for consideration: area test item 18. Results for this item with pupils of average ability are given in table 5.

Item 18 : red oblong; red parallelogram; red geoshape

Place the geoshape over the red oblong so that it fits exactly.
'*This shape (*indicate geoshape*) fits exactly over the red oblong.*'

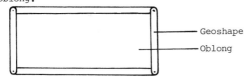

'*Watch carefully.*'
Remove the geoshape from the oblong, elongate it and place if over the parallelogram so that it fits exactly.

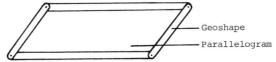

'*The shape (*indicate geoshape*) fits over this red cardboard too.*'
Remove the geoshape to one side. Place the oblong and the parallelogram close to each other.

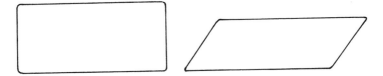

101

18a *'Does this oblong have the same amount of surface as that shape* (indicate parallelogram) *or does it have a different amount of surface?'*

If S answers *'different'*,
'Which has more surface?'
'Why do you say that?'

If S answers *'the same'*,
'Why do you say that?'

If S answers *'the same because one is longer but the other is fatter'* or similar compensatory reason,
'Is there any other reason why they have the same amount of surface?'
If S answers *'the same because they both measure the same round the outside'*, end item. Otherwise proceed.

18b *'Does the oblong measure the same round the outside as that shape* (indicate parallelogram) *or does it measure a different amount?'*

If S answers *'the same'*,
'Why do you say that?'

If S answers *'the same because one is longer but the other is fatter'* or similar compensatory reason,
'Is there any other reason why they measure the same round the outside?'

If S answers *'different'*,
'Which shape measures more round the outside?'
'Why do you say that?'

Table 5: Results for area item 18 (average ability)

Answer	7y5m %	7y11m %	8y5m %	8y11m %	9y5m %	9y11m %
Correct: oblong has greater area	23	22	16	19	14	9
Incorrect: parallelogram has greater area	15	10	4	1	2	O
Incorrect: both have same area	51	56	72	68	80	87
Incorrect: other	12	13	8	12	4	4
Sample size (=100%)	75	72	79	78	79	76

Even the consistent use of one form of argument rather than another does not give a firm indication of the conceptual power of the child. In this test item the child should use the perceptual features in order to arrive at the correct answer. If answers of the reversible type are used e.g. 'The areas must be the same because we can change it back into its original shape' or 'the same because nothing has been added or removed', then the child will in fact be wrong. This particular test item is an important one as it could be argued that Piagetian test situations are illustrative, i.e. they are carefully selected so that conservation based on concrete-logical argument is the right answer. In reality, the idea of conservation cannot be applied generally. I simply present the results of this item and ask 'Have the older children who have used the concrete-logical argument and got the wrong concept "centred" in the Piagetian sense? - they certainly failed to select the right argument'. Have the younger children the concept simply because they gave the correct answer?

Throughout the research the variation in the responses of individuals has emerged as the principal observation and this hinders us from producing a neat and rigid framework for the conceptual powers of other children. I believe that even if Piagetian theory is correct the resolving power of our tools of observation and the dynamic nature of the children's minds will continue to hinder observation of any 'stages' - even if they exist. The idea of growing progressive differentiation and integrative reconciliation suggested by Ausubel (1978) is an attractive one; above all else it is an optimistic view of conceptual development. I am now very wary of researchers who claim to be able to evaluate 'stages' of thinking required by certain topics and deciding whether they should be included or not in school curricula without relating such arguments to research on teaching approaches and tasks used. As for the measurement of developmental 'stages' in adolescents I suspect that individual performances on a range of tasks would vary more than we expect. Much more research is required in this field before any tentative conclusions can be drawn.

Certainly any conceptual power actually measured gives little indication of the potential of the pupil or his speed of future development. Perhaps the introductory work of Rowell, Dawson in Australia (see 'Teaching about Floating and Sinking : An attempt to link Cognitive Psychology with Classroom Practice, 1977) is a development along promising lines. If we are to believe in the constant dynamic state of the pupil's mind at whatever age and level of cognitive development then we need to observe closely the pupil's own reasoning in presented learning situations if we are to improve on the design sequence and structure of those learning situations.

In this context we should heed Milkent's recent comment (1977) that 'It is time that we turn our attention, or at least a major part of it, away from devices external to the students and begin to

examine science from the students' point of view. We should stop
devoting a major portion of our attention to the correct answers
students give and begin listening to the incorrect answers they give.
Like Piaget we may discover a wealth of information, and this should
eventually lead us to greatly improved strategies in the teaching of
science'.

It is my opinion that the measurement of the average ability of
an age group or a group of pupils does not supply information of any
great worth. Such measurements create a restrictive view of the
performances of individuals within a group and tell us nothing about
the capabilities of, or the difficulties experienced by, individuals
within the group. The strength of Piagetian research lies not in the
measurement of average performances but in the recording and measurement of individual responses. One must agree with Piaget (1969:
English 1971) when he recommended 'a close union of teacher training
and research, the teachers being associated with the latter right
from the start'.

PIAGETIAN TASKS IN A SMALL-GROUP FORMAT

Robert E. Pearson

In a great number of different research studies, Piaget's tasks
have been used to diagnose the stage of intellectual development
reached by an individual. In most cases these tasks have been administered on an individual basis, one subject at a time, following the
procedures, if not the purposes, described in Piaget's publications.
An increasing number of researchers have developed procedures for
administering the tasks to groups of subjects, allowing the collection
of much more data than is gained from individual interviews, for the
same amount of time and effort. In the individual, or clinical,
method, the task becomes immediate and accessible to the subject,
regardless of whether the subject or interviewer manipulates the
material. It also allows informal discussion between the parties,
through which the subject can ask questions for clarification, and the
interviewer can use supplementary questions, fashioned to the requirements of each situation, to determine how the task is understood.
Much of this immediacy and communication is sacrificed to efficiency
when the tasks are administered to large groups, but little is known
about the level of subjects' performance on the tasks under these
different conditions.

Investigation of the validity of a group method seemed to be a necessary first step in a research project aimed at gaining information about the intellectual development of Ghanaian secondary school students. Some alternative to the clinical method was required in order to collect data from a sample large enough to be considered representative of the secondary school population. In an attempt to retain some of the advantages of the clinical method, I designed a number of Piagetian tasks for administration to groups of about eight subjects at a time. This allows each subject to have essentially the same view of any phenomenon being demonstrated, and permits the interviewer to follow the progress of each individual, and to give whatever assistance may be appropriate. The main purpose of the study reported here was to investigate the validity of the small-group method for assessing the intellectual development of secondary school students.

In most work where group forms of Piagetian tasks have been used, no effort has been made to establish whether or not the results were equivalent to what would have been obtained if the same subjects had been given the same tasks by individual interviews. In those few cases where comparisons between individual and group forms have been made, the design of the experiment usually has not produced evidence of result equivalence, but of some other relationship, such as correlation (Russell,1962; Ankney, Joyce, 1975; Sills, Herron, 1976; Winkelmann, 1976a, 1976b; DeLucca, 1977; Lawson, 1978) or similar factorial structure (Winkelmann, 1974, 1976a, 1976c; Lawson, 1978). Where the tasks are to be used for individual diagnosis, or to collect cross-sectional data, a comparison of the two forms demands an experimental design which allows hypotheses about differences in levels of performances to be tested. Winkelmann (1976b) reported that performance of 5 to 8 year olds was better for conservation of substance and conservation of number when concrete materials were used, than when only drawings were available. Shayer, Küchemann, Wylam (1975) found performance on a group form of the pendulum task (Inhelder, Piaget, 1958) was considerably inferior to achievements by the same subjects on individual interviews. Sills, Herron (1976) compared performances on the combination of colourless chemicals task (Inhelder, Piaget, 1958) and an electronic analog, and found no significant difference. Both Tisher (1971) and Lawson (1978) compared group and individual interview forms of several formal operational tasks, but used different tasks for the two forms, leaving open the question of comparability of performance on two forms of the same task.

Other questions about the procedures for administering Piagetian tasks, particularly in cross-cultural research, arise from the great disparities in performance obtained by different interviewers using different subjects (Ohuche, Pearson, 1974). Great comparability should be possible by more careful sampling and by using common forms of tasks administered in equivalent ways. Even if many of these variables are eliminated, the possible effect of different interviewers remains. While we recognise the advantage of an interviewer from the same culture as the subjects, does an 'outsider' influence performance adversely? Since this question is pertinent to the conduct of the anticipated major survey, this study attempted to determine how the use of different interviewers might influence results.

Selection and construction of tasks

Two main criteria were used in choosing tasks: each should be amenable to construction as a group task in a form similar to the individual task, and the whole set of tasks should cover a wide range of intellectual operations and developmental levels. The following tasks emerged from this selection process:

1. Conservation of weight (Piaget, Inhelder, 1974).

2. Conservation of volume, including displacement of water by metal cylinders of equal size but different weights (Piaget, Inhelder, 1974).

3. Class inclusion and the principle of duality (Inhelder, Piaget, 1964).

4. Horizontality of water level (Piaget, Inhelder, 1956).

5. Quantification of probability (Piaget, Inhelder, 1975).

6. Curves of movement (Piaget, Inhelder, Szeminska, 1960).

7. Combination of colourless chemicals (Inhelder, Piaget, 1958).

Each task was preceded by an introduction which attempted to set the task into a relevant cultural context. In many cases, subjects were asked several introductory questions, to establish the nature of the task and the method of responding to questions, which in all cases was very simple. Where necessary, further explanations and discussion were provided.

Design of the Experiment

The study was devised as a 2 x 2 x 4 factorial design, with form of task (individual or group), educational level of subject (first or third year in secondary school), and interviewers (four individuals) as fixed effects. This allows investigation of the two main effects of interest (form of task and interviewer) and of possible interactions of these effects with each other and with educational level of the subjects. The interviewers were two Ghanaian men, a Malaysian woman, and an American man. All were university graduates in science, with experience in science teaching in Ghana. Each interviewer spent 30-60 hours in a training and practice programme, spread out over one month.

Subjects

A sample of 192 subjects was chosen in equal numbers from each of four secondary schools in the vicinity of Accra, the capital of Ghana. The schools were chosen according to their abilities to provide the facilities for undisturbed interviewing, and to obtain a sample of students from a relatively wide range of socio-economic and geo-graphic backgrounds. Subjects from each level in a school were chosen at random and assigned to each set of conditions (form of task and interviewer). Different forms of each task were not given to the same subjects, so as to avoid experience on one form influencing per-formance on the other form. Each subject was tested in two sessions, each lasting about one hour, separated by two weeks. Within each session, there was partial randomisation of the order in which tasks were presented.

Results of study

For each task, patterns of responses corresponding to Piaget's descriptions and analysis were assigned to specific developmental levels. Other patterns were assigned to the same, or intermediate, levels, as seemed appropriate. By this means each subject's perform-ance could be assigned to a developmental level. The developmental range from 1B (pre-operational thought) to 3B (complete formal opera-tional thought) was divided into eight different levels, which were assumed to lie roughly on an interval scale. These were converted to numerical scores, as shown below, for the statistical analysis.

1B	1B/2A	2A	2A/2B	2B	2B/3A	3A	3B
1	2	3	4	5	6	7	8

In table 1 are recorded the mean and standard deviation for each task. Note that most of the tasks did not cover the entire range of developmental levels.

Table 1: Means and standard deviations for performance on tasks
(Group and individual forms combined)

Task	Year 1		Year 3		All subjects	
	Mean	S.D.	Mean	S.D.	Mean	S.D.
1. Classification[a]	4.32	1.30	4.76	1.11	4.54	1.23
2. Conservation of weight[b]	4.58	0.74	4.64	0.65	4.61	0.69
3. Conservation of volume[c]	4.85	0.89	4.97	0.83	4.91	0.86
4. Quantification of probability	4.62	1.65	5.12	1.46	4.88	1.57
5. Horizontality of water level[a]	4.51	1.46	5.17	1.02	4.84	1.30
6. Curves of movement	4.10	1.60	4.74	1.63	4.42	1.64
7. Combinations of chemicals	5.10	1.29	5.42	1.36	5.25	1.33

a. Upper limit = 6   b. Lower limit = 3, upper limit = 5
c. Lower limit = 3, upper limit = 6.

F-values resulting from the analyses of variance are given in table 2.

Table 2: Results of analysis of variance : F-values for each task

Task	Interviewer (I) $(df=3)*$	Form of task (T) $(df=1)*$	Yr. in Sch. (Y) $(df=1)*$	IxT $(df=3)*$	IxY $(df=3)*$	TxY $(df=1)*$	IxTxY $(df=3)*$
1. Classification	3.79[c]	14.02[e]	6.87[d]	2.09[a]	0.54	0.76	0.36
2. Conservation of weight	1.92[a]	1.92[a]	0.28	2.93[c]	0.43	2.51[a]	0.22
3. Conservation of volume[f]	0.18	1.64[a]	0.35	4.01[d]	0.08	0.02	0.24
4. Quantification of probability	2.20[b]	1.98[a]	4.66[c]	1.28	2.07[a]	0.04	0.16
5. Horizontality of water level	0.10	1.14	12.52[e]	0.58	0.48	0.91	0.74
6. Curves of movement	1.06	1.04	7.30[d]	0.68	0.96	0.16	0.69
7. Combination of chemicals[g]	1.07	0.08	2.44[a]	0.99	0.93	0.99	0.98

* N = 176

a. P <0.25
b. P <0.10
c. P <0.05
d. P <0.01
e. P <0.001
f. df of denominator = 167
g. df of denominator = 166

108

In drawing inferences from these results, we must be particularly careful not to commit a type II error, that is accepting results as being equivalent, where they are in fact different. The probability of making such an error was calculated for each of the tasks for which the effect of form in the analysis of variance was not significant at $P = 0.25$. Assuming that the actual value of the mean of the group task was one level above (or below) that of the individual task, all probabilities of a type II error were less than 0.01. For a difference of 0.5 levels, probabilities ranged from 0.02 to 0.40.

Although the group forms of the tasks will be used to obtain average results for samples of students, the tasks might also be used to characterise individuals. For such a purpose, the reliabilities of the tasks need to be known. To this end, individual questions within each task were assigned scores, and the reliability calculated for each of four tasks (Winer, 1971). Table 3 gives the reliabilities of these tasks, as well as the correlations between the summed scores for each task and the numerical value of the developmental level used for the analysis of variance.

Table 3: Reliabilities of tasks

Task	No.of items	r_{xx}(ind)	r_{xx}(group)	S_e(group)/ levels	Correlation of marks & scores
Probability	4[a]	b	0.86	0.62	0.89[c]
Horizontality	4	0.86	0.72	0.79	0.93
Curves	6	0.53	0.50	1.17	0.90
Combinations	5[a]	0.67	0.54	0.84	0.90

a. Calculation of reliability based on selected items, which were used as main criteria for assigning developmental level to each subject.

b. Not all items were used with every subject on the individual form.

c. For group form only.

The correlations among these four tasks, with level in school partialed out, are given in table 4.

109

Table 4: Intercorrelations of tasks

Task	Horizontality	Curves	Chemicals
Probability	0.032 (0.261)[a]	0.120 (0.195)	0.012 (-0.006)
Horizontality		0.388 (0.529)	0.040 (0.241)
Curves			0.220 (0.367)

a. Correlations of individual forms are given in brackets;
the other figures are for group forms.

Discussion

For a task to be suitable for use in small-group testing, it first
of all must have a relatively high probability of being equivalent to
the individual form. The classification task does not meet this
criterion, but horizontality of water level, curves of movement, and
combination of chemicals do, with F-values for the effect of form of
task small enough that $P > 0.25$. The two conservation tasks and
quantification of probability show larger differences. The former can
be ruled out due to the substantial interactions between interviewers
and forms of task. A related criterion for selection is the power of
the task, or probability of avoiding a type II error. This exceeds
0.99 for a hypothesised difference of 1.0 between group and individual
means for all of the four tasks still under consideration. Finally,
apart from quantification of probability, these four tasks given equivalent results with different interviewers ($P > 0.25$). This effect on
the one task was due to an enhanced performance by first year students
interviewed by the Malaysian woman. This trend was noted in some
other tasks, but the differences were smaller. Since the effect was
not sufficiently strong or pervasive to lead to any definite, practical conclusion, it was not used to reject the task. No interactions
for the four tasks reached the 0.25 level of significance.

Quantification of probability was still suspect, due to the
difference in performance on the two forms of the task. The task was
revised, and group and individual forms given to different halves of
a new sample of 110 students drawn from the first four years of a fifth
secondary school. The means and standard deviations for the results,
marked as before, were 4.62 ± 1.38 and 4.89 ± 1.45 for the individual
and group forms, respectively. In testing the hypothesis of no difference between the two forms, $P = 0.31$. The power, calculated as before,
is greater than 0.99 for a difference of one level. Thus the revised
form of this task meets these criteria for acceptance. The reliability
for the group form is 0.68, with a standard error of 0.82.

The values of the reliabilities of the tasks should be regarded as approximate, since the calculations are based, not on the actual method of scoring, but on an alternative method which correlates highly with it. These reliabilities are high, considering the small number of items on each task, but relatively low for an instrument to be used in assessing the performance of an individual. If one can accept a substantial probability of misclassifying an individual by one level, but a low probability of erring by two levels, then no higher reliabilities are needed.

The low values of the correlations between tasks suggest that the different tasks are measuring different abilities. Other investigations of correlations between Piagetian tasks requiring the use of formal operational thinking have produced a variety of results. Although Lawson (1978) found high correlations and Shayer reports similar results at this seminar most other studies have produced values below 0.5 (Bady, 1978). Factor analyses by Hughes (1965); Lovell, Butterworth (1966); Lovell, Shields (1967); Bart (1971); Lawson, Renner (1974); Lawson, Nordland (1976); Lawson, Karplus, Adi (1978) produced substantial loadings for formal operational tasks on a single factor, while Ross (1973), Gray (1976) found no unifying factor. It may be that some tasks which apparently require the characteristics of formal operational thought are more closely related than others, and most workers who have investigated the relations among these tasks have sampled only those from one cluster. Such a procedure was deliberately avoided in this study. Perhaps no unified structure of thought underlies formal operations, or if one does, several of the tasks used in this study, because of the different contexts in which they are set, may introduce factors which are required for solution, but which are extraneous to the logical operations involved. Considerable evidence has accumulated to indicate that performance using formal operational skills is influenced greatly by familiarity and meaning of the task. These differences may run deep enough to give rise to different factorial structures in different cultural environments, but this possibility is still untested.

The four tasks have several features which distinguish them from most other group tests using Piagetian tasks.

1. The small-group format provides immediacy and communication.

2. A wide range of content areas is covered.

3. Each task covers a wide range of developmental levels; three of the four extend to the 3B level.

4. Responses are very simple; almost no writing is required.

5. All of the tasks involve examination and discussion of the first responses, and a gradual progression from easy to more difficult items of similar type. This may help to overcome unfamiliarity with the task, and to promote the application of operatory structures which otherwise might not be used. Dasen, Ngini,

111

Lavallée (1979), in their training studies, found that performance of some subjects in concrete operations was greatly enhanced by a minimum of stimulation, such as a retest or one or two brief training sessions.

Conclusions

Of the several Piagetian tasks which were designed for administration to small groups of pupils, four have been found to give results which are essentially equivalent to those obtained from the same tasks given as individual interviews. The fact that not all tasks exhibited equivalence between their two forms shows that equivalence must be tested experimentally for any task, rather than assumed. The four tasks which are acceptable for group work are most suitable for assessing group performance. The experimental design does not allow deductions to be made about individual performance on the two forms of each task. In any case, the low reliabilities would allow only crude classification to be made of an individual's performance on a specific task. Individual performance across the range of tasks is so variable that in few cases would a general classification be justified.

Although the effect of interviewer was fixed, rather than random, the results indicate that in Ghana, at least, different interviewers who are competent and well-trained should be able to administer the selected tasks to secondary school pupils without influencing the results adversely.

Acknowledgements

Stephen Atakpa, Kwadzo Nyavor and Pushpa Sinnadurai were my most obliging and valued colleagues in the field work. The study was supported by a research grant from the University of Ghana, and by the Ghana Education Service, which provided two of the interviewers. I am indebted to many people for their helpful suggestions at various stages of this work, but wish to acknowledge in particular the contributions of Gustav Jahoda, Kenneth Lovell, Michael Mitchelmore, Kwosi Odoom and Michael Shayer.

Discussion

The issue of the very low correlations reported between tests was raised. One point of view from the floor was that this was not unusual and in fact was often desirable in a test battery, but this was countered by a suggestion that this would not be the case in a matching exercise. Pearson's view was that the low intercorrelation reflected the true picture. He made no claims for the battery other than to achieve gross measures on groups of pupils, acknowledging that the tests could say nothing useful about the performance of an individual. Another view from the floor was that the three tests could be used for the prediction of science performance. In this case, the lower the correlation between tests the better, provided they all correlate with the area one wishes to predict. Also on the technical issue of test construction, the circularity in constructing a test to bring out high intercorrelations of items, the test then being used to prove developmental synchrony, was raised. It was commented from the floor that it proves easier to find individual 'formal operational responses' than formal operational pupils.

SECONDARY SCHOOL BIOLOGY STUDENTS' REACTIONS TO LOGICAL FALLACIES IN SCIENTIFIC AS COMPARED WITH EVERY-DAY CONTEXTS

E. Jungwirth and A. Dreyfus

Introduction

One of the main arguments for the necessity of teaching science in schools is based on the notion that it enhances the development of certain intellectual skills, which are then transferable to, and thus usable in, every-day situations (e.g. George, 1967; Lawson, 1969; Masey, 1965). The implicit assumption appears to be that parallel logical structures (in school, or curricular vs. every-day) are indeed perceived by pupils to be equivalent i.e. that horizontal transfer is not hampered by contextual factors. Wason and Johnson-Laird (1972) sum up a series of experiments which lead them to conclude that, of all performance variables, item-content (i.e. the context in which the logical structure is embedded) is 'vitally important' for successful response. Their experiments were based in the main on syllogistic reasoning, comparing responses in abstract with those in concrete situations, etc., finding little evidence of transfer, but better success with items based on concrete situations.It is probably because of findings like those - as well as commonsense intuition - that every-day situations are recommended for use in science teaching to illustrate scientific principles and principles of scientific methodology (e.g. Riesman, 1962). The motivational aspects of using 'problems of the real world' (Mayer, 1974), or presenting subject matter 'closely related to every-day experience' (Coulson, 1966) 'showing the obvious relationships of science to real life' (Nuffield, 1970) should also be mentioned. This three-pronged two-way tie-in of every-day situations with science teaching in both the cognitive and the affective domain is thus of immediate concern to science teachers.

The study reported here relates to the cognitive aspect of this interconnection only, namely - pupils' perception of the logical structure of situations, by comparing certain of their intellectual skills i.e. their propensity to accept or commit logical fallacies, one aspect of what is commonly termed 'logical thinking ' - in curricular and 'real life' situations. 'As a root-notion, critical thinking is taken to be the correct assessing of statements' (Ennis, 1962). Martin (1972) states that the well-trained scientific mind should consider...the relevant evidence in considering an answer to a problem. Dressel and Mayhew (1954) list, among others:

- willingness to face facts, to revise judgment...in the light of appropriate evidence

- to recognise when...data support and do not support a given hypothesis

- to recognise when evidence used in context is adequate for the drawing of a conclusion

(all emphases added).

According to Cronbach (1963) critical thinking boils down to 'the disposal of unsound proposals'.

Eight 'logical fallacies' (Burton,Kimball, Wing, 1960), or 'potential pitfalls' (Ennis op.cit.) were selected for this study, because the committing of any of them would invalidate any scientific report, analysis, conclusion, or experimental design. The prevention of such errors is one of the objectives of any modern science-curriculum.

1. Assuming that events which follow others are caused by them ('post-hoc' reasoning);

2. Drawing conclusions on the basis of an insufficient number of instances (sample too small);

3. Drawing conclusions on the basis of non-representative instances (sample not representative of population);

4. Assuming that something which is true in specific circumstances is true in general;

5. Imputing causal significance to correlations;

6. Drawing inferences about individuals from the mean of the population;

7. Drawing conclusions on the basis of small and fortuitous differences;

8. Using similar propositions to prove each other i.e. circular reasoning.

Procedure

A set of four 14 item multiple-choice tests was designed (all based on the same eight logical fallacies):

1. The BIO-test, based on curricular biological subject matter.

2. The LIFE-test, based on 'the world of the pupil' e.g. school, home, or peer relations of the pupil.

3. The BION-test, paralleling the BIO-test, but containing Nonsense terms in key positions.

4. The LIFEN-test, paralleling the LIFE-test, but containing Nonsense terms in key positions.

The purpose of the BION- and LIFEN-tests was to examine pupil behaviour in situations where the possibility of their relying on previous knowledge was prevented. Pupils were informed that the nonsense terms would not interfere with their ability to respond.

The four tests were constructed according to the same pattern (see below). Pupils were asked to give a reasoned explanation for their choice. This explanation, as will be shown later, constituted the most important part of the pupils' response. One set of items illustrating the 'post-hoc' reasoning and the general item-pattern is given below:

BIO-test

Some pupils grew tomato plants in the laboratory. One day there was a gas leakage, which was soon repaired. The plants continued to grow, but purple spots appeared on the leaves. What is your opinion?

a. The gas caused some disturbance in the plant and the purple spots were the result.

b. The gas interfered with the chlorophyll, and as a result the leaf-colour changed from green to purple.

c. No conclusion can be drawn from this event, since the kind of gas used in laboratories has no influence on plants.

d. My opinion is different, because...

LIFE-test

Jane had been John's girl friend since the beginning of the school year. After Easter she was severely punished at school for cheeky behaviour. When her parents learned about this, she was punished at home too. At the end of that week Jane wasn't John's girl friend anymore. What is your opinion?

a. Jane and John split up, since Jane was very nervous and upset because of her punishment.

b. They split up, because John's opinion of Jane had changed for the worse after the incident.

c. The story shows that punishment at school has some influence on the personal relations of pupils.

115

d.   My opinion is different, because...

BION-test

Mice which were kept in a school laboratory developed difficulties in breathing. This happened just after the mice had been given
an addition of Daypoon in their food. What is your opinion?

a.   Since the trouble started after the mice ate Daypoon it is
     reasonable to think that the Daypoon caused something which
     made breathing difficult.
b.   One should be careful before adding Daypoon to the diet of
     small animals, since they are very sensitive creatures.
c.   Adding chemicals like Daypoon to food may be dangerous.
d.   My opinion is different, because...

LIFEN-test

Bill was the best pupil at school in goornistry. One day during
the second term the teacher asked him to do a long series of plasnocations. Soon afterwards Bill's classmates noticed that he had
lost interest in goornistry. What is your opinion?

a.   The many plasnocations caused Bill to lose interest in goornistry.
b.   Bill's interest in goornistry became weaker because the many
     plasnocations caused him to see goornistry in a different light.
c.   The story shows that different work methods have some influence
     on pupils' interest in school subjects.
d.   My opinion is different, because...

It can be seen that, since the tests were logically equivalent,
context was the independent variable.

Test-administration

The population numbered 344 9th grade biology students in
eleven schools. 200 girls and 144 boys. All pupils were given I.Q.
and reading comprehension tests, after which each class was divided
into two groups matched for sex and I.Q. One group took the BIO-,
the other the LIFE-test. Two weeks later the BIO-group took the
BION-, and the LIFE-group the LIFEN-test. This design permitted
independent examination of both contexts.

Results

The results were analysed in two stages:

1.   Determination of the number of 'correct choices'.
2.   Analysis of the types of reasoning employed.

116

Table 1, below, will show population details, test reliabilities and numbers of correct choices per test:

Table 1: Means and standard deviations of the number of 'correct choices'

Test	N of pupils	Mean (out of 14)	S.D.	%	*Reliability
BIO	171	6.23	2.36	44.5	.56
LIFE	173	7.75	2.64	55.4	.62
BION	167	6.41	2.79	45.8	.70
LIFEN	163	6.57	2.85	46.9	.68

*Cronbach's alpha coefficients.

Table 1 shows an apparent pupil-superiority on the LIFE-test (every-day situations without nonsense terms), but it will be seen later that this was no more than an 'optical illusion'. The data shown so far do not throw any light upon the main point to be investigated in this study i.e. the type(s) of reasoning associated with pupils' choices - both 'correct' as well as 'incorrect'.

Types of reasons-for-choice as found in pupils' scripts

1. No explanation (or unintelligible explanation).
2. Reasoning based on content i.e. pupil pays no attention to the logical structure of the situation.
3. Pupil accepts the logical fallacy.
4. Logically sound reasoning.
5. Complete misunderstanding of the situation.

Reasons 2 - 4 accounted for approximately 85% of the responses. Table 2, below, will show the reasons-for-choice's distribution in all four tests:

Table 2: Percentages of occurrence of reasons-for-choice in all tests

	No explan- ation	Misunder- standing	Content- based	Logical fallacy	Logically sound
BIO	15.96	2.43	25.69	33.12	22.81
LIFE	9.12	1.42	45.41	19.32	24.73
BION	15.54	3.33	8.25	45.62	27.29
LIFEN	12.09	1.91	22.43	40.64	22.91

Examining the data in table 2 - the apparent pupil-superiority on the LIFE-test fails to reappear. 'Logically sound' responses can be seen to be of the same order of magnitude in all four tests. The low percentage of 'no explanation' and 'misunderstanding' in the LIFE-test, which might indicate that pupils had felt more secure and more involved in 'real life' situations,was not followed by a higher percentage of logically sound responses. It cannot, therefore, be concluded - in contra-distinction to Wason and Johnson-Lairds' (op.cit.) findings - that performance was better in concrete situations. It should be recalled, however, that the test situations here had been rather different from those of Wason and Johnson-Laird.

There was, however, a striking difference across tests of the proportions of 'content-based' as compared with 'logical fallacy' responses. Figure 1, below, will illustrate this phenomenon graphically.

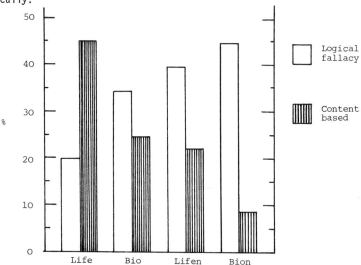

Figure 1: 'Logical fallacy' and 'content-based' responses

The difference between reasons-for-choice according to the measure of pupils' familiarity (real or imagined) with the context of the situation can be readily seen. When the use of the content-based reasoning was prevented by the introduction of meaningless key-words, students did not reason more logically, on the contrary, they committed more logical fallacies. Pupils, whose reasons-for-choice were nevertheless content-based in the BION- and LIFEN-tests, had reasoned by analogy, or after first 'translating' the nonsense term into a similar, meaningful, one. Pupils' familiarity-with-content (real or imagined)-with curricular biological material content being less developed than their familiarity with every-day situations - their content-based reasoning was higher in the LIFE- and lower in the BIO-test, with logical fallacies showing the opposite trend.

The level of 'logically sound' responses was correlated with I.Q. They were all of the same order of magnitude (0.33 - 0.46) indicating a very weak functional relationship.

Discussion

The apparent superiority of pupils' critical thinking on the LIFE-test, when measured by 'correct choices' alone, which disappeared when pupils' 'reasons-for-choice' were taken into account, is by itself a phenomenon worth mentioning. Had reasons-for-choice not been asked for, an entirely erroneous picture would have emerged - confirming the desirability of every-day situations in science teaching as relevant to this study. This is a peculiar weakness of multiple choice tests' diagnostic capacity, which has been found before (e.g.Jungwirth,1971). With reasons-for-choice, however, the conclusion emerging from the data is that every-day situations do not bring about a greater amount of critical thinking, so that their advantage in this respect has not been proven. This study does not, however, have any statements to make as regards the affective, motivational domain, except, perhaps, that intense involvement with content (context) may have a deflecting influence away from the logical task.

Some further remarks about pupils' response-patterns seem to be warranted. It has been shown that the 'content-based' and 'logical fallacy' response types' proportions varied inversely - according to respondents' familiarity-with-context. Some clarification as to the nature of these response-types might be useful: whereas the logical answer is based upon a search for evidence to test (successfully or unsuccessfully) the validity of a given statement - a logical category, the 'content-based' answer involves 'the recruitment of a theory' (Gibson, Abelson, 1965) to support the acceptability of the given evidence - an evaluation category. The subject fails to accept the logical task, and does not distinguish between 'a conclusion which is logically valid, and one with which the subject agrees' (Henle, 1962). In addition, the logical structure of the test-situations (all tests), which did not justify any of the offered conclusions, called for only one possible response: the suspension of judgment for lack of sufficient evidence (after 'disposing all the unsound proposals'). It appears that this response-type of 'not enough evidence for a definite conclusion' might have been alien to this population. The development of just this ability is, however, regarded as of extreme importance especially in real-life situations, and definitely deserves fostering.

The principal question to be answered by this study, namely whether pupils perceive equally structured logical situations as equivalent, when presented in different contexts - must be answered in the negative in spite of the very similar percentages of sound logical answers.

Teaching is a process of communication. Formal logic is impersonal, but when a logical issue is presented to pupils the problem and its context tend to interact with the pupil and the problem may be dealt with, as has been shown in this study, in a very personal manner indeed. When the elements of dissimilarity in a problem situation are permitted to outweigh the elements of similarity (the logical structure in our case) there is no generalisable principle left for transfer. As long as this tendency persists, much transfer of what has been called 'critical thinking ability' from one contextual area to another (curricular to every-day or vice versa) is not really to be expected. Teachers should thus not take the 'non-specific transfer value of critical thinking processes' (George op.cit.) for granted unless or until they have indeed assured its existence in their particular pupil-population.

It has been said (Kastrinos, 1962) that 'there are few studies at any level of education which indicate that students can be taught to think critically', citing various authors to show that very little change had taken place in the last thirty years as to 'any systematic attempt being made to develop critical thinking ability' (ibid.). This depressing diagnosis should not, however, deter science-educators (and not only science-educators) from future 'systematic attempts'.

Discussion

The discussion following Jungwirth's presentation was helped by a clarification of a semantic issue, with the suggestion that since probabilistic reasoning was in fact logical, the polarity of reasoning described might be better expressed as a deterministic-probabilistic dimension. Both types of reasoning are logical but start from different premises, and have different degrees of certainty.

On a methodological point it was questioned whether a pencil and paper test of a largely verbal nature, conducted in a school setting could be considered a reflection of a real-life situation. Jungwirth acknowledged these limiting factors and pointed out that even under these conditions, differences were apparent, though he would not wish to extrapolate children's responses to events in their lives. It was also queried whether the nonsense items were really nonsense, as in many instances in the classroom children could be seen to be assigning meaning to unknown words. Jungwirth pointed out that he was not presenting children with nonsense situations, but nonsense key-words, and the histogram revealed a gradual influence across the four conditions, not a total transformation of behavioural pattern.

120

Jungwirth stressed the implications of the findings in an educational context. Conventional wisdom recommends that pupils' experiences should be carried into school, but his research supported the suggestion that culturally disadvantaged children might usefully be detached from their life experiences in the school setting.

LANGUAGE LEARNING AND LOGIC

F. Lowenthal

Introduction

The object of this research is to study the development of logical abilities in children. How does this development occur? Can it be influenced? Can it be hastened?

We think that the main factor of cognitive development is manipulation of representations. We also believe that these representations have to be non-ambiguous and that the child must execute them in contact with other children or adults (Bruner, 1966).

Contrary to Piaget, Inhelder (1966) we think that the use of verbal language to study cognitive development is a faulty technique. Indeed words may not represent the same idea for the child and the adult. On the contrary, when children use a precise formalism, made concrete by schematic and iconic representations, they must obey precise technical constraints. They are obliged to understand the exact meaning of the terms and phrases they use (Lowenthal, 1977).

The formalism

We introduced during the 3rd grade a non-verbal formalism which is suggestive of a logic (Lowenthal, Severs, 1979a). This formalism is based on the use of New Maths, and involves the use of multicoloured diagrams derived from automata and graph theory; it stresses the fundamental operations of thought: sorting and relating. The main techniques used in modern teaching of mathematics are really limited to the use of sets (for all sorting problems) and multicoloured networks called here 'diagrams'. In the latter case dots represent the objects under discussion and the arrows of the diagram represent the relationships between these objects, each colour symbolising a relationship very clearly defined and fixed by the convention binding the author and the reader of the diagram; the convention could be altered but the logical structure of the message has to be respected.

121

The sample and the use of the formalism

We worked with 7 different classes, comprising 164 children. They were primary classes, not specially chosen and in ordinary schools. Two classes were in an industrial environment, one in a school applying methods inspired by Decroly's works and the other 4 classes were in city schools, in Brussels. In each case we started our work in January, in a 3rd grade (children 8 to 9 years old) and we carried on for at least 18 months. In each case we gave a weekly lesson of 50 minutes.

During the lessons, we used games with rules and representations of games, for two reasons: first, such games are reassuring and amuse the children and also playing is for them a serious activity, an activity in which, at that age it is easy to introduce notions such as 'law' and 'rules' (Bruner, 1972).

Five steps were used:

1. learn a game and play it,

2. give a verbal description of what happened in the first step,

3. describe all possible plays of the game with a multicoloured diagram (a 'play'is a succession of moves according to a given set of rules of a game, such that these successive moves lead to a conclusion),

4. forget the initial game and modify the diagram arbitrarily,

5. describe and play a game illustrated by the new diagram (or tell a logical story which corresponds with the new diagram).

Steps 1 to 3 constitute a learning phase, step 5 a creation phase and step 4 is an iconic-symbolic bridge between learning and creation.

An example

We will demonstrate the children's progress during 18 months by means of one example. To simplify the account we will only use one game. These are the rules of the game.

'Two players : White (W) and Black (B) play the game of goose. The course has 3 boxes only, called box a, b and c. The two players start with their pawns in box 2. They throw alternatively a die which has 3 red faces and 3 green ones. W always starts.

The player who gets green must move forward one box, the one who throws red cannot move his pawn. The first player to reach box c is the winner. The play immediately stops.'

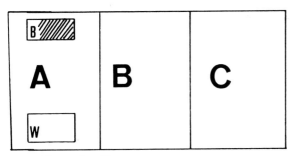

Figure 1: The course

First we asked the pupils to have a play and then to describe
verbally what happened. Then have another play of the same game and
describe it...Then all the possible plays of that game.

This is too involved: there is an infinity of possibilities.
We then suggested to them to note all the different positions the
pawns W and B could be in (Kohl, 1974). This gave us table 1 (the
position of W is always indicated first).

Table 1:   Positions
                        (a,a)
                        (a,b)
                        (a,c)
                        (b,a)
                        (b,b)
                        (b,c)
                        (c,a)
                        (c,b)
                        (c,c)

The pupils realise then that this is not sufficient to describe
all the possible plays: 'If both pawns are in box b, as we don't
know what happened previously, we don't know who has to play next!'

We must remember that the children have been playing often and
reached the position (b,b) through many different combinations. They
come to the conclusion that one has to name the player who is due to
play. This gives us table 2.

123

Table 2

Positions	W must play	B must play
(a,a)	1	2
(a,b)	3	4
(a,c)	5	6
(b,a)	7	8
(b,b)	9	10
(b,c)	11	12
(c,a)	13	14
(c,b)	15	16
(c,c)	17	18

The numbers 1 to 18 are simple code-numbers. Each indicates three facts: the position of W, that of B and the name of the player who has to play next. These numbers are called <u>states</u>, they are only codes and do not imply any order of succession.

We also helped the children by suggesting that they should represent the moves by arrows joining the original state to the resulting state. The pupils chose red arrows (represented here by dotted lines) to represent 'the player throws the die and gets "red" ', and green ones (represented by plain lines) to represent 'the player throws the die and gets "green" '. These arrows and table 2 were used to build the diagram shown in figure 2. (The double arrow is used to show the starting state.) This diagram summarises all possible plays according to the rules of our game.

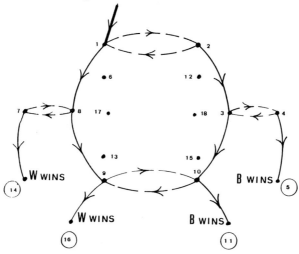

Figure 2: <u>Original diagram</u>

We then asked the children to arbitrarily modify the diagram. One sees in figure 3 the result of their collective work.

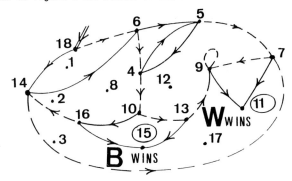

Figure 3: Modified diagram

Finally we asked them: 'What can one do with this?'
They answered: 'Play!'

- 'How?'
- 'By following the arrows!'

And they did play, but needed from 11 to 18 months to succeed in expressing what they were doing (Lowenthal, 1979a). We must here emphasise that we always started with a simpler game (Lowenthal,1978). The game we described above has been offered to the children 7 months (of which 2 were holiday months) after we started our work, immediately at the beginning of term. The diagram shown in figure 3 was created by the children after 3 months of discussions concerning the game: shape of the course, construction of the diagram shown in figure 2, individual attempts to create a new diagram.

Results

The children very quickly realise that the rules of a game form an ordinary social convention which can be altered by a simple 'majority vote'. As we mentioned vote, we must talk about the numerous social interactions in the classroom: the children discuss freely, they learn to listen to each other, they attach considerable impor- tance to corrections made by the other children, and to avoid these corrections they try to formulate their sentences as clearly as possible.

From a verbalisation point of view they learned to formulate explicitly and as synthetically as possible the new rules laid down by the new diagram.

1.   From the start they were able to play by manipulating the pawns on the course but without being able to describe the rules. The new diagram did perturb them slightly as the arrows had changed their meaning, but they were able to interpret well enough to manipulate the pawns correctly.

2.   Three months after the commencement of the experiment, the children concentrated more and more on the diagram and did not bother about the pawns.

3.   After 5 months they discovered certain traps: they said that in the diagram shown in figure 3 '6 is a trap because B plays and if he plays red he must play again'. Some children mentioned the fact that the arrows no longer had an absolute value ('go forward' or 'stand still') but a relative value: green from 18 to 14 means that B goes back 2 boxes and must play again, but green from 14 to 6 means that the pawns exchange places and that B plays again.

Finally the pupils said that 'the rules are in the diagram'. They already tried to formulate verbally those rules when the summer holidays interrupted their efforts.

4.   Two months later we started work again (with another game). All the children were now conscious of the 'relative' value of the arrows in the altered diagram. They discovered the existence of 'security zones' and of 'critical points'. For the diagram shown in figure 3, they said: 'There is a kind of symmetry. One can divide the diagram in two, one part W wins. When he reaches 7 he is certain to win, it is not worth playing anymore'.

Here 7 and 9 are in W's security zone, whilst 13 is a critical point: it is W's turn, if he plays red he reaches his security zone, if he plays green he makes B win. 5 and 14 are also critical points, because if the player plays red the game reaches ' W's camp ', but...

5.   Shortly after the pupils discovered all the possible strategies, with the help of the diagram, they started to formulate verbally, explicitly, all the rules of the new game. Those who were the first ones to understand helped the other ones to discover sentences as involved as: 'the play is at point 14, it is B's turn (the state [c,a]). If he plays green the game reaches point 6 (the state [a,c]) it is B's turn. If he had played red he would have gone to point 7 and (the state would be [b,a]) it is W's turn.' According to the child and also to his teacher, he has needed 11 to 18 months to be able to get along by himself, with the diagram. At the age of 10 nearly all the children (129 out of 164) were able to do so. They had at their disposition two representations for the same object and they knew that they were equivalent. But those who had already succeeded after 11 months told us: 'It is nevertheless more practical to use the diagram'.

6.   We continued our work with a group of pupils, after 18 months
training in logic with the help of diagrams. During a year devoted
to reasoning by induction and the use of axioms, these pupils
succeeded in formulating unaided different complex mathematical statements, one of which was Pick's theorem (Liu, 1978). Some pupils were
also able to discover the proof of this theorem. They then explained
it to others who had found the formula, verified it experimentally,
but had not been able to prove it (Lowenthal, Severs).

At this stage of our work we cannot assert that there is a bond
between the intensive training in logic, with the help of diagrams,
and the subsequent results in mathematics.

Discussion and conclusion

It is evident that our formalism makes it possible for us to
observe certain reactions of children faced (as a group) with different logical problems amongst which is the search for strategies
through a multicoloured diagram. We can do this, even though the
children's verbal language is not sufficiently developed to resolve
these problems. Some of these problems seem to belong to the domain
of formal thinking, and the children are only 10 years old. Something
happened, besides natural maturation. We cannot yet describe the
processes which are involved and research is proceeding with children
taken individually (Lowenthal, 1979b).

Our formalism can undoubtedly be used in schools: it can be used
to ask the children to tell a story whose logical structure is fixed
on a relational plan. The diagram can then be used to make the children discover equivalent expressions in which pronouns, subordinate
propositions,...,are used; in one word to illustrate the grammar
course. Research is going on in that field.

Our formalism can perhaps be used to encourage the development
of logical abilities to such an extent that the children manage to
state and prove collectively very complex mathematical problems,
before they reach the age of 12. We have no information in connection
with other sciences.

To try to explain the results observed, we can only mention an
advantage of our formalism: this non-verbal support of thought allows
to formulate connections between concrete objects (e.g. give the rules
of a game) in a language other than the natural one, whilst the
assessments of the value of these connections (expressed in the diagrams) are still done in usual language. There is, hence, a clear
difference between language (the diagrams) and metalanguage (the
usual language), whilst habitually the usual language must serve
simultaneously as language and as its own metalanguage, which habitually complicates the child's life.

Discussion

Are the children thinking formally when they use the graphs which represent the rules of the game, or does the fact that they use the graphs indicate that their thinking belongs to the concrete stage? It was noted that children of this age (8-9 years) do assimilate the rules of games and that this was because there was a concrete representation in the objects of the game which was equivalent to the signs and arrows of the graphs. In reply to this it was stated that the use of the 'if...then' construct to describe complex sets of consequences which would result from particular 'game-states' was a strong indicator of formal thinking, as also was the ability of children to give different interpretations to the arrows of a particular graph. To what extent, then, could the graphs be applied to real structures, for example, electrical circuits or the grammar of a language? This had to be done with language.

A further criticism of the analysis concerned a point of technique. In order to facilitate analysis the diagrams were modified by removing relations so that they became acyclic. The criteria for this seemed arbitrary, but apparently the use of three different criteria had made little difference to the outcome of the analysis.

Methodological Issues in Investigating Meaningful Learning

JOSEPH D. NOVAK

Introduction

My thesis is explicit: I believe educational research can be a rational enterprise. I will attempt to describe what I believe to be crucial issues relevant to such an enterprise.

We need to agree on what constitutes a rational enterprise. Here I shall draw upon the work of Thomas Kuhn, Stephen Toulmin and D. Bob Gowin. Kuhn (1962) has made a good case for the important interplay between paradigms that guide research and the eventual 'overthrow' of paradigms as a discipline advances. Toulmin (1972) has been perhaps more descriptive in showing the crucial role of concepts and the 'evolutionary' nature of concepts that guide scientific enquiry. More recently, my colleague Gowin (1978) has developed a simple heuristic device to show the important interplay between the theories and concepts we hold, the events or objects we observe and the record making and record transforming procedures we employ. Gowin, in my view, transcends epistemological issues discussed by Kuhn and Toulmin to show the educational relevance of the nature of knowledge and the process of knowledge production. Gowin's work contributes a key epistemological element to my thesis.

The primary achievement of a rational enterprise is the invention of concepts. Gowin defines concepts as regularities in events or objects designated by some sign or symbol. Dog, for example, is the sign English speaking people use to designate the variety of living things that have four legs, a tail and bark. Truth is a more elusive regularity to define, but we all have a functional meaning for this concept label, albeit jurors may debate at length on what is the truth in a given litigation. Records we will define as what we note when we observe objects or events.

Any rational enterprise operates on the assumption that the universe is not capricious, that objects or events have been, can be, or will be characterised in some predictable fashion. The challenge

129

is to invent descriptions to the regularities that occur in ways that have progressively more parsimony or greater predictability. Gowin (1978) has assembled key elements operative in a rational enterprise in the form of an 'epistemological V', as shown in figure 1. The 'point' of the V is where any rational enterprise must begin, the objects or events that occur in the world, or that can be constructed (as in experiments or in the field of mathematics). On the left side of the V are the 'thinking' elements or those things that humans are uniquely capable of inventing. Nothing on the 'left side' is discovered, in the sense that we discover gold or oil; it is all constructed by the human mind. On the right side of the V, we have procedural or methodology elements of a rational enterprise. These too are invented by people, and they are largely a product of the philosophy-theory-concept aspect of human understanding. In many cases, our recording or data-processing devices (such as oscilloscopes or analysis of variance) are also products of conceptual invention, only the invention has been in some other relevant discipline (e.g. electronics or statistics).

The question is often raised, why does Gowin use a V form? One colleague has suggested that the form of a ladder might be better. Or a U or O form might be used. Gowin's epistemological V is a heuristic device and therefore other forms might be equally able or more powerful to represent the epistemological elements and their relationships. However, Gowin chose the V form partly because it 'points to' the events and objects in the universe where our thinking (left side) and doing activities (right side) come together. The lines are not meant to be vectors, since we proceed in knowledge making both 'up and down' the left side and the right side of the V. Also, every element on the left side interacts with every element on the right side, as well as with the objects or events we construct or choose to observe. It is important for students to acquire an understanding of this interplay between our procedural activities and our conceptual or thinking activities. Moreover, they need to recognise that our theories and concepts control what events or objects we construct or choose to observe. One does not set out to sail around the world when one holds the concept that the world is flat.

In our work with junior high school and college students, we have found that the most critical area of Gowin's V is the 'bottom' portion: concepts, objects or events, and records. It is confusion at this point that it most often troublesome in applying relevant principles or theories or in reaching valid claims. Partly for this reason, we often ask students to construct a 'concept map' of the salient concepts that guide their observation of events or objects. Further discussion of concept mapping is given below.

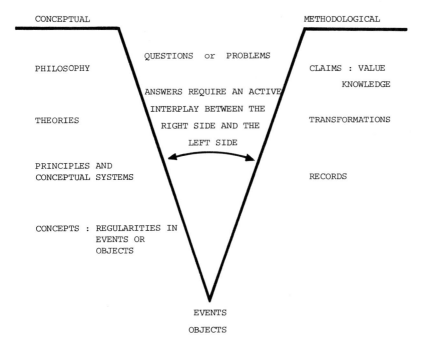

Figure 1: Gowin's (1978) epistemological V can be used as a
heuristic for viewing the nature of science for
the science of education

One aspect of genius is to select what objects or events are of
interest to observe and what kind of records to make. So it was
Mendel's genius that led him to a theory which guided him to select
pea flower, colour, height, etc. to observe and to record the frequency
of these traits in progeny. Watson's and Crick's genius led them to
construct alternative molecular models for DNA. The product of such
genius is new concepts (new regularities) such as Mendel's factors and
Watson's and Crick's double helix, and reformulation of the guiding
theory which may subsequently be stated more explicitly and more
parsimoniously. New concepts lead to new ways to observe old objects
or events and new ways to select new objects or events worthy of

131

scrutinising and recording. New concepts also give new ways to observe, record or transform records (e.g. R.A. Fisher's t statistic*).

We need to recognise that often our record making or record trans- forming procedures or devices are complex and the product of other knowledge production ventures. Even a simple balance assumes we accept Galileo's conclusion that the earth pulls all objects with the same force. Oscilloscopes, complex statistical procedures or bio- chemical analytic techniques are themselves resultant from the knowledge claims of other 'epistemological Vs', and we tacitly accept these knowledge claims when we employ principles, techniques or devices to guide our record making and record transforming activities. One of the problems in educational research, especially in the United States during the 1960s and 1970s, has been the blind application of complex statistical procedures in the hope that new meaning could be pumped into relatively meaningless records, such as the test scores or questionnaire responses cranked into factor analytic matrices. Rarely do researchers employing these techniques ask, what events led to creation of these records? My concern with the new tests of Piagetian cognitive operations constructed by the Chelsea College group is that scores on these tests will be treated as if they are the students' cognitive activity rather than a particularly biased repre- sentation of that activity.

We have also applied the V heuristic in other fields and our students report enthusiasm for the usefulness of the V in clarifying their thinking in areas as diverse as mathematics and literature. Mathematics represents something of a special case in that events constructed by the mathematician may have nothing to do with the real world. One of the reasons students have difficulty with word prob- lems is that they fail to see that real world events occurring in the word problem need to be translated into mathematical events repre- sented by an equation or some function. For mathematics, we might add an event-event connection to help to emphasise this translation problem.

The debate as to whether or not the discipline of education be- longs to basic or applied sciences, or even if it is akin to the sciences, has a long history. Several times a year this issue emerges in publications or meetings of the American Educational Research Association, with a good article published recently by Shaver (1979). Although Shaver presents a more contemporary view of science, accom- modating many of the activities some would classify as technology, there remain serious deficiencies in Shaver's view of science as he describes it, deficiencies that I believe are overcome in Gowin's V heuristic for characterising science.

---

*Also known as Fisher's z^r transformation

Gowin's V as an epistemology for education

We can use Gowin's V as a tool to study the nature of knowledge and knowledge production in education. This assumes, of course, that we consider education to be a rational enterprise, and that we hold a philosophical view that the study of educational objects or events can be rationally conceptualised, as suggested in figure 2. Many teachers and 'professional' educators tacitly operate as though education occurs by some mysterious force and their educational epistemology is no more related to rational disciplines than astrology is related to science. If Gowin's V has some validity, we should find it possible to use this heuristic to examine the process of knowledge making in education.

In figure 2, I have suggested some of the elements that should be considered under the general theory of reception learning, with special reference to mastery learning (see Bloom, 1968, 1976). The events under study are the interplay between learning modules, pretests for knowledge of physics, intuitive and analytic ability and criterion-referenced tests for achievement on study modules. Sample data transformations and knowledge claims would be as shown in figure 2, and also a sample value claim. The research 'mapped' on to the 'V' in figure 2 would be studies of the type reported earlier (Thorsland, Novak, 1974; Naegele, 1974; Castaldi, 1975).

The major question, or as Gowin (1978) suggests, the telling question of some of our research studies has been, 'Does individualised instruction enhance learning?' This is the telling question because it 'tells on the phenomenon of interest'. The events and objects we are concerned with in figure 2 are those involved in individualised instruction; student paced learning; clear specification of learning objectives; accommodation for learner variables; 'mastery' units instruction; criterion-referenced evaluation. Telling questions are usually addressed through a series of 'key questions', and for our research programme, some of they key questions have been: (1) Does learning time vary according to previous knowledge and how is learning time influenced by intuitive* and analytic ability (Thorsland, Novak, 1974; Naegele, 1974; Castaldi, 1975)? (2) How is learning efficiency (test score divided by study time for a unit) influenced by prior

---

*We have used various forms of intuitive and analytic ability tests, constructed on the theoretical basis that high intuitive performance will be characterised by subjects who begin problem attack with broad basic concepts, whereas high analytic subjects prefer to use specifically relevant concepts or facts. For further discussion of intuitive and analytic abilities and relationships to creativity see Novak (1977a).

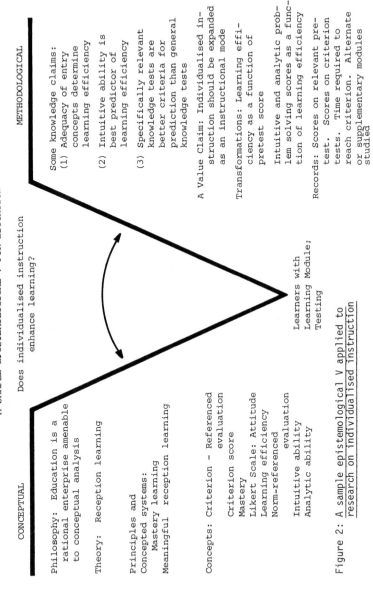

A SAMPLE EPISTEMOLOGICAL V FOR EDUCATION

CONCEPTUAL

Does individualised instruction enhance learning?

METHODOLOGICAL

Philosophy: Education is a rational enterprise amenable to conceptual analysis

Theory: Reception learning

Principles and Concepted systems:
Mastery learning
Meaningful reception learning

Concepts: Criterion - Referenced evaluation
Criterion score
Mastery
Likert Scale: Attitude
Learning efficiency
Norm-referenced evaluation
Intuitive ability
Analytic ability

Learners with
Learning Module;
Testing

Some knowledge claims:
(1) Adequacy of entry concepts determine learning efficiency

(2) Intuitive ability is best predictor of learning efficiency

(3) Specifically relevant knowledge tests are better criteria for prediction than general knowledge tests

A Value Claim: Individualised instruction should be expanded as an instructional mode

Transformations: Learning efficiency as a function of pretest score

Intuitive and analytic problem solving scores as a function of learning efficiency

Records: Scores on relevant pretest. Scores on criterion tests. Time required to reach criterion. Alternate or supplementary modules studied

Figure 2: A sample epistemological V applied to research on individualised instruction

134

knowledge and intuitive and analytic ability? (3) How does manner of tutoring (Castaldi,1975) influence achievement? (4) How is achievement influenced by standard study guide versus a study guide prepared in accordance with Gowin's V (Chen, 1979)? Some of the knowledge claims that emerge from our research are shown in figure 2. What we cannot show explicitly is the constant interplay that takes place in our seminars and research conferences as to why Ausubel's theory, or mastery learning strategy, dictates the need for certain kinds of test questions, or a certain form of instructional unit. It is this dialogue regarding theory, past research claims, practical educational issues and broad research goals for our programme that lead us to construct the objects and events of our inquiry, the evaluation materials and procedures and the record transforming procedures. In an ongoing programme of research, Gowin's V serves as a useful schematic to chart 'where are we now as regards our telling questions and key research questions?'

Ausubel's learning theory as a preferred framework to guide research

Since 1964, we have endeavoured to use Ausubel's (1963, 1968, 1978) cognitive learning theory to guide our research. I say 'endeavoured' because Ausubel's theory was not easy for our group to grasp. It took almost a decade before I began to feel comfortable with key ideas in his theory, partly as a result of our own research data that tended to confirm aspects of his theory and thus to help clarify (to us) the nature of the theory. This interplay between theory and research methodology led in time to some modifications in the theory (see Ausubel, Novak, Hanesian, 1978). Even when preparing manuscript in 1976-77 for key chapters in this work (e.g. chapters two to five), I found myself still checking with Ausubel to get a better grasp on such theoretical ideas as advance organisers, superordinate learning, subsumptive learning, representational learning, and concept assimilation. Ausubel's critics maintain that the difficulty lies in the ambiguous nature of his theory and/or his abstruse writing style. In my view, the difficulty lies in the profound and comprehensive nature of his theory, and educators and educational psychologists are not known for the dogged pursuit of the profound. It is also true, of course, that any theory becomes more refined and more explicit as it is used, amended and given numerous illustrations through its applications. The best way to extend one's grasp of a theory is to use it to guide research or instruction. There is the old adage, 'Don't knock it if you haven't tried it', that applies here also.

One of the important distinctions Ausubel has made in his first book (1963) was between rote reception learning and meaningful reception learning. The label 'reception learning' has been given a variety of interpretations, so for the purposes of this paper, I will define reception learning as that form of learning where the regularities to be learned and their concept labels are presented explicitly to the learner. In contrast, discovery learning in its pure form requires that the regularities in objects and/or events are first discovered by the learner, abstracted from the general context in which they occur and perhaps given a concept label, although the latter is not part of discovery learning per se. In actual practice, discovery learning occurs primarily with very young children in the process of concept formation, as when children discover that all things with four legs, a tail and bark are called dogs by older persons, or when new discoveries are made in a discipline. Most discovery learning in school settings is actually various levels of guided discovery learning, and we have a continuum from a pure reception mode of learning to pure discovery mode of learning.

However, we must also consider the cognitive functioning and psychological set of the learner as new knowledge is internalised. Here we must distinguish between rote learning wherein new knowledge is arbitrarily incorporated into cognitive structure in contrast to meaningful learning wherein new knowledge is assimilated into specifically relevant existing concepts or propositions in cognitive structure. Since the nature and degree of differentiation of relevant concepts and propositions varies greatly from learner to learner, it follows that the extent of meaningful learning also varies along a continuum from almost pure rote to highly meaningful. Figure 3 schematises the rote $\longleftrightarrow$ meaningful learning continuum as distinct from the reception $\longleftrightarrow$ discovery mode of information acquisition. A clear distinction between these two continua has been one of the important contributions of David Ausubel's (1968, 1978) learning psychology. Description of the major elements of his theory go beyond the scope of this paper and can be found elsewhere (Novak, Ring, Tamir, 1971; Novak, 1977a, 1977c). Some of the key elements of his theory as they relate to a paradigm for science education research are discussed below.

The use of Gowin's V to examine the epistemology underlying any educational inquiry is not dependent on the use of any specific theory. However, we cannot legitimately work in the framework of one theory and then invoke principles or concepts that are derivative from another theoretical framework. One of my criticisms (Novak, 1977a, pp.125-128) of Gagné's learning model (1965, 1970) is that it derives from behaviourist theory that eschews consideration of concepts, and then proceeds to employ concepts from cognitive learning theory to explain concept learning, rule learning and problem solving. The eclectic researcher who invokes whatever concepts are convenient on the 'left side' of the V to explain what happens on the 'right side' is building on epistemological quicksand. The concepts employed must be consistent with the general theory guiding the enquiry; there must be consistency between the elements on the left side of the V.

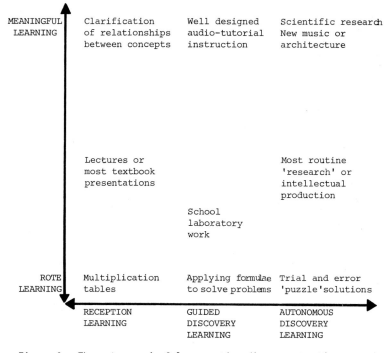

	RECEPTION LEARNING	GUIDED DISCOVERY LEARNING	AUTONOMOUS DISCOVERY LEARNING
MEANINGFUL LEARNING	Clarification of relationships between concepts	Well designed audio-tutorial instruction	Scientific research New music or architecture
	Lectures or most textbook presentations		Most routine 'research' or intellectual production
		School laboratory work	
ROTE LEARNING	Multiplication tables	Applying formulae to solve problems	Trial and error 'puzzle'solutions

Figure 3: <u>The rote-meaningful, reception-discovery continua</u>
<u>(From A Theory of Education</u>, p.101, 1977. Reproduced
with permission.)
Too often in the past, science and maths educators
have confused discovery learning with meaningful
learning and reception learning with rote learning.
Ausubel's (1978) theory helps us to design meaningful
learning experiences that are either reception or discovery types of instruction.

Perhaps one of the most popular theories applied to education
studies today is the developmental psychology of Jean Piaget. One of
the reasons for the success of Piaget's developmental theory is the
power and consistency it has shown for critically observing selected
educational events, guiding the record making (clinical interview)
and record transforming processes and the development of knowledge
claims. The genius of Piaget has been analagous to that of Mendel
who carefully selected traits to be observed, devised clever ways to
record and transform data and showed the consistency between theory
and evidence. Useful as Piaget's work has been, I have argued

elsewhere (Novak, 1977a, 1977c) that there are alternative theoretical models that are more relevant to learning events and to a generally broader array of other educational events.

Information processing psychology, the most popular reception learning theory today, derives from earlier 'cybernetic' (Smith, Smith, 1966) theories and is rapidly becoming embraced by many psychologists who previously were ardent behaviourists. The cybernetic learning theories had their origins in the early 1950s and have advanced in part through their identification with computer models for learning which have experienced tremendous impetus from the exponential rate of advance in computer technology. However, early pioneers such as Estes (1950) suggest caution in hoping for too much too soon from information processing theory (Estes, 1978, p.6).

> Though anyone's judgement at this point is necessarily speculative, my own is that the computer analogy has proven to have definite merits and has been of substantial value in the early stages of a new approach to cognitive psychology. But this analogy also has sharp limitations. In important ways it seems that the human brain and the computer operate on different principles (see, for example, Anderson, 1977). In some current theorising by the most enthusiastic devotees of the information-processing approach, we are beginning to see the results of trying to rely too strongly on an analogy of limited validity. But over the greater part of the field, we are seeing instead the emergence of new combinations of theoretical ideas and methods that may be considered inelegant in terms of the inhomogeneity of their origin but that are dictated by the demands of new findings.

While we hope that information processing theories as a basis for learning studies do not achieve the blatant dogmatic adherance that characterised behaviourist theories in the 1940s and 1950s we would encourage careful study and consideration of this theoretical view as an alternative for science education.

Another important characteristic of Ausubel's learning theory is its consistency with what we regard as key principles from modern epistemology, curriculum theory, and instructional theory. Firstly, meaningful learning, a key concept in Ausubel's theory, is dependent upon the idiosyncratic concepts individuals hold, which in turn are derived from the current concepts held in the society impinging upon the individual. There is close harmony between the central role of concepts in current epistemologies and the role of concepts in Ausubel's description of the process of meaningful learning.

Secondly, Ausubel's description of 'advance organisers' and their role in facilitation of meaningful learning, together with the emphasis on concept learning as the central learning task, is highly compatible with Johnson's (1967) model for curriculum. Johnson defines curriculum as an ordered sequence of intended learning outcomes (ILO's) where the major ILO's are the concepts the teacher selects from the discipline under study. Johnson's distinction between curriculum and instruction, where the latter invokes selection of specific examples or activities designed to achieve the ILO's of the curriculum, nicely complements the emphasis in Ausubel's theory summarised as (1968, p.iv):

> If I had to reduce all of educational psychology to just one principle, I would say this: The most important single factor influencing learning is what the learner already knows. Ascertain this and teach him accordingly.

The challenge of the instructional designer is to select examples or activities that will allow the learners to assimilate new concepts to be learned (or new elaboration) into the idiosyncratic conceptual framework they already have.

An example of a research study guided by Ausubel's theory of meaningful reception learning is Kuhn's (1967) study on the use of advance organisers in college biology. Figure 4 shows how this research would be viewed under Gowin's epistemological V heuristic. We see that Kuhn's research was guided by the general learning theory framework proposed by Ausubel (1963) and that it employed the system of concepts governing the use of advance organisers and also the statistical procedure of analysis of variance. Some of the relevant concepts utilised are also shown in figure 4. It is obvious that the structure of the events observed as well as the data analysis procedure are guided by the Ausubelian theory and a theory of statistical inference. In turn, the knowledge claims have relevance to Ausubel's theory and relevant concepts, providing significant validation. Thus we see the inextricable interplay between theory, observations and knowledge claims, and the important relevance Ausubel's theory has to curricular and instructional planning.

Thirdly, Ausubel's theory supports and elaborates some of the concepts in Carroll's (1963) model for school learning, later elaborated by Bloom (1968) in his ideas on mastery learning and Bloom's research findings reported more recently (1976). Although Ausubel recognises important genic differences in learning capability, the quote above points out that careful consideration of the 'anchoring' concepts a learner has will influence the rate and quality of meaningful learning. Carroll and Bloom's view that most students can master most school subject matter if they are guided and given time to master relevant concepts necessary for later learning is explainable through Ausubel's learning concepts on the nature and role of advance organisers, progressive differentiation of concepts and integrative reconciliation of concepts.

139

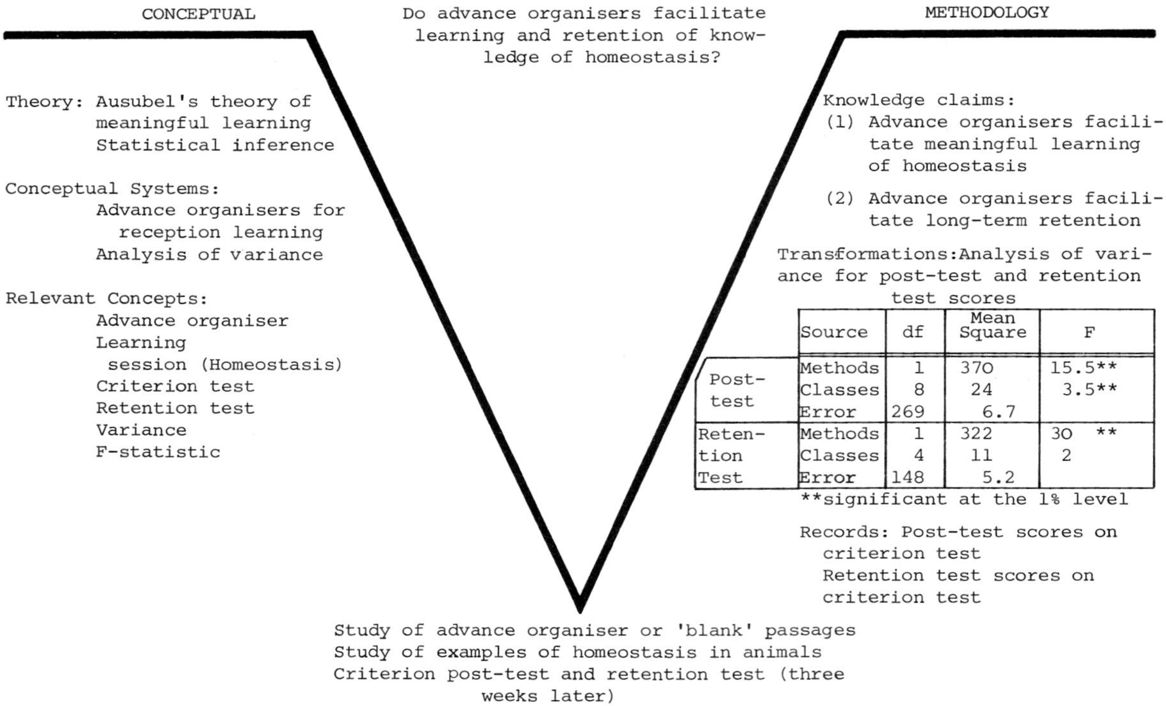

CONCEPTUAL

Do advance organisers facilitate learning and retention of knowledge of homeostasis?

METHODOLOGY

Theory: Ausubel's theory of meaningful learning
Statistical inference

Conceptual Systems:
Advance organisers for reception learning
Analysis of variance

Relevant Concepts:
Advance organiser
Learning
session (Homeostasis)
Criterion test
Retention test
Variance
F-statistic

Knowledge claims:
(1) Advance organisers facilitate meaningful learning of homeostasis

(2) Advance organisers facilitate long-term retention

Transformations: Analysis of variance for post-test and retention test scores

	Source	df	Mean Square	F
Post-test	Methods	1	370	15.5**
	Classes	8	24	3.5**
	Error	269	6.7	
Retention Test	Methods	1	322	30 **
	Classes	4	11	2
	Error	148	5.2	

**significant at the 1% level

Records: Post-test scores on criterion test
Retention test scores on criterion test

Study of advance organiser or 'blank' passages
Study of examples of homeostasis in animals
Criterion post-test and retention test (three weeks later)

Figure 4: Kuhn's (1967) research study of the use of advance organisers shown as represented on Gowin's V

Finally, there is also the affective domain to be considered and here Ausubel's theory provides important guidance in the positive affective results that accrue from competence or achievement motivation that derives from successful meaningful learning. While other factors also influence positive affective growth, the primary avenue through which schools can contribute, he would contend, is through encouragement of practices that augment meaningful learning.

Another example from our research programme that illustrates the usefulness of Ausubel's reception learning paradigm is a study done by Naegele (1974). In this piece of research, Naegele focussed attention on the role of prior knowledge for the facilitation of learning, as predicted under Ausubel's theory. Facilitation of learning means that students will score higher on a criterion test, or learn a unit of study material in less time. Naegele combined these two parameters into an index of learning efficiency, where the latter is defined:

$$\text{Learning efficiency} = \frac{\text{Test score on unit test}}{\text{Study time for unit}}$$

Figure 5 shows the resulting learning efficiencies for students who entered study with different competencies as measured by a pretest for knowledge of physics. We see that students with higher physics pretest scores appear to be more efficient learners in units 1, 2a and 2b. However, by unit 3, the students with low physics pretest scores are significantly more efficient learners than those with high pretest scores. At first this appears to be an anomaly until one considers the following relevant curriculum factor. Units 1, 2a, 2b and 3 all deal with kinematics and unit 3 is highly dependent on concepts introduced in the three preceding units. The data suggest that the low physics pretest group may have been less efficient in learning early units but their extra study effort did result in acquiring specifically relevant concepts needed for unit 3. Since the source was a 'mastery learning' programme, time was available for the low physics pretest group to master relevant concepts. Students' natural tendency to 'coast along' in study units for which they have already considerable knowledge (units 1, 2a and 2b) probably contributed to the high physics pretest group's less than significantly higher learning efficiencies in these units and their significantly lower learning efficiency in the more demanding unit 3. The same significant 'reversal' effect on learning efficiency was observed again in units 4 and 15, also units at the end of a conceptual sequence building on earlier units. The results are both explainable by Ausubel's reception learning paradigm (adequacy of prior relevant concepts is the most important factor influencing learning) and also give credence to the importance of careful planning of learning sequences stressed in Johnson's (1967) curriculum model. The value of Bloom's mastery learning strategy is also illustrated in that there was a general trend in both groups to become more efficient learners and differences between the high pretest knowledge group and the low pretest knowledge group were essentially zero in the final summary unit, R1 (which was a 'tough' unit and took everyone more time). Naegele's study is one kind of research study schematised in figure 2.

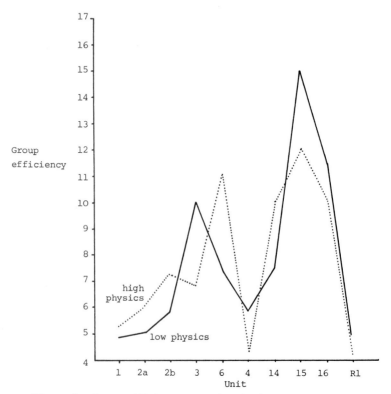

Figure 5: Group efficiency on each unit for two pretest groups; low math-low physics vs. low math-high physics. (From A Theory of Education by J.D. Novak, p.237, 1977. Reproduced with permission.) Notice that for units 3, 4 and 15, which are final units in a sequence of related units, the group scoring low on a physics pretest exceeds the group scoring high, demonstrating in part the importance of prior, specifically relevant learning on new learning and in part the effectiveness of a mastery learning approach.

142

Gowin's epistemological V and Ausubelian theory applied as strategies for learning to learn

My first research study (Novak, 1958) was directed at what I saw then as a crucial aspect of rational human behaviour-problem solving. Then, as now, it seemed to me that if we could improve the average level of people's competence in problem solving, desirable social consequences would ensue. The difficulties as I viewed them in the mid 1950s were that we needed more than a better psychology of learning; we also needed a better philosophy of education and a complementary set of instructional strategies. What I believe has changed significantly in two and a half decades is power and complementarity of new ideas in these three areas. Undoubtedly, a quarter of a century hence we will see important new advances, but my gut feeling is that we have today the set of complementary ideas that did not exist in the 1950s or any time previous to this, and these ideas could lead in a decade or two to a quantum improvement in education. This is not my current optimism; this is my first enthusiasm for what can become a rational basis for the improvement of some of the conceptual tools we believe can augment learning. We are involved with studies with junior high school and college students that include explicit instruction in key learning concepts, Gowin's epistemological V and related ideas for textbook or instructional programme interpretation. Our major effort at the present time is with junior high school science students.

The starting point of our 'learning to learn' programme is to guide students to see the differences between rote learning and meaningful learning, and to recognise that these forms of learning are on a continuum, depending on the extent of potential meaningfulness in the learning material and the adequacy of relevant concepts the learner possesses. We use simple word lists or short stories as examples showing how much learning and recall is facilitated when word lists have an inherent relationship or an idea is presented to serve as an 'organiser' for the material. For example, students could make no sense out of a short story describing the necessity to sort items into piles, doing batches, etc., unless they were given the lead sentence, 'This paragraph is about washing clothes'.

We proceed to demonstrate that a concept represents some regularity in other concepts (word lists) or events or objects, and that meaningful learning is a function of the number and quality of relevant concepts we hold. Sometimes we include brief discussion of current ideas about human memory, but we do not pursue this in detail. Next we move to a consideration of how knowledge is made, or more explicitly how concepts function in knowledge production. It comes as a bit of a surprise to students that knowledge is made like clothes or automobiles and not discovered like oil or gold.

Gowin's V is introduced in conjunction with an experiment, demonstration or set of observations. We first have students identify the events or objects under study (and we simultaneously define events and objects and 'redefine' concepts as regularities in events or objects). Students are then asked to list concepts that are needed to 'make sense' out of the events or objects we are studying. We discuss records and record transformation (such as averaging and graphing) and show how concepts guide us in making records or transforming records. Principles are introduced as relationships between two concepts, such as 'grass is green' or 'sunlight provides energy for photosynthesis'. Principles also guide our observations, record making and record transforming activities. We show how the activities on the 'right side' of the V lead to new knowledge claims, which in turn may become principles to guide future inquiry. The sequence concepts and principles, new knowledge claims, new or revised concepts and principles is illustrated with concrete examples from the materials they have been studying. This sequence becomes increasingly apparent as the course progresses. Figure 6 shows an example of a V constructed in a seventh grade science class for three levels of exercise activity with pulse beats as the records.

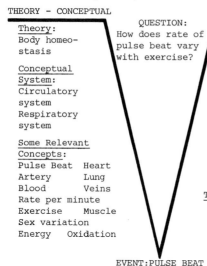

THEORY - CONCEPTUAL

Theory:
Body homeo-
stasis

Conceptual
System:
Circulatory
system
Respiratory
system

Some Relevant
Concepts:
Pulse Beat   Heart
Artery   Lung
Blood   Veins
Rate per minute
Exercise   Muscle
Sex variation
Energy   Oxidation

QUESTION:
How does rate of
pulse beat vary
with exercise?

EVENT:PULSE BEAT

METHODOLOGY

Knowledge Claims:
Pulse rate varies considerably
among individuals

Pulse rate increases with
activity

Boys have lower pulse rates
than girls

Increasing pulse rate supplies
more food and oxygen to muscl-
es, and removes more CO_2

Value Claims:
Exercise can be good for you

Transformations:

Average Pulse Rate			
	Rest	Some Exercise	Vigorous Exercise
Boys	64	88	120
Girls	72	102	140

Figure 6: Lab exercise on pulse rate 'mapped' on to Gowin's V. The data shown were obtained by students in the class.

Records: Pulse beats per min. for each boy and girl when at rest, after moderate exercise, and after vigorous exercise

The data transformations (averages in tabular form) was done on the blackboard and then 'mapped on' to Gowin's V along with other items during class discussion, using an overhead projector.

144

To emphasise the interrelationships between concepts, we ask students to construct concept maps (see Stewart, Van Kirk, Rowell, 1979; Bogden, 1977; and Moreira, 1979). Students begin to see that while all concepts are related in some way, and many concepts have at least some explanatory relevancy to a given set of events or objects, it is possible to pick out the 'most' salient concept(s) and concepts of secondary or tertiary relevance. Figure 7 shows a concept map constructed by a seventh grade student from a section of their text dealing with different kinds of plants. We have given 'concept mapping homework' assignments and find that all students are successful in producing reasonable maps, albeit the maps may vary substantially. We point out to the student that there is no 'ideal map', but some maps perhaps better represent the structure of knowledge, as it is presented in written material or a lab activity, and better show the mean of 'connections' between the concepts. We point out that each line connecting concepts may represent one or more principles, and some of these principles can be indicated by 'labelling the lines'.

In our early work with concept mapping in a college genetics class (Bogden, 1977), we prepared maps for each lecture and provided copies to the students. We found that preparation of maps was very challenging to the professor and to Bogden, and valuable in their planning for lectures and exams. However, many students gave unenthusiastic or negative reactions to the concept maps. We learned that the best maps were those that were relatively simple, with only 8 or 10 concepts and with the lines labelled. Also, students who tried to construct their own maps were much more enthusiastic about the value of concept mapping. Thus in our current work we use almost exclusively simple maps as the students prepare them. A student map on acetate projected on an overhead projector can lead to a lively discussion as to what is 'right' or 'wrong' with the map. We have found students to be generally enthusiastic about 'concept mapping' when they prepare their own maps. The construction of concept maps can serve as a powerful technique for showing students the idiosyncratic nature of meaning, and consequently the varying patterns that meaningful learning can produce, in contrast to rote learning. They also begin to recognise better the complex interplay between concepts, principles and theories, or the mental inventions illustrated on the left side of Gowin's V.

By the time the students have worked through a few experiments or textbook sections constructing concept maps, they are prepared to construct fairly elaborate V's for an experiment or textbook topic. The first V we present is usually constructed on an overhead projector in dialogue with the class (see figure 6). After a few such demonstrations and work with concept mapping, students can construct V's for other experiments or for textual material. In our experience, they become disturbingly aware of the theoretical nature of science as it is taught in elementary and junior high school classes (or high school and college classes also). They begin to see why the study of science has so often meant rote memorisation of concept definitions,

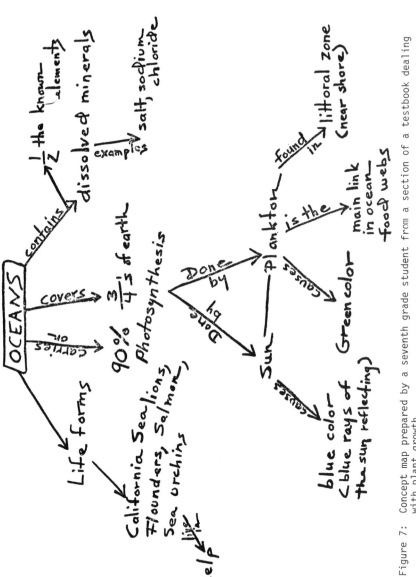

Figure 7: Concept map prepared by a seventh grade student from a section of a testbook dealing with plant growth

principles or knowledge claims. They begin to see that what they
thought were facts (which they equate as absolute truth) are really
knowledge claims whose veracity is dependent upon the events or objects observed, records and record transformations made and the
concepts, principles and theories that guided the knowledge making
process. It becomes evident to them why scientists sometimes disagree
on the 'facts'; they begin to see that truth seeking is an elusive
search, but the best that rational beings can do.

Initially, we had planned to compare the relative success of
seventh and eighth grade students in acquiring the psychological and
epistemological strategies. It became increasingly apparent that all
students in 'average' seventh or eighth grade science classes can
demonstrate satisfactory understanding of concept mapping, Gowin's V
and correlated psychological and epistemological concepts. Through
class, homework and structured clinical interviews, we saw consistently
that all students in the two pilot programme classes we worked with
demonstrated understanding. And this was achieved in less than thirty
hours of class time during which the same science content usually
taught was also being presented.

Currently, our attention is turning to questions of attitude
change and the influence of the learning strategies on problem solving
success when students are presented with novel situations for which
concepts previously taught are applicable. We hope to compare the
problem solving success of students presented with learning strategies
with comparable students studying the same programme, but without
these learning strategies. We also plan to monitor long-term (6 months
or more) retention on the learning strategies and (hopefully) their
influence on later learning and problem solving.

It should be evident from the above that we are moving the locus
of our efforts from the development of theory to the application of
theory to improvement of classroom learning. Thousands of research
studies in education have shown the general futility of preparing
alternative teaching materials or alternative teaching strategies,
with the usual conclusion that no significant differences in pupil
achievement resulted. We are trying something different; we are
providing students with metalearning, with instruction on the nature
of knowledge and the nature of learning. Our research is currently
in progress, so I cannot say what effect our metalearning strategies
will have over the long term on pupils' attitudes toward science,
grasp of basic concepts in science or long-term facilitation of new
science learning. We do know now that all normal seventh and eighth
grade students can acquire these metalearning strategies, and they do
so enthusiastically. Furthermore, we see no reason why these strategies could not be taught together with any presently used science
curriculum, or any curriculum in any other subject matter field. While
our work shows that both students and teachers can easily locate
serious gaps or omissions in their present curriculum, it is not
necessary to first rewrite all of the curricula in use in schools, as

we have tried to do in science and mathematics over the past two decades at great expense.

The potential power and simplicity of better, theory based meta-learning strategies for improving learning success are the primary basis for my current optimism regarding education and the promise it holds for solution of crucial social problems faced in the world. We will try to provide further information on these strategies to interested persons in the future.

In summary, I have tried to show that research in education, as well as in the design of instruction, can be importantly influenced by the paradigm that guides our work. As Kuhn (1962) points out, and Lakatos (1976) better elaborates, advances in a discipline arise from systematically employing a paradigm to guide work and there are at any time competing paradigms. The crucial factor is that we are guided in our work by some paradigm, for ultimately all paradigms are modified or discarded and the issue is not whether our guiding paradigm is true but whether it is useful. My contention is that Ausubel's paradigm for cognitive learning, together with an epistemological framework that places emphasis on concept learning, can be enormously useful to education. The value of other relevant paradigms are brought together in A Theory of Education (Novak, 1977a).

RESPONSE by Pinchas Tamir

Novak has been a long time advocate of Ausubel's theory of meaningful verbal learning, also known as assimilation or subsumption theory. His reasons for adherence to Ausubel's theory may be stated as follows:

1. Ausubel's theory is comprehensive and relevant to a wide array of educational events.

2. It has a powerful heuristic value for designing educational research in terms of guiding the selection of educational events for study, types of assessment measure to use, alternative ways to transform data and the interpretation of relevant knowledge claims.

3. It has provided a useful and parsimonious framework for interpreting results of educational research regardless of whether or not this research was originally planned according to this theory.

4. It is consistent with key principles from modern epistemology.

5. It is highly compatible with key principles of curriculum theory.

6.   It is highly compatible with key principles of instructional theory.

7.   In the last 15 years Novak and his associates performed a number of research studies and developed a variety of instructional units based on Ausubel's theory. This personal experience combined with the many welcome opportunities to argue in favour of Ausubel's theory and against its rivals has certainly created an attitude of personal comfort towards Ausubel's theory, one that many researchers acquire while working continuously within the framework of a particular paradigm.

Personally, I look at all of these seven points with great sympathy. I consider myself a student of both Ausubel and Novak and I often find myself thinking in terms of Ausubel's theory. I do have, however, several reservations regarding the interpretation and utilisation of certain issues as I understand them to be presented by Novak. I shall deal with three issues mentioned in his paper and one which he has evaded.

The first three issues are advance organisers, Piaget's theory and the rote - meaningful, reception - discovery interrelationships. The last, ignored issue is the role of the teacher as mediator in the learning process.

I do not intend to discuss Gowin's heuristic device known as the epistemological V. The reason is that even when I examine carefully the examples provided in Novak's paper I don't find the model especially helpful. To me it is significantly less useful than Carroll's (1963) model of school learning or the recent model suggested by Gagné and White (1978) regarding memory strategy and learning, and by far less useful than either Bloom's (1976) recent theory on human characteristics and school learning or, certainly, Ausubel's own theory. It should be pointed out that my attitude towards the epistemological V does not imply in any way disagreement with Gowin's definition of concepts or with the validity of sentences such as Novak's 'One aspect of genius is to select what objects or events are of interest to observe and what records to make'. Upon examination of his figure 2, I still need to be convinced how the listing of all these variables in specific spaces along the V can help me in the conceptualisation of the general theory of reception learning with special reference to mastery learning.

Advance organisers

In a recent article Ausubel (1978, p.253) makes it clear that he considers advance organisers as his original discovery of a novel pedagogic device and that he will not tolerate any attempt to discredit him of this important discovery. His whole paper goes on to show the value and merits of advance organisers on the one hand and, on the other hand, the ignorance and misconceptions which have been

149

associated with them among educational researchers.

I find the manner in which advance organisers are introduced in
Novak's paper somewhat misleading. My criticism is directed at two
specific points. First, his sentence 'Ausubel's description of
"advance organisers" and their role in facilitation of meaningful
learning is highly compatible with Johnson's model for curriculum'
reads as if this compatibility is the main merit of advance organisers.
Such a restrictive implication, in my mind, does injustice to advance
organisers. Second, the study on advance organisers by Kuhn (1967)
which is presented as an example of a research study guided by
Ausubel's theory on the use of advance organisers in college biology
does not appear to me to be such a good example.

I shall begin by a general discussion of advance organisers and
then deal with the two points mentioned above. The idea that preparing
the cognitive structure of the learner for the new learning task will
facilitate the learning of this task follows from the basic premise of
Ausubel's theory that 'the most important single factor influencing
learning is what the learner already knows. Ascertain this and teach
him accordingly' (Ausubel, 1968, p.iv). There are many ways by which
this adjustment and matching can be made. For example, teachers'
questions can be very useful for this purpose. Free exploration of
batteries, wires and bulbs may serve as an advance organiser for
further more structured learning of pertinent concepts. There may
be a number of pedagogic ways to accomplish this preparation of cognitive structure of the learner for a new learning task. For many
students a well sequenced curriculum will do the job. However,
Ausubel observed that very often existing learning materials as well
as common instructional settings, fail to do this and, consequently,
rote rather than meaningful learning takes place. To remedy this un-
fortunate situation, to bridge the gap between what the learner
already knows and what he needs to know, Ausubel invented (I prefer
invention to discovery) advance organisers.

What is an advance organiser?

'I define advance organisers as introductory material at a
higher level of abstraction, generality and inclusiveness than
the learning passage itself. Further, advance organisers...
(are) relateable to presumed ideational content in the learner's
cognitive structure.

...Expository organisers are used when the new learning material
is completely unfamiliar, as determined by pretests, and attempt
merely to provide inclusive subsumers that are both related to
existing ideas in cognitive structure and to more detailed
material in the learning passage.

...Comparative organisers, on the other hand, are used when the
new learning material is relatively familiar or relateable to
previously learned ideas. In this case the aim of the organiser

150

is not only to provide ideational scaffolding for the specifics
of the learning passage but also to increase discriminability
between the new ideas and the previously learned ideas by
pointing out explicitly the principal similarities between
them'   (Ausubel, 1978, p.252-253).

The major attributes of advance organisers are: They are not
part of the learning material itself. They are designed to match
the prior knowledge of the learner. They are presented in advance of
the learning material. They present highly inclusive ideas which are
capable of creating the anchorage for the subsumption of the specifics
of the learning material.

The purpose of advance organisers is to bridge the gap between
what the learner already knows and what he needs to know and to
increase the discriminability between the new ideas and the previously
learned ones. The intended outcomes of using advance organisers are:
to facilitate meaningful learning, retention and transfer.

Now let me turn to advance organisers and curriculum. The idea
of consolidating and organising existing knowledge as a means for
facilitating learning of new materials is certainly valid for any
approach to curriculum development whether or not curriculum is
defined as intended learning outcomes. When we turn to advance
organisers per se I find them to have especially high potential in
curricula which do not follow Johnson's prescription for careful
sequencing. A curriculum which is built of modules or independent
units which are not carefully sequenced, but which are intended for
free selection by students or teachers can benefit enormously by mindful incorporation of advance organisers, while on the other hand well
sequenced curricula often have built-in advance organisation.

We now turn to the example of Kuhn's study. An examination of
the advance organiser passage compared with the historical passage
used in Kuhn's study (Novak, 1977a, p.271-276) reveals that the
study suffers from a methodological flaw. The advance organiser
passage actually provides abundance of general and specific information on the topic of homeostasis while the blank passage doesn't.
Thus the study suffers from a methodological limitation (lack of
adequate control) which was recognised to be valid by Ausubel himself
(1978, p.254).

As stated above advance organisers, by definition, are not part
of the learning material itself. One may, of course, legitimately
use the principle of progressive differentiation, but this is a different matter. Let me add that the idea of advance organising the cognitive structure of learners for the new learning tasks is, in my mind,
much more powerful than the specific pedagogic device called an
advance organiser. I feel that the teacher may play an important role
in doing just this. For example, an adequate pre-laboratory discussion

may serve as advance organiser and raise significantly the position of school laboratory work on the rote - meaningful continuum shown in figure 3 of Novak's paper. In this figure well designed audio-tutorial instruction appears at the top of the rote - meaningful continuum. This may or may not be so. Erlwanger (1975) reports the results of clinical interviews with several students who ranked in the top 25% of their class and who had successfully passed one unit after another of the mathematics IPI curriculum. He found that some of them had developed weirdly idiosyncratic algorithms for passing the tests; they had simply developed ad hoc inconsistent and in-accurate mathematical theories and rules which somehow got them through the units, but which led them to totally distorted understand-ing of mathematics. Apparently, the nature of the individualised programme in question (and this may well be true of many other individualised curricula) is such that if pupils score well on unit post-tests, they rarely talk to anybody about it. The teacher does not talk to them. And this brings me to a central and important point: we cannot and we should not attempt to circumvent the teacher. It is true that learning is an activity of the learner. However, in most school settings today teachers still run the show. The decisions of teachers and their actions are often the single most influential factor affecting the meaningfulness, efficiency and general nature of learning.

Piaget's work and its implications for education deserves more than Novak's statement 'Useful as Piaget's work has been...there are alternative theoretical models that are more relevant to learning events'. Novak's reservations from Piaget's theory may be explained by his contention that 'we cannot legitimately work in the framework of one theory and then invoke principles and concepts that are derivative from another theoretical framework'. Perhaps when one deals with a highly formal discipline this argument is valid. Yet, even physicists find it possible to work simultaneously within the frameworks of two alternative theories, wave theory and particle theory. Education as already observed by Schwab (1971) is a prac-tical discipline, much richer than any one theory can encompass. The art of the eclectic is the one that helps educators in seeking and obtaining the best guidance in each particular event. Piagetian studies continue to dominate research on learning in science and mathematics. We find three types of investigations:

1. attempts to replicate Piaget's studies with new samples or new tasks and to develop new measures for locating individuals at particular developmental levels;

2. attempts to demonstrate (in the form of training experiments) acceleration of transition from lower to higher stages;

3. attempts to use Piaget's concepts or methods to anticipate cognitive difficulties students may encounter in learning concepts in science and mathematics.

I believe that those Piagetian studies included under categories 1 and 2 are irrelevant to science education. The goal of science education is not to move children ahead on Piaget's developmental scale. The major problems of science education are those of <u>horizontal decalage</u>, of enriching and differentiating students' understanding within a level of development. Piaget has little to say about that. As Doyle, Lunetta (1977) suggest, science educators should view Piaget in perspective. While we need no more studies in categories 1 and 2, we should welcome category 3 studies which deal with concepts that are intrinsically important to science and mathematics learning and <u>not</u> those that Piaget or his disciples chose to fit their psychological interests.

A recent study by Nussbaum and Novak (1976) on the development of the concept of Earth in young children provides a good example of this approach. Despite its obvious educational relevance, the concept Earth has no intrinsic importance to cognitive developmental psychologists. They are concerned with and could make use of a concept like conservation, which can help to categorise students into discrete developmental categories. While awareness of these categories may help educators in matching learning tasks with intellectual readiness, their usefulness for science teaching is limited. As observed by Klausmeier (1977, p.179):

> Children appear to acquire concepts and other outcomes in the cognitive domain gradually, rather than abruptly, although qualitatively different cognitive operations are presumed to emerge which make possible successively higher levels of concept attainment...Focussed instruction clearly aids students to attain concepts to successively higher levels during short time intervals and also to use their concepts in understanding principles and in solving problems...The quality of an educational experience exerts a strong influence on both the rate and the final level of cognitive development.

Let me finish with another general comment. In an attempt to highlight and emphasise the central role of concepts, Novak plays down the complementary component, namely, the methods and processes of dealing with concepts. To use Schwab's terminology he is stressing the substantive structure and de-emphasising the syntactical structure. It should be made clear that learning to use the processes of meaningful learning, namely, progressive differentiation and integrative reconciliation, is no less important than the concepts themselves. Inquiry learning and problem solving should be regarded as special cases of meaningful learning. Yet, as far as science education is concerned there is no substitute for these 'special cases' if we wish our students to study and view science as enquiry. Verbal reception learning, important as it is, is only one way of learning. The value of other ways cannot and should not be denied.

Discussion

Discussion was initially focussed on alternative representations of Gowin's epistemological V. Some felt that the close relationship between methodology and the learner's conceptual framework would be better represented in some other way, such as a continuous line. Others argued that concepts, records and methods should all be regarded as events. Many participants felt that, whatever the mode of representation, the elements of the V should be maintained as they highlighted the relationship between claims, events, records and concepts. Observation of events leads to claims about them which then become the principles guiding the study of further events. The elements of Gowin's V emphasised that claims are not 'truth', but only have validity in the context of the events observed, the records made, and the concepts involved. It was reported that high school pupils had used the V to analyse the relationships between the concepts they were studying. This had helped them to understand the notion of meaningful learning.

The degree of meaningful learning was stated as being dependent on three factors. Firstly, the material being learned must be understandable, otherwise rote learning took place. Secondly, the learner must adopt a meaningful learning set. Thirdly, the extent of meaningful learning depended on the degree of differentiation of the subsumers into which the new material was being incorporated. Thus the position of audio-visual presentations and laboratory work were not necessarily as shown by Novak in his figure 3. In testing for the occurrence of meaningful learning, it was felt that the learner's ability to incorporate yet further related material at a later date should be investigated.

The remainder of the discussion involved a comparison between the Ausubelian and the Piagetian approaches. Both agreed that 'what the learner already knows' is of central importance. Piaget has provided a methodology for teasing out some of the elements whereby children hold ideas together. It is thus possible to identify the logical structures that enable differentiated concepts to be related to one another and progressively differentiated. But Piaget is concerned with gross cognitive development and not with individual learning situations. His tasks slice through broad areas of cognitive structure that have relative stability. If narrower slices are taken, this stability may not be apparent, as was demonstrated in Hughes' paper.

It was asserted that children are as formal in their thinking as their concepts allow. If 'formal' is defined strictly in Piagetian terms, then very few children below the age of twelve are formal. But if a broader description is used, as has been done by Nussbaum (1979) a significant proportion of even younger pupils exhibit formal thought. Many studies have shown the similarities of the misconceptions in adults and in children. The difference is that adults have a broader conceptual framework that is more differentiated and more integrated than that of children. This change takes place by continuous progression rather than in stages.

In conclusion, it was suggested that the lesson to be learned from Ausubel's theory, and the best advice one could give to a teacher at the start of their career was to be considerate and understanding of the learner as an individual, and teach so as to assist progressive differentiation and integrative reconciliation.

The Nature of Mathematical Learning

A. W. BELL

Many aspects of mathematical learning can be illuminated by comparing them with the learning of language. The formation of algebraic equations and the interpretation of graphs are two such aspects. This paper will describe some pieces of research and development work done at Nottingham recently on these topics, and will also draw comparisons with research on the improvement of reading (Lunzer, Gardner, 1979) and on the making of judgments (Peel, 1971). Reference will also be made to the attempts of the Assessment of Performance Unit at the Department of Education and Science to evaluate children's developments in mathematics, language and science in a broad educational context, that is, seeking to identify what general outcomes of the learning of these subjects are visible as broadly usable general acquisitions.

The general conclusion from these considerations will be that the teaching methods traditionally adopted in mathematics classes place far too much emphasis on the acquisition of local skills and concepts and too little on the general development of mathematical awareness and power, and that improvements might be made by drawing on some of the methods seen as normal in the learning of language.

Reading - does it comprise sub-skills?

The Schools Council Project on the Effective Use of Reading began by visiting classrooms and studying the extent to which reading was used as a means of learning in the various subjects of the curriculum. It was evident that this happened to a comparatively small extent, particularly in the secondary school. Subsequently, attention was focused on the possibility of improving the reading ability of pupils and it was initially assumed that the way of doing this was to identify the range of sub-skills involved in the reading process and to devise teaching exercises to practice and develop these sub-skills. Tests were devised, consisting of passages with a number of comprehension questions attached, the questions being of eight types. These types were word meaning, words in context, literal comprehension, drawing inferences from single strings and from multiple strings, interpretation of metaphor, finding main ideas and forming judgments. This categorisation includes certain hierarchies, for example, the third, fourth and fifth represent situations where a question has to be answered, in the first case by a direct reading of a phrase or sentence, in the second case by an inference from such a sentence and in the third case from two or more statements appearing in different parts of the text. From another point of view, the early categories, particularly the first two, can be seen to concern a knowledge of the meanings of particular words, while the last categories require judgments about the comparative importance of different ideas referred to in the text. It was thought that a factor analysis applied to the results of such tests might group these categories into a number of distinguished sub-skills, which would enable a profile of attainment for individual pupils to be drawn, showing how some perhaps excelled in vocabulary, whereas others were particularly competent in making inferences although having a rather smaller vocabulary. However, the results showed no such differentiation and it appeared to be possible to describe pupils' performance as being good or poor on the test as a whole, little or nothing being added by any further distinctions.

If we put this result alongside the fact that, for example, the Raven Progressive Matrices non-verbal Reasoning Test and the accompanying Millhill Vocabulary Scale are often used side-by-side with a fair but by no means total correlation between scores, and that this is typical of psychological practice in testing general intellectual abilities, we are forced to conclude that in the interpretation of a passage of text and in the mass of prior learning which leads up to this, vocabulary and inferential ability interact so extensively that they cannot be distinguished. Better reasoning ability, in fact, means that an individual will learn by inference the meanings of more terms and, conversely, in the making of inferences from the data in the passage, the level of vocabulary knowledge of the terms involved is a significant factor.

Improving reading

The methods adopted in the attempt to improve reading skills did not deal separately with the eight types of task identified above. This decision was no doubt prompted by the failure to find distinct sub-skills leading to profiles of attainment. The question, whether teaching which aimed at developing techniques relevant to each of the eight categories would have been more or less successful than those actually adopted, remains open. The methods actually used were based on a consideration of the different purposes which a reader might have in approaching a passage, that is, gaining an overall impression of content or of line of argument, memorising details, verifying and criticising assertions or arguments. The main formula for developing reading was a technique known as SQ3R (Robinson, 1946). This consists of an initial <u>survey</u> or skim reading, a formulation of <u>questions</u> which the text might be expected to answer, a <u>read-through</u> of the passage, a <u>reciting</u> of the answers to the questions posed and finally a <u>review</u>, which might be seen as a checking and gap filling exercise. <u>Other</u> exercises consisted of cutting up a passage into sections which were then mixed and had to be re-arranged in proper order, the reading of passages from which a number of words had been deleted and which had to be supplied; and the adaptation of each of these techniques to a group discussion situation, the latter enriching the environment of possibilities and interpretations of which the individual pupil is aware, as well as providing a social stimulus to the work.

Mathematical comprehension and power

What light does this throw on the problems of mathematics? First, we need to ask, in what respects is mathematical activity similar to reading, and secondly, how do the teaching methods compare? On the first point, if one looks not so much at the mathematics in the traditional classroom but at the employment of mathematics elsewhere, one finds a number of close parallels. In the terms used by the Assessment of Performance Unit, one is considering mathematics across the curriculum and mathematics as a line of personal development. The concept of mathematics across the curriculum implies that when in physics a law is expressed as a mathematical formula, for example $pV = $ constant, or $E = IR$, that the form of the functional relationships expressed is understood. It implies also being able to read graphs with some degree of fluency, for example, to tell the story implied by a hysteresis curve or by a decaying wave. In geography it probably most often implies being able to interpret a table of numerical data and to draw relevant conclusions from it. These activities might well be described as mathematical comprehension. They may or may not involve an element of calculation as a subsidiary task but clearly no calculation can be performed until it has been decided what calculation is relevant and, for example, in the case of interpreting a table of data, a comparison of relevant magnitudes by eye, (i.e. with the aid of a number of quick mental calculations), is probably what is required. Similarly, in the graphical case, the ability to plot a graph from a formula or from data is not at all the same task as being able to interpret a given graph. Thus the concept of mathematics across the curriculum is essentially that of mathematics as a language, implying the ability to read material expressed in terms of mathematical concepts and in mathematical symbolism, and conversely to express and describe situations using mathematical concepts and symbolism. The concept of mathematics as one of the lines of a pupil's development suggests again the comparison with language,

that is it suggests a developing ability to read material of increasing
degrees of sophistication and to express oneself with increasing
subtlety and precision and in an increasing range of different ways.
Mathematically it suggests a developing ability to recognise mathematical properties of the environment and to use mathematical transformations to gain further insight into them. Thus the concept of a
line of development implies powers which are actually applicable over
a broad range of the person's experience, and an awareness by the
person of the possession of these powers. The analogy with art is
also a valid one. A person's developing powers of drawing and representation, if not neglected, like mathematical powers can be put either
to practical uses or serve simply for enjoyment. The solving of a
geometrical problem or the establishment of a number pattern or number
property can yield the same satisfaction as the ability to make a
sketch of a person or landscape.

Reading, thinking and mathematics

The above discussion has been conducted as if reading were an end
in itself, but it is clear that the implicit purpose of the reading
activity is the acquisition of information. What was under discussion
in fact, was a set of skills for acquiring information from written
material. The process of thinking is inevitably involved since an
essential part of the process is assimilation of the new material into
existing knowledge. Facts picked up in one part of the passage are
compared with those from another and the phrases take their meaning
from the relationships they have to things which are already known.
The questions which are therefore provoked by this attempt at comparison with mathematical thinking are whether the methods of survey,
question and read and the method of discussion are appropriate to
mathematical thinking and learning too. Although they may well be
applicable to the reading of mathematical material, mathematical
activity is in general not the acquisition of information, but the
processing of it; it is thinking rather than reading. Also, whereas
language learning is non-specific in regard to context, mathematics
is particularly concerned with relational concepts, and mathematical
learning or development consists of the acquisition of relational concepts which are of use in thinking about the world. It also includes
the acquisition of a set of strategies for thinking which are particularly appropriate to thinking with relational concepts. Some of
these particular strategies derive from the fact that relational concepts are interconnected with each other by deductive links, expressed
in some cases as algorithms, and this enables transformations of the
relational information to be made to expose some insight which was
not previously available, for example, a list of different records
with their prices before and after different discounts may be studied
and the percentage discounts calculated, and this gives some additional insight into which records give the biggest reductions proportion-
ally.

Language in the broad sense is the medium through which all

communication takes place, including the self-communication involved in thinking. Mathematics is special in that it employs in addition to the words of ordinary language, special symbolic forms such as that as for algebra, and diagramatic ones, of which graphical representation is an important case so that there is in mathematics a language learning task which is in some ways similar to that of learning a foreign language although in other ways profoundly different. In particular, the mathematical languages tend to be much more condensed than natural languages and comparatively small changes in them represent profound changes in meaning. The problem of translating to and from mathematical languages has been treated in two pieces of research which I wish to discuss. Before doing so however, I would like to draw attention to one or two other potential parallels between language learning and learning of mathematics. The passages of literature or descriptive material which are commonly used for comprehension exercises in the English classroom generally allow comprehension at different levels so that there is some challenge for pupils of a wide range of ability. Both discussion and exercises of the kind discussed above provide the stimulus to pupils to reach the highest level of comprehension of which they are capable. Corresponding mathematical passages are very rarely used but it is certainly possible to envisage suitable extracts containing a good proportion of mathematical content which could be treated in similar ways. The mathematics teacher probably needs far more material which ranges across particular mathematical topics and is not simply confined to the exercise of one skill or concept which is currently being learnt. Some material relevant in this way has been produced in recent years by the Leapfrogs Group (1975, and subsequently).

The learning of thinking and judging

Another approach to the development and training of those higher level thinking skills associated with the making of judgments is given in Peel (1971). Here, the specific ingredients of the making of judgments are given as (a) the detection of inconsistencies and partialities, (b) the ability to examine a situation formally and structurally as opposed to circumstantially and merely content-wise, (c) the capacity to relate the test material to the offered hypothesis, (d) a capacity to reason propositionally, (e) a mastery of language in relation to reason. As relevant teaching methods, Peel quotes the Inquiry Training of Suchman (1964), in which films of a scientific phenomenon were shown and the pupils had to attempt to explain each phenomenon by formulating and asking questions of the teacher, who would answer only yes or no. He also mentions the general problem solving programme of Crutchfield and Covington (1963) which was based on the discussion of mysterious happenings and the solution of the problems by a detective. At various points in each lesson, the learner himself was challenged so that he had to make various problem solving responses. Both of these methods developed general thinking and problem solving skills which generalised to other contexts. One of Peel's own collaborators, Anderson, devised a judgment training

programme based on developing some of the sub-skills listed above.
The pupils were first taught how to recognise inconsistencies, in-
compatabilities, irrelevancies and partialities. Two questions discussed in this sequence are: If you are judging a girl's dancing, does
it matter if she can cook?, and, Can a coloured magazine be dull?
Other topics were concerned with reasoning from propositional statements and focusing on the distinctions betwen true, false and
inconclusive reasonings and with the properties of all and some.
This programme was shown to be effective.

All the teaching methods so far discussed for developing reading,
learning and thinking skills could be broadly described as putting the
pupil in a situation where the skill is demanded, providing some means
by which the skill is picked up either from direct instruction or
through discussion, and finishing with a reflection on the nature of
the process which has been used, possibly with the naming of process
or of features of the process. A further refinement of this general
method would consist of a judicious concentration of attention on a
particular range of skills before moving on to another so as to make
a suitable compromise between concentration and the necessary final
flexibility of use. These methods may be compared with those investigated for the improvement of mathematical problem-solving; these
have tended to lean heavily on the sub-strategies identified by Polya,
(see Bell 1979).

Words into algebra

We now turn to the two research studies before mentioned. Galvin
and Bell (1977) studied the formation of equations from verbally described situations by fifteen-year olds of above average ability.
Among a number of general misconceptions regarding the difference
between natural language and mathematical language, two particular
kinds of error stood out. Both of these involved a too-mechanical
translation from one language to the other. One involved reading a
statement such as $r + 6b = 23$ as 'one red pencil plus six blue
pencils cost 23 pence', the other involved the translation of a statement such as, 'there is one more rabbit than there are hutches' by
$r + 1 = h$. In the first example, some subjects wrote down what was
the correct equation but gave it the meaning described above, as the
following extract shows:

$$1r + 6b = 23$$

E	-	What do r and b stand for?
BW	-	Oh! Red and blue!
E	-	What does 6b stand for?
BW	-	6 Blue pencils
E	-	And this (1r) stands for 1 red pencil?
BW	-	Uh Uh.
E	-	And what does this stand for? the equals sign?
BW	-	How much it costs.

This was not an isolated case and cannot be simply accounted for by the choice of r and b as symbols. Some subjects who used x and y and defined them correctly still translated 6x as 6 red pencils.

There appeared a strong tendency to attempt to read and write mathematical sentences in a manner too closely analogous to the reading and writing of English. In the sentence, 'Two rabbits were in the burrow', the word 'two' is a numerical adjective and is placed before the noun it qualifies. In a mathematical situation, if r is the number of rabbits, '2r' is certainly not meant to be interpreted as 'two rabbits'. Such an interpretation occurred frequently during the interviews.

Consider the following extracts. They illustrate this tendency to mistranslate among a substantial minority of subjects.

JM's attempt at problem 2 of set 1 -

> There are some rabbits and some hutches. If one rabbit is put in each hutch, one rabbit will be left without a place. If two rabbits are put in each hutch, one hutch will remain empty. How many rabbits and how many hutches are there?

JM - (interprets the second sentence as: 'There is one more rabbit than there is hutches' and writes)

> r + 1 = h.

JM - (having read the third sentence and correctly interpreted it to mean 'There are twice as many rabbits as there are hutches when there are h - 1 hutches', writes)

> 2r = h - 1.

E - How do you read '2r'?

JM - Two rabbits.

BW's attempt at problem 2 of set 4 -

> If 6 pupils are seated on each bench in a classroom, 2 will be left without a place. If 7 pupils are seated on each bench, 3 will remain. How many pupils and how many benches are in the classroom?

BW - (having read the first sentence writes)

> 6p = 1b.

This is a translation of '6 pupils are seated on each bench'.

Approaches suggested for dealing with these difficulties consisted of:

1. setting up a situation in which the pupil was likely to make the error, and then raising the question to be discussed openly so as to make the pupil aware of the possibility of error in that kind of situation;

2. exercises involving the bringing together of exercises in going from natural language to mathematics and in the reverse direction, that is making up stories or problems to fit a given equation or pair of equations (this principle can also be carried into the problem, into the equation solving phase, by having exercises which not only reduce the number of equations by eliminating variables, but also which generate additional equations).

Graphs into words

Janvier (1978) working with us at Nottingham, studied the interpretation of complex Cartesian graphs by pupils. A typical example of the tasks he used is the following, entitled 'Vending Machine', see figure 1. (N.B. This is a simplified version of the graph presented to the pupils.)

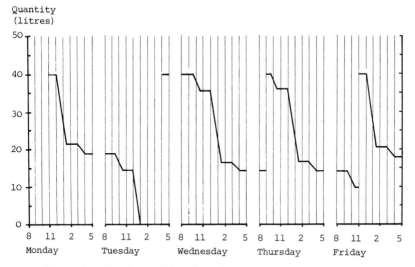

Figure 1: <u>Vending machine in a factory</u>

163

The questions asked included a request to explain the happenings first on Wednesday, then Tuesday (including a refill), then Friday, and going on to ask whether the same amount is drunk at lunchtime on each day, and whether more is drunk in the afternoon or the morning. The task aimed at testing how easily the drops, plateaux and discontinuities could be identified with drinking/not drinking, machine empty/machine refilled and so on, and thus it tested how meaningful graphical features could be handled in questions calling for comparisons and measurements. Janvier's approach to graphical interpretation was that:

'Graphical interpretation is a progressive integration of the various pieces of information conveyed by the graph with the underlying situational background. The basic ingredients are associations: graphical features ──→ situational facts.'

Janvier recognised that whereas most pupils become proficient at the reading and plotting of points on graphs, interpretation of graphs of the type shown above and indeed of the great majority of graphs which appear in scientific and general work, depends on the ability to read global features such as intervals, maxima and minima, discontinuities, rates of increase and so on. Graph reading can in fact be compared with the reading of text, and one can draw a parallel between point reading and the ability to make out particular letters or perhaps to read single words, and similarly between the direct appreciation of global features of graphs and the ability to extract meaning from whole phrases, sentences and paragraphs, with a degree of fluency which does not apparently involve the separate reading of the component parts.

Janvier reports that the responses to the first question on the graph above ranged from less to more systematic and from absolute to relative in the sense illustrated by the following examples-

BAR: 'From 8 till 9.30 there are 40 litres in the machine. At half-past nine, the workers start to drink. They drink...er...35.5...4.5 litres. Afterwards they don't drink till... ...er 12. And then at 1.30, there is 16.5 litres in the machine. So, they drank (a calculation) 19 litres...'

CRA: (Non-systematic, relative) 'It drops quite a lot from 12 till 1.30. But in the morning it does not drop so much...'

JAM: (Semi-systematic, absolute) 'There is 40 litres in the morning and there is 14 at the end.' (The rest goes on with absolute values.)

Other responses simply read off values of the amount of liquid on each hour ignoring the amounts between. Another difficulty lay in

164

the fact that drinking, thought of as a positive action, had to be associated with a fall in the graph. Several responses were of the type, 'the quantity went up from 14 to 40'. The discontinuity on Friday created several problems. By several pupils it was initially seen as a gap where the curve suddenly disappeared and this was accounted for by such statements as, 'It ran out', 'It's empty' or 'It broke down'. Even when the gap was seen to be a jump rather than simply a disappearance, it still proved hard to associate this with a refill of the machine. The comparisons required by the questions whether more liquid was drunk on one day than another and in the afternoon than in the morning, are most directly solved by moving the segment of the graph by eye and comparing it, and a number of pupils learned this skill in the course of answering the nine questions through which they were taken, but in many cases their earlier responses showed the phenomenon of attraction to high values which was also seen elsewhere in this work. In this case this meant the assumption that the graph which began higher was the one associated with the greatest consumption (i.e. Friday afternoon as against Thursday).

Teaching graphical interpretation

Janvier's work included two teaching experiments and it is instructive to compare the methods adopted with those discussed above for the improvement of reading. His main method was called a language approach and described as follows:

We have tried to devise a rich setting in which the pupils would be encouraged to speak meaningfully the graphical language rather than to write a systematic series of lessons which would 'grammatically' present a set of identified skills. To 'speak meaningfully' means to use (and learn) a language in relation to a rich environment in which the links between the language and the situational facts are diversified and numerous while both get mutually richer and more complex as a result of the ongoing feedback process involved in learning any language.

A language approach is in essence indirect and natural. The best analogy we can use to characterise it is that of a child learning his mother tongue. No lists of words are referred to by his mother, no catalogues of grammatical forms. But, the contact with his environment 'supervised' by his mother 'makes it happen'...

Having in mind to use this approach, we organised, with a science teacher, a series of experiments to be carried out in a science laboratory and during which the pupils would have to use graphs meaningfully (in relation with the experimental facts). For instance, in one experiment they were asked to heat up water and take the temperature every thirty seconds. This gave a graph for each group of pupils (2 or 3 pupils). The shape of the graph was then discussed, the various gradients were related to the 'hotness' of each flame. Also, the 'graphical consequences' of not stirring, of reading too late the thermometer, of adjusting the flame..., were equally discussed. In short, in comparing all the graphs, the teacher and the pupil 'spoke' the graphical language in relation with the experimental facts.

A control group carried out the same series of experiments but recorded their results as tables rather than graphs but discussed them in the same way with their teacher and classmates. The results of the teaching, measured by differences between pre and post tests comprising tasks similar to the one already discussed, showed that both groups made similar improvements. Janvier says that it appears that the changes in the temperature and in the rates of increase were more noticeable on the tables, since they appeared as numerical differences between the values, and, given the pupils' greater familiarity with numbers than with graphs, these proved more directly readable. This difference also affected the motivation of the two classes, and the demands made on the pupils' concentration by the class discussion of various members' graphs proved too great. One aspect in which the graph group did better than the tables group was in recognising the difference between the symbolic meaning of a graph and a pictorial interpretation of it. This was seen in the responses to a question in which the speed of a racing car going round a track was displayed (it showed three dips), and the pupil had to select which of a number of offered shapes of track was the one to which the graph corresponded. Here some pupils were strongly distracted and tended to choose the shape of the graph itself as the shape of the track. It was this distraction which the pupils of the graph group were more able to resist. Among his conclusions, Janvier says that:

> More analytical ingredients should be injected in the graph language approach, which stresses synthetic elements. The occasional use of tables is such an analytical element... Also sometimes complex graphs should be introduced and analysed in graphical terms without reference to situations... More attention should be paid to reading skills including grid reading.

In the discussion above of methods adopted for the improvement of reading and of judgment, we contrasted the approach of identifying and separately teaching sub-skills with that of providing more holistic meaningful tasks in which the sub-skills might be learnt indirectly. The approaches to reading were in general of the latter type whereas the methods used in training for judgment, leaned towards the former. Janvier began by adopting the holistic approach but concluded that more attention could usefully be given to the identified sub-skills. However, he is of course still far from suggesting that sub-skills should be taught in an isolated fashion. This more direct teaching is still seen as taking place within the context of a meaningful task of interpretation. Janvier notes that the process of successive extraction of meaning from these graphs was strongly dependent on verbal mediators between the graphical features and the situational features and such a continual movement back and forth between graph and situation was necessary. He quotes in support Olson (1970), who claims that acts such as drawing, constructing and speaking provide the occasions for elaborating and revising ones perceptual information.

A teaching unit on sequences

The unit now to be described is an investigation of number sequences, in the course of which algebraic and graphical representations of the sequences are used. The ways of developing the translations between these different languages are discussed.

A List of Sequences

S_1 =	6, 10, 14, 18, 22	S_{18} =	4, 8, 14, 22, 32
S_2 =	3, 5, 7, 9, 11	S_{19} =	2, 20, 38, 56, 74
S_3 =	1, 5, 9, 13, 17	S_{20} =	$\bar{8}, \bar{7}, \bar{6}, \bar{5}, \bar{4}$,
S_4 =	2, 4, 6, 8, 10	S_{21} =	4, 2, 0, $\bar{2}, \bar{4}$
S_5 =	4, 4, 4, 4, 4	S_{22} =	4, 12, 24, 40, 60
S_6 =	1, 4, 9, 16, 25	S_{23} =	$\bar{3}, \bar{3}, \bar{3}, \bar{3}, \bar{3}$
S_7 =	10, 8, 6, 4, 2	S_{24} =	11.7, 17.3, 22.9, 28.5, 34.1
S_8 =	6, 24, 54, 96, 150	S_{25} =	95, 89, 83, 77, 71
S_9 =	4, 7, 10, 13, 16	S_{26} =	2, 7, 15, 26, 40
S_{10} =	23, 28, 33, 38, 43	S_{27} =	2, 4, 8, 16, 32
S_{11} =	3, 6, 9, 12, 15	S_{28} =	1, 9, 25, 49, 81
S_{12} =	4, 12, 20, 28, 36	S_{29} =	57.4, 89.7, 122, 154.3, 186.6
S_{13} =	3, 12, 27, 48, 75	S_{30} =	$\bar{2}, \bar{8}, \bar{18}, \bar{32}, \bar{50}$
S_{14} =	3, 5.2, 7.4, 9.6, 11.8	S_{31} =	3409, 3195, 2981, 2767, 2553
S_{15} =	1, 3, 6, 10, 15	S_{32} =	$\bar{5}, \bar{4}, \bar{2}, 1, 5$
S_{16} =	6, 16, 30, 48, 70	S_{33} =	3, 6, 12, 24, 48
S_{17} =	1, 1, 1, 1, 1	S_{34} =	16, 13, 9, 4, $\bar{2}$
		S_{35} =	5, 8, 14, 26, 50

The lesson sequence (Bell, Rooke, Wigley, 1979) begins by giving the pupils the List of Sequences. What kinds of sequence are there? How can you describe these different sequences? Describe their differences and their similarities. In the course of discussion it emerges that some of them are taken from multiplication tables, for example S11 - 3, 6, 9, 12, 15, and S4 - 2, 4, 6, 8, 10, and so on. There are some consisting of the same number repeated - constant sequences. There are some which go up and some which go down, increasing and decreasing, and there are some which go up but at an increasing rate and we can distinguish these as soon as we consider the differences between successive terms. For example S3 has common differences of 4, while S6 has differences of 3, 5, 7, 9. In the case of S6 the second differences are equal to 2. It is natural at this point to invite the pupils to consider the relation between the different sequence types which they have identified and their graphs. They draw a number of graphs and the conclusion of this section of the work is a write-up where they say that the proportional sequences, that is the ones forming multiplication tables, have graphs which are straight lines and pass through the origin, and other sequences with constant differences give straight lines, constant sequences give straight lines parallel to the x axis, decreasing sequences have graphs which slope downwards as you go from left to right, and the sequences with changing differences, which at this stage we simply call non-linear, have graphs which are not straight lines. Bear in mind that it is these general connections which the students are investigating. They are choosing their own examples to graph as they derive these general conclusions.

The second phase of this unit of work consists of relating sequences to formulae. The objective is first to be able to recognise the type of formula which corresponds to these different types of sequence, and secondly to be able to construct the formula for a given sequence. This is the skill development phase of the unit. In getting the formula for linear sequences, such as S12 - 4, 12, 20, 28, 36, we know by this stage that we need a formula of type An + B and we need to know that the coefficient of n, the A, will be equal to the common difference so here we need 8n + B and we find the B by substituting n = 1, so here we have 8n + B = 4, 8 + B = 4, B = -4, and we can check in a couple more terms that this is correct. After a first trial of this we felt that a better approach is to start by making the easy transformation, that is, given the formula, generate the sequence, so we now give a collection of formulae and ask for the corresponding sequences to be generated. We then look at the results we have together and it is very clear that the linear formulae correspond to what we have called linear sequences and that the common difference is the coefficient of n. We have begun to learn the recognition of algebraic form and we have taken a useful step towards being able to move from sequence to formula. In a similar way we learn a skill for finding formulae for the quadratic type of sequence, working from the row of second differences.

The next piece of investigation to be done with the aid of the formulae is to study what happens when sequences of the same or different types are combined, for example what happens if you add a linear and a proportional sequence, or two proportionals, or if you multiply a linear and a proportional, or if you add a linear and a quadratic, or multiply a linear and a quadratic. As before, this is posed as a general investigation; the students choose a particular type, or a pair of types, to consider, choose their own examples from the set of sequences, combine them and see what kind of sequence they have at the end. This can of course be done either using the numerical forms of the sequences or their formulae. The tendency of the students, (ours were aged about 14 and were quite a good set) was to prefer to use the numerical form - we had to push them fairly hard to see that the task could be accomplished much more efficiently using the formulae. In this task, as in so many of these situations, there was again the interplay of empirical and deductive work. Numerical checks of one or two sequences convinced the student of the result, for example, that a linear plus a quadratic always gave another quadratic sequence, and in fact one with the same second differences. But to prove this in general one needs to say that linear sequences are of the form $An + B$, a quadratic is $Cn^2 + Dn + E$, these added give $Cn^2 + Dn + An + B + E$ which is still quadratic.

In this work it can be seen that sequence, graph and formula are all manifestations of the same concept, that is, of different kinds of growth of numbers. The state of mind which it is desirable to reach is that in which any one of these can be read and associated with any one of the others, for example, the formula $4 - 3n$ needs to be immediately recognisable as a linear expression, as corresponding to a straight line graph though not through the origin, and to a sequence of steadily decreasing terms. Exercises in translating each one of these three into the others need to be performed to achieve fluency. The investigation requiring the study of combinations of sequences provides the opportunity for this.

Reading algebra

The ability to read a considerable amount of meaning into an algebraic formula is also something which needs to be developed; for example, to look at the formula $A = \frac{a + b}{2} \times h$, to read this as multiplying the average of $a + b$ by h, and so to interpret it as the area of a rectangle whose length is the average of the two lengths a and b; also to recognise how a and b appear in a symmetrical way in the formula. These represent higher levels of comprehension of the formula than the mere ability to substitute numbers for the letters and calculate the result. Similarly, given a formula like $\frac{1}{R} = \frac{1}{R_1} + \frac{1}{R_2}$, to be able to consider what might happen to R if R_1 remained fixed but R_2 varied; to realise that with R_2 very small, R varies while remaining very close to R_2, but with R_2 large, R remains

virtually constant and equal to R_1 - this again represents a high
level type of comprehension. The point is that these are ways in which
the fluent mathematician will treat these formulae, and that they are
more likely to be satisfactorily recognised and dealt with in the
course of learning if they are seen as problems of reading, than if
formulae are simply regarded as condensed summaries of rules for
calculating with substituted numbers. A further point which arises
here is that the development of fluent reading of algebraic and graphical material depends on direct association and for this to happen, the
language itself must be familiar. This suggests caution with non-
standard notations, such as arrow diagrams instead of Cartesian graphs,
or arrow notation for functions instead of the traditional algebraic
notation (e.g. $n \xrightarrow{\times 4} \xrightarrow{+3}$ instead of 3 - 4n). While these certainly
have their part to play, not least in that translation to and from
them forces a degree of understanding of the underlying concepts,
nevertheless, most of the work which is done needs to be in the
notation which is standard and which is going to be met in subsequent
work. Another example of this concerns work with numbers in other
bases than ten. Whereas this may undoubtedly be used to expose
and provoke dimensions of understanding, one also needs to develop
rich associations with particular numbers, like 12 for example, or
say 63, as three 21's, a multiple of 9, seven below seventy and so on.
These associations are not being reinforced during work which is done
in other notations.

The topic Sequences involves a pure mathematical investigation,
that is in this case the study of a situation involving numbers. I
should like to give also an example of a piece of 'real problem solving'
where a question arises in an everyday situation for the solution of
which some mathematical ideas and techniques have to be used. This was
collected by Hugh Burkhardt and will appear in his forthcoming book
The Real World and Mathematics. As set out here it is a comprehension exercise but, for the girls originating it, it was a piece of
expressive - even persuasive - writing.

Keeping a Pony

Ellen is 13 and keen on horses. She wants a horse of
her own but her parents say it is far too expensive.
Ellen's friend, Alison, has the same problem. They
each get £2 per week in pocket money and for odd jobs.
They claim they can pay for a horse out of this money.

(a) Fill in the smudges in their report, and

(b) find out if they are right.

Pony Problem   by Alison and Ellen

Food amount and cost

HAY   -   For 14.2h horse will a ton of hay a year
           There are 45-50 bales of hay in a ton at
           60p per bale.
           1 ton ▮▮▮▮▮▮ 12 months a year = £2.25 per mo.

PONY
NUTS   -   4 lbs of nuts a day for 7 months.
           ½ cwt of nuts = £3.00 which will last for 14 days
           £6 per month for 7 months = £42 per year
           12 month a year = £3.50 per month

OATS   -   4 lbs of oats a day for 7 months
           ½ cwt of oats = £3.00 which lasts for
           14 days
           £6 per month for 7 months = £42 a year
           12 months a year = ▮▮▮▮▮▮ per month

FIELD - £2.00 a week   SHOES = £3.50 for removes
         ▮▮▮▮▮▮▮   £5.50 for new shoes
                                        need   removes 6 times
         Insurance £2.50 a month   a year
                                        need new 3 times a
                                        year
         Vet - £2.50 a month   12 months a year ▮▮▮

Conclusions

In this paper I have identified the following ways, suggested by
the comparison between mathematics and language, in which the teaching
of mathematics might be brought into closer relation with the real
nature of mathematical activity.

1. The interpretation of symbolic expressions and graphs is a reading
    activity, an extraction of meaning. This involves levels of
    competence ranging from the need to interpret each individual part
    of the expression or graph and then to perform a more or less
    conscious act of integration, through to the immediate apprehension

of meaning, rich with associations, which is characteristic of fluent reading with understanding. The acquisition of such fluency in mathematics needs building up by practice leading to familiarity; a useful kind of practice consists of translating in the various possible ways, between different symbolic languages and natural language.

2. The appreciation of literature through reading, discussion and reflection could have its parallel if more mathematical literature of a suitable type was available and was used. For example, exposition of the seven strip patterns, of divisibility tests, of the various aspects of Pythagoras' theorem, numerical and geometrical, could all be offered for appreciation and enjoyment without any necessary demands to learn a theorem or a technique or to solve a set problem.

3. The comparison with language helps one to see how, just as competence in the use of language involves not simply knowledge of vocabulary and of grammatical rules but also general abilities, such as those to infer from multiple sentences or phrases, to identify key ideas and to make judgments, mathematical activity in fact has a similar breadth which should be reflected in the classroom. The use of mathematical processes in the making of a judgment is illustrated in the Pony Problem above, and the possibility might well be exploited of using comprehension exercises in mathematics, of the same degree of breadth as those discussed above in relation to reading. Thus, one might present an extensive mathematical situation and invite the discussion of what is immediately given in it and what is obtainable by inference.

4. The next question is whether a broad activity like reading or mathematics, or indeed the making of judgments in general, is best learned simply by tackling whole tasks with discussion, or with some other means of provocation to reflection (such as the method of supplying missing words or of re-ordering a passage cut into sections) - or by the identification and separate learning of sub-skills. The former method was used in the reading project and was successful, at least in so far as it engaged the enthusiasm and apparent interest of both pupils and teachers and showed, in at least some cases, measurable gains on tests. Peel and his associates, in their studies of adolescent judgment, used training methods involving the learning of sub-skills. These too proved effective. The informal Galvin study of translation to and from algebraic language, though it made no evaluations, certainly implies that common errors in the translation from natural language to algebra, such as that arising from the phrase 'more than', and the interpretation of 2r as two rabbits rather than something more abstract - that these need to be brought to the pupils' awareness if there is to be any real hope of avoiding them. Janvier, we noted, moved towards the view that a teaching method

drawing attention to specific sub-skills was desirable. However, in all these cases there is nowhere the suggestion that it is sufficient to teach sub-skills in isolation, in fact the general implication is that the learning of particular sub-skills would be done in close and continuous relation to exercise of the total activity. This closer relationship may be seen in the teaching unit 'Sequences' discussed towards the end of the paper, and of course in the problem of Keeping a Pony.

RESPONSE by J.R. Hartley

This wide-ranging paper attempts to deal with an ambitious topic - the nature of mathematical learning. The argument is that insights into the processes of such learning, and their management through teaching, can be provided by studies in language acquisition and reading comprehension. By way of illustration, two or three studies on 'mathematics comprehension' (interpreting equations, symbolic expressions and graphs) are outlined. Their conclusions, hardly novel when stated in the general terms of Bell's paper, seem to argue for teaching to expose and develop relations (knowledge structures) and to encourage fluency in comprehension through wide-ranging practice, e.g. in translation between symbolic and verbal statements. However, such generalities, while providing useful aims, tend to ignore or obscure complex issues of theory and technique. Other questions on whole-part task learning and the role of general/particular skills training are raised in later sections of the paper, but are left largely unresolved.

Thus, Bell highlights several matters for discussion. First, there is the relevance of language studies to mathematical learning, and the extent to which such research can provide a theoretical underpinning and a guiding framework for research experiments in mathematics teaching. In what respects is the process of understanding prose, the process of understanding mathematics? Second, there are the research studies of Galvin and Bell, and of Janvier, and how well they delineate fundamental problems in mathematics learning and comprehension. Third, do the suggested teaching procedures relate to these learning problems, link to a theory of instruction and generate evidence of their validity?

Although Bell makes reference to research on reading, and argues the analogy to mathematics comprehension, he is somewhat uncritical and patchy in his selections, and does not underline several issues which experimenters have found to be important. For example, the Robinson SQ3R technique for reading, or PQ4R (Thomas, Robinson, 1972) in a more modern guise, encourage the pupil to preview/skim the passage and then formulate salient questions. This helps him to attend to important aspects of the material on subsequent reading. But the situation is not as simple as this. Studies almost always show subjects do better at answering comprehension test questions if they have used the same or similar questions either before, or during, or even after the passage is read (see Anderson, Biddle, 1975). In fact, when the to-be-tested questions are different from priming questions, subjects seem to do better only when the primers are asked after the reading. Attention can be too exclusive. Further, providing a focus is not the only purpose for priming questions, for altering the distribution of the questions (e.g. interspersed by paragraph or by page within the text) also influences performance (Frase, 1967). The reason is that questions force the pupil to process the text in certain ways, perhaps by requiring him semantically to rephrase, exemplify or integrate the material.

Current reviews of reading (e.g. Reder, 1978) also stress the need for giving more attention to the elaborative aspects of comprehension, for this is a variable which consistently distinguishes between good and poor readers. Such processing is influenced by the type of material (e.g. its concreteness and familiarity), its structure and if the pupil can utilise the implied/implicit material of the text to engage his previous experience. In summary, the extent to which a passage is comprehended is not solely a function of the text or the reader, but their interaction through the learning/teaching situation. The different processing demands placed on the student develop different cognitive structures and different memory.

Thus a closer consideration of the reading literature shows a learning situation more complex than Bell reveals. Paradoxically, through its emphasis on cognitive processing and the knowledge brought to the task by the student, the reading analogy returns the mathematics researcher to cognitive psychology on the one hand, and to an analysis of mathematical tasks on the other.

Because of time limitations, I treat the next sections of Bell's paper in a summary fashion and make only two comments. First, the reference to the National Assessment of Performance Programme being mounted by DES raises large measurement issues which deviate from the main purposes of this discussion. Of course, mathematics and quantitative methods are applied in a wide variety of subject areas, for it is advantageous that the abstract laws of mathematics work independently of context. However, their valid use relies heavily on an understanding of the concepts underlying the subject matter of application, otherwise incomplete or incorrect models are set up. Thus, notions of 'across the curriculum' mathematics need careful interpretation. Second, the references to relational thinking and to the work of Peel and Suchman invite us to stray into the vast and difficult area of judgmental learning and problem solving. Bell asks what materials and teaching techniques should be used? Many studies from language emphasise the importance of elaboration in building up better comprehension. This suggests that placing congruous information and related examples in the text will aid the process, and research supports this conclusion. However, in Suchman's work, a hurdle was placed in the way of the students' ready comprehension. They were not told, but had to hypothesise and ask. More closely controlled experiments (e.g. Auble, Franks, 1978) support the value of this method provided the learner eventually reaches a conclusion. So which method, or mix of methods, results in the better understanding? Answers or hypotheses on this question cannot be stated simply; they involve subject matter, students and learning objectives. [The weight of evidence, though, does not support the view that either method can develop general context-independent problem solving skills, or even that such skills exist. Indeed, we are not even clear on how to represent problem solving performances and the complex interplay of procedures and knowledge they involve (see Newell, Simon, 1972, for an attempt which uses an information processing approach).] Thus, looking for generality, or asking large questions in this field, is not likely to prove profitable.

Now to consider briefly the research studies in mathematics learning and teaching which are cited by Bell. Galvin and Bell are concerned with pupils' ability to formulate equations from verbal statements. The researchers complain of linguistic processing being too closely applied when pupils set up their mathematical sentences. Space prevents Bell from giving details of the experiment (these are available, no doubt, in the reference), but it would be helpful to know of the pupils' perceptions of the task. Perhaps it is not likely, but they may have thought the experimenter wished for close translation. But I wasn't too shocked at confusion about the representation of r (whether one red pencil, a collection of pencils, or the pencil's cost); maybe the operational understanding of the pupil was adequate and verbalisation was the principal difficulty. The rabbits and hutches problem suggests similar queries. Perhaps the way pupils conceptualise the situation is psuedo-diagrammatic. Putting a pair of rabbits in a single hutch when previously they occupied two, saves a hutch. Since two hutches were to be saved, four rabbits were needed. When giving a more formal representation, the pupil must consider relationships and procedures - how he is solving the problem. Providing a sequence of sentences and asking for a mathematical translation affects, perhaps even discounts, the total conceptualisation of the problem and emphasises, not procedures, but declarative translation statements. Do the experiments hit the nail on the head?

Some suggestions are made for improving the teaching of these 'translation' skills. But cognitive psychologists would underline the importance of the representation which the teacher, and hence the pupil, gives to the underlying subject matter or problem solving contexts. Setting up formal equations derives from an understanding of the problem solving situation, and representation influences the procedures and type of processing in which the pupil can engage, and even governs the effectiveness of the feedback given to him. [See, for example, Greeno (1976) on techniques and some consequences of giving spatial, set-theoretic or numerical representations to fractional quantities; or see Mayer, Greeno (1972) who showed differing types of learning outcomes between formal and concrete-elaborative representations used in the teaching of probability.] So, in this case of Galvin and Bell, has the language analogy distracted attention from more fundamental issues?

After describing Janvier's experimental study, a comparison is suggested between text reading and graph reading. But is this analogy helpful and advantageous? Surely there are many differences between the two in both the representation given to the data and the process of analysis. The study showed wide differences in the pupils' explanations of the graph, but while accepting this, it would be interesting to know of their perceptions of the task. 'Explain the happenings' is a vague instruction, and perhaps pupils were unsure of the precision, level of detail, or type of explanation which was required. The teaching treatments I found hard to operationalise, but would like to make two comments on their effects. The first concerns the representation of data (graphs v. tables); the second, the advantages of providing a relational framework - in this case a series of laboratory experiments. The suggestion that changes in data and their rates of increase were more noticeable from tables than from graphs, seems surprising, as the pictorial highlighting of features is one of the oft-quoted reasons for employing graphs. Representing data through graphs should allow different considerations (e.g. scaling) and different activities (e.g. easier suggestion of possible explanatory hypotheses, and extrapolation). Therefore, treating data (tables and graphs) 'in the same way' might not exploit the potential of graphical forms. Janvier attributes differences in performance to the knowledge/ previous experience which pupils bring to the task - perhaps the most important variable in learning and comprehension. He claims they have a greater familiarity with numbers than with graphs, though whether this was an experimental variable or a *post hoc* hypothesis is not clear.

The value of providing a relating framework for learning (in Janvier's case through experiments) has received much experimental support. How pupils build up their conceptual organisations from connected discourse, and other materials such as diagrams, is being actively researched. For example, in a geographical context, as part of a series of studies on the learning of maps, Shimron (1975) had an experimental group read stories which used the map as a background of events. The treatment was contrasted with an equal time spent looking at, and re-drawing, the map. Post-tests showed both groups learnt the map's features, but on questions which required associations between cities and routes, or spatial organisation, the story group were significantly the better.

A further important topic which Bell raises from his analogy with language learning is the development of fluency through practice. But what types of practice are useful, and how should they be integrated within teaching sequences? The example of the teaching unit on sequences contained interesting suggestions, but the related complexities of whole-part task learning and general/specific skill training, I find daunting. The literature is large, the issues difficult to set out, and teaching guidelines, such as they are, owe more to intuition than experimental data. Even when narrowing the discussion to the role of practice in developing new concepts and cognitive structures, the issue is more complex than Bell reveals.   Some ways of practising, e.g. rehearsal, increase retention, but usually add little to understanding and transfer. Other ways of practising, e.g. same-context tasks, clarify and make fluent but are less effective in promoting later transfer than varied-context examples. However, these latter type of tasks can cause confusion in the early stages of learning. The experiments of Nitsch (1977) demonstrate the value of hybrid practice schemes in overcoming some of these difficulties. These comments are not to devalue   Bell's   references to language learning (indeed, Nitsch's experiments were set in this field), but to point out some issues which further analysis necessarily reveals. Again, translating these ideas into mathematics experiments will not be easy. It will require careful examination and definition. What are mathematical fluency and flexibility in thinking? How are we to represent these notions (and the pupils' cognitive structures on which they depend) at the level of detail needed by experiments?

In conclusion, I believe the best way forward in mathematics learning and teaching will come from detailed studies of the cognitive processing which pupils undertake when working through mathematical tasks. The supporting framework for this research should not be limited to studies in reading, but draw on cognitive psychology more generally. (The beginnings of such a framework is available and its emphases include, representation, processing and structure. Within this scheme, mathematics learning will have its own distinctiveness. It will differ from language learning since its representations are often abstract, its processing relates to a different body of knowledge, and its structure comes from inference rather than narrative.) Further, if teaching principles are to be developed systematically, attention must be given to technical matters which Bell ignores. e.g. ways of representing subject matter structures and pupils' knowledge. Otherwise, we can do no better than proceed pragmatically and use the techniques of experienced teachers. Of course, research into the nature of mathematical learning has to prove its worth, or be an act of faith. Either way, experiments which are not adequately related to theory, or firmly attached to teaching practices, are wasteful.

Discussion

Bell explained why he had devoted the paper to a discussion of a comparison between language and mathematics.

An important aspect of the task of clarifying the nature of mathematical learning is the distinguishing of the content of particular mathematical ideas from the general processes which characterise the subject. These processes of mathematics need to be analysed and their learning studied, and means need to be devised for evaluating their attainment.

An extensive discussion of these matters appears in The Learning of General Mathematical Strategies (Bell, 1976), and a paper surveying existing work appeared earlier this year (Bell, 1979).

Perhaps representation is the most characteristic aspect of mathematical activity - for example, the use of symbols and diagrams. Mathematics uses symbols in a special way - it manipulates them spatially. Science does something similar with circuit diagrams and chemical equations but to a smaller extent.

The crux of mathematical skill in this area is the ability to switch between thinking simply of the symbols and their spatial movements, and being aware of their meanings. It may be important, therefore, to study pupils' perceptions of symbolic expressions and graphs, and to see how they develop from step-by-step attention to local features to the ability to recognise forms and to read global features with fluency.

In the context of this seminar, it was thought particularly appropriate to raise for discussion an aspect of mathematics which appears to mark it off as distinct from science, yet makes it an essential tool in scientific inquiry. The point of the paper is that it may be profitable to look particularly at tasks where the relation of symbol manipulation to symbol meaning is a key feature. There is little developed theory in this field. Readers may find useful the additional references, to the work of Krutetskii (1976) and Davis et al. (1978).

Much of the discussion concerned itself with the question of language, both mathematical and other, and the value of the analogy suggested by Bell between learning mathematical symbolisation and the learning of reading. Although the analogy was accepted by some contributors as being usefully suggestive of possible lines of investigation there were many who felt that there were dangers in pursuing it too far. There were, for instance, several essential differences between the writing of mathematical material and ordinary language. The first is clearly a more active process involving the development of new knowledge and conceptual frameworks at the same time as the symbolic representation is constructed whereas the learning of reading

178

is comparatively passive in the sense that it is the process of acquiring the ability to match a symbolic representation to an already
well-known spoken language. Learning mathematics is not essentially
the learning of symbols but the development of ideas which necessarily
need to be symbolised in order that they may be communicated. The
process of symbolisation is not so closely related to the content as
is the case in symbolising an already known spoken language and,
moreover, the form of the symbolisation used in mathematics need not
be unique (for example, the use of Reverse Polish Notation as an
alternative to 'common' algebra). There is little doubt that pupils
have problems in going from statements written in ordinary language
to their mathematical embodiment. Often there seems to be a place
for softening the transition by the use of some non-standard representations of the type that children generate for themselves as reported
by Bell referring to the research of Janvier. It was therefore
suggested that children might be allowed more freedom to produce non-
standard symbolisations or to be encouraged to work with various
alternatives (e.g. $8 \xrightarrow{+5} \boxed{13}$ and $\left.\begin{matrix}8\\5\end{matrix}\right\}$ 13 as alternatives to
8 + 5 = 13) before being required to use the normal conventions. The
main problem to resolve is that children may well use representations
in symbolic form that are quite reasonable and meaningful to them on
their own terms but are inconsistent with usual practice. The idea
of 'encoding' problems in order to gain greater understanding and an
ability to manipulate ideas is not, of course, confined to mathematics
courses and, as Dienes (1978) has argued, may well be an important
general skill that should be encouraged more widely even though it is
of crucial importance in mathematics.

Despite these problems which are related to the value, or otherwise, of the analogy that Bell introduced, there was considerable
interest expressed in research that might elucidate the difficulties
children have in using mathematics as a language. The process of
going from a mathematical idea to its representation is clearly a
complex one and several contributors stressed the importance of
research in this area. It is also useful to consider the language
analogy in studying the process by which a person goes from symbol to
meaning. Among other remarks it was suggested that more time needs to
be spent by children discussing mathematical ideas before the introduction of symbolisation. Thus the use of the child's natural language
in exploring mathematical understanding may well be an important
subject of research. The use of symbolisation too soon may inhibit
children's understanding and it is therefore important to know what
thinking processes are involved when a child works with mathematical
statements. Linked closely is the problem, discussed by Bell, of
the need to investigate the 'translation' techniques involved when a
child is required to mathematise situations arising in problem solution. These matters are aspects of the process dimension of
mathematics which, from the mathematician's viewpoint, is possibly
more important than the content dimension although, it was suggested,
the content dimension may well be seen to be by far the most important
by users of mathematics who treat the subject as a tool.

179

The particular place of graphical representations in the context of children's thinking in mathematics was also felt to be an important issue. A report was given of evidence obtained in the work of the CSMS project suggesting strongly that children saw graphs as pictures rather than representations of relationships, thus supporting the work of Janvier reported by Bell. It seemed highly likely that graphs for some children were distracting rather than an important means of providing understanding. There have, of course,been a number of useful investigations of pictorial representations in mathematics learning and there is a useful summary of issues involved in Plunkett (1979). Once again the importance was stressed of the value of allowing children to talk in their natural language and at length about graphical representations in order to clarify their mathematical under-standing of the relationships involved before being required to express these relationships in symbolic form.

Some concern was expressed about the nature of mathematical objects and there was some discussion (inevitable in a group whose members were from both mathematics and science oriented backgrounds), about the differences between mathematics and science. It is clearly difficult to identify the source of mathematical objects. Nevertheless it is important to see mathematics as knowledge about those objects, knowledge which must then be expressed in some form which is usually referred to as the language of mathematics. This language, however, should not be confused with mathematics itself. The symbols in the language are not themselves mathematical objects but only representative of those objects or of the relationships between them. Children are therefore faced with the problem of translation between symbols and objects which may well be an extremely difficult process particularly if the objects are not well understood. The symbolism is then open to grave misinterpretation. Mathematical objects themselves are construc-ted after a long period of concept formation and the slow process of abstraction, a process which was acknowled   to be common to many subjects although, in discussion, it seemed apparent that the nature of abstraction itself varied between different subjects. In using the language of mathematics, therefore, it is important to know what mathematical objects children think of and what are the generally held misconceptions in their thinking.

Here there is further opportunity for research activities and it was suggested that much of this research might best be conducted using the teachers as the source of information for 'practitioner-based' findings rather than necessarily seeking solutions to the problems involved within a general theory of learning.

Studies of Conceptual Development in Mathematics

LEARNING THE CONCEPT OF A FUNCTION : AN ANALYSIS OF THE RELATIONSHIP
BETWEEN MOTIVATIONAL VARIABLES AND PREVIOUS MATHEMATICAL KNOWLEDGE
OF PUPILS AND TEACHING STRATEGIES

Erika Schildkamp-Kündiger

I am going to introduce a running research project, the aim of
which is to get a better insight into students' learning processes at
school. The subject matter taught is the introduction to functions.
A pilot study with two classes and a main study with 8 classes have
been accomplished. The students belonged to technical and trade
school classes.

Learning and teaching processes can be looked upon from a lot of
different standpoints (Dunkin, Biddle, 1974), therefore it is necessary to state some essential aspects of the theoretical background.

The chance of a pupil to follow a lesson and to reach the
achievement goal is seen to depend on two sets of variables:

a. his antecedent knowledge and abilities and motivational
    variables concerning mathematics;

b. the teaching procedures of which two aspects are of interest:
    the subject matter aspect and the motivational aspect.

    The subject matter aspect includes: the strategies the
    teacher uses to reach the learning outcomes e.g. starting
    with concrete, special examples, moving to abstract, general
    definitions; which antecedent knowledge he assumes.

    The motivational aspect includes: the teacher's way to
    motivate the pupils by encouragement, evaluating their

answers, demonstrating the usefulness of the mathematical
topic taught for pupil-relevant objectives; e.g. getting
a certain mark, solving physical problems, developing
abilities necessary for a desired profession.

To analyse the relationships and dependencies a variety of
student's and teacher's variables were involved. The lesson sequence
'the introduction to functions', that in the main took 4 x 1½ hours,
was recorded on tape and an instrument for coding the lessons was
designed.

Some results of the pilot study will be reported. They refer to
antecedent and subsequent mathematical knowledge and some relationships
between motivational variables.

Two classes of the 'Vorklasse zur Fachoberschule' were involved
in the pilot-study ($N_1 + N_2 = 40$). To be eligible for this type of
class one must have finished an apprenticeship. It is the
first step to get a certification that is equivalent to that from
an intermediate school and moreover opens the way to enter a technical
college.

The curriculum

The mathematics curricula at technical and trade schools in the
FRG usually are not built upon the internal structure of the subject
matter, but they are a sequence of practical problems assigned more or
less as they are used in other subjects. In North-Rhine-Westphalia a
new curriculum has been developed that integrates the practical demands
of these special schools and the structure of the mathematical science
(Andelfinger 1979a, p.67ff; 1979b, p. 86ff). The curriculum consists
of 'building stones', which are relatively complete teaching units.
Some of these units deal with basic knowledge, relevant for all classes, others concern special aspects relevant to different branches only.
This curriculum was tested with great success and it is an essential
step forward towards a greater possibility to pass from a more practically orientated educational system to high school and vice versa.

One 'building stone', belonging to the area of basic knowledge
deals with functions, the first section of which is relevant for this
research project. The curriculum segment: the introduction to
functions starts with relations; functions are then introduced as
special relations. The teaching is based on a concrete approach as
Orton (1970) proposed. The concepts are taught by means of six word-
problems: a relation is given and has to be represented in different
ways; thereafter special relations are identified as functions and
it is discussed how this can be recognised. Two definitions of functions are presented (type of relation; set of ordered pairs).
Detailed curriculum materials exist for the teacher. This makes it
possible to construct a pre- and post-test in advance corresponding to
this sequence.

The pre-test

The first task is concerned with different representations of sets and operations on sets. This matter was already taught in a previous sequence and is presupposed for the sequence 'introduction to functions' (items 1a, b, c, d, e, f, g).

The second task is concerned with equations (items 2a, b) and an inequality (item 2c). In the third task percentages are to be calculated (items 3a, b). Knowledge of the last two tasks will be helpful to solve the problems of the sequence 'introduction to functions'.

The tasks 4, 5, 6 are admitted to get to know what students know already about marking points in a Cartesian graph, about relations and about functions.

The post-test

The tasks can be related to three areas.

I   Basic knowledge of relations.
    Relations are to be identified from given sets of numbers and criteria for non-relations have to be stated (task 1a). The relation 'is the brother of' has to be represented by a set of ordered pairs (task 2a) and by an arrow diagram (task 2b).

II Basic knowledge of functions.
    Relations in all of the major representations are given, functions have to be identified and the criteria for the decision have to be stated (tasks 1b, 3a, b, c, d). Examples of functions (task 6a) and relations that are not functions (task 6b) are asked for, as are definitions of functions (task 6c).

III Word problems.
    Three word problems were given (tasks 4, 5, 7). They were formulated in analogy to the examples taught during the sequence. 4th task: the relation between force and elongation of a spring is given by table; the graph (item 4a) and the equation (item 4b) are asked for. 5th task: verbal description of the relation between initial costs of a car and the amortisation is given; the table (item 5a) and the graph (item 5b) are asked for. 6th task: there are two washing machines of different capacity and different running-time; the problem is, how many possibilities there are to wash a certain amount of washing in a given time; the table (item 6a) and the graph (item 6b) and the decision whether this relation is a function or not (item 6c) are asked for.

Results of the pre- and post-test

The mistakes the students made were analysed and a classification was developed with reference to van Dormolen (1978, p.100ff).

Type 1 : solutions which make no sense.

Type 2 : wrong strategy, wrong computation rule, wrong formual used.

Type 3 : partly correct.

Type 4 : right with regard to the content, but wrong mathematical symbols or expressions.

Type 5 : mistakes due to inadvertence only.

For each task the different types of mistakes are defined separately, so that differentiated information of a student's knowledge is available.

The pre-test

In table 1 the frequencies of right solutions (including solutions with a mistake due to inadvertence) are listed.

Table 1: <u>Pre-test; frequencies of right solutions (including solutions with a mistake due to inadvertence)</u> N = 35

Sets							Equations Inequality			Percentages	
1a	1b	1c	1d	1e	1f	1g	2a	2b	2c	3a	3b
32	1	25	1	-	-	8	13	12	-	29	19

First task: representations of sets and operations on sets. Three of the seven items were solved relatively often, these are:

item 1a : the set members of a finite set that was described verbally shall be enumerated,

item 1c : the set members of a set diagram shall be enumerated,

item 1g : the empty set as solution of an intersection of two sets shall be found.

There were 2 students having 4 correct answers and 3 students having 3 correct answers, all other students solved fewer items correctly. The overall impression is that the previous knowledge of sets is not very good. Most students failed when mathematical symbols are used e.g. item 1b: $C = \{2n \mid 0 < n \leqq 4; n \in N\}$ or are asked for. In the main study some more items were included to examine if this is a problem in general or if this depends on the special symbols used or asked for.

Second task: two equations and one inequality. No student solved
the inequality - $\frac{x}{5}$ ≤ -3 correctly, two students gave a partly correct
answer.

6 students computed both equations correctly, 8 students computed one
equation correctly.

Third task: percentages (2 items). 14 students computed both items
correctly, 16 students computed one item correctly. Only three students solved at least 3 items of the 1st task, 2 items of the 2nd
task, 2 items of the 3rd task.

The students with relatively good results in the pre-test all had
good marks in mathematics; the inverse was not true. The overall
impression is that the antecedent knowledge of the students is not
very profound even if it is considered that the students were not
prepared for the test.

Antecedent knowledge concerning the sequence 'the introduction
to function':

One student knew the subject matter already;

12 students knew how to mark points in a Cartesian graph and a
further 8 students had obviously once learned this matter, but
there were only vague impression ideas left.

The post-test

Very often word problems are the most difficult ones for the
students, this is not true for this sample as can be seen from table 2.
Probably this is due to the fact that the students came in contact
with the concepts of a relation and a function by solving word problems. A more detailed analysis of the relationships between the
achievements in the three areas: basic knowledge of relations, basic
knowledge of functions and word problems (table 3) showed that it is
possible to have average (2 or 3 correct solutions) or good results
(more than 3 correct solutions) in the area 'word problems' without
having understood very much about a relation or a function. According to the logic of the subject matter as it was taught, the
concept of a function was not understood without knowing the concept
of a relation.

The overall result is not very encouraging and the results of the
main study as far as already available confirm this impression. The
opinion Hart states in her paper for the Cognitive Development Research Seminar is confirmed, that there is only a small group which
succeeds in mathematics and that there are many pupils who fail. The
mistakes made show that very often the concepts of a relation and a
function were mixed, in such a way that relation and function are two
excluding concepts, or that every relation is a function (these results
agree with those of Orton, 1970).

185

Empirical researches confirm the obvious relevance of previous knowledge to antecedent. In this study too, those students with good previous knowledge succeeded in the post-test, moreover these students had good or very good mathematics marks in the last school report. More detailed information about the learning processes will be available after a thorough analysis of the teaching procedures in the classrooms.

Table 2: Post-test; frequencies of correct solutions (including solutions with a mistake due to inadvertence) N = 35

Basic know-ledge or relations	Basic knowledge of functions	Word problems
Items 1a 2a 2b	1b 3a 3b 3c 3d 6a 6b 6c	4a 4b 5a 5b 7a 7b 7c
12 11 9	9 11 7 15 19 12 4 6	25 0 21 27 4 2 8

Table 3: Number of correct solutions (including solutions with a mistake due to inadvertence) N = 35

Number of correct solutions	Basic knowledge of relations	Basic knowledge of functions	Word problems
0	17	7	3
1	10	9	3
2	4	6	9
3	5	3	14
4		5	5
5		2	0
6		2	2
7		2	0
8		0	

Relations between motivational variables

If a student has not reached the antecedent achievement goals, this has two different impacts for the learning processes to come. Firstly, a more subject matter directed one: assuming the subject matter is structured hierarchically the student's deficiency means that his chances of reaching the following goal are lessened because of his fragmentary antecedent knowledge; cumulating deficiency will appear, the more the subject matter is hierarchical in nature and is taught in this way.

Secondly, a more motivational directed one that can be described when cognitive achievement motivation models (Weiner et al.,1971;

Weiner et al., 1972) are adapted to school situations (Fuchs, 1978; Kornadt, 1975). It is assumed that during the years at school a student has developed a subject matter related self-concept of his abilities, associated with causal attributions of success and failure. This developing process can be described in a simplified manner as follows. The information about his achievement level, e.g. by a teacher's remark or a class exercise, influences the student's further achievement expectations. Failure can lead to two different reactions: it is possible that he makes more efforts to compensate the deficiency and, if his efforts lead to success, his learning potential for the next learning step is strengthened and his achievement motivation too; if his efforts fail and if this occurs over and over again, a failure cycle begins and is maintained by a defence mechanism to avoid achievement situations. This mechanism becomes obvious e.g. by day-dreaming, aggressive behaviour in the classroom, the setting of unrealistic achievement goals, or difficulties in concentrating during the learning task, and so on. The negative motivational development and the lack of knowledge relevant for the next learning step are affecting each other. In analogy to this failure cycle a success cycle can be developed.

When motivation theories are applied to school situations it must be considered that learning is embedded in a social pattern of relations and personal goals (Schildkamp-Kündiger, 1974, 1979). The persistence a student develops to master difficulties on the one hand depends on his experience of the efficiency of his efforts and on the other hand on the relevance the subject matter has for the student. These relationships can well be described by Ausubel's theory of relevant cognitive structures (Ausubel, Robinson, 1969).

These learning processes briefly described above are essentially influenced by the teacher's behaviour. That is why he should have some knowledge about the motivational situation the learning of his students is embedded in.

Theoretically the processes based on the interaction between student, teacher and subject matter leads to certain types of learners on the side of the students. The extremes may be characterised as the achievement motivated student; good knowledge, positive self-esteem of his mathematical abilities, success will be attributed to his own ability and efforts, failure not to lack of ability but to internal or external variable causes, e.g. lack of efforts or bad luck, the fear to fail student; poor knowledge, negative self-esteem of his mathematical abilities, success in mathematical tasks is not attributed to ability but primarily to external reasons such as good luck and easiness of the task, failure or lack of ability.

Having in mind the importance of the perceived effectiveness of one's efforts that there may be a group of students with average or only sufficient grades, learning self-assured of their own success, because they perceive their achievement levels as success within reach by personal efforts. To get to know which groups can be found in natural school settings, it is necessary not to use grades as criterion variable but to start from motivational variables.

Results based on the following motivational variables will be reported.

M_1 Causal attribution of good and poor class exercises in mathematics. [Two questionnaires with 6 items each. The causes stated for success are (M_{1S}): ability, good luck, facility of the task, much learning, concentration during the exercise, sympathy of the teacher. The analogue causes are stated for failure (M_{1F}).]

M_2 Efforts in connection with the achievement goal. [Questionnaires with 6 items. Causes stated for efforts: to improve one's achievements, to keep one's achievements, to fill up gaps. Causes stated for non-efforts: achievement goal in reach without efforts, efforts have no influence in achievement, achievement in mathematics of no personal importance.]

The items of the questionnaires M_1 and M_2 have 3 possible answers: correct, partly correct, not correct.

M_3 Self-esteem of one's own mathematical abilities, compared to the students of the class. (Degree to be marked by a cross on a scale.)

34 students answered the items.

To find groups of students with different motivational patterns a statistical model that is based on linear relationships e.g. correlation, regression or factor analysis is inadequate, therefore the data were analysed by cluster analysis. An algorithm published by Späth (1970, p.70ff) (the KMEANS algorithm) was used. Starting from an initial assignment the individuals are shifted to other clusters until the distance function achieves a minimum. The algorithm finds relative minima. 6 clusters lead to a well interpretable result. One cluster consists of only two students who answered all items in the same way. They obviously did not answer the questionnaire seriously. They are not considered further. The two items concerned with the influence of the teacher's sympathy on success or failure of the causal attribution questionnaire (M_1) were always answered as not correct except by two students, so these items lead to no differentiation between the groups.

In the main all causes to make efforts are accepted partly and those to make no efforts are negated. Success as well as failure are attributed less to ability and luck but more to the characteristics of the tasks, own preparatory training and possibility to concentrate during the class exercise. The mathematical abilities are estimated a little better than average.

188

Two of the five remaining groups (groups 1 and 2) can roughly be looked upon as groups of self-assured students. They differ with regard to the readiness to make efforts and the relevance they believe diligence has for a good mark. Students of groups 1 and 2 have good or at least average marks in mathematics.

Groups 4 and 5 are failure students. These two groups differ mainly in respect to their self-esteem of mathematical abilities; students of group 4 think to have average abilities, students of group 5 think to have poor abilities and logically the last group accepts that a poor mark is due to lack of ability besides other factors, not so students of group 4. Students of these groups have average to poor marks. Group 3 takes an average position; this is true for the marks also.

It is obvious that the groups differ in respect to their causal schemata (Kelley,1972).

To get the final number of groups and the characteristics constituting them, the results of the main study have to be awaited. The pilot study has demonstrated that the methods used are qualified for detecting groups of students with different motivational patterns. In a further stage of the evaluation of the results the relationships between motivational background, knowledge and classroom behaviour are analysed.

Discussion

In response to a question, the speaker explained that students completed questionnaires on attributes placed in three categories:

a. Attributes making for success (six attributes were given including ability, easy work, good luck). Corresponding attitudes making for failure were also given. Students marked on a three point scale of true, partly true, false.

b. Six attributes listed in connection with achievement goals which were marked on the same scale.

c. Mathematical self-esteem marked on a five point scale.

Five groups of students were isolated by the means indicated in the paper. For each group the mean and standard deviation were recorded diagrammatically. It was thus possible to see quickly the variety of motivational patterns arising from the mathematical attitudes and work of these groups of students. In the case of some responses, more weight was given to such causes as concentration in class, personal preparation and the kind of tasks in relation to success or failure than to mathematical ability.

The speaker confirmed that the self-evaluation of students was checked using interviews, information from the teacher and the scores from the pre- and post-tests, and also added that some students do not see themselves as being poor at mathematics; there is a conflict between their aspirations and their results. Discussion also brought out the point, noted in the paper, that the results are in line with the views expressed in Hart's paper that only a small percentage of students are successful in mathematics.

The matter was raised of the teachers' reactions to the work. The speaker remarked that she had discussed the motivational aspects and teaching materials with teachers and intended to have further discussions with them on the implications of the study.

In conclusion the speaker suggested that her work had differentiated achievement motivation between groups of students and that the procedure could well be applied to other subject areas in school. It has to be appreciated that a complete analysis has not been made and so all aspects could not be considered.

DIDACTICS AND ACQUISITION OF 'MULTIPLICATIVE STRUCTURES' IN SECONDARY SCHOOLS

G. Vergnaud

Our research group is concerned with 'multiplicative structures', i.e. classes of situations and problems in elementary arithmetic for the solution of which multiplications or divisions are needed. The term 'structure' is here taken in the wide sense of 'space of problems'. Geometry, technical devices, physics and ordinary problems in arithmetic contain such 'multiplicative structures'. We distinguish two main structures that we consider relevant to study the acquisition of concepts and skills by students from 7 to 16 (we are presently working with secondary school children).

The first structure is the 'isomorphism of measures', which covers all situations in which two measure-spaces are directly proportional to each other. The reason why we call it 'isomorphism of measures' instead of 'proportion' or 'linear function' will be explained below.

The second structure is the 'product of measures' which covers situations in which one measure-space is the product of two other measure-spaces.

Examples of 'isomorphism' : quantities of goods and prices, durations and distances when the speed is uniform...

Examples of 'product' : area, volume, Cartesian product...

Our hypothesis is that 'product' is a very difficult concept which cannot be perfectly understood until it is analysed as a double or treble proportion (bilinear or trilinear function) and until some kind of dimensional analysis is performed, at least intuitively.

Another hypothesis is that the isomorphic properties of the linear function are more easily 'appropriated' (or found evident to be used) by young students than the canonical property of the linear function $f(x) = ax$.

Actually, this formula means that a is a quotient of dimensions,
$$a = \frac{f(x)}{x} \text{ (like speed} = \frac{distance}{time}).$$

So, if you need to calculate $f(x)$ given x, you have to multiply by a, which is a quotient of dimensions; and if you need to calculate x given $f(x)$, you have to divide by the quotient a or multiply by the inverse quotient.

This is more difficult than using the isomorphic properties,
$$f(x + x^1) = f(x) + f(x^1)$$
$$f(\lambda x) = \lambda f(x)$$
or even $\quad f(\lambda x + \lambda^1 x^1) = \lambda f(x) + \lambda^1 f(x^1)$

In other words, 'scalar' aspects are more easily grasped than 'functional' aspects, as will be shown below.

It explains why I introduced a new terminology: isomorphism of measures.

Most situations met by students can be easily analysed with these two structures and one can distinguish several classes and sub-classes of problems with different levels of difficulty, according to the value of the different quantities and parameters involved and to the nature of the measures referred to.

But 'multiplicative structures' do not merely cover classes of problems to be solved. They include also important concepts like rational numbers, linear function, dimensional analysis, vector-space, which must be made meaningful through these classes of problems. And this brings us to the main problems of didactics.

Not only must we know:

- the success rate of students of different ages or forms for well-defined classes or problems,
- the procedures that students find more natural to use and the main errors they make.

We must try to know also:

- how to help them to become conscious of the relationships they deal with, correctly or incorrectly,
- how to help them to elucidate and understand the general properties of these relationships,
- how to use symbolic representations such as tables, diagrams, graphs or algebra in a way that helps them to understand these relationships and to solve problems that they would otherwise fail to solve.

This brings us to the problem of building up appropriate situations, theorising about them, observing what happens, and modifying one's views; and to the problem of repeating the same didactic sequence in different classrooms and saying something reliable and transmittable about the goals aimed at, the behaviour observed and the interpretation.

I would like now to focus upon that problem in the second part of this paper.

Research work in didactics involves a variety of methods: large-scale inquiries, individual interviews, experimental work in the classroom, etc.

Our research group uses these different methods according to its purposes. When we need to establish the hierarchy of difficulty of different classes of problems we use written questions because we have to make experimental designs with many variables. When we want to go more deeply into the understanding of a specific concept for which a clinical approach is first necessary, we use interviews.

For instance, we have just finished interviewing on volume 80 students from the 'sixième' to the 'troisième' (age 11 to 15). The results are now being analysed.

In another kind of experiment, we have planned to show that 'scalar' aspects of proportion are better used than 'function' aspects.[1]

---

1 (Note) Since this paper was written, L. Lybeck has communicated some of his results to me; although he starts from different theoretical considerations, his idea is essentially the same as the one that has inspired this experiment, and his results confirm ours.

Given two durations a and c and the consumption of oil b = f(a) of a house central heating, find x = f(c).

durations	consumptions
a	b = f(a)
c	x = f(c)

We have used four different situations.

The first two situations make it easy to find a 'scalar' ratio λ and apply it to n_2 (λ = 3 or 4).

S_1

durations	consumptions	examples	
n_1	n_2	7	84
λn_1	x (× λ)	21	x

S_3

durations	consumptions	examples	
λn_1	n_2	32	104
n_1	x (/ λ)	8	x

The other two situations make it easy to find a 'function' ratio and apply it to n_2.

S_2

n_1	λn_1	8	32
n_2 (× λ) → x		104	x

S_4

λn_1	n_1	21	7
n_2 (/ λ) → x		84	x

Of course, we have used different triplets (λ, n_1, n_2) for S_1, S_2, S_3 and S_4.

We wanted to draw a picture of success rates and of procedures used by students for these different situations.

193

Table 1: Success rates

Classes \ Situation	S_1	S_2	S_3	S_4
6ème	39%	39%	29%	16%
5ème	64%	55%	59%	36%
4ème	65%	69%	69%	35%
3ème	82%	85%	74%	56%
	63%	63%	58%	36%

The progress is not bad over four years but the final level is still not very high, especially for the last situation S_4. Table 1 shows anyhow that there are good reasons to pay attention to that sort of situation in secondary schools.

We have observed as many as 30 different procedures and classified them into different categories.

SUCCESS   S - scalar   : calculate $\frac{c}{a}$, then apply it to b.

           F - function   : calculate $\frac{b}{a}$, then apply it to c.

           V - unit-value : calculate $\frac{b}{a}$ as the unit-value (consumption in one hour), then apply it to c.
This procedure is ambiguous because it consists of the same arithmetical operations as F, but has a scalar character, as can be seen in the diagram.

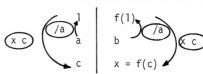

           R - rule of three   : multiply b and c, then divide by a.

      DS - scalar decomposition : find λ and λ^1 so that
$$c = (\lambda + \lambda^1)a, \text{ then}$$
$$x = f(c) = (\lambda + \lambda^1)b.$$

FAILURE S^1 - scalar 'degenerated' : attempt with a scalar aspect.

$\quad$ F^1 - function 'degenerated' : attempt with a function aspect.

S^1F^1 - both scalar and function degenerated.

$\quad$ P - erroneous product.

$\quad$ Q - erroneous quotient.

$\quad$ I - inversion of the relevant ratio ($\frac{a}{c}$ instead of $\frac{c}{a}$ for

$\quad$ A - others. $\hspace{5cm}$ instance).

Table 2 shows clearly that scalar aspects are better taken into consideration than function aspects. It also shows that the rule of three is very seldom used and that there are many ways to tackle a rule-of-three-problem.

Table 2: Analysis of results-categories of responses

Procedures / Situations	S_1 (n_1 | n_2 / λn_1)	S_2 (n_1 | λn_1 / n_2)	S_3 (λn_1 | n_2 / n_1)	S_4 (λn_1 | n_1 / n_2)
SUCCESS — S	41%	32%	38%	16%
SUCCESS — F	11%	14%	6%	8%
SUCCESS — V	9%	14%	10%	5%
SUCCESS — R	1%	1%	2%	1%
SUCCESS — DS	1%			4%
FAILURE — S^1	8%	6%	20%	5%
FAILURE — F^1		1%	4%	10%
FAILURE — S^1F^1	10%	9%		5%
FAILURE — P	3%	4%	1%	3%
FAILURE — Q	3%	4%	2%	1%
FAILURE — I	2%	2%	1%	11%
FAILURE — A	11%	13%	16%	31%

Let us turn now to the problem I raised before: experimenting in classrooms.

We usually have two purposes at the same time:

- design and experiment with didactic situations enabling students to develop different mathematical activities and understand different relationships, properties and concepts,
- observe in a reliable way the main behaviours one can expect in such situations.

The question I raise is the following: how can this experimental work be 'repeatable' by ourselves and by other research groups, and how can we come to reliable assessments and scientific discussion?

A very important point is to make as clear as possible the goals aimed at, and the reasons for the choices made. There is a tremendous number of situations one can think of and the only way to clarify the problem of choice is to analyse the cognitive tasks involved and try to link them to the didactic goals.

Let me give some examples.

1st example. Suppose you hypothesise that setting out the data spatially and especially in tables is a good way of explaining the relevant relationships and consequently of being more efficient in problem solving and in understanding the properties of the linear function. You have several ways to experiment. We found it helpful to introduce tables with problems containing much data and no question, so that the students' task was to sort out the data and formulate questions.

The area of a farm is 254.5 ha. Half of it is assigned to corn-growing. The average croft is 28 'quintaux' (hundreds of kilograms) to the hectare. You need 1.2 kg corn to make 1 kg flour; 1.5 kg flour to make 4 loaves; and a loaf is the average daily consumption of 2 persons.

What are the questions you can think of? Can you arrange the data (written on pieces of cardboard) on the table?

This table shows a possible outcome:

area	corn	flour	loaves	persons	
1	2800		e		a. *How much flour can you get from the farm?*
	1.2	1	b		b. *How many loaves can you make with 1 kg flour?*
		1.5	4		c. *How many persons can you feed with the corn-croft of the farm?*
127.25		a		c	d. *How much corn do you need to feed 10000 persons in one day?*
	d			10000	e. *How many loaves can you make with the croft of 1 ha?*

Of course there are many possible questions. It is not trivial to formulate them unambiguously, to place them with the data in a table, or to find the questions that one might ask about any point in the table. They are very important tasks: they imply the capacity of identifying two independent dimensions of the table and of the set of data and questions.

2nd example. Suppose you hypothesise that children are able to use different proportions (isomorphic proportion for instance) without being able to explain them properly. We found it helpful to build up situations in which they would perform these calculations and we asked them to explain, and eventually to represent in the table, the 'theorems in action' that they had implicitly used. The concept of 'theorem in action' is very important because:

- although the theorem seems to be evident to the student who uses it, it cannot be easily made explicit, and if the attempt is made, the explicit formulation may actually be wrong,

- the best criterion of 'appropriation' of a theorem is the use of it in action.

The 'Aquitaine' is a direct train Paris-Bordeaux. It leaves Paris at 17.53. It runs through les Aubrais, Blois, Saint Pierre des Corps, Chatellerault, Poitiers, Ruffec, Angoulême, Coutras and Libourne. In 6.4 minutes, it covers 16 km.

	distance	duration
Paris		
	116	
Les Aubrais		
	58	
Blois		
	58	
St Pierre		
	64	
Chatellerault		
	32	
Poitiers		
	64	
Ruffec		
	48	
Angoulême		
	88	
Coutras		
	16	6.4
Libourne		
	36	
Bordeaux		

As can be seen on the table, it is sometimes very easy to calculate the times. We wanted to get explicit explanations and also diagrams or algebraic representations of them.

For example:

$$x\ 2 \left(\begin{array}{cc} 32 & x \\ 16 & 6.4 \end{array}\right) x\ 2 \qquad f(2 \times 16) = 2\ f(16).$$

or

$$\begin{array}{cc} 16 & 6.4 \\ +\quad 32 & +\quad 12.8 \\ \hline 48 & x \end{array} \qquad f(16 + 32) = f(16) + f(32)$$

or

$$\begin{array}{cc} 32 & 12.8 \\ 16/4 = 4 & 6.4/4 \\ \hline 36 & x \end{array} \qquad f(32 + \tfrac{1}{4} \times 16) = f(32) + \tfrac{1}{4}\ f(16)$$

198

3rd example. Suppose you consider that the concept of rational number essentially includes an understanding of the concept of an infinite class of ordered pairs, although it may have been made meaningful through concrete situations such as the ones mentioned before.

It is not just a boring task to generate such classes of ordered pairs. For instance, in the farm-problem, we asked students to generate all possible ordered pairs of whole numbers describing the correspondence between corn and flour.

corn	flour	
1.2	1	*What about 18-15 or 6-5?*
12	10	*What about the operator that goes from the left to the right, or from*
24	20	*the right to the left?*
36	30	*What about the generator of the whole class? of ordered pairs? and so on.*

My last point will be the problem of repeating such experiences and discussing what is going on.

When a psychologist interviews individuals, he usually finds patterns of responses and behaviours that give him a reasonable picture of what is going on, of what is representative or anecdotal, of what is difficult for 11 year-old children and easy for 15 year-old children.

Is it possible to imagine that we get such reliable patterns for the behaviour of a whole class?

Of course, the answer is not straightforward because there are many conditions interfering. Yet, if we manage to describe properly and unambiguously these conditions, there should be repeatable facts, at a certain level of description and analysis.

We found it necessary to come to an agreement inside our research group about what was going on in a group of four students (or even in the whole class), by watching and watching again the videotapes. This was usually possible. After that, we repeated the same sequence of lessons in different classes of the same level, or at different levels. And we did actually find repeatable facts among all the differences that you can imagine.

For instance, we found that organising data in spatial array, when the table is not given, is not trivial at all; and that the number of measure spaces involved in the questions asked is significantly bigger for 14 year-olds than for 12 year-olds.

We found also that some situations could not be meaningful before a certain level, although they did not seem to involve any previous

199

mathematical knowledge. We found persistent difficulties for the
students in mastering the notion of function when it is not of the
trivial case f(1) given and f(1) > 1.

But this is just a beginning and I am not pretending that we have
yet established the important didactic facts and theories it would be
helpful for teachers to know about multiplicative structures. I just
want to express my confidence in the possibility of moving from prag-
matism to scientific arguing in the new field of didactics.

Note

This short paper refers essentially to the following report,
available at IREM d'Orléans, Domaine Universitaire de La Source,
45045 Orléans Cedex.

Vergnaud, G., Rouchier, A., Ricco, G., Marthe, P., Métregiste, R.,
Giacobbe, J. (Mars, 1979),
Acquisition des 'structures multiplicatives' dans le premier cycle du
second degré,
Publication de l'IREM d'Orléans et du Centre d'Etude des Processus
Cognitifs et du Langage.

Discussion

In reply to a question on insights into pupils' learning, the
speaker said that, in line with the findings of Hart and Lybeck,
children find it easy to double or halve and even to multiply by
3 or 4 or 5 as necessary.

It was pointed out that in the U.K. the method of practice was
formerly taught to children who then memorised it. As it was considered too rigid the method was dropped. The speaker took this up
in connection with his theorem in action. He explained that this concept is important and is appropriated by children to solve problems.
But the method of working cannot always be stated clearly by pupils.
A theorem in action tends to be functional and is used as an algorithm.
It is a way of working built up piece by piece by a pupil who finds
it difficult to describe and justify. People's words and practices
represent their theories and they are not always explicit. It is even
possible for pupils to use a good procedure and to describe it in-
adequately or wrongly. One member interjected to say that there is the
notion of a 'locked up theory' inside you which does not seem to issue
in action.

The discussion went on with a question on the misinterpretation of
a theorem in action. In reporting on a correct procedure, the speaker
suggested that some children rationalise their practice.

A question was raised about the interdependence between these structures as seen by pupils. In particular it was asked if these structures support each other. The speaker commented that the distinction they had made seemed justified. He illustrated this by saying that the practice in some French primary schools of introducing multiplication by the Cartesian product seemed to cause confusion. At the secondary level older pupils had considerable difficulty with volume problems where say one dimension was doubled and another trebled. The unspoken implication seemed to be that multiplication difficulties at primary and secondary levels were interdependent. If it is the case that from an early age children work out their personal strategies then early misconceptions of operations will distort concepts and skills and attitudes.

AN INVESTIGATION INTO THE UNDERSTANDING OF ELEMENTARY CALCULUS IN ADOLESCENTS AND YOUNG ADULTS

A. Orton

Introduction

Calculus is an important subject area within mathematics but many students appear to find it difficult. A major purpose of the study described in this paper was to investigate difficulties experienced by students in coming to understand elementary calculus.

In Britain there has been a continuing debate about when calculus, meaning differentiation and integration, should be introduced. Nowadays, many able students meet calculus around the age of 15 years, that is within the period of broad general education which ends at 16 years. However, because of the variety of examination syllabuses available, not all able students meet calculus as early as 15 years of age.

Many mathematicians have considered that some understanding of limit is a necessary prerequisite for studying elementary calculus. Also, the approach to calculus in schools has been based on considerable understanding of rate of change. It was therefore considered important to test students' understanding of both limit and rate of change. It was also considered that the study would throw light on students' difficulties with the essential background algebra involved in learning calculus.

In carrying out the study it was decided that, in a subject area in which extensive research had not previously been carried out, individual interviewing of students and not a written test should be used

to provide the raw data. It was also decided not to interview students
in the 15-16 age range because those students were being prepared for
their first major public examination. The study was based on individual interviews with 110 students in the age range 16-22 years.

Design of the experiment

The subjects of the study came from school sixth forms or from
colleges concerned with teacher education. All of the students had
chosen mathematics as a major subject in their own studies. Sixty
students were selected from four mixed secondary school sixth forms,
and were chosen to represent the spread of ability normally found in
present-day mathematics classes. Some such students were very able,
others were really too weak to be embarking on advanced studies, but
all students had previously studied for a public examination in
mathematics which included calculus. The fifty college students were
attending two mixed colleges and were undergoing courses of initial
teacher education with mathematics as their main teaching subject.
All of the college students had studied calculus at school. In both
school and college groups students were chosen from all years, that
is from a variety of different stages in their education. In the
school sample there were more males than females, the reverse was the
case in the college sample, but in the complete sample of 110 there
were 55 males and 55 females.

The tasks were presented in four sections, two sections in each of
two interview sessions. Section A aimed to test the understanding of
limits in a variety of mathematical situations independent of calculus.
Section B developed the idea of integration as measuring area; the
section also included some questions involving routine indefinite and
definite integration. Section C introduced rate of change using both
graphs and tables of differences, eventually leading to differentiation.
Section D dealt with a number of simple applications together with certain aspects of the introduction of calculus which it had not been
possible to introduce earlier. Figure 1 illustrates the subject areas
and interconnections reflected in the choice of tasks. Many of the
tasks were directly related to customary school approaches to calculus,
but some deliberately presented unusual situations. The tasks were
given to students on cards and were also read out. Wherever appropriate supplementary oral questions were applied to gain further
insight into the level of a student's understanding.

Some of the tasks comprised a variety of questions based on a
single mathematical situation and they therefore often incorporated a
number of skills and concepts which needed to be looked at separately.
These same skills and concepts may also have appeared in several different tasks. For the purposes of scoring student performance, responses
to appropriate subdivisions of the tasks were re-grouped to form items,
each item relating to just one aspect of elementary calculus. Thirty-
eight items resulted and these are listed in table 1, together with
the means of scores obtained by students on each item. Scores were

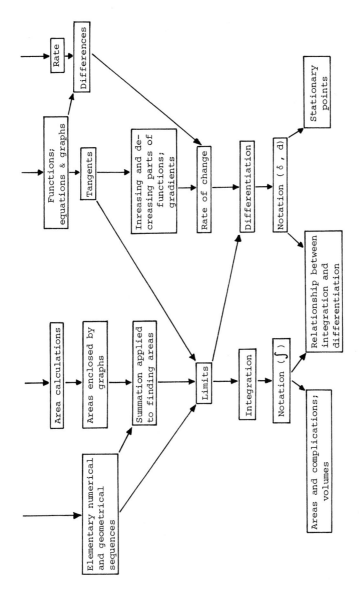

Figure 1: Subject areas and interconnections reflected in tasks

obtained by assessing responses on a five-point scale, for each item separately. The score of 4 was reserved for the best responses, those judged to be as good as students could be expected to achieve after a first introduction to calculus. The score of 0 was used when no progress was made by a student. Intermediate scores were allotted to categories of response which were defined for each item after a careful scrutiny of all responses. Naturally, the scoring scales which resulted were not evenly spaced linear scales, but they did provide a useful guide for studying and discussing responses.

Analysis of the results

Table 1 shows the mean scores on items for school and college students separately. These means show that the two groups of students experienced similar successes and failures with the items. Particularly difficult or easy items may be identified from the table, as can those items which were more successfully answered by one of the two groups of students. Amongst the easier items were limits of number sequences (Item 1),easy graphical questions involving areas (Items 5, 6 and 9), routine integration and differentiation (Items 15, 31 and 32), simple graphical interpretation (Items 21 and 22), elementary rate of change (Item 23) and some of the simplest applications of differentiation (Items 35 and 36). The difficult group of items included the introduction of integration based on the sequence of approximations to areas under the curve (Items 12, 13 and 14), graphical items concerning rate of change (Items 27, 28, 29 and 30), some applications of integration (Items 17 and 19), an application of differentiation and integration (Item 38) and some important items in understanding differentiation (Items 33 and 34).

Levels of responses in the scoring scales for the items were analysed to determine whether formal or concrete operational thinking was required. This analysis was obviously based first and foremost on what was directly available from Piaget. Clearly, in the subject area involved, study of Piaget's work only provided a beginning and so the final interpretation was the writer's own. In table 2 it was not considered appropriate to include level 0, since this represented the absence of any worthwhile response. The gaps in the table are because it was considered unnecessary to include the level of thinking required for lower scores when a higher score demanded only concrete operational thinking. The abbreviations used were defined as late concrete (2B), early formal (3A) and late formal (3B). An overall measure of the cognitive demand of items was obtained by converting the scale 3B, 3B/3A, 3A, 3A/2B, 2B to the numerical scale 5, 4, 3, 2, 1 and summing. This measure of cognitive demand was compared with the mean scores for items using rank correlation, and the coefficient obtained was 0.90. Thus there was a high and statistically significant degree of correlation between scores measuring the difficulty experienced by students and scores measuring the cognitive demand of items.

Table 1: The items and mean scores

	Item	Mean Score School	Mean Score College
1	Limits of sequences of numbers	3.28	3.06
2	Limits from general terms	2.82	2.90
3	Infinite geometric sequences	2.88	2.56
4	Limits of geometric sequences	2.92	2.78
5	Area under graphs y=k	3.87	4.00
6	Area under graphs y=kx	3.17	3.20
7	Heights of rectangles under graphs	2.68	3.42
8	Use of previous heights in a new situation	2.40	3.12
9	Calculation of areas of rectangles	3.03	3.62
10	Simplification leading to sum of areas of rectangles	2.43	3.52
11	Sequence of approximations to area under graph	2.18	3.22
12	Limit of sequence equals area under graph	0.78	1.00
13	Limit from sequence of fractions and from general term	1.67	2.48
14	Explaining integration	1.57	1.62
15	Carrying out integration	2.98	3.40
16	Definite integration	3.02	3.16
17	Integral of sum equals sum of integrals	1.10	0.60
18	Complications in area calculations	2.55	2.78
19	Volume of revolution	0.95	0.88
20	Linear equations	2.75	2.50
21	Substitution and increases from equations	3.32	3.68
22	Increasing and decreasing parts of a graph	3.13	3.24
23	Elementary rate and rate of change	3.13	3.12
24	Use of differences	2.55	2.28
25	Rate of change from differences	3.02	2.74
26	Constant rate from graph, equation and differences	2.50	2.48
27	Rate of change from straight line graph	2.22	2.02
28	Rate, average rate and instantaneous rate	0.88	1.18
29	Average rate of change from curve	2.22	1.92
30	Instantaneous rate of change and tangents	2.02	1.46
31	Rate of change by differentiation	3.38	3.62
32	Carrying out differentiation	3.62	3.50
33	Differentiation as a limit	1.88	0.95
34	Use of δ-symbolism	1.52	1.40
35	Significance of rates of change from differentiation	3.43	3.62
36	Gradient of tangent to curve by differentiation	3.63	3.76
37	Stationary points on a graph	2.30	2.54
38	Relationship between differentiation and integration	1.78	1.20

Table 2: Levels of responses in scoring scales for items in relation to the Piagetian stages of operational thinking

Item	Level 4	Level 3	Level 2	Level 1	Measure of cognitive demand
1	3B	3A	3A	3A	14
2	3B	3B	3A	3A	16
3	3B	3B	3A	3A	16
4	3B	3B	3A	3A	19
5	2B				4
6	3B/3A	3A	3A	3A/2B	12
7	3B/3A	3A	3A	3A/2B	12
8	3A	3A	3A	3A/2B	11
9	3A/2B	3A/2B	3A/2B	2B	7
10	3B/3A	3B/3A	3B/3A	3A	15
11	3B	3B	3B	3A	18
12	3B	3B	3B	3A	18
13	3B	3B	3B	3A	18
14	3B	3B	3B/3A	3A	17
15	3A	3A	3A	3A/2B	11
16	3A	3A	3A/2B	3A/2B	10
17	3B	3B	3B/3A	3A	17
18	3B	3B	3B/3A	3A	17
19	3B	3B	3A	3A/2B	15
20	3B/3A	3B/3A	3A	3A	14
21	3B/3A	3B/3A	3A	3A	14
22	3A	3A	3A/2B	2B	9
23	3B/3A	3A	3A/2B	3A/2B	11
24	3B	3B	3B/3A	3A	17
25	3B	3B	3A	3A	16
26	3B	3B	3A	3A/2B	15
27	3B	3B	3A	3A/2B	15
28	3B	3B	3B/3A	3A	17
29	3B	3B/3A	3A/2B	3A/2B	13
30	3B	3B	3A	3A/2B	15
31	3A/2B	3A/2B	2B		6
32	3A/2B	3A/2B	2B		6
33	3B	3B	3B/3A	3A	17
34	3B	3B	3B/3A	3A/2B	16
35	3A	3A	3A/2B	3A/2B	10
36	3A	3A	3A/2B	3A/2B	10
37	3B	3B	3B/3A	3A	17
38	3B	3B	3B/3A	3A	17

The major skills underlying the understanding of integration and differentiation as represented by the content of the tasks, were analysed separately by means of factor analysis. The method of principal components was applied, the criteria used to decide how many factors to extract were those suggested by Kaiser and Cattell (the scree test) and the six components thus obtained in each analysis were rotated by the varimax method to obtain the final factors. The factors obtained are listed in Tables 3 and 4.

Some tasks and students' difficulties

It is not possible to present all of the tasks and the enormous amount of detailed information obtained concerning students' difficulties, but some examples are considered briefly under five headings.

1. Elementary algebra

    TASK : *Find the coordinates of the point or points on the curve*

    $y = x^3 - 3x^2 + 4$ *at which there is a turning point*

    or stationary point. Determine also what kind of

    point you have found.

This was a calculus task, but it illustrates how elementary algebra was also being tested. Within the task the solution of the equation $3x^2 - 6x = 0$ was required, and twenty-four students were unable to solve it correctly. Twelve students lost x = 0, six students factorised into $3x(x - 6) = 0$ and hence obtained x = 0 and x = 6, and the other six students committed a variety of errors. Teachers of algebra will be only too familiar with such errors, but here they were being made by intelligent and mature students of mathematics.

Other examples of difficulties with algebra were the inability to find a simple linear equation from a table of values and a graph, the inability to substitute values of x to find heights of rectangles under a curve, the inability to expand $3(a + h)^2$ correctly and the inability to simplify the sum of areas of rectangles. School students experienced rather more difficulty with algebra than did college students, but in both groups the incidence of difficulties with algebra was higher than expected.

Table 3:   Factor analysis:integration

Factor	Description	Percentage of variance
1	General intellectual/educational factor reflecting understanding of the approach to areas under curves as the limit of a sequence of approximations obtained by summing rectangular areas	23.3
2	Limits from sequences of numbers and from general terms	9.2
3	The technique of integrating	7.4
4	Rectangular areas in relation to graphs	7.3
5	Integration as the limit of the sum of increasingly narrow sections	6.7
6	Integral of a sum equals the sum of integrals	6.2

Table 4:   Factor analysis:differentiation

Factor	Description	Percentage of variance
1	General intellectual/educational factor reflecting understanding of rate of change as a simple ratio and of derivative as rate of change but with no involvement with substitution or with limits	17.4
2	Average rate of change and instantaneous rate of change on a curve by substitution	9.0
3	The differentiation process and symbolism	8.3
4	Applications of differentiation to gradients and stationary points on graphs	6.8
5	Limits of number sequences	6.7
6	Elementary rate of change	5.4

2. Rate of change

TASK : *The graph of y for a certain equation for x = 0 to x = 6,*
is shown in figure 2.

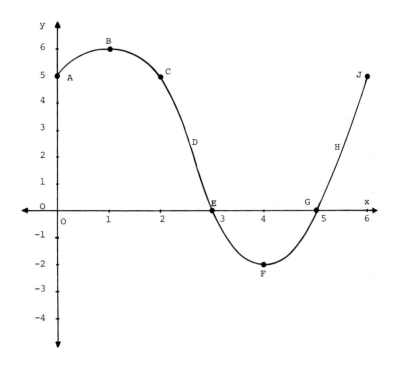

Figure 2: Graph for task 2

What is the average rate of change of y with respect to x

(i) From A to B? (ii) From B to E? (iii) From A to J?

In part (i) thirty-nine students did not obtain the answer 1.
In part (ii) twenty-five students divided correctly but omitted the
negative sign; a further eighteen students appeared to divide the
correct y-increment by the x-coordinate of E and again nine of these
students also omitted the negative sign; another fourteen students
could give no answer at all. In part (iii) there were incorrect
answers from fifty-one students, of whom eighteen could give no answer
and ten gave an answer involving both 6 and 5, the coordinates of J
being (6, 5).

Many tasks on rate of change were included in the study. Tasks which involved calculating a ratio, y/x, always caused problems, and rate of change at a point on a graph proved to be a particularly difficult idea, even when the graph was linear. It was clear that rate of change was particularly badly understood by many students.

3. Limit

TASK : *Figure 3 shows a circle and a fixed point P on the circle. Lines PQ are drawn from P to points Q on the circle and are extended in both directions. Such lines across a circle are called <u>secants</u>, and some examples are shown in the diagram.*

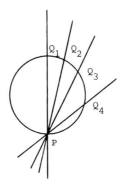

Figure 3: <u>Diagram for task 3</u>

(i)   *How many different secants could be drawn in addition to the ones already in the diagram?*

(ii) *As Q gets closer and closer to P what happens to the secant?*

Some students gave numerical responses to (i) and to similar questions in other tasks. Five students said '∞ - 4', and the answers '176' and '356' given by individual students appeared to be related to angle measurement. Some responses suggested concern about the practicality of carrying out the task, for example some students said, in effect, 'You'd get more the finer your pencil lines'. In part (ii) 43 students were unable to state that the secant eventually became a tangent despite encouragement to say more through further questioning. Typical responses included 'The line gets shorter', 'It becomes a point', 'The area gets smaller', 'It disappears'. It seems that, in the normal approach to differentiation, students may need considerable help in coming to understand the tangent as the limit

210

of a set of secants.

In general, in geometrical limit tasks, the infinite nature of the processes involved did not appear to be understood by many students. In both numerical and geometrical tasks it was common to find students using ∞ as if it were a number. On the whole, however, limit was not so poorly understood as rate of change.

4. Elementary calculus

   TASK : *Calculate the shaded areas in the graphs of figure 4, if possible. If it is not possible, explain why not.*

(a)

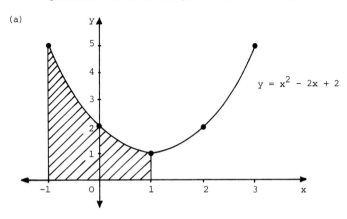

$$y = x^2 - 2x + 2$$

(b)

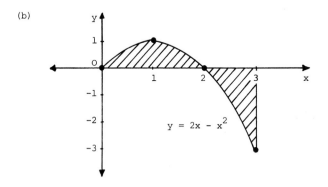

$$y = 2x - x^2$$

Figure 4: Graphs for task 4

In part (a) thirty-one students committed errors in the arithmetic, sometimes more than one error. After integrating, the students should have written

$$\left(\frac{1}{3} - 1 + 2\right) - \left(\frac{-1}{3} - 1 - 2\right)$$

but seven wrote

$$\left(\frac{1}{3} - 1 + 2\right) - \left(\frac{-1}{3} + 1 - 2\right)$$

and some other students had a different incorrect number in the second bracket, for example + 2 instead of - 2, or - 1 instead of -1/3. Five students made errors because they would not be persuaded to use brackets. From there on many errors were made, e.g. $\frac{1}{3} - 1 + 2 = \frac{2}{3}$ and $- 1 - (-1) = + 2$.

Six students obtained negative answers and were asked to explain what this meant; two said it was because the curve had a negative gradient, one said you disregard the sign, one said it was because it was the area underneath a curve and the other two were frankly puzzled.

Part (b) presented a familiar complication at school level, and it produced enormous variety of confused responses. Thirty-three students were convinced that the integral must be calculated in the two separate parts, but they could not explain why. Six students said they would do it in two parts only because 'that's the way we were taught to do it'. Eight students thought it was prudent to calculate the area in two parts because they were suspicious of what might happen if they did not, and four others thought negative areas might complicate matters but were not sure how. Four students thought that $\int_0^3$ gave the area shown in figure 5, and two others appeared to be thinking along similar lines but did not provide a diagram.

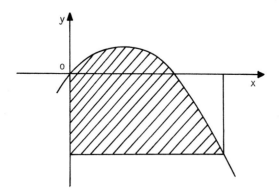

Figure 5: <u>Incorrect shaded area given with some responses to task 4</u>

212

One student said $\int_0^3$ would give an area that was too large, another
thought $\int_0^3$ would miss out the area from x = 2 to x = 3. Three
other $\int_0$ students expressed concern that the area from x = 2 to
x = 3 was not enclosed by the curve, without explaining why working
out two separate areas would solve this problem.

Another five students were confident that $\int_0^3$ would give the
answer, proceeded to calculate the area, obtained zero, and were then
able to explain why this had happened. A further seven students
explained the method of working out two separate areas but, in reply
to a question, said that you could alternatively work out $\int_0^3$. One
of these students when asked why, in that case, she would work
out the area in two parts said 'Well, that's the way you are taught
to do it, the other way is what you get on to later'. The sixteen
students who were judged to have made no progress with part (b) included nine students who claimed that the area from x = 0 to x = 2
could be worked out in the normal way, but they either thought it was
impossible to work out the rest of the shaded area, or they did not
know whether there was a method.

This discussion of responses to this task illustrates the great
variety of answers and statements given by students to tasks concerned with elementary calculus.

5. Symbols

TASK : *Explain the meaning of each of the following symbols:*

(i)	δx	*(iv)*	dx
(ii)	δy	*(v)*	dy
(iii)	$\delta y/\delta x$	*(vi)*	dy/dx

(vii) What is the relationship between
$\delta y/\delta x$ and dy/dx?

The symbols which caused the greatest problems for students were
dx and dy. This was expected in the sense that the symbols are not
really meaningful except when used together as dy/dx or when used in
integration. Twenty-nine students explained dx as 'the differential
of x', or 'the differentiation of x' or 'the rate of change of x'. A
further twenty-five students explained dx as 'the limits of δx as
$\delta x \to 0$'. Another twenty students thought that dx was 'an amount of x'
or 'an x - increment' and was, in other words, more or less the same
as δx, though some students were careful to point out that one of dx
and δx was a little bigger than the other. Twenty students could give
no response at all for dx and dy.

The majority of students were able to explain δx and δy satisfactorily. However, seventy-one students could not give a correct
response for $\delta y/\delta x$. The largest number of these students gave an
answer involving rate, for example 'rate of change of y/rate of
change of x', 'rate of change of gradient', 'rate of change at a point',
'a small increase in the rate of change'. Another large number of

students gave unacceptable responses which referred to 'small changes' and twelve students gave vague replies which included mention of the word 'gradient'.

As far as the students were concerned, part (vi) was the next easiest after parts (i) and (ii), though forty-seven students gave unacceptable responses of a wide variety. In part (vii) seventy-eight responses were completely incorrect and the following two types were common, 'they are the same' and ' $\delta y / \delta x$ gets smaller until it becomes dy/dx'. Overall, it was clear that the level of understanding of the δ and d symbols was extremely poor.

Teaching elementary calculus

It is difficult to sum up the findings of a major study in a short section; only a few observations can be made. Looking at students' responses as a whole, it was certainly not only a small group of weak students who had difficulties. Taking item scores of 0 and 1 as an indication of failure on an item, more than half of the students failed in 10 or more items. Some items were easily identifiable as causing problems even for very able students whose total scores were high. Four such difficult items concerned integration (Items 12, 14, 17 and 19) and another four concerned rate of change and differentiation (Items 28, 30, 33 and 34). It seems that, even for able students, there are areas of mathematics which need special attention in a teaching programme.

Looking briefly at some particular subject aspects of the study, it appeared first that care needs to be taken that difficulties with algebra do not stand in the way of the development of students' understanding of calculus. It may be that, in the future, using an electronic calculator to lay a firm base in arithmetical approaches to calculus will lead to fewer problems with algebra. Secondly, rate of change was poorly understood by very many students, and many older students understood less than younger ones, possibly because they had ceased to encounter problems and discussion concerned with rate. Thirdly, limit has been somewhat neglected as an idea to be developed throughout the main school mathematics programme, though there are many ways in which even young pupils can be encouraged to think about limits and limiting processes. Comprehensive treatments of both rate of change and limit are important if they are to form a base on which calculus is to be built. Finally, it appeared that some students had learned the rudiments of elementary calculus in an abbreviated or even algorithmic way and may not have been taken back to reconsider any underlying mathematics. If calculus is introduced in the fifth year in British secondary schools, it seems important that mathematics students in the sixth form should go back to the beginning and look in greater depth at the development of calculus.

Discussion

The matter was raised of the relation between the levels of response in the scoring scales and the Piagetian stages. The speaker took the view that the literature offered some help with this difficult task but that Piaget had not investigated understanding of this sort of mathematics. He had made decisions partly based on his own knowledge and experience. In doing so he had tried to ignore all knowledge of how children react.

One member enquired about the desirability of using the facility aspects of tasks to help to establish the levels of responses. The speaker had some reservations about this.

Discussion next centred on the mathematics curriculum. Mention of the spiral curriculum raised problems of 'steepness', 'flatness' and frequency of return to a given idea or skill. The view was strongly expressed that calculus work was rushed through too quickly at O-level without a spiral build-up and it seemed almost as if the sixth form students did not return to basic principles but moved on.

Again in relation to levels of understanding it was suggested that a cluster analysis would be helpful provided that the ideas came out of the data. A crucial thing is how you define distance on the scales.

Studies of Conceptual Development in Science

A STUDY OF THE UNDERSTANDING OF TRANSPORT MECHANISMS AMONG NIGERIAN
SCHOOL CERTIFICATE* BIOLOGY CANDIDATES

Eunice A.C. Okeke

Introduction

Recent emphasis on the quality of children's thinking has prompted many research efforts. Of those based on Piaget's theory of cognitive development some were replications of Piaget's experiments while
some others tried to relate the theory to school subjects. Among the
latter are Pella and Billeh (1972), Lawson et al. (1975), Hewetson (1975);
these are in the area of biological education. This study is focussed
on children's understanding of a biological area, the transport mechanisms in living things. The degree of understanding of any given
concept is said to be determined largely by the cognitive stage which
the child has reached. Thus according to Piaget's model, a concept
requiring formal operational thought cannot be mastered in an analytic
sense by a pupil who has only reached the level of concrete thought.
Nonetheless, some intuitive level of understanding may be possible.
Though Piaget's model has not met universal acceptance, it provides a
useful framework for examining the quality of thinking of which pupils
are capable at different age levels.

---

*The West African School Certificate is an external examination admini-
stered by the West African Examinations Council. It is regarded as
being of approximately equivalent standard to the Ordinary level of
the British General Certificate of Education (GCE) which is taken by
higher ability students at the age of 16.

This investigation (see Okeke, 1976) has, among other things, tried to identify levels of understanding demonstrated by School Certificate candidates in one biological area. It also used Piaget's model of cognitive development to analyse candidates' responses to tasks dealing with the transport mechanisms of living things. The objective is to determine how freely School Certificate biology candidates employed concrete or formal operational modes of thinking in tackling biological tasks.

It was intended that the investigation would find answers to the following questions.

1. What levels of understanding of the basic concepts and ideas concerned with transport mechanisms have the candidates acquired?

2. To what extent does Piaget's developmental psychology provide insight into candidates' difficulties?

3. What fundamental misconceptions do pupils hold in this area?

4. What implications does the investigation have for the teaching of biology?

In addition it sought to provide answers to the following questions.

5. Is there any significant difference between the performance of boys and that of girls?

6. Is there any significant difference in the performance of candidates in urban schools compared with those in rural schools?

It was hoped that by exploring the answers to these questions, some insight would be gained into the problems and difficulties associated with the learning and teaching of biology up to the School Certificate level.

Method

One hundred and twenty candidates were questioned orally using prepared tasks in order to test their understanding of concepts and ideas subsumed under the heading of transport mechanisms. Their answers were classified using predefined criteria.

Piaget's theory of developmental psychology was used as a framework for determining candidates' possible levels of cognitive functioning. Piaget's view is that intellectual development goes through a number of stages whose order of emergence is constant but whose time of appearance may vary with the individual and with the society. Readers are referred to Inhelder and Piaget (1958) for a detailed account of the theory.

217

Following Piaget's indication of the possible age at which children begin to employ formal operational thinking, one would expect that a majority of School Certificate candidates would be in the stage of formal operations. The question then is how freely do School Certificate biology candidates really use formal operations when dealing with biological concepts which demand such thinking skill?

Selection and analysis of the biological area

The area of transport mechanisms was chosen because it incorporates several basic physical and biological concepts such as diffusion, pressure and transpiration. Also the topic is given prominence among questions set at the West African School Certificate examination.

Basic concepts and ideas within the area were identified. There were thirteen as follows:

T_1 The necessity for transport mechanisms with reference to the ratio between surface area and volume.

T_2 The functions of transport systems in living things.

T_3 Diffusion expressed in terms of molecular movement.

T_4 Pressure.

T_5 Osmosis.

T_6 Plasmolysis and turgidity in living cells.

T_7 The selectivity of a living cell membrane.

T_8 The mechanism of transpiration pull.

T_9 The mode of transport of food in plants.

T_{10} The relationship between the blood vessels and the cells in the body.

T_{11} The idea of the parallel distribution of blood in the mammalian body.

T_{12} The function of valves in the mammalian blood system.

T_{13} The function of the lymphatic system in transport.

Each of these ideas was analysed in terms of levels of conceptualisation demanded. For example T_1, the necessity for a transport mechanism with reference to the ratio of surface area to volume of an organism required relating this to the efficiency of diffusion as a means of transporting materials. An understanding of this involved second degree relations, that is formal operations.

218

As another example in T_2, the functions of a transport system in living things, demands that candidates demonstrate knowledge of the sources and destinations of materials transported in the body. Such a degree of understanding involves only concrete operational thinking since it deals with concrete and observable data.

The other eleven ideas were analysed in the same way considering the level of understanding expected of School Certificate candidates. The entire analysis utilised the experiences of practising biology teachers, the syllabus, and past West African School Certificate biology questions.

Construction of tasks

Several tasks were devised to test candidates understanding of each of the thirteen ideas. For each task one or more questions were framed. For example to test T_1, the necessity for a transport mechanism...the task was as follows:

Suggest two reasons why it is necessary for some organisms, for instance an earthworm to have a transport system whereas it is not necessary for another organism such as an amoeba.

Another example is in T_2 - functions of a transport system, where several subquestions were constructed as follows:

1. Name two types of substances that are transported in the body of animals.

2. From where in the body of an animal are these substances transported and where are they taken to finally in the body of the animal?

3. Name two types of substances that are transported in the body of plants.

4. From where in the body of a plant are these substances transported and where are they taken to finally in the body of the plant?

These tasks were scrutinised for validity by two biology experts.

Constructing the scoring key

In order to classify pupils' answers into levels of understanding a 5 point scale of answers was constructed for each concept or idea. In this scale the generalised pattern was as follows:

a score of 1 represented 'I don't know' or a totally wrong answer.

a score of 2 represented answers containing a few isolated but relevant facts.

a score of 3 represented answers including all the important sub-ideas but without necessary explanations, or generalisations.

a score of 4 represented answers including the relevant ideas with some evidence of knowledge of relationships or generalisation.

a score of 5 was for answers including all the relevant ideas and relationships, generalisations, applications or explanations as considered adequate at the School Certificate level. This scoring scale was defined in more precise terms for each of the thirteen ideas. For example, the scoring key for T_1, the necessity for a transport mechanism with reference to the ratio of surface area to volume, was as follows:

a score of 1 for 'I don't know' or a totally wrong answers.

a score of 2 for a partial reason but without explanation.

a score of 3 for an answer such as the multicellular nature of a bigger organism, with some attempt at an explanation.

a score of 4 for an answer explaining the necessity for a transport system in higher organisms in terms of an increased number of cells, increased size with an explanation regarding the effect of the increase.

a score of 5 for an answer which explained correctly the necessity in terms of the ratio of the surface area to the volume of an organism.

Pilot trial

The questions and the scoring key were tried out on English GCE biology candidates for 1975 in the Leeds Metropolitan area. The questions were written out on cards and administered orally and individually to the sample. Follow-up questions were also used to probe further into the candidates' level of understanding or to seek further clarification of their answers.

These interviews were recorded and later transcribed and scored using the already prepared scoring key.

From the result of this pilot run, some questions were modified for greater clarity and the scoring key amended to take account of additional information contained in the candidates' answers.

The main experiment

The main experiment was carried out in Nigeria from mid-January to the end of May 1975.

The population consisted of secondary school pupils in Nigeria who were enrolled for the School Certificate biology examination of June 1975. One hundred and twenty pupils were selected from a sample of eight single sex secondary schools in the East Central State of Nigeria. A stratified random sample method was used in selecting the eight schools based on sex as well as an urban/rural dichotomy.

To make each school sample representative of the ability range of the candidates in the school in respect of biology, a stratified random sample technique was again employed. Each teacher rated each of their candidates on a 3 point scale of ability in biology, so that the fifteen candidates selected from each school could be said to be representative. Thus a total of one hundred and twenty pupils altogether were selected from two boys urban, two girls urban, two boys rural and two girls rural schools.

The procedure for administering the task was as in the pilot run. Each session lasted for about forty-five minutes. The subjects cooperated. The only difficulty that could be regarded as a limitation in this study was the subjects' poor ability in the use of the English language. However, it should be pointed out that English is the medium, both for instruction, and examination in the secondary schools of Nigeria.

The answers were scored as in the pilot trial. Out of the one hundred and twenty candidates, responses from a random sample of thirty were scored by an independent biology teacher. Correlation co-efficients between the two sets of scores for each concept or idea ranged from .73 to .97. This increased the confidence in the reli-ability of the instrument.

Results and discussion

Levels of understanding demonstrated by candidates

Table 1 shows the performance of candidates indicative of the levels of understanding reached by them in respect of each of the thirteen broad ideas. In each case the mean and median scores are given in addition to the total number scoring 4 or 5 compared with the total number of candidates scoring 1 or 2. These data as shown suggest probable levels of understanding possessed by these candi-dates. Except for T_2 and T_3 where the mean or median score reached 3.1 and 3.0 respectively, the performance of these pupils in respect of the other ideas was low. One could state with some degree of confidence that these candidates performed below the average level expected of School Certificate candidates.

The application of Piaget's model of intellectual development

Each of the questions and levels of answers in the scoring key was analysed to determine the conceptual demand. This is presented in Table 2. With the except of T_2 and T_9 the other eleven ideas demanded formal operational thinking to achieve a score of 5. Of these eleven ideas, seven $(T_4, T_5, T_7, T_8, T_{10}, T_{11}, T_{13})$ also require formal thought even for a score of 4.

Table 1: Data relating to scores on the thirteen ideas

Concept or idea	Raw scores – frequency					Mean scores	Median scores	Total no.of pupils scoring 4 or 5	Total no.of pupils scoring 1 or 2
	5	4	3	2	1				
T1	O	2	23	29	66	1.7	1.4	2	95
T2	15	31	34	32	8	3.1	3.1	46	40
T3	17	24	31	34	14	3.0	2.9	41	48
T4	9	22	36	38	15	2.8	2.7	31	53
T5	8	18	23	38	33	2.4	2.2	26	71
T6	9	26	11	22	52	2.3	1.9	35	74
T7	O	12	1o	86	12	2.2	2.1	12	98
T8	9	18	34	38	21	2.6	2.5	27	59
T9	5	19	42	36	19	2.6	2.6	24	54
T1O	6	17	33	25	39	2.4	2.3	23	64
T11	12	16	18	47	27	2.5	2.2	28	74
T12	7	23	43	19	28	2.7	2.8	30	47
T13	1	13	11	44	51	1.9	1.7	14	95

Grand mean score 2.5   N = 12O

The candidates' scores were examined for evidence of concrete or formal operational thinking. The number of candidates who employed formal reasoning relative to the tasks is also shown in table 2. The highest number of candidates who demonstrated formal thought in any of the ideas demanding such skill was thirty-one and this was in T_4. This represents just about 25% of the sample. In other words in no task did more than 25% of the candidates demonstrate formal operational thinking. This result is close to the findings of Shayer (1976) who noted that, by the age of 14, only 20% of English children have achieved early formal thinking.

The temptation may be to conclude that most of these candidates are largely still in the stage of concrete operations. This conclusion would be misleading since in this type of investigation the degree of understanding shown by candidates may depend on factors other than the possession of the appropriate cognitive structures. One example of such factors is effective teaching. The researcher believes that administering Piagetian tasks to these candidates might have yielded

valuable information for a more generalisable conclusion. The main
problem in this regard was the non-availability of suitable and
reliable tasks validated with Nigerian children. Even then experiments using Piagetian tasks have not yet demonstrated whether the
individual who demonstrates the use of formal operational thinking in
one situation will transfer this skill to every other situation. The
alternative is that an individual may demonstrate formal operational
thinking in one situation and revert to a lower level of thinking in
another situation. Here the familiarity of content has been known to
be one important factor in the use of formal operational thinking
(see Lovell, 1974).

In short the results of this study are only indicative of a
possible level of cognitive functioning common among these subjects
with reference to biological concepts. In other words, it can be
stated that these candidates failed to demonstrate formal reasoning
in biology tasks that demanded this skill, but any generalisation that
these candidates were at that stage incapable of this level of thinking
may be misleading. The best, in fact, one can claim is that there is
a close relationship between pupil difficulty and the conceptual difficulty of the ideas investigated. A rank order correlation of pupil
difficulty with conceptual difficulty of the thirteen ideas yielded
$r = 0.60$ which is significant at .05 level. Thus the application of
Piaget's developmental psychology can throw some light on pupil difficulties in understanding biological concepts. The implications of
this to the teaching and learning of biology are discussed later in
this paper.

Table 2: Classification of the scale of answers in terms of
conceptual demand together with the number of
instances of formal thinking (n = 120)

Ideas	Mean Score	Score				
		1	2	3	4	5
T2	3.1	–	–	–	–	–
T9	2.6	–	–	–	–	–
T1	1.7	–	–	–	–	10*
T3	3.0	–	–	–	–	17*
T6	2.3	–	–	–	–	9*
T12	2.7	–	–	–	–	7*
T4	2.8	–	–	–	22*	9*
T5	2.4	–	–	–	18*	8*
T7	2.2	–	–	–	12*	0*
T8	2.6	–	–	–	18*	9*
T10	2.4	–	–	–	17*	6*
T11	2.5	–	–	–	16*	12*
T13	1.3	–	–	–	13*	1*

* Demands formal operational thinking
– Demands concrete operational thinking

223

Differences in Scores due to Sex and Locality

To test the significance of the factors of sex and location of schools, a two-way analysis of variance was carried out (see table 3).

Table 3: Results of a two-way analysis of variance for sex and locality

Ideas and Concepts on Transport mechanisms	Mean scores				F Ratios		
	Boys (Urban)	Boys (Rural)	Girls (Urban)	Girls (Rural)	Sex	Local-ity	Inter-action (S L)
1	1.8	1.5	1.9	1.5	.1	7.7	.1
2	3.4	3.0	3.4	2.6	.8	8.4	1.5
3	3.2	2.8	3.1	2.7	.2	2.6	0
4	3.1	2.8	2.5	2.7	2.4	.2	1.5
5	2.4	2.1	3.0	2.2	2.8	5.2	1.1
6	2.0	1.9	3.2	2.1	2.2	1.1	4.3
7	2.4	2.0	2.5	1.8	.1	15.9	.6
8	2.4	2.4	3.6	2.1	3.5	.9	15.2
9	2.6	2.5	3.1	2.3	.8	5.3	3.1
10	2.8	1.8	2.9	2.0	.6	17.1	.1
11	2.9	2.2	2.6	2.3	.3	4.5	.9
12	3.0	2.5	2.7	2.6	.1	1.9	.8
13	1.8	1.6	2.3	1.9	4.3	2.8	.1
Sum of mean scores	33.8	29.1	36.8	28.8	.79	12.3	.79

F ratios with single underlining are significant at .05 level, those underlined twice are significant at .01 level.

In respect of the sex factor, the results indicate that sex is not significant in the understanding of the transport mechanisms in living organisms. Though boys exhibited formal reasoning in respect of this particular topic ninety-one times while girls did so one hundred and three times the difference is slight. However, it is worth a mention that girls included in their answers fine details which showed evidence of good understanding.

The findings of no difference attributable to sex agrees with those in some other studies involving sex differences in respect of use of formal thought (Lawson, 1975) and in respect of educational attainment (Ogunlade, 1973).

In the case of difference due to location of schools, the investigator is aware of problems of validity in comparative studies on cognition and culture especially as regards difference in environmental or cultural settings (see Hyde, 1970). In this study the results of the analysis of variance for urban/rural location of the schools (by implication urban/rural pupils) reveal that in more than half of the ideas tested there were significant differences in the level of understanding shown by urban and rural pupils in favour of the former. This difference is even more marked when we compare the number of instances each set of pupils demonstrated formal reasoning when the task so demanded. While in urban schools there were one hundred and forty such instances, in rural schools there were only fifty-four. This difference can be interpreted in the light of environmental influences on cognitive development. Other related studies, for example, Poole (1968) observed similar environmental influences. Cole and Scribner (1974) ascribed such differences in cognition not to the presence or absence of formal thought processes but to differences in the ways the different groups of a culture or subculture interpret and classify their experiences, what they termed 'life style'. Whatever is the case, the performance levels shown cannot be absolute since other factors such as the effectiveness of teaching, motivation, and proficiency in the use of the English language were not controlled. However, the results have given some insight into the forms of reasoning common to candidates in different environmental settings and such knowledge is valuable to any teacher.

Principal misconceptions

Doran (1972) stated that 'a knowledge of common misconceptions related to science phenomena and principles can be of extreme value to the curriculum developers and classroom teachers since it enables them to know where the student is.' With this in mind principal misconceptions were noted and these are in the area of 'diffusion', 'osmosis' and 'the operational mechanism of valves'. In describing osmosis, a majority of the candidates stated that the 'strong solution draws in the weaker solution', that is both the solute and solvent of the weaker solution move into the stronger solution. These candidates did not seem to understand that osmosis is the movement of water molecules across the selective membrane obeying the law of diffusion. Another example is in the operational mechanism of valves in the blood circulation. Many pupils were unable to explain this. When presented with valves in a sheep's heart, many resorted to unscientific explanations such as ascribing the valve with in-built ability to open or close. These misconceptions have implications for teaching.

Implications for teaching

Three major implications are discussed:

1. Sequencing and structuring of the ideas considered: It is necessary to take into account the conceptual difficulty of each idea while following the logical order of presentation. In order to do this certain ideas need to be treated at two levels. Some concepts must first be treated at the intuitive level and later the analytic level. Also a mapping out of interconnections between the various ideas and concepts facilitates the construction of meaningful learning and teaching sequences.

2. The role of practical work: Practical work should be geared to helping pupils understand better the ideas introduced in the lessons. This is because most of the pupils would be operating more frequently at the stage of concrete operations than formal and so require constant use of concrete referents. By constant use of laboratory and other practical experience and building on the intuitive understanding of concepts revealed by pupils, teachers may encourage them to develop that analytic level of thinking which characterises what Piaget has called formal operational thought. Indeed Piaget pointed out the value of concrete experiences in enhancing the development of formal operational thinking skills.

3. Evaluation: A new form of evaluation needs to be introduced which will emphasise the ability to reason out or explain biological phenomena. Even in objective test items pupils could be asked to explain why they selected a particular alternative as the correct answer. This will indicate whether or not candidates do in fact possess the level of understanding expected of them. By adopting such evaluation methods and using more challenging questions pupils and teachers alike would be persuaded to engage in learning experiences which will lead to a better understanding of biological concepts and ideas.

Summary

This investigation was aimed at investigating the levels of understanding of the transport mechanisms in living things as demonstrated by School Certificate biology candidates in the Eastern part of Nigeria. Piaget's developmental psychology was used as framework.

The findings show that many of the ideas involved in this area of biology were poorly understood and some even misunderstood. While there were no differences attributable to sex, there were significant differences due to location.

Implications of such findings for teaching were discussed. These implications are related to sequencing and structuring of the ideas, providing practical experiences and employing forms of evaluation that would test pupils' performance at higher levels of cognition.

Suggestions for further research

It would be profitable to carry out this type of research on a much wider scale so as to bring out the many more misconceptions of biological concepts among Nigerian secondary school students. It is suggested that practising teachers could be involved in this exercise in order to acquaint them with possible misconceptions.

Acknowledgement

The author acknowledges with thanks the help and guidance given to her in this investigation by Professor K. Lovell, and by Colin Wood-Robinson, both of the University of Leeds where this research was carried out.

Discussion

There was some debate about the procedures necessary to ascertain the Piagetian cognitive level of demand of each concept or idea. The procedure adopted had been for three independent workers, after reference to the literature, to rate each concept or idea and then compound their ratings in discussions.

In discussing the selection of schools, it was pointed out that the observed sex difference might not have been repeated if some co-educational schools had been included in those sampled. It was also noted that only some 25% of the population attended secondary schools at this level. Hence the population studied might not be fully representative of the population as a whole. When asked about the possible application and use of her research findings, Okeke maintained that she saw her role as making as precise a diagnosis as possible of widely held misconceptions. Her findings would then be reported as widely as possible so that teachers could use the information in planning their approach to the relevant area of biology.

AN EMPIRICAL STUDY OF THE UNDERSTANDING BY 16-19 YEAR OLD STUDENTS
OF THE CONCEPTS OF WORK AND POTENTIAL IN PHYSICS

Fred Archenhold

Abstract

The aim of the study was to ascertain the degree of understanding
of the concepts of work and potential by sixteen-to-nineteen year old
students who had studied these concepts whilst following Advanced level
physics courses (Joint Matriculation Board, 1972, pages 150-155;
Nuffield Advanced Physics, 1971, pages 16-18) in sixteen Secondary
Schools of different types in the North of England.

The sample contained seventy-nine students, sixty male and nineteen female. All had passed the General Certificate of Education
Ordinary level* examinations in physics and mathematics, 63 per cent
of them with grades which placed them in the top 5 per cent of the
ability spectrum (Department of Education and Science, 1970). The
ages of the students ranged from 16 years 6 months to 19 years 3
months, with a mean age for the sample of 17 years 9 months.

Twenty-five pre-tested tasks (See Appendix on page 235) were
presented to each student in an individual interview, which lasted
approximately forty minutes. After transcription of the recorded
conversation, the responses to twenty of these tasks, specifically
designed to probe understanding of work done and potential in a
variety of theoretical and practical situations, were assessed on a
defined five-point scale, using specified criteria written for each
task. Two experienced physics teachers each re-assessed twelve different protocols using the same criteria for assessment as in the study.
The Pearson product moment correlation coefficient between the original
assessments and the re-assessments of these 24 protocols, i.e. 480
tasks was r = 0.80.

The mean scores on tasks involving work done were significantly
better, at the one per cent level, than scores on tasks involving the
concept of potential. About one response in eight was judged to reflect a full understanding of concepts associated with work or
potential. Five-eighths of all responses were judged to indicate either

---

*The General Certificate of Education (GCE) Ordinary level is an
external examination taken at the age of 16 by higher ability
students.

'no understanding' or 'some knowledge, but little understanding'.
Many misconceptions came to light, indicating the difficulty most
students have in reaching a full understanding of precisely and
analytically defined abstract concepts.

Relationships were established between the students' total scores
on the test and their O-level grades in physics and mathematics. The
highest correlation ($r = 0.47$), significant at the one per cent level,
was obtained between the total test scores and O-level grades in
mathematics, emphasising the importance of mathematical competence
when dealing with abstract and precisely defined concepts. There was
some indication that students taking mathematics and further mathematics as part of their sixth-form curriculum performed rather better
(at five per cent level significance) than students not taking the
further mathematics option.

Principal components analysis (Child, 1970) revealed a strong
intellectual/educational component. Varimax rotation of the principal
components based on raw data isolated two major factors containing
tasks associated with potential and work done, whilst Varimax rotation
of principal components based on dichotomised data resulted in the
sub-division of the factor associated with potential into two factors,
one reflecting concepts of equipotential and potential gradient, the
other being associated more with tasks designed to assess the basic
understanding of the concept of potential.

Eleven students were re-interviewed some 10-12 months after the
main study. The mean scores on both work done and potential increased,
although compared with their earlier scores, the difference was not
significant at the five per cent level. The difference between scores
on work done and potential remained significant at the one per cent
level in the re-test study.

Introduction

To understand a state, according to Piaget, requires the student
to know the transformations which brought the particular state into
being. This definition of understanding was extended in this study
to include the ability to use the state, i.e. apply the concept to a
variety of problem situations. The term concept was used in the sense
of a 'scientifically and analytically defined state', such as force,
work, energy and potential.

The study was open ended and not related closely to any particular theory, although the Piagetian conceptual framework was used as a
backcloth in the sense that the concepts being tested did not deal
with firsthand reality. Students were required to think at the third
level of abstraction, characteristic of formal operational thought
(Lovell, 1974).

The 'Hauling Weight on an Inclined Plane' experiment described by

Inhelder and Piaget (1958, pages 182-198), indicated that 'formal stage' explanations in terms of work were only given by adolescents who had grasped the principles of 'proportion'. The ability of a student to deal with proportionality appears to be crucial to an understanding of precisely defined concepts such as work done = force x distance, electrical potential = work done per unit charge and gravitational potential = work done per unit mass. A hypothesis in this study was that any hierarchical order of concepts, logical or psychological (Driver, Easley, 1978), would place potential at a higher order than work done because potential includes the concept of work done and a further concept i.e. charge or mass.

A possible hierarchical model might be made up of a 'central pillar' of major concepts with 'branches' containing related concepts, all at the third level of abstraction (figure 1).

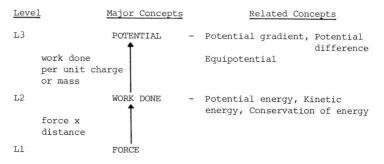

Level	Major Concepts	Related Concepts
L3	POTENTIAL	- Potential gradient, Potential difference
	work done per unit charge or mass	Equipotential
L2	WORK DONE	- Potential energy, Kinetic energy, Conservation of energy
	force x distance	
L1	FORCE	

Figure 1: Possible hierarchical model of concepts leading to the concept of potential

Only concepts associated with proposed levels L2 and L3 were tested by the twenty assessed tasks in this study, ten tasks on work done and ten tasks on potential.

Tasks and criteria for scoring

Three phases of a pilot study involving 10 students were used to improve the clarity of the twenty-five tasks (two starters, three linking questions and the twenty tasks to be assessed) which were presented to the students in the main study. All tasks had been written to match particular task objectives. All but one of the tasks were amended at some stage during the pilot study - mostly by rewording to produce a clearer and crisper question, which left the student in no doubt as to what was expected and which consequently eased the assessment of the protocols.

The responses of the seventy-nine students to the twenty tasks were assessed on a five-point scale specific to each task. The highest score of 5 was awarded for responses which teachers and examiners regard as being entirely satisfactory at GCE A-level* standard, while the lowest score of 1 was reserved for no answers, or responses based on false reasoning which indicated no understanding of the concept. The general specification for scoring is shown in figure 2.

Score	Response
5	Very good, shows complete understanding and sound reasoning.
4	Good, but understanding and reasoning not complete.
3	Average, shows some understanding and some power of reasoning.
2	Weak, some knowledge but little understanding.
1	No answers; no understanding, false reasoning.

Figure 2: General specification for scoring

It must be appreciated that such a five-point scale is not necessarily an equal interval scale but that it has been defined according to the stated criteria. It follows, therefore, that a certain assumption is made in using the t-test of significance under these conditions. An example of a task, with its stated objective and scoring criteria, is shown in figure 3.

---

*The GCE A-level is an external examination taken at the age of 18 by high ability pupils. Three, or sometimes four, subjects are normally attempted.

TASK 1c

OBJECTIVE   To assess understanding of the meaning of work done in a uniform field; the student lifts a ½kg mass from the floor on to a table.

TASK   To lift the ball on to this table...just do that please...you have to do work. What do you understand when I say 'you have to do work'?

SCORE	RESPONSE
5	Work done = force x distance moved in the direction of the force, the definition is applied correctly in this example, or, work done is a measure of the transfer from chemical to potential energy.
4	Work done = force x distance moved in the direction of the force, but no application to the example under discussion, or work done is a measure of the gain in potential energy of the ball.
3	Work done = force x vertical distance, or, work done equals energy used in moving the ball from the floor on to the table.
2	Work done = force x distance, or, energy has to be used to move the ball.
1	No answer, or, no understanding of the concept of work.

Figure 3: Example of a task (1c) with stated objective and scoring criteria

    Examples of responses by five different students to task 1c on work are shown in figure 4 with an indication of the score awarded.

Student number	Score Awarded	Responses to task 1c transcribed from the recorded interview
36	5	'In doing that, I've used up energy and given the ball energy in lifting from there (floor) to here (table). I've used up energy and given the ball potential energy.'
31	4	'When the ball is picked up, you apply a force to the ball, and when a force moves its point of application, here from the floor to the table, then it is said to have done work.'
70	3	'You have to exert a force on the ball through a certain distance, and it gains potential energy.'
42	2	'In order to lift this (the ball) from a lower to a higher position, I have got to use some energy, so the ball now has energy because of its position.'
43	1	'Work is the movement of a mass through a distance; in this case, work is required to lift the ball from the floor to the table.'

Figure 4: Examples of responses to task 1c showing the score awarded based on the scoring criteria

Analysis of results

The mean scores per task on the ten tasks which were postulated to test work done (L2) and potential (L3) were 2.78 and 2.04 respectively, indicating a better average overall performance by the seventy-nine students on tasks involving the concepts of work done and energy than on tasks involving the concepts of electrical and gravitational potential. The 'null hypothesis', i.e. that the true difference in means was zero, was tested using the method of difference pairs (Lewis, 1967, pages 119-122). The calculated value of t was 8.57, above the t-value of 2.65 required to reject the null hypothesis and accept the difference in sample means as significant at the one per cent level.

Table 1 shows the number of students with score differences in the stated ranges between scores on tasks involving work done (L2) and potential (L3).

Table 1: <u>Score differences between tasks involving work done</u>
<u>(L2) and potential (L3). (The maximum possible score</u>
<u>difference is 40)</u>

				Score difference			
	O	1-5	6-10	11-15	16-20	21-25	6-25
L2-L3		12	21	17	8	4	50
L3-L2		8	4	1			5
L3=L2	4						

It is seen from Table 1 that 50/79 (63.3 per cent) of the students scored between 6 and 25 marks (in a range of 40 marks between 50 and 10 marks) more on tasks postulated to assess understanding of work done than on tasks postulated to assess understanding of potential; 24/79 (30.4 per cent) scored within 5 marks on both concepts and 5/79 (6.3 per cent) scored at least 6 marks more on potential than on work done.

Selecting those students who scored 30 or above on work done, and who may be said 'to have shown some understanding and some power of reasoning' (see figure 2, 76.5 per cent (26/34) scored between 6 and 25 marks more on work done than on potential, compared with 63.3 per cent when the whole sample is considered. It appears from this sub-sample of 26 students (one-third of the main sample) that even if a student has 'some understanding of work done', this does not imply a similar degree of understanding of potential, i.e. potential is a higher order concept than work done, though both are at the third level of abstraction.

Only eleven of the seventy-nine students scored 30 or above on potential, and of these eleven students, nine also scored 30 or above on work done and the other two scored 28. Hence it would appear from this small sample that 'some understanding of potential' is accompanied by scores on work done which also reflect 'some understanding', i.e. above-mean scores on potential were only obtained by students who also made a satisfactory showing on tasks assessing their understanding of the concept of work done.

A brief summary of other results is given in the abstract of this paper; further details, including points of misunderstanding related to the concepts of work done and potential, are contained in the thesis by the author (Archenhold, 1975).

234

Discussion

Not only the statistical analysis, but also the scrutiny of protocols, point to the conclusion that a representative sample of sixth-form students studying GCE A-level physics find considerable difficulty in understanding the concept of potential, and to a lesser degree, the concept of work done. Many students confused concepts of force, field, work, energy and potential, e.g. 38 students confused gravitational potential with gravitational potential energy, and 24 students confused gravitational potential with gravitational pull or force.

It would seem essential for teachers to provide students with sufficient practice in the use of abstract concepts to enable them to build their own conceptual schemes. Any teaching strategy must give students the time to acquire concepts, both in a qualitative and quantitative sense. The advantage of face-to-face discussion, as adopted in this study, compared with a written test, is that the teacher (or interviewer) can more easily require the student to provide reasons for answers given and probe any weaknesses in the thinking strategies being adopted to tackle a particular problem.

Results from this study suggest that the concepts of work done and energy transformations in both uniform and non-uniform fields must be understood before going on to potential. The absence of significant increases in scores of the eleven students in the re-test study ten to twelve months after the original test suggests that frequent use, discussion and testing of certain key concepts may be required during a physics course to ensure that the student retains familiarity with the concepts and has the time and opportunities to incorporate the concepts into his own conceptual scheme.

Appendix - Tasks in study

Note: Task numbers marked ^{o} were not assessed. These tasks were regarded as 'starters' or 'linking questions'.

Question 1

1a^o The earth pulls on a mass of 1kg with a force of approximately 10 newtons (10^6 dynes). Here we have an iron ball, of mass ½kg, at rest on the floor. Tell me the size of the earth's pull on this ½kg mass.

1b^o Can you tell me the size and direction of any other force acting on the ball?

1c   To lift the ball on to this table...just do that please...you have to do work. What do you understand when I say 'you have to do work'?

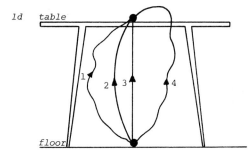

1d table

Do you think that the size or magnitude of the total work done against the earth's pull depends on the path along which the mass is moved from the floor to the table (along paths 1, 2, 3, 4 in figure 5)? Give me reasons for your answer.

Figure 5

1e Let us assume the vertical distance between floor and table is 1 metre. What is the size or magnitude of the work you did in lifting the ½kg mass from the floor on to the table?

1f Now push the iron ball over the edge of the table and explain carefully in terms of work what happens in this experiment.

Question 2

2g In question 1 we were mainly concerned with force and work done. Can you tell me the connection between work done and energy changes when a mass moves through a vertical distance on the earth?

2h Explain carefully in terms of energy what happened when you pushed the iron ball over the table.

2i^{o} What is the actual change in energy of this ball, mass ½kg, when it falls through a vertical distance of 1 metre?

2j When you lifted the ½kg ball on to this table through a vertical distance of 1 metre, you did 5 joules (5 x 10^7 ergs) of work against the earth's gravitational pull, and the ball gained 5 joules of potential energy. What was the size of the potential energy of the ball on the floor, if the potential energy of the ball on this table is 5 joules? Explain your answer carefully.

2k The following table shows the values of potential energy of various masses 1 metre above the floor:

mass (kg)	½	1	1½	2
potential energy (J)	5	10	15	20

Using this table, or otherwise, can you explain what the gravitational potential is at this level (on the table), 1 metre above the floor?

21   This table shows the values of the potential energy of 1kg mass at various levels above the floor:

height (m)	½	1	1½	2
potential energy (J)	5	10	15	20

Using this table, or otherwise, can you explain what you understand by gravitational potential?

Question 3

3m   This question is about the concept of electric potential.

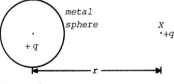

The force of repulsion F between two charges $+q$ and $+q_o$ distance r apart is given by Coulomb's law

$$F = k\frac{qq_o}{r^2}$$ where k is a constant.

Figure 6

Explain to me how you would derive an expression for the work necessary to move charge $+q_o$ (say a small test charge) from infinity, to point X, distance r from the centre of the metal sphere carrying charge $+q$.

3n   What do you understand by the phrase 'electric potential at point X'?

3o   Tell me what would be the effect on the potential at point X if the small test charge $+q_o$ were halved in magnitude?

3p   Suppose now that the test charge is on the sphere (pointing to figure 6). No work is required to move the test charge $+q_o$ from one point on the charged metal sphere to any other point on the sphere. What conclusion do you draw about the potential difference between those two points? Give me reasons for your answer.

3q   Suppose the charge on the sphere were doubled. Would this affect the potential gradient at X? Explain your answer carefully.

3r   Two horizontal parallel conducting plates are a small distance apart and carry opposite charges. Explain why there is a potential gradient between the plates.

3s   The idea of difference in electric potential is an important one in the study of current electricity. Tell me what you understand when I say 'The potential difference across a car headlamp is (say) 12 volts'?

237

Question 4

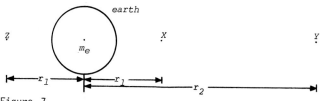

Figure 7

The force of attraction F between two masses m_e and m. distance r apart is given by Newton's law of gravitation $F = G \dfrac{m_e m}{r^2}$

where G is the gravitational constant.
Explain to me how you would arrive at an expression for the work necessary to move mass m (say a space probe) from X, distance r_1 from the centre of the earth, to infinity?

4u   The expression work done = $Gm_e m (\dfrac{1}{r_1} - \dfrac{1}{r_2})$ tells us the work

done against the earth's gravitational field when mass m is moved from X, distance r_1 from the centre of the earth to Y, distance r_2 from the centre of the earth. Tell me what the change in potential energy is when mass m is moved from X to Y?

4w   Tell me how the expression given in the last question (4u) is affected if you imagine point Y to be at infinity, and what this new formula means?

4x   What do you think is meant by the phrase gravitational potential at X? (Reference to point X in figure 7).

4y   What do you think is the gravitational potential at point Z, which is the same distance from the centre of the earth as point X?

4z°   There are many other points all at the same distance from the centre of the earth. Tell me how much work is done in moving around these points at constant speed...give me reasons for your answer.

Discussion

In introducing his paper, Archenhold indicated his approach to such aspects as the role of theory, placing concepts in a hierarchy and scoring the responses to the tasks he used. While the concepts of work done and potential are at the third level of abstraction, his findings supported the view that knowledge of potential implies knowledge of work done, but the converse is not necessarily true.

The ensuing discussion first focussed on the use of language to express the meanings of terms like energy. In physics energy is transmitted, but in ordinary life energy is used up. Concepts like work, energy, potential are used at a higher level in physics as they are strictly defined and expressed in symbols. It was pointed out that a corresponding confusion of use occurs in mathematics with the meanings of ideas like 'similar'.

Discussion then centred on the scoring procedure. Archenhold explained that he used a five-point scale where 5/5 meant a very good answer in terms of what is expected at A-level in the U.K. On his scale 1/5 meant no understanding or an answer riddled with false reasoning. In support of his scoring procedure, it has to be remembered that the use of twenty tasks (scored in this way) enabled the concepts to be examined over many situations and, further, some partial checking was done independently by two experienced physics teachers.

Finally, there was some discussion over the meaning and nature of a hierarchy of levels of abstractions. Comments ranged inconclusively over the criteria for levels, the relations between levels, the starting points for the lowest levels and the justification for a hierarchy.

TEACHING STYLES AND COGNITIVE SELECTION RELATED TO DIFFERENT TYPES OF BIOLOGICAL CONCEPTS

P.J. Kelly

Introduction

This paper reports on some preliminary ideas that have arisen from research which attempts to elucidate the reasons for pupils' difficulties in learning biological concepts. The research was prompted by the realisation that biological concepts have rarely featured in studies of cognitive development and that there was a need for more studies of how the form of teaching varies with the concepts being taught and how this influences the selection and understanding of the concepts by the pupils.

The starting point of the work arose from questions such as: Is there a particular type of concept which we can justifiably call 'biological'? Are there features of biological ideas which distinguish them from those in other areas of scientific study? There is, of course, a considerable literature in philosophy which compares the content and procedures of biological sciences with those of the physical sciences. It is not always very helpful to the educator because of the high level of abstraction and generalisation with which it deals. However, biologists such as Pringle (1963) have pointed to

the range of types of ideas in biology and, in particular, have
stressed the dichotomy between those aspects of biology which are
similar to those of the physical sciences and those which clearly are
not. Pringle indeed refers to the 'Two Biologies' to emphasise the
distinction. Physical science-based biology is one in which it is
relatively easy to undertake controlled experiments and in which, for
example, we are concerned with how the bodies of organisms work.
Essentially it involves the same approach as the study of inanimate
material. In contrast to this there is the biosocial sphere of biology
concerned with phenomena which have their roots in the physical make-
up of an organism but which are expressed in a social context. In
studying them we ask questions of a different sort: What is the
function (purpose) of a particular feature of an organism or its
behaviour? Why did the feature become what it is? These are questions
which we ask much less in the physical sciences.

Biophysical and biosocial concepts

By adapting the general tenets of Pringle's analysis it is
possible to suggest two categories of biological concepts, biophysical and biosocial.* The former relates to physical science-
based biology, the latter to studies of social and evolutionary perspectives of life.

We have scrutinised these two categories of concepts in order to
identify those logical and psychological characteristics which might
influence learning. They appear to differ in four such respects which
are summarised in table 1.

Table 1: Four differences between biophysical and biosocial
         concepts

Biophysical concepts	Biosocial concepts
Stable	Unstable
Additive	Holistic
Little influence from intuition	Strong influence from intuition
Low affective load	High affective load

*These categories are not necessarily exclusive of each other, nor of
other categories. For example, categories of concepts related to
holistic perceptions of individual organisms or of life processes
rather than life entities could be included.

In order to illustrate the differences we can take a biosocial concept natural selection and a biophysical concept respiration. Note that both can be expressed at different levels of complexity. Natural selection can be in the form of a simple Darwinian statement or beset with the complexities of population genetics. The concept of respiration can be based on a simple equation summarising the oxidation of sugar to carbon dioxide and water or Krebs' cycle. The differences we are concerned with are not to do with complexity or the load of information contained in the concept.

Respiration as a concept is tightly-knit and invariable because it is capable of little reorientation. It is not possible easily to formulate the concept in different ways. Hence it is described as stable. The conceptual structure of natural selection consists of a number of integrated constituent concepts - reproduction, adaptation, selection and survival - which can be orientated in different ways. You can, for instance, emphasise the processes of selection or, alternatively, adaptation. The concept is variable in its formulation and, hence, unstable.

Respiration is described as additive because as a help to understanding, it can be broken down into discrete parts which can be examined separately. The formulation of the full concept comes from adding these parts, one to another, in a particular order. With natural selection, on the other hand, the essential nature of the concept is holistic. These are not parts you can add together. The distinction is similar to that between knowing the alphabet (which can be achieved by 'adding' the letters A to Z together) and knowing a sentence (which cannot be achieved by adding the letters or, indeed, not just by adding the words: it is the meaning of the whole sentence that matters).

The distinctions 3 and 4 are closely related. In essence they are saying that our understanding of biophysical concepts is relatively less influenced by our feelings than our understanding of biosocial concepts. Motivation, of course, can be an influence in both cases. However, biosocial concepts tend to be of (or allied to) phenomena which are close to personal experience and, in a non-scientific context, we understand intuitively. Deadman (1976), for example, has described the explanations of evolution by 11-14 year-old schoolboys as being Lamarkian rather than Darwinian. In his extensive interviews with the boys he was invariably told that changes in the forms of animals was due to their changing 'needs', 'wants' or some unspecified internal forces within the animals helping to 'make them better'. It is salutory to learn also that Brumby (1979) has recently shown that with first year University students reading Human Biology and Nursing Studies there is a not too dissimilar tendency to give Lamarkian interpretations. An explanation for this, I suggest, is that change in other organisms is interpreted by reference to the sense of change we have for our own personal activities. In this respect it is an intuitive understanding related as much to feeling as to cognition. Such modes of understanding are less obvious in relation to biophysical concepts.

Given that this analysis is valid it is suggested that, assuming there are equal levels of complexity and loads of information, bio-social concepts are likely to be more difficult to learn adequately. They will tend to be more easily confused and less easily memorised than biophysical concepts. Also, they will require different styles of teaching and students are likely to respond to them differently.

Conceptual structure and teaching style

Investigations have been undertaken of the styles adopted by teachers when teaching biophysical and biosocial concepts and of the perceptual and cognitive selection processes of the pupils being taught.

In outline these investigations entailed discussing with teachers the differences between the categories of concepts and obtaining their agreement to teaching a topic in each category. Immediately before a lesson each teacher was interviewed in order to establish what conceptual structure they intended to communicate to pupils; recording the verbal and non-verbal (e.g. gestures and the use of illustrative materials) communication by the teachers associated with particular concepts; analysing the classroom environment (other than the teacher) for possible associations with the concepts of being taught; and interviewing pupils after the lessons in order to ascertain the form of concepts they had derived from the lesson and their reactions to the lesson.

My associate, Cynthia Millband, has been responsible for this investigation. Continuous audio-recordings were taken of both the teachers' talk and pupils' responses by recorders in fixed positions. At the same time still photographs were taken of the classroom itself and of materials and activities during the lesson. Comments on activities were recorded on a personal tape recorder by Millband.

The analysis of the data collected is currently underway. Partly it consists of mapping the occurrence of concepts during a lesson and the relationships between them. This is termed the conceptual stream of a lesson. In this way one is attempting to relate the conceptual structure of the teaching to the structure of the type of concept (biophysical or biosocial) being considered and, in turn, to the structures of the concept retained by the pupil. In parallel to this the data are being scrutinised for indications of the role of affective influences on the teaching and learning of the concepts.

At this stage we have only a few tentative comments to make on the results analysed so far, but the following may be of interest.

1. So far it has been difficult to discern different teaching styles related to the different structures of the concepts. If anything the teachers tend to teach biosocial concepts as they do bio-physical ones. Irrespective of the topic a tightly-knit, relatively invariable structure is imposed on a concept and it is characteristically broken into discrete units which are dealt with in a step-by-step, additive fashion.

2. A characteristic of much of the teaching observed is that it is expository rather than conversational, and deals with a high load of information. This mitigates against the portrayal of a concept as either unstable or holistic.

3. Especially when dealing with biosocial concepts there is a tendency to use metaphors and theatrical presentations. This heightens the affective load of the concepts and becomes a distraction rather than the help to understanding or boost to motivation which it was intended to be. It re-enforces teleological and similar intuitive conceptions in the pupils' minds.

Discussion

In introducing his paper, Kelly expressed his concern with the social transmission of knowledge, the diffusion of new curricula at various levels, and how ideas changed in the process of transmission and diffusion.

There was some debate about the use of language in the discussion and Kelly indicated his preference for the term 'conceptual structures' rather than concepts in this context. It was agreed that the dichotomy between biophysical and biosocial studies was not complete. The study of Krebs' cycle might have a holistic element, even though it was essentially biophysical. In the study of the human body both approaches were relevant. The distinction was made between motivation, which might be discussed in relation to any piece of biological work, and the affective feelings about ideas which were more characteristic of the biosocial aspects.

It was suggested that in teaching biosocial studies, stress might be laid on synthesis rather than analysis. Teachers of the humanities might provide a better model than teachers of science.

It was pointed out that some ideas about biosocial issues, e.g. students' preference for a Lamarkian rather than a Darwinian model of evolution, reflected the historical growth of ideas on the subject. It was also suggested that there might be a third type of biology centred on mathematical modelling and cybernetics.

Studies of Pupils' Alternative Frameworks or Misconceptions in Science

IDENTIFYING SCIENCE STUDENTS' CONCEPTS : THE INTERVIEW-ABOUT-
INSTANCES APPROACH

John K. Gilbert and Roger J. Osborne

Introduction

Donaldson (1978) tells the story of the disgruntled child who
complained to his mother after his first day at school,

'They never gave me the present.'
'Present, what present?'
'They said they'd give me the present.'
'Well now, I'm sure they didn't.'
'They did! They said: "You're Laurie Lee, aren't you? Well
you just sit there for the present." I sat there all
day but I never got it. I ain't going back there again!'

Undoubtedly this typifies one of the most difficult and subtle problems in teaching and learning. Where a student believes that
understanding of what has been said or read has been achieved, but
where this understanding or interpretation is quite different from
that which was intended. While the problem is prevalent in the
early years of schooling it is undoubtedly common in more subtle
ways at more advanced levels.

Where the interpretation achieved by the student is different,
to a greater or lesser degree from that intended by the teacher or
textbook writer, the student is likely to encounter learning difficulties at a later date. The problem of misinterpretation is not
uncommon, but words used in everyday language e.g. velocity, power,
displacement and even words like potential and electric current, when
used in a subtly different way in science, are a particular problem

for the novice science student. While all teachers are aware of this problem, lack of time, and the framework of normal classroom interactions, tend to prohibit a teacher acquiring a real understanding of the word meanings that students bring with them to science classes, and the word meanings that students subsequently take away from science classes.

In this short paper, we give an outline of a method for the investigation of concept understanding, present examples drawn from pilot work, and provide discussion on its scope and application.

An approach to investigating concept understanding

The views of Klausmeier et al. (1974) and Markle, Tiemann (1970) suggest that concept attainment is closely related to the ability of an individual to categorise instances (not previously encountered) as instances, or non-instances of a particular concept. This led us to the idea that it may well be practical and effective to investigate a student's understanding of a particular concept using an interview situation and a set of simple line drawings to depict instances. The method we have evolved uses a set of approximately 20 cards for each concept, each card depicting an instance or non-instance of the concept under consideration. To gain a good appreciation of students' understanding of the concept, the student is asked to categorise each instance and then asked to explain the basis on which the categorisation has been made.

There are at least two different aspects of concept understanding which can be investigated by this interview-about-instances (I.A.I.) method. Firstly, there is the understanding of a particular concept as evoked in a student's mind by the use of the word in a particular communication context, e.g. via teacher or textbook. A student may not understand the concept in the way it is intended in the communication. Alternatively, the student may understand the intended concept, but the particular context may evoke a different concept or may evoke a limited generalisation of the intended concept. For example, 'pen' may evoke the concept of a 'small enclosure' or a 'fountain pen' respectively rather than 'a writing instrument which usually uses ink'. Apart from the problems of a student not understanding a concept, these additional problems can create hidden learning difficulties. Secondly, there is the student's actual domain of understanding of a particular concept in situations where the concept is explicitly given by a formal statement or definition, which is accepted by the student as being 'understood'.

With regard to the first aspect of understanding, what is evoked in a student's mind by the use of a particular instance in an I.A.I. investigation will depend on the context and nature of the instance. However, alternative procedures for investigating concept understanding, which might be used, either do not eliminate this problem or introduce other difficulties. For example, a student may be asked

how he would teach an understanding of the particular word to another
student who did not understand it, or be asked to explain how he or
she was actually taught the concept. In these cases a student's
answer would probably be as much influenced by the student's perception
of the audience, and what the audience required, as by his or her conceptual understanding.

Provided it is appreciated that in the I.A.I. method particular
instances will evoke particular understandings, and hence that the
order of presentation is important, an order can be deliberately chosen
which will make use of this fact to explore the way students tend to
use a word. If each categorisation of an instance by a student is
followed by an interview discussion to establish the reasons for the
particular categorisation, some idea of the intuitive understanding or
aspects of formal understanding that a student has about the particular
concept can be established (see also Dahlgren, Marton, 1978). A
variety of such instances would then give some indication of the understanding and the type of understanding (whether intuitive understanding
or any particular aspect of formal understanding) a student is likely
to invoke when reading a textbook or listening to a lecture where the
word is used.

Some applications of the method

To explore the scope of the I.A.I. method, sets of cards were
developed for the concepts of 'work' and 'electric current'. In the
first phase of each interview, students were asked, for example,
'Would you say, in your meaning of the words "electric current" that
there is an electric current in -' which was followed by 'Can you give
a reason why you think that?'. At the end of this phase students
were asked for their own definition of the concept. If they could not
provide one, we gave them the most commonly accepted form. In the
second phase, the instances were drawn exclusively from 'conventional
physics'.

Whilst details of this work are given elsewhere (Osborne, Gilbert,
1979), some representative results are given below. As we were seeking to explore the scope of the method, and not looking for generalisations in concept understanding, the results must be viewed as being
illustrative only.

Interviews on the concept of 'work'

Twenty students ranging in age from 7 to 17 were interviewed on
this concept. Whilst the same sequence in cards was used, the cut-
off point, which took place when the student obviously had no more to
say, varied. Between 10 and 20 instances were presented, and each
interview occupied 20-40 minutes.

Students found difficulty in separating an event, either in time
or space, from associated events. Thus, one 18 year old insisted that

the force in 'force x distance' was the original force acting on the body. Both 14 year old and 18 year old students were confused between the work being done now as compared to the work done prior to the event under discussion. The work being done by a particular force was not clearly isolated in space from the work done by the reaction forces. For example, in discussing an instance where coal is travelling up a slope on a conveyor belt, an 18 year old stated 'Yes, it is gaining potential energy as it moves up...there is no force as such on it as it is moving at a constant velocity...so there is no accelerating force...not all work needs to be done with a constant force, I should think...I don't think you can do it with force x distance.'

The answers the older physics students gave often differed dramatically from those given by younger students, but were often given without necessary qualifications. 16-18 year olds seemed to consider the questions to be, in their estimation, a part of the idealised world largely unrelated to the real world and their own (expressed) early intuitive understandings. In the 'physics world' intuition tends to be suppressed and rules are applied without qualifications. Thus a weightlifter holding up a bar is not doing work, nor is work being done by somebody pushing a stationary card.

The idealised world of physics, with its unstated simplifying assumptions, is confusing to students. A physics teacher might say that no work is being done on a stationary car. For the very able student, the realisation that the vehicle does not have an infinitely high spring constant, and that energy is being transferred to the car, must be confusing. Many students were unhappy with the idea of frictionless surfaces. Intuitive misunderstandings abounded: two 12 year olds thought that, if you push on the stationary car, the brakes heat up.

Interviews on the concept of electric current

Thirty students, ranging in age from 7 to 48, were interviewed about electric current in a manner similar to that used for 'work'.

Many students of 18 years old, studying A-level physics, showed a pattern of understanding similar to that found in 7-13 year olds who had received no formal teaching in the area. For example, when asked if there was electric current in a battery pictured as sitting, alone, on a bench, answers included:

'Yes, if it has not all been used up' (16 year old)

'Yes...well the thing is built for electric power' (10 year old).

This pattern of age-independence of similarity in answers was broadly observed. Thus the intuitive ideas about what happens when electric current reaches a lamp, are found in all ages, e.g.

q.   *'Where does the electric current, which goes into the lamp, go to?'*

a.   'Electric current goes into the bulb and shines up.'

'I don't really know...well it is not dispersed I know that...
perhaps it would stay there because electrons are infinitely
small.'

'It goes into the lamp to make it shine...it is burnt.'

'It is just staying there and being used up...the electric
current is being pumped up into the light and is being used
up as light.'

'It goes into the light and turns into another sort of energy.'

'It goes through the wires to the lamp (then what happens?) it
lights up (then what happens?) it is all used up and more is
pumped in from the switch.'

'It goes to the surroundings as light (all of it?) and some of
it is used as heat.'

'It just is finished...it doesn't go nowhere...when it reaches
the bulb it is just finished (what becomes of it?) well the
current is used to make the bulb glow so that there is no
more current after it has reached the bulb.'

(students aged 7, 10, 11, 14, 16, 16, 18, 18 respectively.)

The scope of the method
_____

From these exploratory interviews, some defining facets to its
applicability were identified.

(i) It can be used over a wide age range.
     We interviewed students ranging in age from 7 years to 48 years:
from primary school children to mature entrants for the teaching profession. No modifications, other than the degree of progression
through a card sequence, had to be made to accommodate this age and
educational span.

(ii) It was enjoyed by both interviewer and interviewee.
     Naturally, students were apprehensive at the start of an inter-
view. However, our emphasis that 'there are no right answers, we
just want to know what you think' quickly put students at their ease.
For younger students, the card as a focus of attention, rather than
the student, helped reduce tension. For older students, where they
requested it, we went over some of the cards to give our interpretations, using the same kinds of language as they had used. This
equalisation of role frequently led to extended discussions on attitudes to science and such subjects.

(iii) It has advantages over written answers.

In this interview situation, students could not easily omit a question or give an answer without an accompanying reason. It was possible to probe how committed a student was to a particular view.

Questions could be set that were deliberately imprecise and ambiguous. This enabled students to criticise the question, thus revealing a lot about their understanding. As one major scientific skill is that of being able to 'sharpen-up' questions, evidence in this area was also obtained.

(iv) More is gained than by asking for a definition at the outset.

In the I.A.I. method, students are asked to produce a definition of the concept between phase I and phase II of the interview. We found that students who had previously displayed good understanding had difficulty in verbalising a statement. On the other hand, individuals who had displayed a poor understanding were able to produce an accurate, if evidently trite, 'scientific definition'. Many produced definitions that stemmed from their earlier answers and were consistent with those answers.

Accepting the views of Markle, Tiemann (op.cit.), concept understanding is shown by the patterns of classification of instances. A request for a definition at the outset would have produced either a recalled proposition or a verbalised rule built on the few instances that came immediately to mind. By delaying the request, the product more genuinely reflects consideration of a wide range of instances, or clearly reveals a failure to do so.

Whatever the advantages of the method, it does make demands on the research worker.

(i) Care has to be taken in the choice of instances.

Although we are in the process of developing a theoretical rationale for the selection of instances, our current work is pragmatically based. Instances are selected from a consideration of the various attributes and contexts of a word in its scientific form. This is supplemented by consideration of the everyday uses of the word, including situations with which this usage of the word has associations, and consideration of borderline instances. Field testing produces a set of instances blending theoretical analysis, comments from teachers, and the experience of students.

(ii) The ordering of instances is important.

Instances presented early in an interview set the pattern for subsequent responses. If these instances are unduly novel, they may unsettle a student's viewpoint to the extent that subsequent answers are adversely affected. Optimum sequences are best worked out during field trials.

(iii) The arts of the interviewer must be well developed.

Understanding is only elicited in dialogue, which requires mutual trust and open discussion as Snyder (1971) has pointed out. The emphasis on there being 'no right answer' helps build up this trust. The interviewer has the task of extracting information, following up comments, reducing the embarrassment of extended periods of silence, and helping the student to clarify thinking. All this must be done without putting words into the student's mouth, providing clues which would bias an answer, or butting in. This is particularly difficult with 'cue-conscious' students, who will readily change their line of approach if it receives negative feedback.

The use of the method by the student's current teacher may, for these reasons, be particularly problematic. The risk of falling into elicit-response-evaluation talk, a pseudo-language as Stubbs (1975) has called it, is great. Teachers will certainly need special training. Perhaps peer-group use could overcome this problem in schools, provided students with excellent understanding can be found.

Future studies

The pilot work outlined in this paper was completed by March 1979. Since that time, one of us (J.K.G.) has obtained a B.P. Schoolteacher Fellowship to determine the range of understanding of physics concepts in a broad range of students, and is exploring the use of the method for concepts related to the environment. The other of us (R.J.O.) has since been involved in the establishing of the 'Learning in Science Project' in New Zealand. One aspect of the project involves the use of the I.A.I. approach. Within and beyond these activities, there are a number of issues worth investigating further.

(i) Younger students' egocentric view of the world.

This phenomenon was very evident in the pilot studies, e.g. 'nature cannot do work'. The prevelance of these views over a variety of concepts, and the manner whereby students change their orientation, would be of interest.

(ii) The use of scientific language.

As Dahlgren, Marton (1978) observed, increased language sophistication by a student is not necessarily accompanied by a greater depth of understanding of a concept. On the other hand, teachers do tend to use unnecessarily complex language with younger students, perhaps thereby hindering the acquisition of understanding. The I.A.I. method seems capable of extending the work on student-talk undertaken by Suan (1976) and Ogborn (1977).

(iii) Sex differences in concept understanding.

The need to investigate the roots of the differences in popularity of the sciences between the sexes has been emphasised by Ormerod, Duckworth (1975) and Kelly (1976). Some of our data did suggest that boys and girls responded to some instances in different

ways. The nature of these differences needs investigation if they are
to be eliminated.

(iv) Attitudes to the several sciences.
     Many students now pursue combined or integrated science courses
and are forced, at some stage, to choose separate science courses.
We believe that one factor in such a decision is the perception of
'what physics etc. is'. A tentative application of the I.A.I. approach,
built around the concerns of the several sciences, and applied just
before a curricular choice point, showed disturbing evidence of confusion in this area.

Discussion

     In introducing his paper Gilbert explained the choice of work
as one of the topics. It seemed on the basis of Archenhold's study
to fit conveniently in the sequence force/work/potential. More pupils
described work in terms of energy transfer than as force times distance. They were now attempting to develop a similar study within
the field of chemistry, with particular reference to the concept of
stability.

     It was pointed out that the wording of questions was crucial.
The students might respond to cues (real or imagined) and sometimes
consequently adopted positions in which they probably did not really
believe and found hard to justify. It is difficult to select neutral
questions. Both 'which is the heavier?' and 'are they the same?',
for example, might imply a desirable answer to the pupils.

     Gilbert stated that he had not yet developed a systematic mode
of analysis. They attempted to identify crucial phrases and then
categorise them. Possibly systemic analysis based on network
theory and similar techniques might be useful. He suggested that
knowledge about the learner's prior knowledge should help the teacher
but he had yet to develop proposals for a formal teaching strategy
in the light of these responses. He thought that these techniques
might have considerable value for in-service work.

SOME ASPECTS OF CHILDREN'S UNDERSTANDING OF BOILING-POINT

Björn Andersson*

Background and problems

The present investigation explores children's understanding of some 'conservational' aspects of the boiling-point concept. The boiling-point of water, for example, is independent of the time the water has been heated, and the amount of energy transferred to the boiling water per unit time. If a thermometer in a saucepan of boiling water registers + 100°C, the reading is still + 100°C five minutes later, although heat is continuously transferred to the water from the hot-plate. And if water is boiling at + 100°C on a hot-plate, with the switch on 3, the temperature remains at + 100°C if the switch is turned from 3 to 6.

On the other hand, the boiling-point of water depends on the pressure applied. Also, adding an impurity changes the boiling-point.

Swedish textbooks of physics for grades 7, 8 and 9 (ages 13-15) of the nine year comprehensive school typically mention variables that affect boiling-point, notably pressure applied to the liquid. However, they seem to take for granted that children have a physicist's understanding of variables that do not affect boiling-point. At least these variables are not discussed in the texts.

Are the above mentioned 'conservational' aspects of boiling-point trivial or not for the child? In order to explore this question, the following two paper and pencil problems were given to children in grades 6 to 9 (age 12-15).

---

*The research reported in this paper has been sponsored by the National Swedish Board of Education.

Problem 1

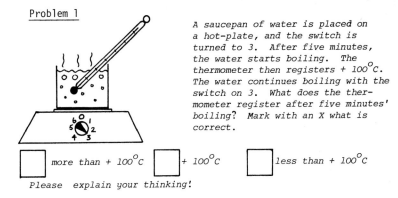

A saucepan of water is placed on a hot-plate, and the switch is turned to 3. After five minutes, the water starts boiling. The thermometer then registers + 100°C. The water continues boiling with the switch on 3. What does the thermometer register after five minutes' boiling? Mark with an X what is correct.

☐ more than + 100°C   ☐ + 100°C   ☐ less than + 100°C

Please explain your thinking!

Problem 2

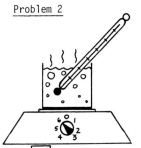

A saucepan of water is placed on a hot-plate, and the switch is turned to 3. After five minutes, the water starts boiling. The thermometer then registers + 100°C. The switch is then turned to 6, making the plate as hot as possible. What happens to the thermometer after the hot-plate has been turned to 6? Mark with an X what is correct.

☐ the thermometer starts going down below + 100°C.

☐ the thermometer remains at + 100°C.

☐ the thermometer starts going up above + 100°C.

Please explain your thinking!

Results - problem 1

The children's explanations have been classified into the following categories:

1. Less than 100°C after five minutes' boiling.
   No subcategories in this group, due to few answers.
   Example - Since it has reached boiling it can't get hotter, it must cool down a few degrees.

253

2. More than 100°C after five minutes' boiling.

   A. No explanation.

   B. The water gets hotter the longer it is on the hot-plate.

      Example - When you let the saucepan remain on the plate it must get hotter.

      - It boils another five minutes.

   C. Remainder (few answers)

      Example - When it gets hot, it becomes easier for the heat to pass through the saucepan.

3. Equal to 100°C after five minutes' boiling.

   A. No explanation

   B. The switch-number of the hot-plate determines the temperature of the boiling water.

      Examples - It is on three all the time, therefore it must be the same temperature.

      - It (the switch) is on the same temperature all the time, therefore it is the same all the time.

      - The water can't get warmer, since the amount of energy transferred is limited.

   C. Explanations expressing that 100°C is an invariant upper limit but without mentioning boiling as a cause.

      Examples - The water can't get above 100.

      - It doesn't matter how long it is on the hot-plate.

      - It can't get warmer than it was, because the water starts evaporating a little later.

   D. Boiling is the cause of the temperature invariance.

      Examples - As long as the water is boiling, it stays at 100°C.

      - The boiling-point is 100°C. When the water goes on boiling, the temperature must remain the same.

      - Boiling water can't get hotter, no matter how much it is boiling.

      - The water can't get warmer than + 100°C when it is boiling. If it gets warmer, the water rises as vapour.

The distribution of the pupils' answers by these categories is given in table 1.

Table 1: <u>Problem 1. Distribution of the pupils' explanations by categories. (%)</u>

	1. Less than 100°C	2. More than 100°C			3. Equal to 100°C			
		A	B	C	A	B	C	D
grade 6 (n = 62)	2	5	35	–	13	26	8	11
grade 7 (n = 138)	4	1	20	3	13	25	11	24
grade 8 (n = 120)	4	2	11	–	13	35	13	22
grade 9 (n = 121)	2	–	13	3	4	32	17	28

Categories

2. A. No explanation
   B. The water gets hotter the longer it is on the hot-plate
   C. Remainder

3. A. No explanation
   B. The switch-number determines the temperature of the boiling water
   C. 100°C is an invariant upper limit but boiling not mentioned as cause
   D. Boiling is the cause of temperature invariance

Results - problem 2

The children's explanations have been classified into the following categories:

1. The temperature goes down below 100°C.
   No subcategories in this group, due to few answers.
   Example - The water evaporates and this cools the water.

2. The temperature goes up above 100° C.

   A. No explanation.

   B. The switch-number of the hot-plate determines the temperature of the boiling water.

   Examples - When you switch to full strength, it must get hotter.

255

- The hot-plate gets even hotter, and then it boils faster, since the water also gets warmer.

- The saucepan was on 3, and 3 is half of 6. On 3 the temperature is + 100°C after 5 minutes. Thus it must be approximately double on 6.

- When you go up to six, it must naturally get warmer, why should we otherwise have numbers on the switch?

C. Remainder

Example - The water starts evaporating.

3.   The temperature stays at 100°C.

  A. No explanation.

  B. Explanations expressing that 100°C is an invariant upper limit, but without mentioning boiling as a cause.

   Examples - It does not get hotter if you increase to six.

   - The water can't get above 100°C.

   - If you turn to six, the water only heats up faster.

   - The heat of the plate goes up, but the heat (of the water) never goes above one hundred degrees, but stays the same.

   - The water can't get warmer than + 100°C without turning into steam, I think.

  C. Boiling is the cause of the temperature invariance.

   Examples - The plate gets hotter for each step, but the water can but boil.

   - The boiling-point is 100°. Therefore it can't get warmer.

   - It is boiling both on the three and the six.

The distribution of the pupils' answers by these categories is given in table 2.

Table 2: Problem 2. Distribution of the pupils' explanations by categories. (%)

	1. Below 100°C	2. Above 100°C			3. Stays at 100°C		
		A	B	C	A	B	C
grade 6 (n = 62)	3	6	71	3	2	8	6
grade 7 (n = 139)	3	9	52	2	3	9	22
grade 8 (n = 120)	-	5	55	-	10	14	16
grade 9 (n = 121)	2	2	49	3	4	24	15

Categories

2. A. No explanation

   B. The switch-number determines the temperature of the boiling water

   C. Remainder

3. A. No explanation

   B. 100°C is an invariant upper limit but boiling not mentioned as cause

   C. Boiling is the cause of temperature invariance

Discussion

Some of the pupils' explanations are quite consistent. Thus, of the pupils in category 2 B on problem 1 (the longer the water is on the hot-plate, the hotter it gets), 80% explain, as would be expected, problem 2 by saying that the switch-number determines the temperature of the boiling water. Of the children in category 3 B on problem 1 (switch-number determines boiling-point), 78% give the same type of explanation on problem 2. Also of the children in categories 3 C and 3 D on problem 1 (C: 100°C is an upper limit, D: boiling is the cause of the temperature invariance), 68% give an explanation in one of these categories on problem 2.

However 28% of the 3 C children on problem 1 change their explanation to 'switch-number determines boiling-point' on problem 2. Possibly, in these cases, behind an answer like 'the water can't get above 100°', there might be a thought of the type 'switch-number determines boiling-point'. Also 21% of the children in category 3 D change their explanation in the same way. This is more difficult to explain. Perhaps they have a very figurative understanding of boiling-point. 'The boiling-point of water is 100°' may be just a phrase for them, and they are easily distracted by problem 2, which demands a more operative understanding. They may also think that a certain boiling-point corresponds to each number of the hot-plate.

It is of interest to know how many pupils there are that give a correct answer and an acceptable explanation to both problems, that is categories 3 C or 3 D on problem 1 and categories 3 B or 3 C on problem 2. Also, it is interesting to see how many pupils are stating, on both problems, that boiling is the cause of the temperature invariance. This information is shown in table 3.

Table 3: Pupils answers to both problems

	grade			
	6	7	8	9
Percentage of children giving correct answer and acceptable explanation to both problems	6	26	24	31
Percentage of children stating that boiling is the cause of temperature invariance on both problems	3	16	13	12

These percentages are quite low, and an explanation is required. How about the sample? The two schools that participated in the testing are in general characterised as 'average' by the teachers. This statement is based on standardised achievement tests that are given in Swedish, Mathematics and English, in all Swedish schools in grade 6 and 8. Therefore, the percentages can't be explained away by saying that the sample is very much below the median.

How about the Swedish way of teaching physics? (Physics is taught as a separate subject from grade 7 onwards.) The syllabus in physics in grades 7, 8 and 9 is characterised by a considerable conceptual density. A new concept is introduced every fifth or tenth minute. Many teachers try to give a sort of 'civics education' in physics by going through, in a short period of time, practically all areas of physics: mechanics, optics, electricity, etc. up to nuclear physics. Astronomy and meteorology are also part of the programme. In addition to this, the physics syllabus is characterised by a marked discrepancy between conceptual demands, which are too high, and the capacity of many of the pupils. In short, physics is quickly taught and quickly forgotten. Conceptual understanding is replaced by memorised bits of information. Therefore, the

Swedish way of teaching physics may very well explain the rather low percentages in table 3.

But there are perhaps more fundamental reasons of a developmental nature. A pupil using formal operations considers reality as a possible manifestation of laws which are both general and necessary. He or she is more inclined than the concrete operational child to go beyond a given situation in search for generalities and abstract principles. When this child reads in a textbook that the boiling-point of water is 100°C at normal air pressure, he or she thinks of this as a principle with some generality, whereas the concrete operational child may be more struck by an illustration, e.g. showing a thermometer in boiling water, and remembers a specific event rather than a principle. The ability, characteristic of formal operations, to sort out and control variables may also be of help, both when searching for a principle, and when solving problem 1 and 2. Thus even such a seemingly simple concept as boiling-point may be quite difficult for the pupil.

Admittedly, this developmental argument suggested as an explanation for the rather low percentages of table 3 is somewhat speculative. On the other hand, it is clear that the pupils' explanations, in all their diversity and richness, are an excellent content to deal with in a physics lesson. Discussions and experiments dealing with this content can increase the pupils' awareness of inconsistencies in their ways of reasoning and contribute to an attitude of searching for invariants and principles beyond what is specific.

Discussion

In answer to a question Andersson reported that the youngest pupils in the study had received no formal education in physics and their misunderstandings could not be attributed to the teacher's explanation being confused by the pupils. In that event it was argued that many of the apparent misconceptions came from the application of good logical thinking, the problem was merely that the pupils had inadequate background knowledge. If they did not know about latent heat it might be a logical belief to think that by increasing the flow of available heat, by adjusting the control knob on the heater, the temperature of the water should rise. Perhaps that was a basis of a good teaching point. The pupils' hypothesis could be tested and the finding that the water temperature did not rise should provoke active thinking on their part.

In answer to further questions, Andersson reported that by interview further information was gained from the pupils, e.g. on the nature of the bubbles seen in the water. Thus more information was available about the models the pupils held.

The relative merit of this method of enquiry compared with the interview-about-instances technique reported by Gilbert was discussed. It was suggested that Andersson's procedures might yield richer information.

As in many other instances, the pupils' misconception recapitulated the variety of ideas known to have been held by man historically.

TOWARDS THE DIAGNOSIS BY SCIENCE TEACHERS OF PUPILS' MISCONCEPTIONS : AN EXERCISE WITH STUDENT TEACHERS

Joseph Nussbaum

Introduction

In the framework of education, it often seems that 'listening to' and 'understanding' are activities required of the pupil exclusively. A pupil's difficulties in comprehending and internalising certain concepts are likely to be ascribed to his failure to listen to and to understand what the teacher has to say.

It is possible that many such difficulties would be avoided if teachers were better prepared to listen to their pupils, understand the nature of their misconceptions and, in turn, make constructive use of this knowledge on the pupil's behalf.

The development of these skills in student teachers should be one of the primary responsibilities of every teacher training programme. Nevertheless, teacher training programmes, in general, have not included explicit and specific activities which would increase the student teacher's skills in this particular way.

An approach to the development of understanding of pupils' thinking in science student teachers (along with the development of other teaching competencies) is to be found in the British Science Teacher Education Project - STEP (1974). This programme is mostly based on group exercises.

Following the STEP model, the author has developed a new exercise for science student teachers with some new points of emphasis. The aims of this exercise are:

1. To develop awareness that it is not enough to evaluate pupils' answers in terms of 'scientific correctness', but, it is also of equal importance to pay attention to the nature of the pupils' misconceptions.

2. To enhance competency in rapidly scanning pupils' written answers and 'reading between the lines' for detection of possible misconceptions.

3. To enhance competency in diagnosing pupils' misconceptions using psychological and philosophical terms and ideas.

4. To increase ability in raising various considerations leading to more appropriate reactions to pupils' misconceptions in the teaching - learning process.

The dominant criterion for evaluating a pupil's cognitive structure commonly applied in schools, and especially in college teaching, is the scientific correctness of the pupil's knowledge of the subject. Student teachers, to whom this exercise is aimed, come to the training programmes freshly influenced by this type of college science teaching. To what extent are they able to relate to pupils' thinking according to the aims suggested above, before they become exposed to a specific piece of relevant training?

This study was restricted to the evaluation of the initial state of student teachers' diagnostic competency, i.e. their pre-exercise level of competence.

Purpose of study

The purpose of this study was to evaluate student teachers' pre-exercise competency in diagnosing misconceptions in pupils' answers.

Procedure

Subjects

The study materials were administered to five (three biology, two chemistry) student teacher sections and to one group of graduate students in science education (M.Sc. and Ph.D. candidates; a mixed group according to science specialisation). The student teacher sections were from various universities and colleges in Israel. All the participants had completed at least two years of university pro-grammes in their specific field of science. No attempt was made to sample systematically the student teacher population in Israeli universities. However, the tutors of these groups felt that they were typical of most student teacher groups in their science area.

Materials

The materials consisted of two supposed explanations of a given physical phenomenon. These explanations were constructed by the author based on findings of a previous study (Nussbaum, Novick, 1979) in which individual pupils' explanations of certain demonstrated physical phenomena were analysed. In that study, the researchers were

261

able to detect various misconceptions of the physical world in different pupils' written explanations. These misconceptions were masked frequently by the pupils' usage of scientific language. A detailed description of the material is included in the presentation of the following section.

Administration

1.   Student teachers were informed that as part of their programme they were going to do an exercise on 'reading pupils' answers. They were told that the exercise would begin by working individually on work sheets and would be followed by small group and whole class discussions.   They were informed that the first part of the exercise would serve some research purpose and that their responses in the work-sheets would be collected.

2.   Student teachers were given worksheet 1 (see copy on this page) and they were asked to read answer A and respond in writing to task 1 within the time limit of one minute. Following this, they were given two more minutes to read answer B and to respond in writing to task 2.

PUPILS' THINKING   <u>Reading pupils' answers</u>   Worksheet 1

The following question is taken from a physics test given to fourteen year-old pupils. Two individual answers are cited.

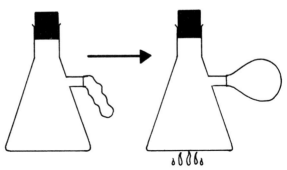

Figure 1

Question : *In a certain experiment a flask full of air had a deflated balloon attached to a side pipe coming out of the flask. As the flask was heated by a flame the balloon inflated (see figure 1).*

Explain this phenomenon using the particle theory.

Answer A: *There is air in the bottle which fills it and also fills some of the balloon which is not blown up. If someone places the bottle with the molecules of the air above the flame then it becomes hot in the bottle and the air expands. The molecules move from the bottle to the balloon and this makes the balloon blow up.*

Task 1 : *Write a short evaluation of answer A and insert an appropriate numerical grade (out of 10 points) in the box*

.... ☐

Answer B: *There is air in the bottle which fills it and also fills some of the balloon which is not blown up. Scientists discovered that the air which is in the bottle contains very small particles which are very great in number. These small particles, which they also found to be like tiny balls, can move and reach every place in the air of the bottle. Scientists called these particles <u>molecules</u>. If someone places the bottle with the molecules of the air above the flame, then it becomes hot in the bottle and the air expands and blows up the balloon. This happens because of the law which says that <u>things expand when they are heated</u> and also because when it becomes hot in the bottle then the very tiny molecules tend to go away from the hot place and so they move from the bottle to the balloon and this makes it blown up. If someone would like to see what would happen if the bottle were cooled down, he would find that the balloon would shrink again because of the law which says that <u>things shrink when they are cooled</u>. But with water it does not happen so since when water is cooled below 4°C then, amazingly enough, it would expand. This is what they call the anomaly of water.*

Task 2 : *Write a short evaluation of answer B and insert an appropriate numerical grade (out of 10 points) in the box.*

.... ☐

As a teacher, which of the two answers (the short one or the long one) would you prefer to receive from your students?

......................Explain why......................

....

3. After the three minutes had passed each student teacher reported his responses to tasks 1 and 2 orally, while the tutor tabulated all the reported data on the blackboard. He then pointed out to the group the great variety which existed among them in their evaluations of the same pupils' answers.

The aims of tasks 1 and 2 and the short group discussion which followed were: (1) to simulate for the student teachers the time pressure which the teacher experiences as he must evaluate many pupils' answers within a short time; and, (2) to raise the student teachers' motivation to read and evaluate the answers again more carefully, by facing them with the great variety of opinions found among themselves.

4. Student teachers were given worksheet 2 (see copy on the next page) and were asked to respond in writing to task 3 and 4. The student teachers worked on these two tasks for about 15 minutes and then the worksheets were collected. The study administration was completed by collecting the worksheets.

It is recommended at this point that the reader devotes a few minutes to doing tasks 3 and 4 by himself before continuing his reading of the paper.

Tasks 3 and 4 were performed as individual work, while in a regular exercise situation they are worked upon by small teams. Some of the exercise activities, though not included in the study, are described below. This additional description should help the reader to understand the desired level of responses to the student teacher tasks and thereby help the reader to follow the analysis of responses.

Upon completion of the team discussion, the tutor conducts a group discussion whose aims are: (1) to clarify the difference between technical or informational errors and misconceptions; and, (2) to elaborate and advance the quality of the diagnoses of the misconceptions made earlier individually by the student teachers. This is done by applying concepts and terms from cognitive psychology and from philosophy of science. The paragraph below highlights briefly the content of the intended discussion.

Each team is asked to report its diagnosis to the whole group and to support this diagnosis with citations from the answer text. The following three conceptual mistakes are expected to be identified by the small team work:

(a)   Air is made of air + air particles.

(b)   Molecules escape from the heat source.

(c)   Things happen because of scientific law.

Following team reports, the tutor conducts a group discussion in which the point is made that answer B reflects some of the pupil's global conceptions, rather than representing some cases of missing or of mistaken information. It is true that these conceptions deviate from the so-called 'correct scientific' ones. The tutor emphasised that for pedagogic purposes it would be better if one viewed them as the pupil's own conceptions which are alternatives to the scientific ones, rather than merely labelling them as misconceptions and assigning them a low score on a test (see Driver, Easley, 1978).

Task 3 : Read answer B again and identify various misconceptions which you think exist in the pupil's mind. Explain briefly the nature of each mistake.

....

Task 4 : What is in your opinion the possible source for these conceptual mistakes?

....

Task 5 : (Remember what you have learned from Piaget.) To what extent has this child performed a mental action of assimilation and/or accommodation?

....

Task 6 : Suppose the answers which indicate these types of misconceptions had been received from only 5 pupils out of the 30 pupils you have in your class. Following is a list of possible ways in which you could react as a teacher. Discuss with your peers the advantages and disadvantages of each:

    a. taking off a few points from the pupils' scores

    b. requiring the pupils to re-read the relevant chapter in the book

    c. requiring the pupils to look at the right answer in a classmate's test

    d. talking to the pupils and explaining the correct answer

    e. talking to the pupils and asking them additional questions

    f. devoting 20 minutes of the next session to discuss the test and its difficulties

    g. _____

    h. _____

These pupils' alternative conceptions can be rediagnosed respectively as follows:

(a) <u>Matter is essentially continuous</u> as opposed to the scientific <u>model which presents matter as particulate.</u>

(b) Dynamic phenomena are conceived through an <u>animistic - teleologic</u> <u>model</u> as opposed to the scientific model which <u>is a mechanistic -</u> <u>causal</u> one.

(c) <u>Science laws are conceived as being separate from nature</u> and are <u>thought to be the determining factor;</u> as opposed to the view that science laws are only a summative description of natural behaviour.

These three misconceptions may stem from the pupil's preconceptions of the world which evolve from a child's naive and highly intuitive view of the world. These preconceptions exist in the child prior to the instruction. The pupil's answer demonstrates that he has not essentially changed his preconceptions through the course of school learning. He has merely incorporated certain new terms and ideas into these existing naive preconceptions without introducing in them any major modification. Discarding a preconception and replacing it with a more abstract and sophisticated conception is a major cognitive revolution. The pupil in such cases experiences some of the cognitive difficulties that great scientists of the past experienced when they attempted to replace existing conceptions by new ones. The tutor brings here relevant significant examples from the history of science. Kuhn's ideas (1962) of the history of paradigms and revolutions in science is relevant, along with Piaget's (1972) proposed analogy between cognitive growth in the individual and the history of mankind's understanding of the physical world. (A good example of how ontogenetic cognitive development parallels the history of science may be found in Nussbaum, 1979.)

In terms of Piaget's theory of intelligence (see Task 5) the pupil assimilated new bits of knowledge (there are air particles; air particles move, etc.) into his existing conceptual framework ('matter is continuous'; 'nature behaves teleologically'; etc.). It appears that the pupil has not accommodated his conceptual frameworks (preconceptions) to any significant extent.

The exercise continues by asking the student teachers to discuss in small teams what actions they would take, had they noticed this kind of answer prevailing among 5 pupils of their class (see Task 6).

Results

Student teachers' responses to tasks 1-4 are summarised and discussed in this section. Table 1 presents their responses to tasks 1 and 2.

Table 1: Student teachers' initial responses to Tasks 1 and 2

Group No.	Preparation for	S's n	Task 1		Task 2	
			Mean score*	Range of scores	Mean score*	Range of scores
1	Teaching biology	17	5.0	2-8	4.0	0-7
2	Teaching biology	13	7.0	6-8	6.0	4-8
3	Teaching biology	22	7.6	6-9	7.2	6-8
4	Teaching chemistry	9	6.5	6-9	5.5	4-7
5	Teaching chemistry	22	7.6	6-9	7.0	6-9
6	Graduate degree in science education	11	7.3	6-9	6.4	4-8

*On a scale from 0 to 10

Most of the groups judged, on the average, that answer B deserved one unit less than answer A. There is an obvious variance between groups in the average score assigned to each answer, ranging from 5.0 to 7.6 for answer A and from 4.0 to 7.2 for answer B. The variance within the groups was similarly high.

In task 3 they were asked to identify and specify various misconceptions which may be reflected in answer B. Tables 2 and 3 present the responses to task 3.

The desired diagnostic ability included specifying the misconceptions using psychological and philosophical terms and ideas. However, in this study every case of detecting a misconception was counted even if the misconception was not diagnosed elaborately as desired. Of the three misconceptions, the one which was detected with the highest frequency was the tendency of pupils to relate 'animism' to dynamic physical phenomena. Even this most frequently identified misconception was detected by only about half of the student teachers (53 out of 94). Each of the other two misconceptions was identified by less than one third of the student teachers (31 and 27 out of 94). Taking into account the low quality of the diagnoses made by the student teachers, these low percents of detection of misconceptions are worthy of notice. In addition, while

267

responding to task 3, the vast majority of the subjects (86 out of 94) made some general remarks supposedly diagnosing a misconception which did not have any diagnostic value. These general remarks came in addition to or instead of suggesting specific diagnoses as expected.

Table 2: Frequency of likely existing misconceptions identified by each group of student teachers (Task 3)

Group No.	S's n	I Structure of matter is continuous (particles exist in a continuous medium)	II Teleologic -animistic view of dynamic physical phenomena	III Science laws exist independently of nature and are the determining factors	Percent of misconceptions identified by each group $(\frac{I+II+III}{3n} \cdot 100)$
1	17	5	6	3	27
2	13	6	8	3	44
3	22	11	9	5	38
4	9	3	9	5	63
5	22	2	14	7	35
6	11	4	8	4	73
Total	94	31	53	27	--

From the total number of 94 there were 21 (22%) who could not suggest any specific diagnosis. Their contribution consisted only of these general remarks.

Table 3 presents the frequency of various combinations of misconceptions identified by each group.

Only very few of the student teachers, 7 out of 94 (7%), identified all three misconceptions. Two misconceptions were identified by 24 (26%) and one misconception was identified by 42 student teachers (45%).

Indeed, it is possible that the variations found between the frequencies of each identified misconception resulted from the degree to which it appeared overtly in answer B. Nevertheless, while relating to the same answer text, the biology student teachers showed lower awareness of misconception 3 (science laws as separate from nature)

268

than of misconception 1 (continuous model for the structure of matter). In the biology groups the frequency of identifying misconception 1 is twice that of identifying misconception 3 (see table 2). At the same time, the chemistry student teachers showed, reversely, a lower awareness of misconception 1 than of misconception 3.

Table 3: Frequency of various combinations of misconceptions identified by each group of student teachers (Task 3)

	Group No.	S's n	None identified	One identified			Two identified			Three identified
				1	2	3	1+2	1+3	2+3	1+2+3
Biology	1	17	6	3	4	2	2	-	-	-
Biology	2	13	2	2	4	1	2	-	-	2
Biology	3	22	4	5	4	3	4	1	-	1
Chemistry	4	9	-	-	2	-	2	-	4	1
Chemistry	5	22	7	-	8	1	-	-	4	2
Mixed	6	11	2	-	2	1	3	-	2	1
	Total	94	21	10	24	8	13	1	10	7

The findings regarding the chemistry groups might look somewhat strange since one would expect chemistry students to be more aware of pupils' misconceptions regarding the structure of matter than biology students. A possible explanation might be that chemistry students are so used to 'thinking with particles' that they do not realise that their pupils might have difficulties in abandoning the continuous model. This interpretation assumes that the larger the cognitive gap between the teacher and his pupil the more apt the teacher is not to notice his pupils' misconceptions and difficulties.

The lower awareness of misconception 3 amongst the biology students might be explained as follows. From the author's informal observation of biology students it seems that they too frequently lack mastery of physics knowledge. They therefore accept physics laws as given and tend to attribute to these laws an explanatory power (as the pupil did in answer B). If this observation is valid, college biology students are more likely to read pupils' answers leaving misconceptions about the nature of science laws unnoticed.

In task 4 the student teachers were asked to propose reasons for the formation of those identified misconceptions. Most of the proposed reasons were an extension of the general remarks which most of the

269

student teachers made earlier in task 3. The proposed reasons may be classified as those related to the pupil and those related to the teacher. Table 4 presents the classified responses to task 4.

The reasons related to the pupil can be subclassified as follows: (1) pupil's inability to abstract; (2) pupil's domination by his own intuition; (3) pupil's failure to understand some important points of what he was taught; (4) pupil's tendency to present his knowledge ambivalently (i.e. superfluous writing and a mixing of relevant points with irrelevant ones).

The reasons related to the teacher can be subclassified as follows: (5) teacher not using enough visual aids in his teaching; (6) teacher including animistic elements in his explanation which misled the pupil; (7) teacher not explaining well enough.

Reasons (1), (3) and (7) were much more frequent than the others.

It is interesting to note that these three reasons are also much more general in their nature than the other reasons. Reason (1) speaks too generally about the 'inability to abstract', since there might be different factors causing this inability. Such factors might be caused by interfering emotional involvement, unavailability of required mental operations, strong miscueing due to incorrect perception of the specific phenomenon, etc. But such factors were not suggested by the student teachers. Reason (3) speaks about pupils' failure to understand the subject matter. But the student teachers did not suggest specifically what might cause the pupils' misunderstanding. Might it be the complexity of the physical phenomenon, or the deficiency of prerequisite knowledge, or the way the teacher presented the topic, or the well-established preconceptions which were in dissonance with the scientific conception presented by the teacher? Reason (7) speaks about the teacher's failure in explaining satisfactorily. There also, the student teachers did not suggest any possible specific teaching characteristics to explain the teacher's failure.

The other reasons were more specific in the way they were stated but they were suggested much less frequently by the student teachers. Reason (2) points to a specific factor, namely, the dominancy of pupil intuition, possibly causing difficulties to the pupil. It is interesting to note that the student teachers referred to this intuitive factor by unconsciously using psychological terminology. Reason (4) is also stated in specific terms as well as reasons (5) and (6). A teacher who is able to hypothesise a specific factor which might cause his pupil difficulty has made the first step toward finding ways to help his pupil.

Table 4: Student teachers' suggested reasons for pupil's misconceptions

Group No.	S's n	Pupil related reasons					Teacher related reasons			
		P. is unable to abstract	P. is dominated by his own intuition	P. misunderstood what he was taught	P. answers ambivalently	Total	T. did not use enough visual aids	T. using 'animism' misled the pupil	T. did not explain well enough	Total
1	12	8	-	5	2	15	1	-	9	10
2	13	4	5	4	-	13	-	1	5	6
3	22	2	1	3	-	6	1	1	3	5
4	9	3	-	3	1	7	-	-	3	3
5	22	6	1	6	8	21	-	1	5	6
6	11	6	4	3	1	14	1	2	3	6
Total	94	29	11	24	12	76	3	5	28	36

Summary

The task of teaching pupils science concepts and conceptions meaningfully is rather complicated and is too often not fulfilled. One of the primary problems we face in teaching this aspect of science is that '...pupils develop misconceptions which can persist in spite of instruction...Not until the reasons for the misconceptions are understood will progress be made in instructional terms.' (Driver, Easley, 1978)

Diagnosing a pupil's misconceptions appropriately is but the first step toward helping the pupil to replace his persistant pre-conceptions with the scientific conceptions. In the present study an attempt was made to learn about student teachers' pretraining competency to diagnose pupils' answers for possibly existing misconceptions. It was found that the student teachers participating in this study before receiving any relevant training by and large are not ready to make appropriate diagnosis of misconceptions. They rather tended to make general remarks which do not have any interpretative quality. The need for inclusion of specific training activities, to develop this desired diagnostic competency, is clear.

Future studies should demonstrate the efficiency of relevant exercises in developing student teachers' awareness, sensitivity and competency for diagnosing pupils' misconceptions.

Discussion

It was suggested that some of the 'misconceptions' which might be identified in the scripts might merely reflect a difference in the frames of reference of the pupils and the reader. Was a description of molecules as 'small balls' acceptable? Did the pupils see the exercise as having the same purpose as the reader? Might the reader hold a personal belief in what was 'true' in science?

Furthermore language might be the problem. The pupil might use a word like 'air' with a somewhat different meaning than the reader.

Nussbaum pointed out that the object of the exercise was to promote student-teacher awareness of possible misconceptions. It was intended that they should be more willing to listen and notice these possibilities. The exact nature and cause of the apparent misconceptions was another issue. Alongside these scripts other evidence, from videotapes, interviews, and so forth was considered.

It was agreed that student teachers might well benefit from such exercises and that their use could be extended to monitor the effectiveness of teacher education programmes.

SPONTANEOUS REASONING IN ELEMENTARY DYNAMICS*

L. Viennot

The scope of this study was to explore and analyse spontaneous reasoning of students in elementary dynamics, from the last year at secondary school to the third year at University.

A set of investigations involving several hundred students (mainly French, but also British and Belgian) showed surprising rates of wrong, or right, answers, which are very stable from one sample of students to another. It seems difficult to attribute these results solely to school learning. But they can be reasonably well accounted for if we assume a spontaneous explanatory system, relatively un-affected by school learning.

In particular, students seem to use in their reasoning two differ-ent notions of dynamics, usually designated by the same word: 'force'. To detect which of these two notions has, in fact, been used, one must look at their properties: one of these 'forces' is associated with the velocity of a motion whilst the other one is associated with its acceleration. Likewise, the part played by energy in these two notions is distinctly different.

It is possible to set up, and roughly classify, the types of questions which give rise to each notion in spontaneous reasoning. This model, where inertial forces are also included, makes it possible, with a minimum of hypothesis, to account for answers on a wide range of topics, such as: free fall, oscillating systems, 'accelerated' frames of references, third law of dynamics.

More generally: when confronted with a physical system, students may first consider the system as it is, with its geometrical and physical characteristics at time t, or consider mainly the evolution of the system, and look for a causal explanation. While compatible in Newtonian formalism, these viewpoints lead students more often to

---

*This is a summary of the paper presented at the Seminar. The complete paper is to be found in the European Journal of Science Education, (1979), 1, (2), 205-221.

right answers in the first case than in the second one, the explanation being then often confused with quasi-animistic arguments, and loosely located in time.

Some teaching consequences can be drawn from these investigations. Some of them, of a relatively technical nature, follow more or less directly from the wrong answers reported here. But the most important one concerns the very principle of these investigations: they provide an opportunity for the students involved to make an extremely useful self-analysis and to learn to distinguish between learned formalism and spontaneous reasoning and, consequently, to master both of them somewhat better.

Discussion

Viennot, in introducing her paper, outlined the aim which was to describe and formulate students' thinking about specific situations and the interest was in verbal explanation rather than in percentages who passed at a given age or level. Concepts of force and motion energy were included. Her research was based on responses from students in France, Belgium and Britain. Pencil and paper tasks focussed on students' predictions about one aspect of the motion of a body. There was evidence for the existence of a form of spontaneous reasoning that is persistent and strong (and possibly subject to its own rules) when used in daily conversation and that contradicts elementary ideas of dynamics taught in schools.

Members agreed on the confusion some students have in handling such concepts as force and energy. These and other ideas have a high degree of abstraction and students need a new framework in which to place their experience. Help should be given to them in making abstractions as it was doubted if students could construct new frameworks for themselves. Discussion went on to the implications for teaching. It was suggested that the presentation of formal concepts is like capping an iceberg. On this view the bulk of the hidden iceberg represents a pupil's internal system of mental constructs which could upset a consistent set of concepts.

As in other sessions the influence of language on thinking was raised. It was pointed out that Norwegian has no term for power, English uses two terms for velocity while France uses one and languages in India and Ceylon lack terms for such notions as force. Where words like force and energy are commonly used in society it seems to be the case that science and mathematics teachers are better supported.

This paper suggest that students adopt an intuitive framework to new situations, but are reluctant to move away from commonsense views of science and its concepts. On the other hand teachers tend to interpret wrong answers in science as due to poor mathematics and not to misunderstanding of concepts.

Classroom Based Research in
Science and Mathematics Education

GOERY DELACÔTE

Introduction

Classroom based research (CBR) has already a long history; it dates back to the beginning of this century. My first reactions, when CBR is considered, are:

- It is an essential part of the research on (science and mathematics) education, which by no means can be avoided.

- It seems to be, beyond the first naive approach, an extremely complicated, tricky, unreliable, disappointing and even frustrating enterprise (in terms for instance of ratio of meaningful information collected versus amount of work done).

- All the questions of why, what, how and when to observe received uncertain answers both on the methodological side (Simon, Boyer, 1970) and the theoretical side (Rosenshire, Furst, 1973). This reflects the complexity of classroom phenomena which parallels the complexity of living things; this reflects also the diversity of educational values underlying the schooling institution.

A certain number of recent reviews have been published on the question. In his paper 'A critical review of science classroom interaction studies' Colin Power concludes:

'Attempting to understand the complexities and realities of classrooms is a long and difficult task upon which we have barely begun. In tackling the task, it is important that we understand the assumptions, strengths and weakness of alternative approaches to studying classroom phenomena and the type of theories and models which might be appropriate.'

(Power, 1977)

In particular Power constrasts the more recent so-called 'interpretative ethnographic' research paradigm with the 'normative-scientific' one. In the first paradigm 'Teaching and learning must be understood in terms of the values, purposes and perception of the participants, rather than in terms of constructs deriving from some prestructured instrument or psychological theory. The theory sought is restricted to particular contexts and is not generalisable. The purpose of the theory is to describe and explain what is happening in a given context rather than to prescribe or predict what should happen.'

This paradigm is now developing, because of the widely recognised failure of process-product CBR, for instance to isolate key teacher competencies. Quoting Power (1977) again:

'The guiding force behind the research (of the "process-product" type) reviewed here has not been the systematic accumulation of knowledge aimed at the building or refining of theory. Rather, most of the research has been generated by a commitment to some relatively simplistic model or claim about what teachers ought to do. These commitments have fared rather badly at the hands of studies designed to validate them. Consistent significant relationships have not been found between counts of a good many seemingly virtuous teacher behaviours and measures of student outcomes. Increasing the frequency of teacher praise, indirectness, higher cognitive questions and of pupil centered inquiry does not invariably lead to increased student achievement and satisfaction. Nevertheless the research does indicate that most students suffer if lessons have no apparent structure or purpose, if much time is wasted due to inefficient management or control, or if the teacher is poorly prepared and plays a passive role in the classroom. But given that the minimal conditions necessary for students to remain on task are met, no simple solution to the problem of improving teaching can be put forward. The effects of any given strategy are complex and vary from pupil to pupil, objective to objective, and unit to unit...Although unintended, one major contribution of process-product research then, has been the debunking of myths about teacher effectiveness. The results force us to question the naive models of teaching and the paradigms for inquiry in education which have dominated educational research, practice and innovation throughout this century.'

In this paper I do not want to repeat, or even complete, the work done by other reviewers on CBR. I prefer to emphasise certain aspects of CBR, which may be, at least from my own point of view, of some importance for the future. The central point shall be the following: my contention is that CBR should progressively evolve from a teacher-centered process-product research toward an 'individual in a group' student-centered finely structured research.

Why do we need an evolution of CBR?

First we already quoted the failure and ambiguity of the process-product research.

In the following two researches reported here the basic aspect has been mainly limited to an analysis of the teacher's behaviours. Any attempt to go beyond this point toward a correlational study (of the process-product type) of teachers' behaviour and student learning outcomes is not very convincing. Even if they are interesting for instance for the training of teachers, those research studies of good calibre do not bring any description or understanding of the students' learning behaviours.

Galton and Eggleston (1979), after having shown that 'those studies which attempted to relate these descriptions of 'good teaching' with pupil achievement, failed to establish significant correlations', claim, with some caution, that they have succeeded where others had failed. They coded science teachers' behaviours (in terms of intellectual transactions) into an 'unambiguous'set of categories. The results were subjected to a cluster analysis and three 'types' of teachers were identified:

The Problem solvers who having the initiative, nevertheless 'challenge their pupils with a comprehensive array of questions, observational, problem solving and speculative in both practical and theoretical contexts.'

The Informers who are characterised by the relatively infrequent use of questions except those demanding recall and the application of facts and principles to problem-solving.

The Enquirers who hand over the initiative to the pupils. Pupil initiated and maintained behaviour is directed toward designing experimental procedures, inferring, formulating and testing hypotheses.

This kind of descriptive result seems to be firmly established and useful for the training of teachers (Dreyfus, Eggleston, 1979). But the correlation (it is not, and not presented as, a causal relation) between teaching styles and pupil learning is more open to criticism in as much as the learning has been evaluated by a pre-test/post-test technique.

Postic (1977) in France has similarly developed a series of observation techniques based on a functional analysis of the teacher's behaviour (three main teaching functions have been identified, 'encadrement', 'information', 'éveil') which allow the interdependence of pupil's and teacher's behaviours to be studied. A double entry category system enables a record to be kept of both the 'pedagogical acts' and the teacher's intention. The basic aim of this study is to allow science teachers to better adjust their own behaviour to their stated goals or intentions. It is essentially an observational system used for the non-normative self-monitoring training of teachers.

In both the studies cited it is clear that the observation is mostly teacher-centered. Classrooms as a whole, but not individual students in their idiosyncrasies, are submitted to the scrutiny of the observers. Whether it is normative or not, this kind of observation may largely contribute to the training of the teachers in terms of more consciousness of the gap which exists between the teacher's personal behaviour and a reference behaviour internally or externally defined. In that respect a purely descriptive, teaching-process-centered CBR may be useful. It is no longer a process-product research.

However we clearly see that this observation does not bring any meaningful information about the process of learning. There is less known about this process, and we would like to collect useful information about it through observation of classrooms. At this point I make three main observations:

First, there is no surprise that much emphasis has been put on observing teachers in classrooms. The teacher is unique, dominant. He talks most of the time, initiates most interactions, asks most of the questions and appreciates alone the student responses and comments. It is rather easy to have access to his set of beliefs. On the whole he is a perfect target to be observed in as much as he occupies the front of the stage. The need for information about both process (modes) and conditions of learning does not eliminate the need for knowing the teacher's behaviour. But this behaviour will be one aspect among others of both types of conditions: the already mentioned 'learning conditions' and the 'observation conditions', the conditions which allow (or prevent) the collection of information about the learning behaviour of the children.

Second, even if one would like to focus attention on teachers' problems, it is necessary to pay more attention to the behaviours of children which may elicit the basic intentions and beliefs of the teacher. A good example is provided by the report on Case Studies in Science Education (C.S.S.E.), (Stake, Easley, 1978). Here the researchers wanted 'to understand the detailed processes or mechanisms which lead teachers in one case to adopt an idea, in another, to reject such proposals as "unworkable in their situations" '. It was hard to get the right data to answer the questions. 'The field observers usually were working on the curricula issues deemed important at the sites, in the classroom at the school building level...and were not usually attempting to probe deeply into the individual teacher's belief system. However the field observers did make many observations of classroom practice which we can now interpret in terms of the perspective that emerges from this quest.' (Stake, Easley, 1978)

It is only after having observed a basic mathematics class working on adding fractions that the observer was able to identify a common student behaviour: 'trying to remember something somewhat like what you are supposed to do'. 'All the attention of the pupil was going so thoroughly on doing the right thing, hence learning and remembering, that there is not at all sufficient time or energy to grasp what is happening in his own terms.'

The field observer recognised here one of the key dilemmas for a teacher: whether to focus on the student's long range needs or their immediate needs. The teacher felt he had to deal with the immediate problem rather than taking a more basic long range approach. The teacher had an internalised concept of what the constraints in the classroom were and why new methods, ones that assume a different pedagogical framework or expository style,were likely to fail.

Third, in the discourse of the teacher, it seems that there is very little use of causal pattern linking experience and performance of the students. This seems to parallel the difficulty of the corresponding research paradigm (process-product type). Chapter 15 of the C.S.S.E. report states:

'It seemed natural to us to expect a conversation to shift easily from "experience" to "performance" - but we seldom found that it did. Somehow, when we were talking about experience, there seemed to be little talk about what the specific results of that learning opportunity were. And when they were talking about student performance there seemed to be relatively little attention to what sort of a situation it was that brought about that pattern of responses. We know that many researchers and others - whether disciples of Professor Skinner or not - are quick to link together the stimulus conditions with the response behaviour. We seldom found a rhetorical linkage between experience and performance in the schools we visited.

Some of our colleagues say that this points to the very trouble with instruction in the schools, that the teachers do not think in terms of causes and effects. We heard plenty of casual talk about causes and effects, but little explicit or rigorous. But rather than conclude that the teachers were falling short in matters of diagnosis and explanation we were inclined to conclude that the simple cause and effect statements that are the basis of research studies are seldom adequately descriptive of the conditions of learning and teaching in the classroom. It seemed to us that teachers were successful in efforts to develop an elaborate discussion of the conditions in which teaching was occurring, and to discuss some of the elaborate patterns of response, but neither they nor we had an adequate language and possibly not an adequate conceptual

system for understanding why the children were learning
or not learning. (Even the descriptions of what they
were learning were satisfying neither to us nor the
teachers.)'

(Stake, Easley, 1978)

How can we manage such an evolution?

It is my opinion that it should be possible to observe classroom
situations in a way which will enable us to say how the learning of
specific students occurs and under what conditions. It will represent already a great step forward to be able to achieve such a
descriptive research task. It has necessarily to rely on a detailed
observation of the pupils' behaviour. Beyond the observation one
should be able to assign meaning to the observed behaviour by using
a network of cross correlated information about the pupils' behaviour.

But here one is facing a severe point of methodology. If one
wishes to collect a large enough amount of meaningful information
about the individual pupils' learning in a classroom, often one has
to remove some constraints of the conventional classroom, such as the
amount to be learned in a given time, the number of pupils in the
classroom and the role of the teacher in taking much of the initiative.
It is hard to believe that these optimum 'observation conditions' will
parallel the optimum 'learning conditions'. Also I am not sure that
most teachers would agree that removal of these constraints would
produce optimal learning. The researcher may therefore set up classroom learning situations which could be optimum for the observation.
But the conclusions drawn from these observations may not apply to a
real learning situation. Vice versa, a real learning situation will
not provide good observation conditions. One has therefore to look
at some kinds of processes more or less independent from the constraints one wishes to remove; or at least one has to guess at the
type of constraint dependence of these processes. For instance, the
different modes of learning may exist at whatever speed you may learn
but the probability of occurrence of the restructuring mode may
greatly decrease when the learning is speeding up.

In the recent literature one may find different examples of
CBR with constraints removed.

1.   Classroom without a teacher (small-group) based research.

In a recent study, Barnes and Todd (1977) investigated the
interplay between cognitive and communication functions of speech in
contexts planned for learning. They also illustrated the way speech
functions as a means by which people construct and reconstruct views
of the world about them.

They studied the talk of thirteen-year-old boys and girls,
recorded while they were working in small groups on tasks which their

teachers had set.

'When children are talking in a group without an adult present, responsibility for the management of the talk falls on themselves. They must negotiate who talks when and how. They must cope with occasional episodes of conflicts and with silences. They must encourage group members with useful contributions to make, and at the same time control any attempts to dominate the talk for irrelevant purposes. They must judge the relevance of contributions and monitor whether they are germane to the problem set; they must also maintain some overall judgement of the quality of the discussion, so as to assess when they have reached a point where it is reasonable to stop.'

In moving control over learning strategies into the learner's hands (in contrast to a teacher's school) the researchers expected to be able to show that a wider range of speech strategies were available to the learner, and that these would include hypothesis forming and testing and the ability to go beyond the given information and to generate new questions and tasks.

One sees here clearly some characteristics of this type of research:

- The tasks to be performed by the pupils are well defined;

- Many constraints are removed (no teacher!) in order to improve the learning situation;

- Extensive use of transcripts are done together with a qualitative mode of analysis.

2. Observing a small group of pupils while teaching a large group (classroom).

This kind of methodology seems to have developed since the early 1970s (Driver, 1973). The basic ingredients are:

- To set up a learning situation which may last a certain number of teaching periods (from one month to a year or more at a frequency of for instance 1 period/week);

- To select by various means some pupils to be specifically observed by narrative instruments (video/audio) and by some observers who may from time to time try to elicit the meaning of the behaviours of the selected pupils (by extra questions);

- To let a teacher control the learning situation with more or less accurate beforehand agreement between teacher and observer;

- To allow in this learning situation, different phases which will be judged useful for the learning. Defining a problem, allowing an experimental or documentary investigation, structuring the acquired knowledge, etc. Among these phases, the most fruitful for observational purposes seems to be the quasi-small group teacher-free learning where only momentary interventions of the teacher interfere with the investigation task of the pupils' groups.

A. Tiberghien did a recent study in this way which is reported later in this Seminar. The study is on the learning of the idea of heat being something which is transferred from a high temperature region to a low temperature region. She was able (by contrasting the detailed behaviour of two 12 year old children working together to detect different modes of learning that Rumelhart and Norman (1976) called 'accretion, tuning and restructuration' modes of learning within a framework of memory analysis on the basis of active schemata.

She also observed the existence or the appearance of so called representations about the idea of heat and other related ideas (conduction for instance)...She found that heat is considered as a fluid (useful idea to build up the idea of conservation), that this fluid may sometimes move at the surface of object (how could a fluid go through a solid material?)...She then articulated these representations with the learning: for instance, the scheme of heat motion is tuned to the more precise but of course erroneous scheme of heat motion at the surface of objects. She observed that different and often contradictory systems of explanation existed simultaneously. 'Coffee pots (aluminium) keep in the heat well' after having learned that 'aluminium is a good heat conductor'...

Children appear to be able to live momentarily with two contradictory views in mind which allows a confrontation and provides a starting point for restructuration.

Her study showed that there are no systematic links between Piagetian type clinical standardised tests and the outcomes of learning which may follow many subtle paths not strongly dependent on the quality of the performance at the tests.

To be able to transfer the results to a conventional classroom would require a speeding up of the teaching process and a stronger interaction with the traditional set of beliefs of the teacher. This is of course one of the natural limitations of such work as previously explained.

In contrast with the previous work, a colleague M.G. Séré was able to follow four pupils during different sessions over a period of two years (first and second year of college, 11 and 12 year old children) and in different disciplines (physics, chemistry, biology, geography) about the notion of air (pressure, air and gas, air in motion, etc.).

The observation conditions (conventional classroom, teacher who had a 'problem solver' profile, compulsory syllabus, problem of marking) were in a sense poorer because of the lower degree of control of the learning situation by the observer. But in the course of the two year period it was possible to detect long term evolutions (or regressions!) specially across the boundary of the disciplines. On the other hand it will be more difficult to identify unambiguously some of the important learning conditions.

Conclusion

CBR has to be a valuable tool not only for the researchers but also for the teachers. We believe that CBR which focuses attention on the transactional behaviour of the teacher can be helpful for the training of the teachers.

In addition CBR which will develop case studies of individual pupils' learning events, processes and conditions may be of rich value for the following reasons:

- In order to acquire some new knowledge on the detailed processes of learning and on the corresponding conditions;

- In order to set up some new hypothesis and instruments for more systematic future research;

- Because it can be directly used as a kind of chronicle by the teachers.

Within this research framework a variety of methods can be used (Vergnaud, 1978) among which only a few have been presented in this paper.

RESPONSE by F.R. Watson

I have had only a short time to study Delacôte's interesting paper and my comments will be brief. This paper deals with issues of central importance to research on how pupils learn; the question of what happens 'out there' in the 'real world' of blackboards, chalk and textbooks, where teachers are sometimes inadequate and pupils occasionally unwilling. What does happen in classrooms?

Professor Delacôte's paper raises for me two major issues. one is implicit - the contrast and relationship between research in classrooms and in 'laboratory' conditions, between the naturalistic and the artificial settings. The second issue is explicitly mentioned - the severe methodological problems associated with CBR - a consequence of working in a realistic situation - which he sums up by describing CBR as 'an extremely complicated, tricky, unreliable, disappointing and even frustrating enterprise...'

Contrast with laboratory-based research

What do we gain or lose by conducting research in 'realistic' settings? Briefly we lose control and we gain typicality. The danger of the laboratory method, which has worked so well in science itself, is that in educational investigations we may create artificial situations so unrelated to the complex world of the classroom that findings are useless.

I should like to propose for discussion two statements:

(i) Though cognitive processes are influenced by their setting, they are sufficiently independent of setting to make it worthwhile to study them in 'ideal' conditions.

A remark: We know that motivation affects cognition. Some experiments may show only a 5% improvement, 'other things being equal', - the experimental effect is swamped by 'noise' in practical situations. But consider the 'feedback' effect, (success breeds success, failure leads to failure) - 5% may make a lot of difference. Consider, too, the difference between 4% and 5% compound growth. Small gains may be worthwhile.

(ii) A major emphasis in classroom research should be the testing in field conditions of ideas developed in 'lab' settings. (Not the only, but a major emphasis.)

Classroom research which examines social control, person to person interaction, etc. is not considered relevant to our purpose; CBR which is focussed on cognition without the benefit of prior 'laboratory' tests of underlying hypotheses is likely to be futile. More provocatively, 'The place to develop theories is the laboratory not the classroom.' On the other hand research undertaken to allow the researcher to explore the area concerned - getting the 'feel' of the problem - even if not producing novel results, is nevertheless valuable.

Methodological problems

Moving now to the second issue, that of methodological problems, we raise the question,'How do we go about finding out what happens in classrooms?' Three problems, at least, stand out: the collection and presentation of data, the underlying theoretical basis and the validity of such studies. The amount of information generated by even a few moments observation of the complex activities of a classroom, must somehow be codified, summarised, integrated to give meaning. How is this to be done? On the one hand are the category systems of Amidon and Flanders and their successors, on the other, the impressionistic, interpretative, ethnographic research paradigm which seeks to get the 'feel' of what is going on.

Underlying the choice of recording and reporting is the second, deeper problem of what theoretical perspective is appropriate to such studies. Some would argue that,'teaching and learning must be understood in terms of the values, purposes and perceptions of the participants, rather than in terms of constructs deriving from some prestructured instrument or psychological theory' (Power, 1977). Is the process-product approach too simplistic? Is the way forward to use a new category system based on a more sophisticated set of psychological constructs which might better mirror the complexity - or should we abandon the whole attempt to formulate general theories? Is it indeed the case that,'the purpose of theory is to describe and explain what is happening in a given context rather than to prescribe or predict what should happen?' Power's (1977) paper gives a very full review of classroom interaction studies in science teaching with a discussion of theoretical bases. To polarise this issue too sharply would serve no useful purpose here - rather I would prefer to ask, 'What can researchers within each paradigm learn from each other?'

Let me mention here a study by Judy Morgan (1977) at Stirling as an example of the interpretative paradigm applied to mathematics teaching.

I make just one other observation on this topic - there is perhaps an assumption of arrogance in using a predetermined 'schedule' to observe a teacher at work. The teacher, aware of his own intentions, knowing his pupils and the social context as the researcher can never do, may be thought to have a more valid perception of the scene. Yet his experience is confined to one classroom - the researcher has a wider perspective and specialised knowledge about learning, about other classrooms, about other observation studies. (It may be worth remarking, though, that interpretative studies do not directly give us the teacher's perceptions, but rather an interpretation by the researcher of what these are, so that the 'scientific' paradigm is not alone in imposing distortions.)

The third methodological problem, which besets all observation studies, is that of validity, in the sense of Campbell and Stanley (1963) - in particular, what they refer to as the 'reactive effect of the experiment'.

In Eggleston   (1975) it is stated:

'It is our experience that, provided the teachers and classes are assured that observation is not judgement, teachers are not threatened by the presence of an observer.'

About 100 teachers were observed, by 40 observers (some of whom are present today, I believe) each teacher being observed three or four times. In many occupations men do their work publicly - or at least with others in the vicinity so that their actions may be over-looked. In this country, once teachers have passed through their initial training period, it is very rare for them to be observed at work by anyone else. It may be many years since an experienced teacher was last 'observed'; to be watched 'in action' is somewhat of an ordeal, as anyone may testify who has given a demonstration lesson. How well founded is this reported confidence that teachers are not threatened? 'Familiarity breeds contempt' but are four visits enough? Perhaps, rather, ' it is our belief (hope?) that teachers are not threatened.' This is an important point for if the behaviour observed was a-typical the whole edifice collapses. (I am not here criticising Eggleston's research, but concerned that the issue of validity seems to be given so little attention.) The report by Judy Morgan, already referred to, demonstrates a sensitive concern for this aspect of teacher observation - one would be happier to see a more widespread recognition of this problem.

Concluding discussion

In the second section of his paper, Delacôte suggests some ways in which CBR may be adapted, both to meet some of the methodological difficulties and to give us more information about children's learning. I look forward to the presentation by Tiberghien which is to follow; Delacôte's mention of the longitudin-al study by Séré illustrates another interesting possibility. It might be helpful to regard observation of a whole class and the clinical interview as (almost) the two ends of a continuum, some parts of which may be useful in improving both validity and data collection on pupils' thinking. Having children working in smaller groups - as in a science practical laboratory or an 'informal' mathema-tics classroom - makes the presence of an additional 'teacher' (the outside observer) more natural. 'Artificial' lessons of teacher or researcher with a small 'class' of three or four (as with micro-teaching), and small groups tape-recorded working without a teacher are other possibilities. (Some examples of the latter have formed part of the S.T.E.P. and M.T.E.P. materials (Watson, 1974; Wain, Woodrow, 1979); though their use was for teacher training, some were based on research work done at Keele by my colleague Ruth Eagle (A.T.M., 1973).) One-to-one teaching (the clinical interview?), individuals 'thinking aloud' into a tape recorder (Watson, 1979), and perhaps even computer-to-one teaching, provide other ways of studying pupils' learning with varying degrees of 'outside inter-ference', and all are useful.

It might be argued that the persons best placed to do CBR are the teachers themselves - an issue which perhaps relates more to tomorrow's session with van Aalst on the research/practitioner interface. Here I would remark only on the teachers' lack of experience, in general, in research techniques, their limited time for research and for familiarisation with other work (a problem, indeed, for those of us here whose University function is mainly in teaching and not primarily in research!). Perhaps crucial is the problem of role conflict - the demands of teaching a class, controlling, organising, are often at variance with those of the researcher - as generations of Education students have found in trying to do small-scale projects in classrooms.

In conclusion, then, may I reinforce two points from Delacôte's paper, which seem to me particularly apposite - his suggestion that we change the focus of CBR from the teacher to the individual pupil in the social learning setting, and that reducing the number of pupils taught - or, in particular the number observed - may be helpful in achieving this. Perhaps if we adopt his suggestions, the task will be less impossible - it remains unavoidable.

Discussion

The discussion of these papers is incorporated with the report of the discussion following the next section.

Studies of Classroom Based Research into Pupils' Conceptual Framing of Scientific Ideas

MODES AND CONDITIONS OF LEARNING AN EXAMPLE : THE LEARNING OF SOME
ASPECTS OF THE CONCEPT OF HEAT

A. Tiberghien

Introduction

We are going to present here a careful analysis of the progress
in learning the concept of heat, made by a small group of children
in the age range 12-13 (2nd year of middle school), in a situation
analogous to that of a class.

We have chosen the concept of heat because it is one of the central concepts in the physical science syllabus for the first two years
of the secondary school. On the other hand, the various effects of
heat are generally very different from mechanical phenomena; they do
not result in movement or deformation, but only in an alteration of
temperature, or eventually a change of state. They are in the domain
of sensation by touch. This idea of heat thus requires on the part of
the subject, a kind of causal reasoning probably different from that
used in mechanics (Driver, 1973).

From a scientific point of view, it is convenient to consider
heat as a transfer of energy, this corresponding to a transfer of
'agitation' (Hachette, 1978). Heat can thus be represented as a flow
of 'agitation', without forgetting that this flow between the two
systems depends on the state of the systems. In this way, the heat
corresponds to an interaction between systems, whereas the temperature
corresponds to the state of a system. Thus heat is essentially something 'dynamic'. It is this general characteristic which we have
studied in these sessions. Moreover, we are limited to a qualitative
approach. It should be noted however that it is very difficult to
introduce this qualitative aspect of conduction, without recourse to
the concept of energy. Heat is not 'stocked' in a system, but is

exchanged between two systems. It is thus necessary to quantify the flows and a balance sheet can only be drawn up by using the quantity of energy or its variation for each of the two systems.

If the quantitative aspect is to be introduced, and first of all conservation of heat, this will most easily be done by a study of calorimetry (Strauss, 1977), which helps to establish a balance by mathematisation of an experimental method, rather than by imagining a mechanism (Jearsain et al. 1978).

In reality, the complete construction of the concept of heat requires at least these two aspects, without considering those which concern orders of size. During these teaching sessions, we have limited ourselves to this essentially qualitative aspect of heat, that of transfer. We have, moreover, introduced the quantitative aspect by some calorimetric experiments. Thus, even if these sessions have been a success, they can only be one step in the understanding of the concept of heat by the children. It seemed important to us to carry out our analysis at this stage of qualitative construction. It is a fundamental stage and is often least studied. In this article, we will analyse the learning for one particular mode of transfer of heat: conduction.

Our aim in this analysis is to show:

1. some of the modes of learning followed by the children, allowing them to change their points of view;

2. some of the varied learning conditions, which have allowed the children to develop, or not, their understanding of an idea such as heat.

The possibilities are innumerable, we could only study some of them. Those we have studied are of different types. We can on the one hand consider the exterior environment of the child and on the other hand the 'internal' state, which belongs to each child alone. Among these external conditions with which the child interacts, we have considered in particular:

- those linked to the teaching contents, the experiments carried out, the available material, the information given...

- those linked to the people taking part in the teaching, the personalities of the other children and the teachers.

Among the 'internal' conditions of the child, we have in particular considered:

- those linked to the global cultural knowledge of the child,

- those linked to the personality of the child.

3.   Among the latter, we have been particularly interested by some of
     the representations or types of interpretations which the children
     give concerning heat, whether they are aids or obstacles to learning.

Experimental methods

     In order to analyse our research, our main reference points have
been the comparison between the points of view and the interpretations
of the children before and after the teaching sessions. This comparison has allowed us to illustrate the different conceptual development
of each child. We have thus considered, for several aspects of an
idea, the development (or stability) of each child caused by the different events occurring during the teaching sessions, which we could
record.

     In the table below are given the main stages of the research,
which will be discussed later.

Stages	Methods
Choice of 8 children: 4 boys and 4 girls (1 good, 2 average, 1 weak, of each, from the point of view of their school work). All the children were from the same secondary school and the same level (5e), but not in the same class.	Requesting volunteers. Questioning the teachers of French, maths and science as to the pupils' levels of ability, their understanding and their contributions in class.
Interpretations given by the children of several experiences before the teaching sessions. Evocation about the word 'heat' by the children.	Individual interviews (non-directive and directive) with each of the 8 children (recorded on a tape recorder).
Analysis of their logical reasoning abilities (after Piagetian theory).	E.P.L.test (logical thought scale) with each of the 8 children (Longeot, 1969).
Organisation and observation of the learning process.	11 sessions of about 1½ hours once a week. 2 children (always the same) were filmed while working together. Another pair were tape-recorded. The whole group together with the teacher was also filmed.
Interpretation given by the children of several experiences after the teaching sessions. Evocation about the word 'heat' by the children.	Individual interviews with each of the 8 children, carried out about 8 weeks after the end of the teaching sessions. (Questioning the same teachers as previously.)

The teaching sessions took place in the studio of the Centre de Documentation Pédagogique de la Rochelle (see note at the end of this paper), which is very close to the children's school.

The teaching was carried out by a science teacher of the school.

We were present at all the sessions and we worked with the children when they were in pairs.

We prepared with the teacher the contents of the sessions.

Comments on the methods used:

1. Choice of children

We picked out children from volunteers and after teachers' reports. We have taken as a criterion the teachers' estimate which seemed to us an important factor. In general, this is linked to the success achieved at school by the child. We would like to elucidate to what extent the development of the children, from the conceptual point of view, during the sessions could or could not be linked to their school success.

2. Individual interviews

We used both a non-directed and a clinical-type directed interview. These are techniques used previouslv by us (Tiberghien et al.1978; Tiberghien, Delacôte 1978), and seem a good method for elucidating

- what types of association the words heat, cold and temperature recall;

- the words used by the children;

- the types of interpretation given by the children in different situations suggested during the directed interview. The actual ideas which were raised by these situations are those which have been studied during the teaching sessions.

By taking into account the level of interpretation given at the beginning in the interviews, a better adaptation of the conceptual level offered during the teaching sessions could be made.

This method has already been used by our laboratory (Guesne, 1976) and work is in progress considering ideas about light and pressure.

3. E.P.L. test

This has been carried out in order to make a comparison between the performances of the children on each of the tests with the interpretations given before and after the teaching sessions and especially with their development during the period. Since these tests are concerned with types of logico-mathematical reasoning, it seems interesting to link the performances of the children on the tests with their interpretations, often qualitative, of physical phenomena. At this stage of our analysis we have only indicated the absence of a systematic relationship between the level of test performance and the amount of the children's development during the period.

The learning sequence:

The table below presents the conceptual progression envisaged during the sessions.

1. Heat transfer

2. Sources of heat

3. Equality of temperature of objects in a room

4. One condition of heat transfer: the difference in temperature

5. Transfer of heat quantities

6. Effects of heat

7. Touch sensation of objects (insulators and conductors) at room temperature

8. Conductors and insulators (repeating the ideas, and making the vocabulary more precise).

We will not comment in this article on the scientific aspect of the suggested progression (Tiberghien, 1979).

We would like to indicate only that from a pedagogic point of view, we have, as far as possible, chosen those activities:

- which put children in situations where their interpretations or expectations are contradicted (if it is necessary);

- which allow the children to ask themselves questions about the interpretations of the phenomena under consideration;

- which would cause discussion among the children.

These discussions were recorded, they were for us an essential key to understanding the children's interpretations.

Results

We are first of all going to present the development of two children during these sessions, for one aspect of the concept of heat, that of conduction. We will then analyse this development, showing their modes of learning and some of the necessary conditions. We will also demonstrate some of the explanations which the children gave.

These two children are girls, Marie-Noëlle and Isabelle and they worked as a pair during the experimental sessions. They were filmed throughout. They came from the same school, but were in different classes.

I   The case of Marie-Noëlle

Teachers' estimate:

At the beginning of the year, she was, according to the teachers, an average pupil, rather timid and not at all relaxed. At the end of the year, the same teachers considered that she was a good pupil, having considerably developed during the year, both from an intellectual point of view and her character, which had become much more determined. She took part in all the sessions.

E.P.L. test:

In the conservation test, she achieved positive results for the conservation of weight and of volume, but she could not dissociate them. This corresponds to an intermediate level (between concrete and formal).

For the three other tests, permutation, probability quantifications and mechanical curves, she was also at an intermediate level.

The initial interview:

From this interview, we are considering on the one hand the kinds of reasoning which Marie-Noëlle used in her answers and on the other hand, the representations of the idea which she gave concerning the heat phenomena under discussion. We have only given here the points from which we will analyse Marie-Noëlle's development.

1.   Kinds of reasoning

Marie-Noëlle analysed certain situations either:

-   in a global manner: she gave her reply in relation to the experience she had had of the objects concerned. For example, to choose a container which would keep water hot the longest, (she had in front of her containers of plastic, cardboard and metal) she took a criterion:

'You drink coffee in that, so it keeps it warm long enough', and 'On his national service, my father had little dishes like that and he put his coffee in it, so it must have kept it warm.'

In consequence, she chose the metal container.

-   in selecting one particular characteristic of the object (in this case, it was the material, but it could also be the shape). This particular characteristic was selected because she connected it with a sensation of cold ('metal is cold'). For example, to choose a container which would keep ice frozen for a long time, she took as a criterion (she had just touched the metal):

293

'Metal cools things, metal is cold.'

She chose a metal container.

It can be seen that she completes her reasoning by a causal scheme: because a metal is cold, it cools things. In the other case, when asked if a casserole, full of hot water, left for a long time in a room would be colder, hotter or the same as the water inside it, Marie-Noëlle replied:

> 'The casserole will be colder than the water...it depends on what the casserole is made of.'

Thus, in these last two examples, Marie-Noëlle gives to the metal the property of being cold, without anything else necessarily cooling down. Or in the first example, the metal itself is a cause of cooling.

2.   Representations of the idea

The initial interview shows that Marie-Noëlle generally interprets proposed situations in terms of state: the state of the situation, the state of object, (hot or cold). Thus she rarely considers the heat differentiated from the object and which moves. This was the case, for example, when she chose containers which would keep ice frozen or water hot for a long time, as indicated in the previous passage. Marie-Noëlle did, however, use the heat once in differentiating the objects under consideration and using it as the cause of the modification of the state of the objects.

> 'The heat will enter...then the wind...afterwards the air.'

But subsequently she did not use this interpretation as a criterion of choice.

Marie-Noëlle also considered the heat in dynamic terms in the case of a situation which seems to us particularly favourable to this type of interpretation. It concerns a metallic bar, heated at one end and along which have been placed wax beads. In this situation, a source of heat (a camping gas flame) recognised as such by the children, is present. The point in question is the change of state of the wax beads, which melt. Marie-Noëlle began to analyse the situation in static terms:

> 'The heat is nearer.'

but very quickly, her ideas developed and she analysed in dynamic terms:

> 'The end is hot, it goes along.'('it' represents 'the heat of the end')

Thus Marie-Noëlle most often interpreted:

-    by considering that the objects act directly, without using the heat as an intermediary;

-    by using a different reasoning of the causal type, for example 'the cold cools', etc.

However, Marie-Noëlle has sometimes used the heat as an existing intermediary in an interaction, but not often, or only in very favourable circumstances.

The final interview:

1.   Kinds of reasoning

In the final interview, for the situations considering heat, Marie-Noëlle most often used one kind of reasoning, where she selected one particular characteristic of the object, here the material. Most often, she considered one property of the material, that of it being a conductor or insulator of heat. For example, to keep the heat the longest, she chose:

'That one, it's plastic, perhaps it's an insulator.'

Another time, she constructed her reply in relation to another situation, using the same characteristics: objects made from the same material. For example, to explain why the handles of two spoons, one of metal, the other of wood, standing in hot water, are not hot in the same way, she said:

'Pans, for example, have wood handles and you can touch them... when you heat the pan...the iron is the material that heats up ...there it's very hot.'

On another occasion, she used exactly the same argument as in the initial interview. When asked to guess the final state after interaction between two systems, in this case a pan full of hot water left for a long time in a room:

'(The pan), it's that kind of material, it will be colder (than the water).'

She considered here that the material is the cause of the temperature of the pan. However, when asked about the equality of the temperatures, read on a thermometer, she changed her mind.

2.   Representations of the idea

The final interview showed that Marie-Noëlle interpreted the situations by considering the heat by itself, independent of the hot objects, distinct from the course, and having the property of moving through the material. For example, concerning a metal container, full of hot water, she said:

'It's a conductor...the hot water's heat will go up the sides...then through.'

She also classified the materials in terms of their ability to conduct the heat more or less well; she used the words conductor and insulator appropriately.

Comparison of the interviews:

1.   Kinds of reasoning

In the final interview, Marie-Noëlle almost never used the type of reasoning which consists of considering the situation globally, for example, by the usual function of the objects. In contrast, she retained the explanation which consists of selecting one characteristic of the situation. However, the type of selection method that she used, differs between the initial and final interviews. The <u>causal scheme</u> was no longer the same (from 'because the material is <u>cold, it cools</u>', she went to 'because the material is a conductor, the heat goes through, etc...').

2.   Representations of the idea

The representations of the idea that Marie-Noëlle used to explain the phenomena of conduction clearly developed. At the end of the sessions, she associated the heat with transfer and considered the materials as a function of their ability to conduct heat. At the beginning, she was often content only to consider the phenomena presented to her in terms of state (hot or cold).

However, and above all in the case where she had to guess the final state of the objects which were interacting, she had developed little. She still sometimes had the tendency to consider the material at the ambient temperature as the cause of the temperature of the object.

Teaching sessions:

Description of child's behaviours

The notion of conduction was introduced in the course of several sessions and with very different types of experiments. We have given here only the different steps followed by Marie-Noëlle.

i   During the first two sessions, Marie-Noëlle carried out experiments to find out which container would keep ice cold and water hot as long as possible. She made a correct classification on testing at the beginning of the second session (the cardboard container conserves the heat better than the metal) and gave as an explanation:

'The material surrounding the ice does it. The cardboard
cup keeps in the heat. For hot water, it's the same thing.'

ii   During the third session, which considered heat-sources, Marie-Noëlle thought that wool was a source of heat. To demonstrate this, she carried out the following experiment: she took two ice cubes, wrapped one in aluminium foil and the other in a piece of wool. She predicted:

> 'That one (ice in wool) will melt more quickly than that one (ice in aluminium); because that (the wool) gives heat.'

She afterwards realised that the opposite had happened and in the course of the general discussion said:

> 'Man gives heat to it and it (the wool) keeps it.'

During the same session, Marie-Noëlle put a thermometer into both the wool and the aluminium foil and noticed the equality of the temperatures. At the test before the following session, she wrote that the temperatures of a piece of cotton and a piece of copper, left for a long time in a room would be the same.

iii During the 7th session, Marie-Noëlle rechecked that the temperatures of the pieces of cotton and copper left in the room were the same and said:

> 'We did the same thing for the heat sources (3rd session), it's just the same.'

The question given during the session was: 'Why do you feel, when you touch a piece of copper and a piece of cotton, that one is hot and the other cold?' Marie-Noëlle replied:

> 'It's the material that does it.'

As previously, she considers the material as a causal agent.

Marie-Noëlle then suggested carrying out an experiment: to put an ice cube in some cotton and in some copper. She said:

> 'We'll see which keeps the heat in.'

She predicted:

> 'I think that, that (the copper) will keep it (the ice) frozen most easily, because that (the cotton) is hotter and keeps the heat better.'

Marie-Noëlle thought that because the cotton is hot, the ice wrapped in cotton will melt most easily (we have again a causal scheme 'because the cotton is hot, it heats', an analogue to 'because the metal is cold, it cools'.

She also carried out an experiment of heating these two materials at one end. She concluded:

> 'The cold of the ice goes into the material (the copper)
> and goes away, and there (the cotton) it keeps it.   That
> one (cotton) keeps the heat more than that one (copper).
> Here (copper) it's all right, it goes away, the heat or
> the cold.'

iv   During the 8th session, after a set of experiments with materials
of varying conductivity, the teacher introduced the words conductor
and insulator to classify the materials.

   In the following sessions, Marie-Noëlle frequently used these
words herself, for example, while working with Isabelle.

v   During the final test, carried out in the eleventh session, in
order to answer a question about the different sensations on touching
metal and cotton, Marie-Noëlle used the fact that the movement of heat
is more rapid in some materials than in others.

> 'The metal spreads out the heat quickly, while the cotton's
> heat stays in the same place.'

   In contrast, for a question based on an every-day experience,(pick
a material for a container to keep soup hot the longest), Marie-Noëlle
referred to a different situation:

> 'Coffee pots keep in the heat well. Aluminium keeps in the
> heat well'.

   She thus chose an aluminium container to keep the liquid hot.

Commentary

Learning modes:

   At the beginning, the stability of Marie-Noëlle's interpretations
was seen, when she was confronted with contradicting experimental
results.   Thus, from the initial interview, she used as a criterion
the feel of the materials.   She retained this type of criterion illustrated by the outline 'what is cold, cools' or 'what is hot, heats', as
a method of explanation, up to the seventh session in spite of several
experiments invalidating her predictions and in spite of a short term
memory for certain results.   For example, she gave correctly the
materials which would keep ice frozen or water hot the longest, one
week after the experiment.   At this stage of the teaching (7th
session), the development in Marie-Noëlle of this idea had only reached
the stage of accumulating information without reorganising her thought;
this is what Rumelhart & Norman (1976) call 'the accretion mode of
learning'.

At the end, however, the development in Marie-Noëlle of the ideas of insulator and conductor could be seen. She had profoundly modified her ways of explaining (heat moves more or less easily through materials, depending on their properties) and cemented this through a new vocabulary (conductor, insulator). Instead of considering the sensation of touch, (the material is hot or cold), she referred to a property of heat, its speed of movement, thus Marie-Noëlle appeared to have reorganised her thoughts. In the terms of Rumelhart and Norman's theory of learning, she has restructured her thought on this concept.

Further, this development shows that in Marie-Noëlle, several types of interpretation co-exist. For example, the final test showed that the old explanatory scheme of analogy: 'Coffee pots keep the heat' could supplant the new method of reasoning in terms of heat transfer and that in spite of their contradiction, these two ways of explaining co-exist in Marie-Noëlle.

Conditions of learning:

This concept is most often taught by questions, put in general first of all by the teacher, but then rephrased by Marie-Noëlle for herself. This personal rephrasing assumes that the right learning conditions are available so that the child can take over the teaching role and ask herself questions about the concept being taught to her. This presupposes that the child must be sufficiently motivated and have an adequate intellectual development to be able to personally ask herself questions, or to restate the questions asked, in her own terms.

In order to answer these questions, the teaching sessions gave Marie-Noëlle the opportunity to carry out experiments, to discuss with other children and with the teacher, and to consider relevant information given by the teacher. The experiments carried out by Marie-Noëlle (7th session) were the occasion of a confrontation between her opinion (invalidated by the experiment) and the opinion of the teacher or another child (confirmed by the experiment). This stage seemed to us to be fundamental, the tension experienced by Marie-Noëlle had allowed her to develop and to reorganise her thoughts. This presupposes teaching conditions which supply the opportunity for this confrontation: this necessitates that, through the teaching, the child recognises an alternative explanation to her own. The teaching must, therefore, clearly give the necessary information, by experiments, explanations by the teacher, by discussions, by reference books, etc. The personality of the teacher must also allow him to accept the tension which is created, that is to say, allow the child to explain herself and to retain her point of view, without correcting her. The teacher must also be able to help the child to overcome these tensions.

It also assumes that the child must be capable of coping with the confrontation. This presupposes that she can make explicit her own interpretations (if they exist), and that she can retain them in order that they can be confronted with others. This has been the case for

Marie-Noëlle, in the context of the idea of conduction.

Marie-Noëlle's original ideas were very far from the proposed model. Moreover, they did not allow her to make correct predictions for the results of experiments proposed during the sessions. These sessions showed that these ideas have been an obstacle for Marie-Noëlle, coming in between the material which constitutes the object and its sensation of touch, and the use of the causal scheme, 'what is cold, cools' or 'what is hot, heats'. We have already met the same type of interpretation with other children (Tiberghien et al. 1978; Tiberghien, Delacôte, 1978).

It causes, as can be seen with Marie-Noëlle, a real obstacle to learning, which can, however, be overcome. However, it can be seen that even when the difficulty has been overcome, it still exists and perhaps it never really disappears. It is only necessary, thus, that each system of interpretation should be in 'its own place', that is to say that its utilisation, or non-utilisation, should be justified by relation to using the other scheme.

Link between development and the teacher's estimate:

In this article, we have only given Marie-Noëlle's development for the idea of conduction, which has been considerable. However, her ability to predict the final state after interaction between the systems has developed less. For example, when predicting the final temperature of a given mixture of warm and cold water, she used the stereotyped phrase 'The hottest wins'. This was the same during the initial interview, midway through the course and at the final interview. However, the course was clearly beneficial to Marie-Noëlle, even if she missed some of the aspects. In her case, the teacher's estimate is in agreement with Marie-Noëlle's evolution during the course.

II   The case of Isabelle

The teachers' viewpoint:

Isabelle was 13.3 at the beginning of the course. At the start of the year, all the teachers considered that Isabelle was mediocre and that she was slow but persistent in as much as she wanted her written work to be neat and tidy.

At the end of the year, the teachers thought her work was still of a mediocre standard, her French teacher, who was also in charge of art and craft, found that she had great difficulty in understanding and always needed support. In practical work she was careful, interested and creative. Isabelle often asked uninteresting questions in French and science, but none at all in maths. She took part in all the sessions but one.

E.P.L. test:

For conservation of weight and volume and differentiation between the two, Isabelle succeeded in the conservation of weight, but not of volume; she was thus at the concrete stage.

For the 3 colour permutation test, she was also at the concrete stage.

For the probability test, she was at an intermediate stage.

The initial interview:

1. Kinds of reasoning

Isabelle analysed some problems by picking out one characteristic of the object, such as thickness, solidity or hardness. She was thus more concerned with the material out of which the object was made, but she could also consider the entire object. This was not one sole characteristic, but in any case, she was imprecise. Isabelle connects this characteristic, which is of a mechanical order, with the possibility that cold or heat can go away. There is thus a causal relationship. Thus to keep an ice cube frozen, Isabelle chose a metal container:

'Because the cold lasts longer, it evaporates less, (the metal) it's harder, it's more solid.'

Isabelle analysed situations by making use of an entity (heat or cold) which is different from the objects and has the possibility of either remaining or going away. This can be seen in the preceding case. Isabelle also used the same method to explain why the handles of two spoons, one plastic, the other metal, whose ends are in hot water, were not equally hot.

'This metal spoon holds the heat, or even the cold, it keeps it.'

2. Representations of the idea

During the initial interview, Isabelle showed that she interpreted the phenomena shown to her in terms of an entity 'hot' or 'cold' (or even 'heat'), which could move. Thus, in relation to the two spoons placed in the hot water, she said:

'It's as if the heat comes up again...that the heat goes into the iron, goes up to the top...in the plastic it goes inside less.'

The heat is similarly distinct from the source. For example, in the case of the metallic bar, heated at one end by a camping gas flame:

'The flame gives off a bit of heat, that goes into the iron
which you put on it and then the heat goes up again.'

In these last two examples, the mode of heat transfer could be
more on the inside of the material. She even envisaged a different
mode of heat transfer depending on the material. However, when considering the case of the containers, Isabelle did not exactly define
the mode of transfer, but only suggested that the heat or cold could
stay or go away.

This sort of interpretation led Isabelle to believe that the
behaviour of metals was the same for heat or for cold.

The final interview:

1. Kinds of reasoning

In the majority of her replies, Isabelle considers one characteristic of the object (its material), with one property of heat or cold;
to go away, stay or scatter. It is the material which causes the
change in heat movement, for example:

Isabelle (talking about plastic): 'The cold stays in a
corner, then it can't go away; in aluminium it goes away
faster.'

2. Representations of the idea

This interview showed the mode of heat transfer considered by
Isabelle. She considers the heat and the cold as separate entities
to which she gives the property of being able to move, similar to that
of a fluid (it evaporates, spreads out). In the majority of cases,
Isabelle considers that this movement is made on the surface of the
material, and not at the interior. For example, in the case of an
ice cube, put in a metal container, she says:

'If you put an ice cube inside it, the cold scatters all
over the surface of the container, and the heat of the room
will go and touch all over the surface, so it will cool
down quicker.'

or, in the case of hot water:

'The heat scatters over all the surface and perhaps it evaporates
quickly.'

Then, when she was asked how a radiator can heat a whole room, she
said:

'This radiator, it's a source of heat, which produces heat
all the time and gives it off...It scatters all over the

302

room...it must come out somewhere...perhaps there are
holes.'

In this case, Isabelle postulated the existence of holes for the
heat to escape through, she could not envisage heat passing through
the metal of the radiator (this was not the case in the initial interview).

Isabelle thus considered that this movement on the surface was
made more or less well, according to the quality of the material.

'On the aluminium, the cold scatters much better than on
the plastic.'
'The heat goes away less (plastic container) than if it
were that (metal container).'

Thus the mode of transfer envisaged by Isabelle was that of an
entity, (similar to that of a fluid), which moved over the surface
more or less well, depending on the nature of the material.

Comparision of the interviews

1.   Reasoning type

The reasoning used by Isabelle had not fundamentally altered, in
the sense that she always connected one characteristic of the object
with the movement of the heat or the cold, this characteristic being
the cause of the displacement. However, the characteristic chosen by
Isabelle was different; instead of being the thickness or solidity,
at the final interview, she considered the nature of the material.

2.   Representations of the idea

Isabelle seemed to have slightly modified her ideas about conduction.

She had established a causal relationship between the nature of
the material and the possibility of heat or cold 'going off' or
'scattering (spreading out)'. In comparison, in the initial interview,
it was the thickness or solidity which was the cause.

She also considered, and at the final interview more accurately,
the movement of the heat or cold. However, in the initial interview,
Isabelle did not seem to have localised this movement to the surface
of the objects, which was the case in the final interview. In both
interviews, but more accurately in the final one, Isabelle gave heat
or cold the properties of a fluid, it evaporates and spreads out or
scatters.

Teaching sessions:

Description of child's behaviours

In the first two sessions, Isabelle carried out experiments to find out which container could keep ice frozen or water hot the longest. She made a correct classification in the test at the beginning of the second session (the cardboard container keeps heat better than a metal one). She said in explanation:

'Because if the ice is in the cardboard, the cold goes away less quickly.'

It seems interesting to note a typical reaction of Isabelle. During the session, her partner (who on that day was not Marie-Noëlle), said to her about the experiments they had performed:

'I think it's going to be the smallest (containers of the same material, similar shapes but different sizes) that the ice will melt first, or I don't know...I don't understand anything about it...There's something which takes the heat, that melts it quicker.'

Isabelle replied:

'We'll find out.'

This reply illustrates a relatively frequent attitude of Isabelle, consisting of not explaining her own point of view, but waiting for a good answer, which might be given by an experiment, or by someone else (teacher or pupil).

ii   During the 4th session, Marie-Noëlle and Isabelle were confronted with the problem of the different sensations to touch of a piece of cotton and a sheet of copper, one seeming hotter than the other. Isabelle explained:

'The cotton, well it catches a bit of heat...Maybe the heat goes in just a tiny bit...and then it doesn't get in there (copper), so it's cold.'

To which her partner, Marie-Noëlle objected.

'How do you think the heat can get inside the cotton?'

Isabelle:

"What I said, it doesn't go right inside, it just stays on top...so it doesn't touch the thermometer, it doesn't go deep inside.'

Then Marie-Noëlle said that Isabelle 'was a bit stupid, because if there is a little bit of heat, it will reach the thermometer, so it must be the material' (which causes the different sensation).

After a lively discussion, the teacher intervened to ask the children to explain their points of view. Isabelle did not mention hers, unlike Marie-Noëlle.

iii During the 7th session, the teacher asked once again the question of the sensation of touch. Marie-Noëlle, Isabelle's partner, restated that the different sensation was caused by the material. Isabelle also took this point of view; when the teacher asked her the question she replied:

'It's the material.'

It is during this session that for the first time Isabelle uses the verb 'to scatter (or to spread out)' in connection with the heat. In a discussion with a teacher and Marie-Noëlle about the comparison between copper and cotton which she had just heated, Isabelle said:

'The heat or the cold scatters much faster.'

There followed a discussion on the role of the extent of surface contact between the hot object and the room's air.

iv During the 8th session, the children had heated several metal sheets having very different heat conductivities. A general discussion took place, and one child explained the difference between the metals (one became hotter much quicker than the other);

'(it's caused by) the inside of the material...it (the heat) goes through it much quicker...that's to say, perhaps there are little holes which let the heat go through much quicker than the other one.'

Isabelle joined in later:

'There's the material or...it (heat)stays just in one place; the other one (on the other sheet), it (the heat) scatters over all the surface.'

A teacher then asked: 'On the surface, only the surface?' Several children replied 'In all the sheet', but Isabelle no longer joined in this discussion.

v In the final test of the 11th session, Isabelle chose a wooden container to keep soup hot longest, because:

'It's because of the material, all the materials can't work the same way, and...I think the heat won't go as fast as in the other materials.'

To the question asking her to choose between several explanations of the different perception on touching metal and polystyrene, she chose the statement 'it is not the same material'.

Comments

Modes of Learning:

Throughout the period, Isabelle has shown a certain stability. Her interpretation, considering the possibility that the heat or the cold will go away, has not changed. Her interpretation, expressed after the 3rd session, that the heat or the cold 'spread out' over the surface is maintained to the end.

Thus Isabelle had initially a type of interpretation of heat transfer approximating to a correct qualitative one: however, at the end of the session, she is suggesting an incorrect model, which she had expressed near the beginning (3rd session) and that she had kept just to the end. Her interpretation is not correct to the extent that she did not recognise conduction, that is to say the passage of heat to the interior of materials. Moreover, she never used the word conductor or insulator (even during the sessions), which would have allowed her to categorise the materials without difficulty.

If we refer to Rumelhart and Norman, learning of this concept of conduction could have been for Isabelle the occasion for a 'tuning'. In the beginning, transfer was not localised (or localised in the inside of the material). This model was refined during the period, the heat moves 'on the surface of the objects', but as can be seen, during the process of adaptation an interference probably occurred with a fluid model of heat which does not allow conduction to be imagined. As all the thermal contacts are superficial, there are no evident experimental means for preventing this interpretation (heat spreads out on the surface).

Learning conditions:

These conditions are similar to those for Marie-Noëlle, except in that which concerns Isabelle personally, her relations to other people, her initial level, her personality (which affects her inter-action with the totality of the teaching).

These sessions show that when Isabelle had rephrased for herself the questions asked, she has rarely confronted her point of view with that of the teacher or of other children. She has, in fact, neither made explicit her point of view (for example, in the 2nd session), nor accepted the confrontation. In the last case, she took the point of view of her questionner, for example, she took over the opinion of Marie-Noëlle: she says that the different touch sensation of objects

306

at the same temperature was due 'to the material'. Alternatively, she kept her point of view, refusing to join in the discussion, for example in the 8th session, concerning whether the heat spreads over the surface or in the inside of objects.

However, the conditions are such that the teaching has not sufficiently aided Isabelle to comprehend and first of all to realise the difference between her point of view and the correct interpretation. This requires the teacher to pay considerable attention to what the child says.

Isabelle is readily influenced and not sure of herself. She changes her point of view, or at least what she says, as soon as she has the impression that she is wrong. This attitude does not encourage her to maintain her own point of view in order to contrast it with another.

The initial interpretation of Isabelle, little different from the correct interpretation, allows her to predict correctly the majority of the experiments suggested. Thus the contradiction between her own interpretation and the proposed model could only have arisen during discussions (and some experimentations). This is less easy than when the contrast arises as the result of experimental evidence.

Link between development and the teachers' estimate:

The teachers' estimate from the point of view of school results is generally poor. This estimate does not agree with the level of interpretation given during the initial and even the final interviews of Isabelle. Those are better than those given by several of the children interviewed. On the other hand, when she will express them, the intuition of Isabelle as to the interpretation of phenomena is often good, and in any case interesting. This estimate agrees with one aspect of Isabelle's behaviour which became apparent during the sessions (Marie-Noëlle often decides instead of Isabelle; during the discussions, the vocabulary of Isabelle is not precise).

Conclusion

The analysis of the learning of the concept of conduction has been made using the categories of modes of learning defined by Rumelhart and Norman. One of the children, Marie-Noëlle, first of all proceeded by accumulating knowledge (accretion mode). She has then restructured her thoughts. In her first interpretations, she used a causal relationship between the given objects (the material of the object) and the sensation to touch for the object (hot or cold). In her final interpretation, she used one property (connected to the heat) of the given objects. The material is a conductor or an insulator of heat. This mode of learning consists in restructuring her thoughts. For these two modes, it can be seen that in Marie-Noëlle, several types of interpretation co-exist, even after the restructuring.

Marie-Noëlle retains her original interpretation which she uses in certain situations. Another child, Isabelle, is an example of the case where learning has occurred through 'tuning' of her type of initial interpretation to that suggested during the sessions, in so far as they have been more or less compatible. When this is not the case, Isabelle has modified her initial interpretation so that she could predict the majority of the experimental results, but introducing incorrect points of view (heat is considered as a fluid, which moves over the surface). Isabelle thus illustrates the case where learning develops adaptation of 'helpful' methods of explanation. That is to say, they allow her to predict correctly in the majority of cases, and to give a correct if rather imprecise interpretation of observations. However, these explanations are false and will probably necessitate a later restructuring.

These sessions have particularly indicated the necessary conditions for learning:

It is important that the child takes over for himself (or takes the initiative) to ask himself personally questions about the inter-pretation of phenomena presented during the sessions.

It is important that the child makes explicit his personal interpretations and confronts them with those proposed (by the teacher, the other children, documents...) or also indicated by the experimental results.

The teaching must allow suitable opportunities for this to occur. In particular, the subject studied must be clearly explicit, and the questions raised. The contents and the organisation of the teaching must allow replies to the questions asked. The means to be used are not limited, those which we have used during the sessions are not the only possible ones. The means could certainly vary considerably for the same subject depending on the people concerned, the material conditions, etc...(these could vary from the subject and the experiments chosen by the children to the problems suggested and resolved, even verbally, by the teacher). However, whatever the means, the teacher must give the children the opportunity to make their own interpretations explicit, to accept them and to try to understand them, which implies that he must not impose his own. He must then help the children to confront the different points of view.

The 'internal' conditions of learning must allow the child's personality and mental development to be such that he can ask questions by himself, give his points of view and confront them with other people's points of view.

This study allows us to know some aspects of mental development of a child thanks to the E.P.L. test. At the present stage of our analysis, the link between the test scores and the results of the learning sessions are not simple. Children having good results, even in one case exceptional ones, have achieved after the sessions types of interpretation which are less good than children with test scores which are on the average. The exception has been the case where a mathematical version of a situation has been given, then the child with exceptional test scores was the only one to interpret the phenomenon rapidly.

These sessions have allowed us to indicate the children's representations and in what sense they can be obstacles to learning. For example, the use of the causal scheme: 'what is hot, heats' or 'what is cold, cools' coming from the touch sensation of the objects at room temperature, can be an obstacle.

On the other hand, these sessions indicate that some children refuse to accept the mode of heat transfer by conduction. The transfer of heat to the interior of a solid object causes a difficulty (some children suggest holes or envisage movement over the surface). Another difficulty was that some children considered heat as a fluid, this is perhaps linked to the problem of accepting heat conduction.

Acknowledgements

I wish to express my gratitude to Mr. Gaucher, Director of the 'Centre de Documentation Pédagogique' at La Rochelle, and to Mr. Fremond and Mr. Batanis. They helped in carrying out this experiment by allowing the use of the television studio and of material, and by taking a technical part in the recording of the teaching sessions.

Without the contribution of Mrs. Boulier, who taught all the sessions, we could never carry out such a work. We gratefully acknowledge her friendly cooperation.

EDUCATION BASED ON A NEW CONCEPT OF TEACHING IN CHEMISTRY

H.H. ten Voorde*

Teaching situations as a source of didactical research

In my capacity as a chemistry teacher on a pre-university level, I have repeatedly been confronted with a communication gap brought about by a lack of overlap between

- on the one side the conversational idiom employed by my pupils when discussing 'chemical' phenomena, and

- on the other side the professionally bound idiom, which I, being a chemically qualified person, was bent on using when I spoke (as a teacher) about the 'same' chemical topics.

This experience has urged me to seek ways of bridging the communication gap. Here I draw on my own teaching/research experience reported elsewhere (ten Voorde, 1977).

In a lesson the pupils have carried out a task, in which they had to give an account of what happens as soon as a piece of thin sheet copper is put into sulphur fumes. Simultaneously they had to check if the observed chemical reaction was of the synthetic type, the decomposure type or a combination of the two. I have recorded the following statements, which are a part of my discussion with the pupils.

Protocol 1   (In all the protocols included in the paper the lines
              are numbered consecutively to allow reference in the
              text. The letters T and P denote teacher and pupil.)

1 T   What have you observed?
2 P   It grew holes.
3 P   Turned black, later on there was fire in the fumes.

---

*The authors of the following two papers have been involved in a project developing science teaching materials which place an emphasis on the role of pupil discussion in learning. In their papers, both authors analyse the discussion that takes place in science classrooms between pupils and teachers and between pupils themselves. From the analysis they indicate the change in level of understanding by pupils produced in the course of the discussion. The first author illustrates this with examples from chemistry, the second from physics.(Ed.)

```
4   P   The copper burned.
5   P   Symptoms of fire.
        (...)

7   T   What happened?
8   P   Oxygen was formed.
        (...)

10  P   It could have formed, couldn't it?
11  T   Out of what?
12  P   Out of copper and the sulphur fumes.
```

In my participation as a teacher (statement 7 and 11), I viewed symptoms of fire as the result of the synthesis occuring between copper and sulphur. A pupil reaches the conclusion 'Oxygen was formed' (statement 8) putting the initial aim of the discussion out of reach.

In this teaching situation the name 'copper' signifies a simple substance to me. To these pupils it could mean a mixture or a composed substance. As teacher, I was confronted with the teaching problem: how do I go about getting across to this pupil that oxygen cannot have been formed in this instance? To that end the first thing I had to know was: What brought about that conclusion for that pupil? In other words: What is he talking about or what reality exists for him?

Didactical interpretation

The development of chemical language (idioms related to chemistry, as e.g. the name 'copper') has an important bearing on chemical education. The aim is then to bring about the significations of a chemical idiom by changes in usage of pupils. This cultivation of idiomatic terms I call idiomcultivation. The teaching situation illustrated by protocol 1 I will refer to as misunderstanding-one-another. Analysing this misunderstanding, we first observe that teacher and pupils can use the same words (e.g. 'copper'), but they may denote different things. The point at issue in such a conversation is different for the teacher and the pupils. Such a point at issue I will refer to as the subject. From a didactic point of view therefore it will be worthwhile to distinguish 'subject for the pupil' from 'subject for the teacher'.

This difference becomes evident by focussing our attention on the choice of other words, used by teacher and pupils in connection with a word such as 'copper'. The teacher will use a word such as 'copper' in different contexts to the pupils. These differences in context denote differences in subjective reality. For teacher and pupils we can notice different language-subject-relations, and often we can notice such differences too between pupils participating in a discussion.

When mutual understanding arises between some of the participants in a discussion, we can say that they are forming a group. If we take the meaning of 'participating in a discussion' seriously, we may consider the participants (group), the language and the subject as 'moments' of the discussion.

I shall refer to the systematic investigation of the process of teaching as didactical research. Situations in which misunderstandings arise between pupils, or between pupil and teacher, have proved to be of great value for research.

Didactical analysis of language fields

The following protocol will indicate that the combination of words used by a teacher or a pupil plays an important role in getting a lasting conversation.

Protocol 2

> *(The aforementioned teaching problem was a challenge to me to try to reach mutual language-subject-relations with my pupils in the following lesson. To this end I attempted to shape the conversation and thereby give it a lasting character by remaining keen for those moments where the conversation lingers. On noticing such moments of misunderstanding-one-another, I attempted to give the conversation new incentive by means of additional questions. In doing this, I tried to turn the reaction between copper and sulphur into a synthesis reaction as an issue for the pupils. The following fragment constitutes a part of that conversation.)*

1 T *Heat is produced. Now we go back to that copper sheet (leaf) and the sulphur fumes. You can see there, that it starts flowing, what's your conclusion?*

2 P_1 *Heat is necessary.*

5   *(silence)*

   T *Why is heat necessary then? Why do you conclude that heat is necessary?*

     (silence)

   P_2 *Well it can't just start glowing, can it?*

10 P_3 *Heat is necessary and heat is being produced.*

   (other pupil): Heat is necessary.

   (Now, T understands these pupils).

   T *Yes, heat is necessary to make the piece of copper glow.*

14   *Where is the heat coming from?*

T(6/7) is in a teaching situation where he realises that his language-subject-relation has not materialised for P_1. T's questioning (3) creates a different language-subject-relation for P_1(4). With the help of other pupils (9-11) a mutual language-subject-relation (12-14) originates for T and P_1, T has discovered T(12) that his choice of words was the cause of P_1's language-subject-relation. The words 'starts glowing' drew the use of the words 'heat is necessary' out.

Such a relation between words, I refer to as a language field. Either a careless choice of words by T or the use of an inaccessible language field was the cause of the misunderstanding here. Certain language fields represent a certain semantic structure such that in the formation of a scientifically disciplined idiom, words out of everyday idiom still remain important. Being mindful of language fields also implies calling our attention to scientific idiom that penetrated into our daily speech. In differentiating between suitable and misleading language fields the teacher is able to offer scientific idiom in such a way as to build up the intended context. By didactical research of language fields we can retrace the significance of words from their context. Changes in language-subject-relations, that are teaching results, can become relatable as a result of such a didactical language field analysis. Possibilities are then created for constructing a curriculum based on the practice of teaching.

Raising the discussion level in teaching

Protocol 3

> *(In connection with the previous excerpt T now tries to get his pupils to formulate the origins of fire symptoms as arising solely from the disappearance of substances present originally and the creation of the product of the reaction. This 'dialogue' drags on with difficulty. After including the burning of a piece of charcoal, with which his pupils are already familiar, in a comparative discussion, he returns to the reaction between copper and sulphur.)*

1   *T*   *If you'll at least cooperate, do you share...then you'll know it all right.*

    P   *Could it be possible, that it is only because of the contact?*
5   *...Just like pouring water on unslaked lime, that that also gets hot?*

    T   *There too, heat is being produced. When water comes into contact with unslaked lime, or water with white copper sulphate. So solely by virtue of two substances coming into contact*
10   *with one another, heat can be produced too. That might be happening here and then you can also compare it to the burning of that piece of charcoal?*

    (...)

```
    P   Simply that that copper starts glowing (as a result of
15      the contact).

    T   So that copper, that piece of copper starts glowing
        because you have contact between...?

18  P   Between the sulphur fumes and...copper.
```

During a troublesome part of the discussion T(1/2) a pupil P(3-5)
is able to combine the intention of T with her own experience with
'heat of reaction' in relation to her own words. She is able to
point out the subject (second 'that' in P) in the words she has at
her own disposal ('contact'). In such cases I will speak of <u>direct
experience</u>.

In this example of direct experience it can be shown that the
productive part of a (teaching) discussion consists of pupils speaking
and listening on the grounds of personal experiences. They can express
those experiences in their own words and thereby contribute to the
conversation.

P(4) raises the question of 'contact'. This question draws a
third reaction ('water with unslaked lime') into the comparative discussion ('copper in sulphur fumes' and 'charcoal in oxygen'). In
these three cases P recognises the same phenomenon. In addition to
this T suggests it to be a rule and mentions a fourth reaction to
stress the point T(7). The discussion progresses - we can say - in a
productive way. This productivity is clearly the consequence of a
tangible event ('starts to glow', 'keeps glowing'). Because of P's
contribution a new mutual language-subject-relation is brought about,
expressing itself in the expressions 'heat is...produced' and 'through
contact'. These expressions, which I call <u>descriptive terms</u> enable the
discussion partners (P and T) to discuss a <u>new mutual issue</u> in previously non-existent context. This change of context I shall refer
to as a <u>raising of level</u>.

<u>Language development in raising the discussion level in teaching</u>

A raising of level, as pointed out in the previous paragraph, is
on the one hand prepared by means of a transition from the conversational language to a basic level and on the other hand this in itself
prepares for a rise to a theoretical level.

a.   Drawing attention to a (chemical) context

We cannot start with chemical reactions because of the misunderstanding we already mentioned. First pupils have to pay attention to
individual substances, each with its own properties. This is a context
within which cultivation of chemical idiom can take place. Such a
beginning in teaching chemistry is distinguishable because of the
absence of reasoning by means of which a (chemical) event can be
described as 'the disappearance and appearance of individual substances'.

It is a period in which the 'conversation of substance' is self-evident as can be derived from the use of language fields. This can also be seen in the next part of a discussion.

Protocol 4

> *(Pupils have filled a test tube as follows: on the bottom a layer of carbon tetrachloride, then a layer of water and finally a layer of oil. First, they must predict the appearance of the contents of the tube after shaking. They expect the return of the three separate layers. The following discussion takes place after they have shaken the tube and they have verbalised their observations by 'It's been mixed' and 'The oil's gone to the bottom'.)*

1 P_1 *D'you know what happened? The carbon tetrachloride has dissolved, for the most part, the oil and that's why it sank. So the carbon tetrachloride is heavy, isn't it?*

    P_2 *Here's a bit more oil.*

5 P_1 *So it's heavier than oil, so that carbon tet is, is sort of, well sort of stuck to that oil and that's taking it down with it.*

    P_3 *The oil and the carbon tet mix, but because of the weight of the carbon tet (a pupil remarks: specific*
10   *gravity) it then sinks right down to the bottom.*

The experiment has taken place in an unexpected manner - there is only one surface boundary visible instead of two. This poses for them a problem of the sort: How is this possible? They seek an explanation for the presence of carbon tetrachloride and oil beneath the water. Their language shows two distinct signs:

- An intuitive-tangible explanation is presented in P(5-7). The expression 'the oil' we can interpret as 'the amount of oil'.

- Although the amount of tetra and of oil isn't visibly present, the conservation of these governs their speech ('...that carbon tet...stuck to that oil...'). The fact that the value of the specific gravity of the lower liquid differs from the change, specifically, as the disappearance of the substances oil and carbon tet and the appearance of a different substance. Then another explanation could have been possible, which cannot be ranked as intuitive-tangible, but one that would have been based on agreements within the group concerning the properties of substances.

b.   The origin of a descriptive net of relations

Three aspects characterise the first rise in level:
1) the analysis, 2) the subject change and 3) the disciplination.

315

As an illustration I have chosen a group discussion that lasted nearly half an hour (the teacher was not present). This discussion started after performing an experiment in which steam passes over heated magnesium until signs of fire are present; gases at the exhaust catch fire. The questions in the instructions for the pupils were aimed at the pupils' tendencies to arrange reactions according to the categories of synthesis and decomposition. They have investigated the combustibility of hydrogen and the reduction of copper oxide with hydrogen. They have also been able to experience that the latter reaction belongs to a different category. In order to formulate a description of the observed phenomena, the group is looking for distinct properties of individual substances so that the names of such substances can be used in the description.

1. Analysis:

Protocol 5

1   Le   *So then...but...so if you then...but magnesium also ignites outside of the tube with just oxygen.*

    Wi   *Sure, I know.*

    Le   *Well, here we only have magnesium and no oxygen.*

5   Wi   *Sure.*

    Le   *Sure, and just using hydrogen.*

    Wi   *Sure...but now we have...well...I thought so too, but that lot's not going to believe that.*

    Ka   *What? That hydrogen...if you ask me the magnesium*
10   *ignites because it gets heated.*

    Wi   *I don't think so...only because magnesium...because the hydrogen's there...and that hydrogen is heated.*

    Le   *Right, you need that heat...to get the hydrogen...*

15   Ka   *Let's start off with...*

    Ro   *For pity's sake, you don't get hydrogen that way.*

    Le   *...and then you get magnesium...but I really can't say how...but I'll assume so anyhow, because Wi said: if you heat steam, you get hydrogen?*

20   *Right?*

    Wi   *Sure, if you heat steam, you get hydrogen...*

    Ro   *If you ask me...no, I don't think so...*

24   Le   *And when hydrogen...then you get gas...*

During the emission of the bright light in the test tube, the magnesium changes into a solid white substance. These pupils call this 'ignition of magnesium' because they had learned to recognise that phenomena Le(1-3). The absence of oxygen Le(4), Wi(5) imposes a problem that does not allow them to label the events with the substance names 'oxygen', 'magnesium' and 'ignited magnesium'. They do not reject this problem, but instead they see it as a necessary step to arrive at a correct description. Together they search for distinct signs for the origin of the emitted light, which to them signifies 'heat of reaction'.

Two changes are discerned here, the 'appearance of hydrogen' and 'ignition of magnesium'. Le(14) considers the heat of the latter reaction as heat of action for the first reaction. The appearance of hydrogen means the 'disappearance of something else'. I call this conception of reactions a relation. The heat of action and heat of reaction are, as far as Le is concerned, certain signs of such a relation. Because Le - regardless of which reaction - has learned to specify chemical reactions as 'disappearance and appearance of individual substances'. Statements such as 'the appearance of hydrogen' and 'the ignition of magnesium' have some relations in a descriptive net of relations. In this manner pupils search for descriptive signs by connecting their experiences with this 'experiment' to earlier experience Le(1), Wi(5). In being objective about their own deductions they are able to describe the unfamiliar experience with previously mentioned relations, such as 'disappearance of steam' and 'appearance of hydrogen' resulting from the heating of steam. In this combined (collective) explanation (analysis) they test newly found experiences with familiar, labelled experiences (facts). However, in this analysis it is Le (17-19) who notices a contradiction in his net of relations between descriptive terms:

-   heat of action is needed to get hydrogen (line 12);

-   this can be the heat of reaction if the event originally labelled 'glowing' can also be labelled 'combustion' Le(1-2);

-   but then we'll need oxygen, which is absent Le(4), Wi(11-12).

This contradiction creates the desire for a new point of view in order to arrive at a correct description, not only with respect to agreements within the group, but also with a correct, consistent chain of reasoning.

2.   Subject change:

Le is looking for reasons enabling him to consider steam as a source of oxygen. Ka and Ro regard the steam as a mixture of water vapour and oxygen (Ro: otherwise it wouldn't boil). Wi considers it possible that the oxygen gets into the tube from the outside somehow. Despite the difference between the individual pupils' opinions, they continue talking and listening to each other.

317

Protocol 6

1 Le ...and hydrogen with uh...oxygen...will...then you get...
       knalgas (= detonating gas), wasn't that the stuff that
       went bang? (...)

   Le It says here...hydrogen is a decomposition product of
5   water (Le is referring to a text of a task set in the
       previous lesson)...so you have steam...and then you
       decompose that...

   Wi Sure.

   Le ...and you decompose the steam in hydrogen and...in
10   other substances.

   Wi Right, that's what I thought.

   Le So now I wonder...in this case...if hydrogen is de-
       composed into steam...now that hydrogen can be
       decomposed out of that steam by heating it...okay
15   so far?...Isn't that so?

16   (silence)

In contrast to the other pupils, Le arrives at a connection between 'appearance of hydrogen' and 'disappearance of hydrogen' in the
experiment he just finished (see protocol 5, Le(14) and protocol 6,
Le (1-3)), in which oxygen is needed for the latter case. Besides
that Le includes Le(4-10):

-    a chosen description view, specifically, arranging reactions
     according to the number of substances disappearing and
     appearing;

-    agreement made concerning the choice of words, to be
     specific,'decomposition reactions', and

-    the thereby relevant indications, out of one substance we get two.

Thus Le develops a reasoning within a descriptive net of relations.

Ka, Ro and Wi continue searching for a description of the events
along the lines of a simultaneous occurrence of two distinct reactions:
ignition of magnesium, with the necessary oxygen coming from outside,
and appearance (evolution) of hydrogen when heating steam. The heat
of the first reaction causes the second reaction.

Le on the other hand, is seeking a description that combines decomposition with snythesis, not being bothered by restrictions to certain
reaction-participants. It is this change in the language-subject-
relation or change in perceptiveness, that I refer to as: subject
change in favour of a descriptive level.

3. Disciplination:

The term 'decomposition product of water' is an indication to Le
for the kind of demands that must be made on the language of a descriptive level: no contradiction between the words employed (protocol 6,
4-7 and 12-15). Because of this, the earlier experiences with the
decomposition of steam into 'detonating gas' gain a new perspective
for Le, as can be derived from Le's statement sometime later on in
the discussion:

> 'Well...isn't just possible that when steam is heated...not
> ...yes...of course...that's it...that's it...it's just
> possible...on heating steam one gets hydrogen and one gets
> oxygen...isn't that the way it goes?

He chooses that reaction as a descriptive view for a correct, factual
description of a relation. The other participants can't (as yet)
accept this as a useful point of view and ask Le to 'prove it'. In
this moment of the conversation Le argues as follows:

Protocol 7

1 *Le That mixture is created instantly...otherwise you could*
       say: on heating steam you get hydrogen...
   (...)

   Le And when that hydrogen meets oxygen, then only...

5 *(...)*

   Le We said so ourselves...on heating steam that knalgas is
7   *formed...and that knalgas is hydrogen plus oxygen.*

The statement Le (1-2) indicates that Le wants to give a correct
description in which previous agreements do not give rise to a contradiction within the terms used Le(6-7). Here again misunderstanding is
possible! Le is not yet able to justify his choice of viewpoint. His
viewpoint 'decomposition followed by synthesis' in describing a relation
between two reactions is clearly a different one to the relation the
other participants are after. They do seek agreement with personal
experience, but as yet do not associate the consequences involved in
using a descriptive term such as 'decomposition product'. On the other
hand Le does make this demand. He is disciplining to another context,
in which the use of controlled language is expected on a descriptive
level. That demand for a consistent use of words has his priority
above the fact that there was no bang audible in the tube.

c. The rise to a theoretical level

For Le the individual relations between terms form descriptive
realities in a consistent chain of reasoning. The reasoning shows
signs of a concentric (closed) descriptiveness. The systematic
approach remains an implicit one because justification of the descriptive views hasn't taken place as yet. If Le were to objectively

319

view this concentricity (in this case its satisfying character) by means of the separately termed relations 'disappear' and 'appear' then again subject change will take place. We could then refer to a transition to a <u>theoretical level</u>, because the discussion would then involve the logical relations between descriptive concepts (realities) in a net of relations. In that context the word 'element' can finally function in a chemical idiom. This type of transition is made by Le a few months later.

EDUCATION BASED ON A NEW CONCEPT OF TEACHING IN PHYSICS

P. Vegting

In our course we want to begin from the experiences of pupils.

In our experiences as teachers we discovered that discussions between teachers and pupils are unsuccessful because they do not understand each other and because teachers often do not observe this lack of understanding, for instance: they are not aware of the pupil's alternative conceptions.

By analysing protocols it has been evident to us that these educational discussions (and thus learning) may arise when tasks are sequenced in a certain way. This is also facilitated by discussions in small groups: pupils can argue in their own language and one can see how pupils are giving each other arguments, criticising each other's contribution.

Following this procedure it is possible to trace the change in pupils' thinking from an initial naive position to a more analytical physical way of viewing phenomena. The naive position is often characterised by alternative conceptions held by pupils, a non-analytical and ad hoc way of describing events and inconsistent reasoning. In the learning situation pupils can come to a more physical way of seeing and analysing events, and achieve a greater consistency in their reasoning.

I illustrate this with excerpts from two teaching sequences. In both cases the excerpt is divided into three parts:

1. Description of the pupils before teaching.
2. Part of the discussion of the pupils.
3. Description of the pupils after teaching.

By comparing 1 and 3 the results of the teaching can be seen.

<u>Excerpt 1 : circular motion</u>

Part 1:

Pupils often say: there is a centrifugal force, not a centripetal force.

In this lesson the pupils try to discover that rotation needs a centripetal force. Two experiments are used:

1. A rectangular container is half filled with water, a pupil pulls the container. The water goes down on the side where the pupil pulls. (see fig.1)

2. A container is put on a horizontal turntable, the turntable is rotated. The water goes down in the 'inside bend'.(see fig.2)

The question now is 'In what direction is the force working'?

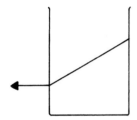   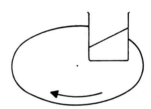

Figure 1   Figure 2

1 T *The issue is in what direction is the force working?*

   A *The water goes outwards.*

   A *In what direction does the force work?*

   S *The force works outwards.*

5 A *Here, it says: when you pull at this side...the water went down at the side where you were pulling.*

   - *When the force is working outward then the water goes up at the outside.*

   E *But this is turning, isn't it? It turns and pulling is in one direction, isn't it?*

A does not see the relation of (1) and (2), and is bound to what she now sees: the water goes outward, so the force is outward. E sees a 'rotation force'.

We call this the basic level: pupils do not see relations and

321

are bound by observation and action.

Part 2:

A   *No! It's silly, I don't see it; when you turn, then the force is outward. But when you pull at that container then the water goes down.*

E   *But to pull is another force than to turn, isn't it?*

10 T   *Yes.*

A   *But when the force goes outward then the water must go down at the outside?*

S   *So there is a force going inward?*

E   *No! The water is swinging outward; now, and the force comes from inside and the water is swinging outward.*

15 A   *But, when here is the turntable and on this side it's lower than there...*

A   *Then you must pull at this side.*

A   *Now, then the force is directed inward.*

18 E   *Yes.*

T   *But how does it come about that if you should sit on that turntable, as it were, that you should have felt that force works outward.*

20 A   *Because it wants to move on.*

The contribution of the teacher is to give tasks: to relate (1) and (2). Now we see that pupils, especially E(18) find the solution. (This is only a short part of the discussion.)

Part 3:

A   *That's the same as we had here: <u>the action force goes inward, but the reaction force goes outward.</u>*

E   *How do you explain that the water in the container goes up in one direction? In doing so think about the explanation concerning the erosion in the curve of a river. (task)*

A   *No, the water wants to go to the outside of the wheel, but it can't go further and <u>therefore it piles itself up</u>.*

E   *Oh, yes, then it piles itself up.*

25 E   *Now (reads the task) give an explanation why you feel a force when you take a curve, for instance, in a car.*

S   *<u>Because you want to move on.</u>*

E   *Yes, you yourself want to move on, and therefore you are*
    pressed outward.

A   *What do you call that force?*

S   *Gravitation force.*

30 A   *No, counter acting force.*

E   *Reaction force.*

After this discussion they are able to make relations as we see in
Part 3. Compare the statements of the pupils before teaching (what
we call the basic level) and after teaching (the descriptive level).

Excerpt 2 : the descent of a parachutist

Part 1:

At first the pupils had the task of designing vectors in the
case of a parachutist who first is in free fall, then opens
the parachute (deceleration) and then falls in uniform motion.

In the last case nearly all pupils say:

'the force downwards is bigger than the force upwards,
because the downward force must overcome the upward force'.

Now comes the following task.

Assertion I

Somebody says that by uniform motion the force downwards is
bigger than the counterworking force up from the air under the parachute. You have to overcome that counterworking force don't you?
Perhaps you said that too.

Assertion II

Look at foregoing tasks: If there is only a weak force working,
then there must be acceleration.

Are both assertions I and II in harmony with each other, or do
they contradict. If yes, explain that and try to solve the problem.

Pupil S had the opinion that assertion II is right, E that I is
the right one. E even adds an argument:

32 *'Equal is not possible because then the parachutist would*
    stand still in the air and that is not possible. There will
    always be a bigger counteraction downwards, because the
    earth has gravitational force. According to me, that's
    like that, isn't it?

Part 2:

The discussion continues without the students convincing each other. Then S enters the discussion with an example of her own:

S *When I lift up a pencil, then there is no force.*

   When I let the pencil fall, <u>that cannot fall in uniform motion</u>.

E <u>*Of course then there is a force*</u>.

35 S *These forces <u>may be</u> equal because it goes by <u>degrees</u> you see, because there is no acceleration or deceleration. When I do like this (acceleration) then the force upwards is bigger.*

E *(S is displaying a uniform motion, with a pencil). No, now the force upwards is bigger.*

S *No, in this case...*

A <u>*Like with the bicycle*</u>, *there you did not need force when you remained bicycling in uniform motion.*

   Now you don't need force to keep it in uniform motion. It is like that, isn't it?

T *You said before.*

   When I lift up that table then I must overcome the counteraction. You are right in a certain sense, but at the same moment is that force that you use bigger, and you try to overcome the counteraction of the table, what moment <u>are you doing that</u>?

40 S *At the <u>moment</u> I lift the table.*

T *At the moment...Yes.*
   It's not so when you are lifting the table?

S *No, not then...*

T *Then it's equal in your opinion.*
   When are they not equal?

A *When it's on the ground.*

45 T *Yes?*

A <u>*When you try to lift it*</u>.

T *Yes.*

E <u>*But when once it is in the air, then it's equal, Oh yes*</u>!

A property of the descriptive level is giving examples of one's own (pencil and table). Now S can distinguish: coming into motion from remaining into uniform motion, an argument that convinces E.

Part 3:

They are now able to see relationships: deceleration is a kind of acceleration:

A *It's curious, isn't it, if there is a decelerated motion, that's an acceleration, that's an accelerated motion...*

50 E *Yes, but <u>they do call that decelerated</u>.*

They can solve the parachutist problem:

51 A *Because the motion is uniform and the forces are equal.*

They see the relation with friction:

52 M *No, of course, if that ball rolls on a smooth road, then will it ever stop?*

- *Of course, it will stop.*

A *But if there is no friction.*

55 E *There is always counteraction.*

- *Then there is always counteraction.*

S *It will always stop.*

A *No, if there <u>should be</u> no counteraction.*

59 E *<u>If there wasn't any counteraction</u>, <u>then it wouldn't stop</u>.*

The pupils then continued to solve a problem about space-travellers and the constant remaining speed of the earth, also relating it to centripetal forces.

Notice that the teacher can contribute to the discussion of the pupils because he tries to speak the language of the pupils. In both excerpts we see a similar process: from the non-analytical <u>basic level</u> with alternative conceptions and without far reaching <u>relations</u> to the analytical <u>descriptive level</u> with relations and physical concepts.

Discussion

The discussion was concerned mainly with the aims and purposes of classroom based studies, their methodology and its relationship to theory. It became clear that a distinction has to be made between two different kinds of research, that concerned with general cognitive development which could, in principle, take place 'in the classroom' and that which seeks to elucidate the ways in which children learn in the classroom. Contributions from the floor reinforced Watson's view that the former was not possible because of the complexity of the classroom; the discussion concerned itself with the latter. Several people pointed out that, in research of this kind, to remove the teacher is to invalidate the whole exercise.

A number of people felt that Delacôte had been too dismissive about the process-product style of research and that its value had to be considered in relation to the intentions of the researcher.

It was suggested that it is important to attack clearly defined problems and that neglect of this point had led to much classroom research being 'a lot of methodology looking for a problem'. It was felt that Delacôte's problem of how a single child's ideas change when he is taught something was clearly defined. It was pointed out that a criticism of a type of research in the area was that investigators had obtained information about pupils' misconceptions without records of the teacher's treatment of the topic and what actually happened in the classroom. Delacôte said that his own research programme was trying to look at:

a. the structures of children's schemes,

b. how the schemes changed during and after teaching,

c. the conditions under which the teaching took place which were related to the schemes.

The discussion on methodology and its connection to theory ranged widely and the writer has felt it helpful to construct a crude model to help represent it.

Much of the discussion can be conceptualised as being about the relationships between the various aspects identified in the diagram and whether the aspects themselves are correct. The numbers in the diagram refer to the following points made in discussion.

1. Methodology must be part of the theory.

2. Research in this field does not have to move between paradigms but could take lessons from one and use them in another. An example given was the sensitivity involved in the interpretative-ethnographic approach.

3. The crucial issue in this type of research is what can be considered as facts. Delacôte commented that, to him, the problem was trying to make sense of the data and the reverse problem of collecting data of which sense could be made. This, he felt, required a theory of the learning process.

4. The process by which the researcher becomes informed was also suggested as important. All research involves filtering of information and this filtering should be considered as an inherent part of the methodology and should be made explicit in the communication with others.

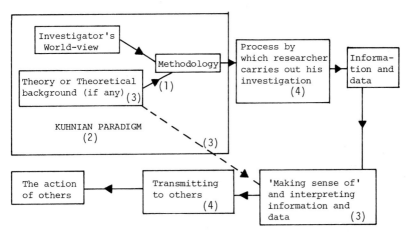

The paper by Tiberghien, who works in Delacôte's group, was naturally the one which related most closely to the issues raised in the discussion. It emerged that the science course upon which Tiberghien's research was focusing was being specifically designed to include experimental tasks which would introduce conflicts with the children's incorrect conceptual schemes. It seemed that this was a constraint on the research which should have been brought out clearly in the paper and that, in general, in classroom research where constraints are imposed, these need to be made explicit.

The work presented by ten Voorde and Vegting has as its main motivation curriculum development. The discussion was curtailed by lack of time so that its relationship to the other papers could not really be explored.

SOME THEORETICAL CONSIDERATIONS AND EXPERIENCES RELATED TO RESEARCH
AND DEVELOPMENTS IN THE TEACHING OF MATHEMATICS AND SCIENCE

Leif Lybeck

Abstract

The theoretical base of the research approach in Science and
Mathematics Education at Göteborg has evolved. It has emerged as
an interaction between theoretical studies and empirical studies in
the science classroom. The discipline Theory of Science and Research
provides us with theoretical tools and the empirical studies are
carried out in close cooperation with the teachers.

The experiences gained from the approach are described and related to research and development activities within the world of the
school system and especially the researcher-practitioner interface
concerning problem generation for future R & D. Some criteria on
knowledge formation in Mathematics and Science Education based on our
experiences are posed. The current and urgent debate in Sweden on
R & D and in-service training in the teaching of mathematics and
science needs a theoretical platform. Our contribution is an attempt
to bring in the point of view of the researcher.

Context

In Sweden, teachers, teacher trainers and educators at university
level have been discussing problems within the field of Mathematics
Education and Science Education over a period of many years. Articles
in Swedish magazines and Government reports from the latter part of
the 19th century point to a tradition that has not resulted in introduction of Mathematics and Science Education at university level.
In the past few decades, the continuous development of curriculum and
study courses has resulted in development projects in mathematics,
biology, chemistry and physics. Especially, research in school
mathematics has been carried out at the Departments of Education.
Similar research on the teaching of biology, chemistry and physics
has been almost nonexistent. However, during this decade the Departments of Education have widened their interest for Science Education
(Lybeck, 1977).

In fact, when I had the priviledge of initiating the BMN project[1], there was no living tradition in Science Education in Sweden with which to connect our research approach. Briefly, our research approach to Science Education at Göteborg has been described by Lybeck (1978a, 1979a). I have used notions introduced by Professor Håkan Törnebohm, The Department of Theory of Science and Research, The University of Göteborg, in order to elaborate our approach. Its theoretical base has been evolved at the Institute of Education at the University of Göteborg. It has emerged as an interaction between theoretical studies and empirical studies in the mathematics and science classroom. The fruitfulness of our studies are themselves evidence for the proposed theoretical base of Science Education and arguments in favour of the applied perspective on science and research adopted from the above-mentioned platform of Theory of Science and Research.

Introduction

In this paper I wish to convey some considerations and experiences on research and development related to the teaching of mathematics and science based on the work in the BMN project. The general theme concerns models on the researcher-practitioner interface.

First, I shall present an essential distinction which demonstrates the separation of two knowledge-producing activities.

Törnebohm (1976) distinguishes between two types of studies which refer to the same area of reality or territory X (Figure 1). In empirical science, research consists of studies treating an area of reality X, e.g. bodies in water (Archimedes' well-known hydrostatic problem). The research here is the inquiring system X̂, which consists of the research group, different types of activities and their organisation (in an extreme case the research group can consist of a single person, e.g. Archimedes). The Theory of Science and Research X̂ studies the inquiring system X̂. (The arrow in Figure 1 refers to hypotheses framed in X̂ and is intended to map features of an object X. There are other relations between X̂ and X. Primary information flows from X to X̂ through various channels, and the work done in X̂ has a steering effect on its territory X.)

---

1. BMN is short for the Swedish name and can be translated as 'Concept formation in mathematics and the natural sciences'. During the school years 1975-79 the project was sponsored by the National Swedish Board of Education. The studies concern mainly mathematics and physics teaching in the integrated upper secondary school, the natural science (N) line and technology (T) line, ages 16-18.

The separation of two knowledge-producing activities

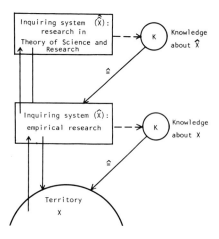

Figure 1:   The relation of studies in theory of science
and research to empirical research

Two different types of knowledge are generated by $\hat{X}$ and $\overset{\star}{X}$ respectively (figure 1). As physicist $\hat{X}$ Archimedes acquired knowledge of
part of the physical reality by studying certain limited phenomena in
X.   Archimedes was able to describe and, to a certain degree, explain
aspects of this reality by introducing concepts such as weight, dis-
placed volume, 'lifting power', 'density', etc. As researcher $\overset{\star}{X}$ we
acquire knowledge about $\hat{X}$ by finding out or reconstructing the method
used by the historical person Archimedes, i.e. by asking questions
such as: How did Archimedes plan his experiments? What theoretical
assumptions did he make (assumptions that are purely hypothetical)?
What instruments did he use to test his hypotheses? What were the
theories that resulted from his activities, etc.? It is important to
note that the reconstruction does not have to concern Archimedes as
an historical physicist but rather the notion of the 'ideal researcher
type'. Other physicists have already developed the Archimedean
research programme. The researcher $\overset{\star}{X}$ wants to ask questions such as:
What importance did Archimedes' hydrostatic theory have for theory

330

development and concept formation? Can the hydrostatic theory be utilised in the development of an aerostatic theory? And if so, how are hydrostatic's 'density' and 'pressure' concepts affected? The Theory of Science and Research forms knowledge on both historical case studies and how research is carried out today.

The human creative activity in $\hat{X}$ leads to knowledge about X. These products or results of the research $\hat{X}$ are lifting power, density, pressure, models, theories, etc. In production, i.e. the research process, the researchers utilise concepts such as hypothesis (H), instrument (I), problem (P), criticism (Cr), tactical plans (Pl), experiment, data, research group, etc. The researcher $\hat{\hat{X}}$ is interested in the researchers' $\hat{X}$ utilisation of these sets of concepts in relation to the phenomenon studied in X. Activities within the empirical research $\hat{X}$ consist of the phenomenon constituting the territory for the research in $\hat{X}$. In order to describe and explain the phenomena within X the researchers in the field of the Theory of Science and Research introduce their own concepts and models, e.g. those shown in figure 1. Törnebohm (1978) has thus developed the triad (H, I, P) or the sequence of triads $\sim$(H, I, P)$\sim$to the pentad (H, I, P, Cr, Pl); the sequence of pentad$\sim$(H, I, P, Cr, Pl)$\sim$represents a running research programme where the pentad $(H_o, I_o, P_o, Cr_o, Pl_o)$ represents an initial research programme. A triad (H, I, P) is to be looked upon as a research result. Sequences of the pentads are models of scientific investigations. We note only that the researchers' paradigm has steering effects on the components of the pentad.

Briefly, we can distinguish three levels. Levels 1 and 2 represent respectively the product and process aspects of the empirical research $\hat{X}$ (let us say related to the levels X and $\hat{X}$ in figure 1). Level 3 corresponds to the reflective activities of the researchers $\hat{X}$ upon themselves and their inquiring system $\hat{X}$. It is the task of a service-oriented Theory of Science and Research to evolve situations, where the researchers $\hat{X}$ articulate their 'knowing' and tacit assumptions as well as previously not articulated knowing on level 3. The dialogue between the researchers $\hat{\hat{X}}$ and $\hat{X}$ concerning level 3, and, of course, levels 1 to 2 may be transformed into knowledge, and the knowledge about the inquiring system $\hat{X}$ is a level 3 knowledge.

Törnebohm's Theory of Science and Research emphasises the content and context dependencies of the researchers' conceptions of knowledge and concepts through their direct relation to the studied phenomenon. For our service-oriented Theory of Science and Research it is a prerequisite that the researchers $\hat{X}$ have intimate knowledge of empirical research of kind X.

I shall now apply the three distinct conceptual levels for the development of theory and studies in Science Education and Mathematics Education.

The levels 1 and 2 correspond to the most important goals for teaching in physics and chemistry in the integrated upper secondary school. Concept formation takes place on two quite separate but concurrent levels, i.e. researcher's product aspect and its process aspect (method of working). Mathematical concepts play a decisive role in this concept formation, e.g. the concepts of proportion and proportionality when concepts such as density, concentration, etc. are introduced. The mathematical concepts are introduced as instrument I in the above-mentioned pentads (H, I, P, Cr, Pl) and influence concept formation within physics and chemistry. Thus, the study of the students' conceptions of concepts in the natural sciences implies a study of mathematical concept formation.

The above-mentioned types of concepts and concurrent concept formations comprise the central part of the content of the BMN project's mapping of the students' spontaneous concepts as they are expressed in interviews or in student-student, student-teacher or student-researcher dialogues in the classrooms and laboratories. In my view, studies of the student-student and student-teacher dialogues constitute the most essential part of the empirical foundation for research in the field of Science and Mathematics Education and its theory development.

Swedish courses of study in biology, chemistry and physics have been influenced by larger curriculum projects (BSCS, CHEM-study, PSSC, HPP, Nuffield, etc.). Behind these projects we can trace the didactic concept 'the student as the small researcher'. It has been criticised, but let us combine it with the idea of the three levels.

The researcher $\overset{\approx}{X}$ and the researcher $\hat{X}$ discuss on the three conceptual levels (let us say related to the levels X,$\hat{X}$ and $\overset{\approx}{X}$ in figure 1). As a consequence of the didactic concept, the model may be introduced (figure 2).

The content of the dialogue on level 1 concerns the product aspect, i.e. concepts such as weight, lifting power, density, etc., while level 2 is thought of as corresponding to the process aspect, i.e. everyday work where concepts such as hypothesis, instrument, problem, criticism, planning, experiment, data, team, etc. are used. By means of dialogues the teacher presents views that enable the teaching process to advance at the same time as the students make their own views known. Thus, the teaching process takes place by means of interaction on the different levels.

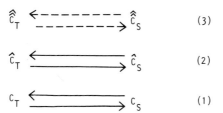

$$\hat{\hat{c}}_T \quad \overset{\longleftarrow -------}{-------\longrightarrow} \quad \hat{\hat{c}}_S \qquad (3)$$

$$\hat{c}_T \quad \overset{\longleftarrow}{\longrightarrow} \quad \hat{c}_S \qquad (2)$$

$$c_T \quad \overset{\longleftarrow}{\longrightarrow} \quad c_S \qquad (1)$$

Figure 2: c is short for conceptual contexts on the different
levels 1-3. They can be separated into one part for
the teacher (T) and another part for the student (S)
on the three levels. $\Longleftrightarrow$ denotes a dialogue and $\dashrightarrow$
a not so well-developed dialogue.

I would now like to present the relation between the notion
'knowing' as it has been used here and knowledge in order to bring
into greater relief the proposed model with special reference to the
practitioner-researcher interface.

Body of views, knowing and knowledge

I now intend to discuss the role of the teacher and of the
researcher in R & D. I shall use the terms body of views, knowing and
knowledge, which were introduced by Törnebohm (1978a), in order to
promote a certain degree of ordered reasoning and in order to be able
to elucidate problems existing in the relationship between practitioner
and the researcher.

A teacher's body of views includes conceptions of how teaching
should be carried on. Similarly, the researcher has a research
paradigm that guides his choice of problems and the way in which they
should be solved. The researcher's paradigm is decisive for the
formation of the problems. The research paradigm that can be shared
by several researchers is one part of the individual researcher's body
of views. It is only by means of a dialogue between the teacher and
the researcher that conscious and unconscious conceptions can be made
knowable (cf. the dialogue researcher $\hat{X}$ and researcher $\hat{\hat{X}}$ or the
dialogue student-teacher in the proposed model in figure 2). The
teacher's and the researcher's knowing is of fundamental importance

and what are decisive are the differences in their knowing and knowledge.

Törnebohm (1978a) divides the individual's knowing into two parts of particular importance in this context as follows:

1. Views acquired by the individual as a result of his own experiences and his own thoughts, and

2. Views formed as a result of reading and teaching (cultural heritage).

In our studies of the students' conceptions of the density concept (level 1) we found that some of them thought that 'a stone sinks because it is heavy' while others were of the opinion that 'the stone sinks because it is heavier than water'. These assertions are examples of qualitatively different conceptions that are part of the students' knowing as well as being part of their individual bodies of views. Their knowing is functional and as a rule is not questioned in the world of everyday physics. These 'knowing forms' or thought forms are adequate in their context.

It is argued therefore that one ought to make a clear distinction between knowing, which is part of the individual's body of views, and knowledge, which is formed through investigations and reported scientifically. As a consequence of what has been said here, one should distinguish between theories concerning knowing and theories concerning knowledge.

We are now in a position to state that a large part of the INOM group's[2] studies concern the individual's body of views and in particular his knowing related to certain phenomena in the physical reality. This means that together we try to form knowledge and theories about knowing. In the BMN project I have called certain forms of knowing thought forms. In the studies, Lybeck (1978b) demonstrated that they have their equivalents in forms of knowledge within the scientific disciplines. This does not mean that I have drawn the conclusion that knowledge and knowing are organised in the same way even if they are related to the same phenomenon. In epistemology one studies the way in which knowledge is organised. A 'knowing theory' should have the task of studying the way in which knowing is organised. The latter task necessitates continued intensive

---

2. A collective name for several research projects at the Institute of Education, The University of Göteborg. INOM is a Swedish abbreviation for 'Learning and the conceptions of the world around us'. The scientific leader is Professor Ference Marton. The BMN project constitutes a part of the INOM group, which activity has been briefly mentioned by Lybeck (1978a, 1979a).

empirical studies as well as theoretical studies based on e.g. the
Theory of Science and Research, the Philosophy of Science, the
History of Science, etc., in order to determine how individuals
transfer their knowing to knowledge, i.e. from something personal to
something public.

I now return to discuss the conceptual contexts presented in
the model in figure 2. They constitute problem fields which, based
on arguments from the Theory of Science and Research, are separable
domains within the field of Science and Mathematics Education.

Problem fields for R & D in the field of science and mathematics
education

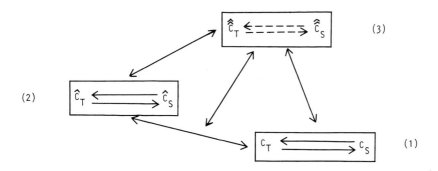

Figure 3: The notations are the same as in figure 2.
←——→ denotes different types of relations.

On each of the levels 1, 2 and 3, the teacher's and the students'
conceptual contexts form problem fields for R & D. The problem fields,
which we perhaps ought to name 'knowing fields', are studied empirically by means of interviews and recordings in classrooms and
laboratories.

In interviews with individual students we are able to map their
knowing with regard to such concepts as density, proportionality,
etc. on level 1 as well as concepts such as hypothesis, instrument,
problem, data, experiment, etc. on level 2. These levels correspond
to the product and process aspects in the human activity (research)
that produce knowledge of the phenomenon studied in its physical

surroundings. The levels 1 and 2 also correspond to the content of the teaching. Similar studies of teachers' knowing on levels 1 and 2 should also be carried out in accordance with our experiences. Level 3 corresponds to the teacher's and the student's bodies of views concerning teaching. The student needs help in expressing both conscious and unconscious conceptions of his knowing concerning the goals of the teaching. It is on level 3 that knowing concerning the method of working is formulated. Level 2 in the model corresponds to the actual teaching process. The student can participate in the teaching (level 2) without necessarily having thought about what its goals are (level 3).

Interviews with students on level 3 constitute a mapping of their knowing concerning levels 1 and 2 as aspects of the teaching. At the same time, their conceptions of the relationship between levels 1 and 2 in the concept-forming and knowledge-forming process in the subject are mapped. Here, it must be emphasised in particular that corresponding mappings of teachers', student teachers' and other adults' knowing on level 3 are not only extremely desirable but also an important part of the approach reflected by the model.

Recordings of the actual teaching provide data that supplement the mappings of the qualitative different conceptions on levels 1, 2 and 3. The two-dimensional category diagram of the students' (ages 16-17) qualitatively different conceptions of the concepts of proportion and proportionality presented by Lybeck (1978b, 1979b) was used in the analyses of student-student and student-teacher dialogues during the actual teaching (1979b, pp 45-47). The classroom recordings show that certain thought forms do not come into play during the teaching itself; this results in some of the students not realising how and why concepts such as density and speed are formed with mathematics as the instrument. Consequently, these students do not participate in the teaching on their own terms. In fact, it can be said that the resources the students themselves constitute are not utilised during the teaching and two conceptual worlds are formed: everyday physics and school physics. Throughout the school year, the researcher and the teachers in our experimental classes recorded discussions with the students and between students during laboratory work and group work. This data generation provides a longitudinal picture of the changes in the students' knowing. An extremely interesting phenomenon is the perspective shifts in the approach of students who have been documented during the school year. These perspective shifts (new insights) must be seen as having great importance for discussions on the method of working in the natural science teaching. During direct teaching or while the teacher is talking with groups of students the teachers sometimes express their conceptions of the teaching on level 3 and state quite clearly why they are partial to certain thought forms on e.g. level 1. On such occasions they articulate, as teachers, intimate knowledge.

By means of interviews with teachers and students and recordings of learning and teaching situations the researcher is able to sketch real pictures. Many ideal pictures and even anecdotes live on in the form of traditions within teacher training. Here, practitioners and researchers have a central and common task, namely to jointly produce real pictures of learning and teaching situations as they actually occur in school. On the practitioner-researcher interface, both sides are responsible for the establishment of fruitful dialogues. One stage in such talks could consist of the researcher describing his view of R & D activities by sketching models as has been done in this paper. In figure 4 I shall sum up some of the essential features of the activities of the BMN project.

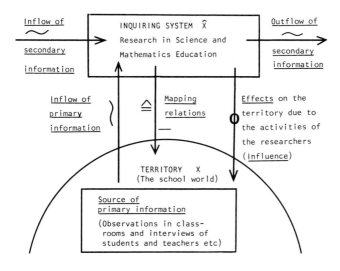

Figure 4: Some features of the research within the field of science and mathematics education.

In our case, the researcher participates in two types of information flow called the primary information flow and the secondary information flow by Törnebohm. The primary information flow is based on the object of the studies. In my opinion, the qualitatively different conceptions of and thought forms around the subject content that can be mapped through interviews and classroom observations are of fundamental importance for the empirical and theoretical development of Science and Mathematics Education. At the initial stage, where we now are, exploratory studies dominate. They can be carried out on the three levels quite separately. These consist of legitimate and purely pedagogical research tasks, e.g. how students and teachers perceive learning and teaching, i.e. on level 3. The dimension in the research activity emphasised by our efforts constitutes strategic planning from level 1 to level 2 and to level 3. This strategy cannot be refined since the levels interact. According to our model, the distinctive feature of Science and Mathematics Education (or History Education, etc.) consists of a focusing on the conceptual content and context dependence. The secondary information flow refers to other inquiring systems. The Natural Sciences and Mathematics are closely related as are other inquiring systems in the field of Science and Mathematics Education. Other closely related disciplines are Education, Educational Psychology, Cognitive and Developmental Psychology, the Theory of Science and Research, the Philosophy of Science, the History of Science and the History of Mathematics. Our import of concepts and intellectual instruments from the Theory of Science and Research is an example of the inflow of secondary information.

I shall now point to some of the demands placed on our research and the criteria as regards its formation of knowledge.

Concerning demands on the research and criteria of its formation of knowledge

We place special importance on the fact that the researcher has an intimate knowledge of the object of the studies. Consequently, the research team should include one or more persons who teach the subjects in question. The researcher should also become well-acquainted with the teaching process involved by attending lessons during a long period of time. Thus, we reject the idea that a person can, from the outside and in a 'neutral way', observe and acquire knowledge of the object of the studies.

Naturally, the researcher often plays the part of a passive observer, but during the dialogues with students and teachers it is not meaningful to consider oneself to be a completely 'objective' and 'neutral' observer since the researcher is in fact a part of the data-generating system. In this context, the researcher can be seen as a measuring instrument with a certain instrument theory. It is particularly important that the researcher's instrument theory is articulated before the actual study. Thus, prior to the Archimedes recordings in the classroom we wrote down our reconstruction based on the platform of the Theory of Science and Research all the knowledge forms that could be considered possible. This, together with developmental-psychological knowledge of the physical phenomena increased the researcher's ability to register logical distinctions in the students' spontaneous statements during the lessons presented by Lybeck (1979b). It should be noted that the instrument theory includes the researcher's intimate knowledge of the teaching, teacher training profession, etc.

An important requirement is that recorded teaching and learning situations must be genuine events that occurred in school. Naturally, it is the teacher who is responsible for the teaching even if the experiments are carried out on the researcher's suggestion. It is during the practitioner-researcher dialogue that the researcher tries to gain approval for the testing of hypotheses. Testing takes place only if the teacher considers the experiment to be consistent with his views of how the students should be taught, otherwise foreign elements might have an undesirable effect on the teaching itself. Furthermore, the researcher has a responsibility towards the students to avoid possible failures. In the dialogues that take place during the duration of the study the practitioner and the researcher develop and exert an influence on their knowing of the teaching process. One can say that their intimate knowledge is going through a refining process. The experimental teachers can be stimulated into renewing themselves and development is carried out while data is being formed for a research task.

In analyses of the students' answers in the study of their qualitatively different conceptions of the proportion and proportionality concepts (level 1) presented by Lybeck (1978b, 1979b), the description was made in terms of the content. Algebra's symbol language was used in the interpretation of the students' verbal quantifications, and aspects of the concept of function, with respect to the general line of reasoning leading to the students' solutions. By describing the students' answers in terms of the content, results are obtained that can be utilised more easily by the teachers. This is thus a practitioner's demand on the research results.

It is a fact that old theories in the instrument theory influence the generation of data. The fact that humanistic knowledge from the Theory of Science and Research and the History of Science and Mathematics has provided valuable ideas and is, as it were, built into the interviewer-researcher's instrument theory does not mean that the production of knowledge takes place in an uncontrolled manner. It is namely the researcher's task when analysing data to demonstrate that the hypothesis can be confirmed in the new context, i.e. in the empirical context of Science or Mathematics Education.

Above, we have given an indication of how the dialogues between the practitioner and the researcher leads to questions that can be made knowable and transformed into problems of two types, namely, problems P_R for the R departments and problems P_D for the D departments. These problems are generated in the world of the school. In the R departments solutions of P_R are accepted as knowledge. These solutions of P_R, knowledge or even new hypotheses can be judged by the practitioners as being relevant or can be rejected. The practitioner's judgment does not necessarily strip the researcher's result of its knowledge status. The problems P_D can be generated by the teachers themselves since they wish to change their knowing. Other P_D's can be produced as the result of practitioner-researcher interaction. Thus, the research results are added to analysis instruments that can be applicable in D work. The analysis instrument for the concepts of proportion and proportionality can be applied in other subjects and in other contexts with the intention of constructing fields of activities. The instrument can also be used in curriculum work. An important aspect of these activities is that the knowledge that is built into the analysis instrument guarantees in advance, so as to say, meaningful tasks that lead to results in D work. The research task is not given the same guarantees. However, D work may lead to alterations in the analysis instrument. In such a case it is a valuable incentive in D work.

During the dialogue between the practitioner and the researcher it is the task of the researcher to try to change the teacher's knowing about teaching by means of his knowledge. The dialogues must be based on insights concerning the different tasks to be carried out by the practitioner and the researcher. These tasks are complementary. The practitioner (teacher) and the researcher are united in an effort to transform knowing about the teaching into knowledge. Questions that lead to problems concerning how certain phenomena in the teaching are to be made knowable may lead to the question: Is the knowable worth knowing? Here, the two sides have a large, joint responsibility. Here, I shall do no more than imply that interested parties outside the school world have reason to make demands on R & D work.

Like teachers, researchers have professional interests and specific professional competence. The former concerns mainly research but also development work. The teacher's competence should, in addition to teaching competence, also include the potential to increase his ability to carry through D work. It is the interests of both researchers and teachers that cooperation can take place in a more planned way.

340

Discussion

Lybeck was congratulated on the elegance of his conceptualisation
of research in science and mathematics education, but was asked to
enlarge on the differences he saw between research carried out under
the paradigm he had described, and that conducted without this framework. Lybeck identified the use of interviews and studies in the
classroom as a means of investigating the variety of, say, concepts
of proportionality, and so of generating hypotheses about their development. He noted that other workers, using rather different methods,
had reached essentially similar conclusions.

As examples of the three levels of conceptualisation discussed in
his paper, he considered ideas of density. At the first level, the
child is not concerned with density as a problem - he may say 'it
sinks because it sinks!'. At the second level, however, the child
becomes aware of his own thinking, and reflects on ways of solving
density problems. Finally the child becomes aware not only of his own
conceptualisations, but of those of the teacher also, and can see the
relation of one to the other. It is the duty of the teacher to be
aware of the child's concepts, and so help to make this bridge.

The problem was raised of how to represent the conceptualisations
that are identified, and Lybeck was asked what method he used for
mapping knowing with respect to, say, proportionality. This was a
very difficult problem to communicate. The method used was still
being developed, and although algebraic methods were used for quantitative aspects, it was hard to convey a flavour of the method to one
who was not working in the group of researchers and teachers.

Studies of Descriptions of Cognitive Structures through Semantic Networks

TOWARDS DESCRIPTIONS OF THE COGNITIVE STRUCTURES OF SCIENCE STUDENTS

Leo H.T. West

Introduction

In this paper I do not intend to describe my own research. I have come as the representative of a group of researchers* with the express purpose of communicating their ideas and results to people here and communicating the work of people here back to the group. I should point out that the group is not a research team in the ordinary sense of a leader of a school and his research team. Each of the people have been working independently for some years, aware of what others were doing but not seeing the close connection. What brought them together was a common need to describe (I hesitate to use the term 'measure') cognitive structure. The group now meets regularly and although there has clearly been a degree of convergence they continue to work independently. In this paper what I want to try to communicate to you is their various approaches to the describing of the cognitive structures of science students.

Description means different things to different people. There are different aspects of cognitive structure on which one could focus. We have tended to call these dimensions of cognitive structure. Some examples of these are extent, detail or precision, accord with reality, and so on. Different individuals aim their descriptions at different points along these dimensions. A neurologist's description would be

---

*The principal researchers involved are Dick White, Dick Gunstone, and Leo West and Peter Fensham (the latter two working together as a team).

very high on precision, relatively low on extent and neutral on accord with reality. An Ausubelian's description would be fairly high on extent but relatively low on precision. Within the group, I think that the description adopted is influenced by a number of factors - the model of cognitive structure that they hold, the methodology for eliciting information that they adopt and the overall purpose that they have. Of course all of these factors influence each other, but I think that they provide a framework for me to summarise for you the approach taken by each of the researchers in this group.

Gunstone, R.

Gunstone is a physics method lecturer, so his primary interest is in teaching. He is interested in finding ways of improving the teaching of physics concepts and sees one avenue to this through increasing the number and kinds of links that students make between the various things they learn. In an experimental sense his inclination was to contrast one teaching method, which aimed to maximise the student's linking of learning to his current knowledge, with a more conventional teaching method (actually a published linear programme). This work derives its theoretical basis from Mayer's work (Mayer, 1975). However, Gunstone was not happy with the high inference research methodologies that have characterised research in this general area (e.g. the advance organiser research) where only learning outcomes are used as dependent variables. Since the aim of the experimental treatment was to change the learner's cognitive structure which should then lead to improved learning, Gunstone wanted to include a measure of cognitive structure as an additional dependent variable. And this needed to be quantitative. Thus his purpose committed him to a summary measure or index of cognitive structure and so his description was to be low on precision. His theoretical model was based on Mayer's internal/external connectedness idea. The experimental treatment aimed to maximise external connectiveness. So the measure of cognitive structure needed to be relatively high on extent - the learning was meant to make linkages fairly widely beyond the specific content of the learning.

Gunstone's methodology for describing cognitive structure was derived from Shavelson's word association approach (Shavelson, 1972). The word association method has potential to examine the extent of linkages made. As used by Shavelson it was restricted in extent, but this need not be so. A major criticism of the Shavelson approach is that words are associated for a variety of reasons and that his method took no account of these differences (e.g. Stewart, 1978). Gunstone overcame this objection by asking respondents to go back and write sentences containing both words (the stimulus and the response word) so that it 'shows the way you see the word being connected with [stimulus word]'. From this he derived a series of indices that were simple counts of numbers of external relational links of particular types. These indices he used as additional dependent variables.

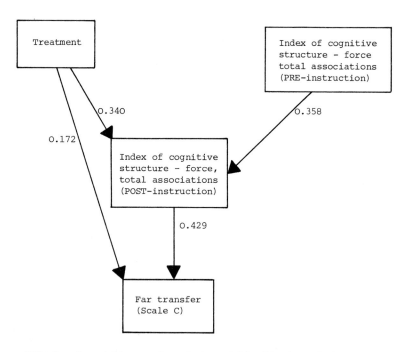

Effects of variables on dependent variable (Far transfer)

	Direct effect	Indirect effect
Pre-Index of cognitive structure	0	0.193
Post-Index of cognitive structure	0.429	- 0.015
Treatment	0.172	0.146

Figure 1: Path analysis from Gunstone's research (all paths with path coefficients less than 0.1 excluded).

Gunstone's results have not yet been published, but I will in-clude just one set here. It is expressed as a path model with only those paths (and variables) that have path coefficients greater than 0.1 included. The index of cognitive structure used in this case is the total number of associations made with the stimulus word 'Force'. The other dependent variable is a measure of far transfer. The result is shown in figure 1.

This result shows that the treatment (experimental contrasted with control) has increased the extent of external connections (as measured by the word association index) and has led to better learning on this as measured by his test of far transfer. It also shows that a substantial part of this better learning is mediated through the increased extent of external connectedness.

White, R.T.

I really need to consider White in two ways. His earlier work concerned developing (with Gagné) a model of cognitive structure (see Gagné, White, 1978) and subsequent research based on that model. His recent work has centred around examining a range of dimensions of cognitive structure.

Considering first his model work: the purposes were quite clearly related to improving learning outcomes, especially retention and transfer of learning. This purpose can be seen most strongly in the direct link made between specific memory structures and specific performance outcomes (see figure 1 in Gagné, White, 1978). For this reason the dimension of primary interest is what specific types of memory element are present. (Gagné and White defined four types of memory element: propositions, intellectual skills, images and episodes.) This is reflected in the research of his graduate students.

Atkinson, interested in the role of practical work in chemistry, sought to discover if practical work led to a greater number of stored episodes, whether these episodes were linked with other learning and whether such increased linking led to better performance. This led her to compare two teaching methods, one involving the students in actually doing the practical work (and so increasing their chance of storing episodes) and the other involving demonstrations of the practical work. Because it was specific episodes and their link with performance that was of interest, Atkinson used interviews and protocols as the methodology for describing cognitive structure. She found no difference in performance between the two groups, although there were differences in the number of episodes stored, so it was not possible to examine whether any differences in performances were due to different cognitive structures.

Mackenzie conducted a similar experiment in geography, concerning an excursion as the episode-providing condition. However he included one excursion mode that included a 'vigorous interaction' with the environment in order to heighten the importance of the episode. (As an example, by chewing the leaves of plants these students measured differences in salinity of plants as a function of proximity to the sea.) He chose to measure the cognitive structure with a pencil and paper test, asking students to choose options that represented different types of linkages between topics learned and potential episodes. His findings strongly support the notion that the building of links between episodes and other memory structures will enhance the

345

retention of learning related to those structures. Mackenzie's 'vigorous interaction' group formed many greater linkages with episodes and retained their learning (12 weeks later) much better than either comparison group (one also taking the excursion and the other receiving only classroom instruction).

White interprets these findings as showing that if episodes are to aid retention, they need to be strongly linked with the verbal knowledge and intellectual skills from the subject matter, and that such linking does not come about easily. Events need to be dramatic, or teachers must work at bringing students to form the links, before episodes are likely to be important in retention.

White is currently concentrating on the dimensions of cognitive structure and an evaluation of the many methods for eliciting informa- tion about cognitive structure against these dimensions. This work is likely to lead to a clearer understanding of what is being assessed by each of the methods currently being used. It may also provide a method of collapsing the very rich information about an individual's cognitive structure in a form that retains a good deal of that rich- ness.

Fensham, P.J. and West, L.H.T.

Fensham and West are interested in learning in higher education, with a particular interest in chemistry. Their original orientation was neo-Ausubelian (West, Fensham, 1974, 1976) and their earlier research (see also West, Kellett, 1979) used methodologies that were high-inference with respect to cognitive structure. However they have found those methodologies inadequate and so have turned their attention to more direct measures of cognitive structure. Hence their immediate purpose has been to explore methods for eliciting informa- tion about and describing the cognitive structure of individual students. Given the Ausubelian origins of their model of cognitive structure, their description demands high emphasis on extent and less on precision. So they are less interested in the nature of memory elements and more interested in their interlinking or structure. For the present they have been using Gagné-and-White-like elements (propositions, intellectual skills and images) but they generally accept that the element size is variable.

Their major technique is the clinical interview. However, unlike Pines et al. (1978) who have tended to use a very flexible approach, Fensham and West have imposed more structure. They partitioned the students' cognitive structure into three separate (although artificial) parts, (a) the 'curriculum' part which relates to a specific teaching/ learning segment, (b) the linking between this and other formal learn- ing: prior, concurrent and indeed subsequent, and (c) the linking with the learner's general knowledge of the world.

346

Investigation of the curriculum part began with testing of specific propositions, intellectual skills and images that the learner should have stored as a result of the learning sequence. The linking between the propositions is achieved in a structuring task similar to that used by Champagne et al. (1978) where the cards correspond one-to-one with the propositional test items. The links between intellectual skills (and images) and the propositions is effected using matching tasks of the intellectual skills test items (and cards containing drawings of the demonstrations) with the propositional test items.

Exploration of the links between 'curriculum knowledge' and the student's general knowledge of the world has been undertaken using Pines et al. (1978) interviewing procedures where the stimuli used were general things like photographs of icebergs floating in the sea, a pressure cooker, etc., (for a learning sequence on phase diagrams). An example of the results of this approach is shown in figure 2.

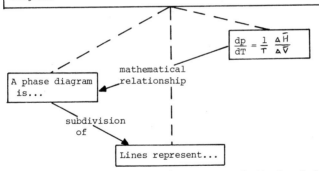

Icebergs are made of ice, floating in water where the water temperature is about zero. They are in equilibrium with water. The sea-iceberg system would be on the liquid-solid line of the phase diagram. A solid should be more dense than its liquid but in the case of ice this is not so (therefore icebergs float). The fact that they float has something to do with the angle of the liquid-solid line on the phase diagram.

$$\frac{dp}{dT} = \frac{1}{T} \frac{\Delta \bar{H}}{\Delta \bar{V}}$$

A phase diagram is...

mathematical relationship

subdivision of

Lines represent...

Figure 2: <u>Some links formed between a student's knowledge of ice, icebergs, flotation, etc., and the curriculum (one component phase diagram) part of his cognitive structure.</u> The text was formed by transforming the interview transcript into propositional format (following Pines, 1977) and reforming the propositions into prose.

347

This student can make some links between aspects of his general knowledge and elements of the curriculum part of his cognitive structure. The prose in the diagram, which is represented as one of a set of 'satellites' related to aspects of the curriculum part, was generated from the interview by first transforming the transcript into propositional format (Pines, 1977) and then reforming the propositions into prose. Compared with his internal linking within the curriculum part, this student has some well-formed links with his general knowledge of the world. However, most other students interviewed showed much less interlinking with their general knowledge.

An attempt to find relationships with the curriculum part and other formal learning was made using Gunstone's 'word association tasks followed by sentence writing' approach. At this stage this method has met with little success and further experimenting with it and other methods is proceeding.

Fensham and West plan to use this overall approach to monitor the learning of students as they proceed through the teaching of a course. However such longitudinal studies will need to find a way of dealing with the problem of the influence of the measurement on the student's cognitive structure. Most of the students who took part in this research were enthusiastic about how the experience helped them to understand the learning so much better. This form of assessing cognitive structure may indeed have more potential as a teaching method than as a research technique.

Concluding comments

In such a short time, it has only been possible for me to convey a brief pen picture of the thinking and work of the members of the Monash group. In conclusion, let me emphasise that their common goal is the description, representation, measurement (call it what you like) of the learner's knowledge and its structure. There are now, both at Monash and elsewhere, a range of methods for eliciting information from students about their cognitive structure. The difficult task that we all face is to find a method of data reduction, of summarising the mass of information in a manner that does not distort it and in combining information from more than one student in a manner that is meaningful and useful.

Discussion

In introducing his paper West set the work described in the context of similar studies. One common problem was that the testing itself, in many cases this was in the form of an interview, affected the students' learning. The interview was a learning experience as students began to relate ideas more effectively and that process might be transferable. It was argued that in essence this was merely demonstrating the value of individual tuition. West pointed out that the interviews were held outside the class context and the interviewer did not normally teach the students concerned.

One feature emerging from the work was the low standard commonly found in university teaching.

There was some discussion whether descriptive statements were satisfactory or whether a quantitative measure was necessary. It was argued that processes of change could only be adequately described and measured by the use of quantitative measures. Other information, e.g. from achievement tests, was available about the students involved in the exercise.

COGNITIVE STRUCTURE FROM DIGRAPH ANALYSIS OF LANGUAGE

R. Maskill and D. Pereira

The Problem

A current preoccupation in education, psychology and psycholinguistics is with setting up a viable model for cognition. From an educational point of view the need for an understanding of why learners experience difficulty should underpin any discussion of how teaching might be improved. This understanding of learning difficulty has to be couched in terms of what is in the learner's mind and this clearly needs a basis in psychology.

Models of cognition are often structural in nature and the notion of cognitive structure, a hypothetical construct, is often used to stand for the knowledge which an individual carries around with him and uses in his thought processes. In trying to understand why some learners experience difficulty and why others do not, the nature of what each knows is an obvious starting point. Unfortunately the cognitive structure construct is hypothetical and unmeasurable and so the goal of knowing what is known is at present unattainable. At best what the learner does or does not do is measurable with some precision. Knowing why this behaviour rather than any other was produced is guesswork. The assumption underlying cognitive psychology is that ways may be found of externalising 'what is known' in order to make the guesses realistic and sensible.

Some Presumptions

The true nature of the internal representation of knowledge will never be known. The best that can be done for the purpose of studying and rationalising cognition is to set up a model which can be tested and validated against performance data. There have been a number of arguments in the literature on the nature of the best representation (Anderson, 1978). This debate will be sidestepped here by assuming that the nature of the representation in use at any moment will reflect the nature of the task being solved (Schank, 1976). Thus the nature of the learner performance used as the probe for the knowledge structure will govern in large part the way the knowledge will be represented. A number of psycholinguists (e.g. Kintsch, 1974) do make the claim that words and their organisation may be as close as it is possible to get to an accurate model for the concepts of mind. This may or may not be so. For the purpose of this investigation the presumption was made that by analysing the responses to simple communication tasks, a structural description of what is known will be produced which might be shown empirically to have some general educational usefulness. It is not being claimed that concepts are necessarily propositional in nature, though it should be said that interrelationship between language and thought (Vygotsky, 1962), between language and ideation (Feldman, 1977) and between language and culture (Whorf, 1964), is so close that this assumption would probably not lead to any great loss.

The process/content debate is also avoided by accepting as a reasonable working hypothesis Newell and Simon's (1972) view that it is the nature of the mental or conceptual organisation that an individual constructs in response to a given task which is the principal determinant of the process of thought. Thus knowing what is known will probably tell us a great deal about the way thought takes place.

The Technique

The technique used is based upon that developed by Shavelson (1974). In summary, each sentence in a piece of discourse is converted into a digraph by means of a set of rules (see figure 1). A piece of prose produces a set of digraphs, one corresponding to each sentence. The full set of digraphs is summarised in an adjacency matrix (see figure 2). This is a square matrix with entries 1 or 0 depending upon whether the corresponding points are adjacent in the digraph representations. In this way the structure of a piece of text can be conveniently described in a simple mathematical way and the techniques of digraph theory (Harary et al., 1965) can be used to analyse it. The rules for producing the digraph from

Sentence (1)   The atoms were in reaction with the molecules

Digraph (1)

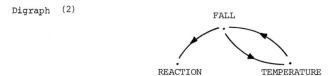

Sentence (2)   The fall in temperature slowed down the reaction

Digraph (2)

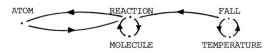

Overall digraph

Figure 1:   Digraphs from sentences

	Atom	Molecule	Reaction	Fall	Tempera-ture
Atom	O	O	1	O	O
Molecule	O	O	1	O	O
Reaction	1	1	O	O	O
Fall	O	O	1	O	1
Temperature	O	O	O	1	O

Figure 2:   Adjacency matrix for the overall digraph of figure 1

351

the text are a matter of choice of definition. The wisdom of the
choice will be reflected in the pragmatic value of the results they
produce.

The mathematical analysis proceeding from the adjacency matrix
can be as complex or as simple as required. The type of structural
idea investigated will depend upon the supposed (hypothetical) congru-
ence between the psychological and the mathematical constructs such
as distance, vulnerability or point basis. The value of the analyses
must then be judged by the criterion of intuitive common sense applied
to the results obtained. Some results, obtained in what must be seen
as a preliminary investigation, will now be described. These results
are mostly based on the distance between points in the digraph. Distance is the minimum number of links separating one point and another.
Thus in the overall digraph in figure 1 atom is distance 1 from
reaction, distance 2 from molecule but an infinite distance from
fall and temperature since no path exists to these latter two points.
All points are distance zero from themselves.

Results

Two experiments have been conducted. In both, third year secondary school pupils were asked to read and learn from two short texts,
texts A and B, on very basic chemical kinetics. One week later the
same children were asked to write what they could remember of the
subject matter in a teach-back situation. Essays and texts were
analysed and compared using the digraph technique.

(i) Conceptual order of essays and text

Any digraph can be made acyclic (i.e. having no cycles) by
suppressing particular lines. In learning terms, the relation in
a digraph of an essay which occurs first, or alternatively which
appears in the same order of occurrence as that of concepts in the
text, is hypothesised to be the primary relation between the two
concepts. Others (i.e. those producing the cycles) are suppressed.
The reason for making this conversion is that acyclic graphs have a
unique order of points called the 'upper triangular order' (Harary
et al., 1965) which is the order of points such that lines to any
point come only from points preceding it in the order. We have
called this order simply the conceptual order. It was found in the
first experiment that the conceptual order for text A was (A) in
figure 3. Intriguingly the orders in the essays of 60 children
((a) in figure 3) were consistent and meaningful, leading from factors
via predicates to products, but different from that of the text
from which they had been learned. This does not indicate that the
text was a poor teaching document or that it was badly written: it
was produced by the teacher of the children, checked by two other
subject experts and pretested on an appropriate similar group of
children before the main experiment. It simply indicates that the
directionality of the conceptual relations perceived by the experts

	(A)		(a)
	Atom		Temperature
	Rate		Concentration
	Reaction		Surface
	Temperature		Size
	Weight		Volume
	Molecule		Atom
	Speed		Molecule
	Volume		Rate
	Concentration		Weight
	Closeness		Area
	Surface		Reaction
	Time		Speed
	Collision		Closeness
	Size		Time
	Area		Collision

Figure 3: The conceptual order of text A(A) and the conceptual order of the essays based on it (a)

when describing the message of the communication was different from that perceived by the learners. This leads to the speculation that the order manifested in the essays had some learning significance, and made a replication study essential.

(ii) Conceptual order as a teaching order

A second text, text B, was written based on text A but with slight reorganisations of the structures of a few sentences to make the conceptual order of text B more congruent with that of the essays of the children who had learned from text A. In this second experiment, as before the essays and text were structurally analysed for their conceptual orders. These are given in figure 4, (B) being that of the text. Once again the orders of the 27 children's essays were highly consistent, being given as (b) in figure 4. Thus this same order has been reproduced by two different groups of children at different times, establishing its validity.

353

(B)	(b)
Temperature	Temperature
Concentration	Concentration
Atom	Surface
Rate	Size
Reaction	Atom
Weight	Molecule
Molecule	Volume
Speed	Area
Surface	Weight
Time	Rate
Closeness	Reaction
Collision	Time
Size	Collision
Area	Closeness
Volume	Speed

Figure 4: The conceptual order of text B (B) and the conceptual order of the essays based on it (b).

In order to test the order as having some teaching significance, a second matched group of 26 children were taught using the original text A, and the two groups were compared. In many respects there were no differences but there was more consistency in the conceptual order for the group who had learned from text B.

The changes made to text A, in producing text B, were relatively minor, being the slight adjustment of only 9 out of the 62 sentences of the text. Clearly, in this case, any effect it might have had has not been a determining influence.

(iii) Other results

(a) Concrete and abstract concepts

In general the concepts whose distances to the other concepts correlated most highly with similar sets of distances from the same concepts in the text were the real/concrete concepts. Those whose correlations tended to be lowest were the more abstract concepts (see table 1). The technique seems to be sensitive enough to separate those concepts where the gap between expert (text) and novice (essay) might be expected to be greatest from those where a lesser difference is anticipated.

Table 1:   Correlations between distances in essays and distances
           in texts, frequencies of forgetting and distances be-
           tween concepts

	Text A Group			Text B Group		
	(i)	(ii)	(iii)	(i)	(ii)	(iii)
Rate	1.61	0.82	0	1.54	0.76	0
Reaction	1.91	0.86	0	1.99	0.83	0
Weight	2.48	0.78	4	2.40	0.82	2
Time	2.30	0.78	2	2.25	0.76	2
Atom	2.13	0.62	1	2.10	0.70	0
Molecule	1.92	0.72	1	1.95	0.69	0
Collision	1.84	0.88	0	1.77	0.92	0
Size	2.29	0.85	1	2.30	0.80	2
Surface	2.67	0.86	0	2.58	0.88	0
Area	1.97	0.87	0	2.00	0.83	0
Volume	2.52	0.80	12	2.76	0.79	8
Concentration	2.15	0.84	1	2.16	0.77	0
Closeness	2.20	0.91	3	2.31	0.89	3
Temperature	2.52	0.93	1	2.22	0.95	0
Speed	2.07	0.84	5	2.20	0.78	1

(i)   Mean average distance to other concepts

(ii)   Correlation between text and essays

(iii)   Frequency with which the concept is forgotten

(b) Clustering analyses

    The clustering analyses carried out in earlier work (Shavelson,
1974; Johnson, 1976) used a simple clustering metric, based on single
distances. This worked well on averaged distance matrices, produced
from a large number of essays, but failed with single texts because
of the large number of common values. An alternative clustering
method (Ward, 1963) has been found to be more useful, as well as
psychologically more intuitive, and also an adjustment to the simple
distance measure, based on frequency, has been devised. The results
are shown in figure 5 and figure 6 for the clustering analysis of
text A, and for the essays written by those children who learned from
it respectively.

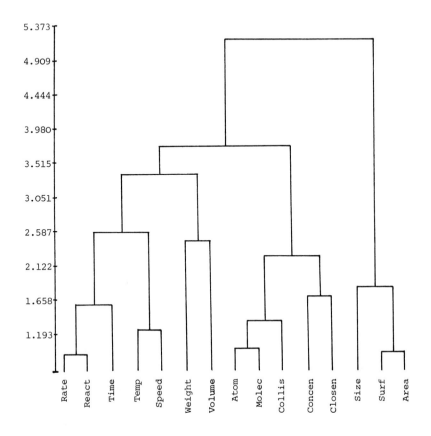

Figure 5: Group A Essays

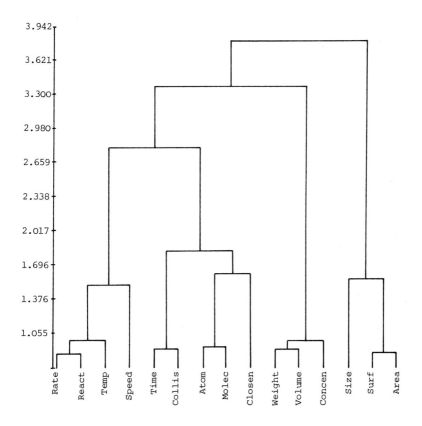

Figure 6: <u>Text A</u>

The clustering patterns make good chemical sense being, by and large, those groups of concepts to be expected. One very interesting difference between text and essays is the position of concentration. The children link it to closeness and to collision, which is sensible since it is concentration which brings about closeness and which, among other things, brings about collisions. The text, on the other hand, links concentration to volume and weight, which again is sensible since volume and weight define concentration. This difference seems to suggest that the expert is concerned with defining his factors whereas the learner does not worry about this, being more pre-occupied with qualitative factor properties.

(b) Forgotten Concepts

Many of the children left out of their essays, concepts described in the texts. It was found that there was a correlation (r = 0.58, p = 0.05) between frequency of forgetting of a concept and the average distance of the concepts from others in the essays. In other words, the concepts most readily forgotten were those most tenuously connected to the main structure as measured by the digraph method (see table 1).

Summary and Conclusions

The results presented here are very preliminary and their significance is only tentatively suggested. The likely psychological meaningfulness of the mathematical constructs, such as the simple distance measure or in more sophisticated fashion the clustering and the conceptual order analyses, rests entirely at this stage on whether or not the results make sense. Since the whole purpose of the exercise was to search for a tool which would, in the results it produces, offer insight into the nature of the concepts in learners' and in the experts' minds, whether or not the results make sense depends upon expected differences between experts and learners.

The clustering results (figures 5 and 6) and the results of the conceptual order analyses (figures 3 and 4) are both readily interpretable with this criterion in mind. In both cases the results show consistency across the individual learners and meaningful differences between expert (text) and learner (essay). These results are particularly encouraging since there is little or no possibility for experimenter bias in the analyses and the differences found were not anticipated.

Further development and testing of the techniques is being carried out.

Acknowledgement

We gratefully acknowledge the financial support (to DP) from the Calouste Gulbenkian Foundation which made this research possible.

Discussion

One result of the digraph analysis is the 'conceptual order' of
terms occurring in the analysed text. Why were there differences
between the order resulting from expert text and that consistently
found from the children's essays? Does this latter order reflect
the 'cognitive structure' of the children and should teaching texts
take this into account? Little explanation was offered for the
phenomenon nor of the observation that within the conceptual order
of the children there existed 'nice' groupings of ideas. It might be
that the ordering reflects, not cognitive structure, but rather the
objectives of the writer. The expert in attempting to teach, the
child to report. If the author of the teaching text was trying to
link new concepts to existing, as suggested by Novak based on the
Ausubelian paradigm, then it would seem reasonable to expect a different conceptual order from that produced by a concise report of acquired knowledge; and consequently it would be unwise to argue that the
children's conceptual order had implications for teaching.

The analysis itself can be criticised in that the 'arrows'
of the digraph have no semantic content and therefore the results have
ignored significant data. This was defended on the grounds of maintaining a simple mathematical technique, otherwise the analysis would be
intractable. It was noted that the views of Kintsch and Schank as
to the relative significance of 'semantic' and 'episodic' memory
should be considered.

A further criticism of the analysis concerned a point of technique. In order to facilitate analysis the digraphs were modified
by removing relations so that they became acyclic. The criteria for
this seemed arbitrary, but apparently the use of three different
criteria had made little difference to the outcome of the analysis.

SOME USES OF NETWORKS OF OPTIONS FOR DESCRIBING COMPLICATED
QUALITATIVE DATA

Jon Ogborn

We have all learned to live with the fact that the more realistic
our data is, the more impossible it becomes to say what there is in it.
If we interview children about how they think, we get a strong impression of understanding rather better what is going on, but an equally
strong sense of despair at ever being able to capture it without
losing its essential complexity. The same could be said for any
number of lines of research. This paper is about a methodological
tactic for chipping away at a corner of the problem, so I have to ask

you to suspend for a short time your natural disbelief that anything can be done about it.

What has all this to do with language and learning? Firstly, some of the most intractable data there is, is what people say. How should one go about analysing it? Secondly, it happens that the method I shall be discussing derives from the study of language itself (from systemic linguistics, in fact), though I do not think that its uses elsewhere depend on whether or not one agrees with the systemic linguists. Thirdly, it evolved for me personally out of confronting recorded speech data (in university physics tutorials, and then in interviews with university students), and trying to find out how to handle it. Fourthly, and much more tentatively, there may be some cases when some of the linguists' analytic categories have uses elsewhere.

Systems of options

The fundamental insight of systemic linguistics is very simple, almost obvious: meanings can be represented as choices. That is, in French, to use 'tu' is to have chosen not to use 'vous' or 'on'; a choice, and so a meaning, that we do not have in English. To begin a letter 'Dear Sir' is to have chosen one out of a finite range of options, including 'Dear (first name)', (Dear (last name)', 'Sir', etc. The options are not the same in French and English, and correspondingly the meanings of options are different (to write 'Monsieur' is not the same as to write 'Sir'). We may express the idea more precisely by saying that a meaning is represented as one particular complex configuration of choices, out of a finite range of possible configurations, in a given environment which allows those choices.

Some notation

Let me illustrate the notation which we have borrowed from systemic linguistics to represent possible options, and do so by using it to tell you what kinds of things I want to say in this paper.

Firstly, I want to say that I shall give examples, each one simultaneously illustrating a particular kind of application, and some general type of problem. So I write:

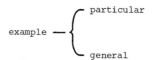

The bracket means 'both at once'. What particular cases will I discuss, you may ask? So let me elaborate the notation:

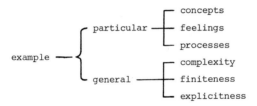

The bars mean 'one at a time'. Together, the combination says (rightly or wrongly) that any example may be understood as one of just nine possible configurations: about dealing with concepts and referring to the problem of complexity, about dealing with concepts and referring to finiteness...any allowed pair. Formally, the 'network'

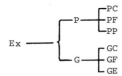

asserts the existence of just the options PC GC, PC GF, PC GE, PF GC, PF GF, PF GE, PP GC, PP GF, PP GE.

Just these two pieces of notation suffice for many purposes, although there are others (three more, to be exact).

Complex concepts

My first example is rather straightforward. Harry Elliot, working at Chelsea on students' solutions to chemistry problems, wated to be able to describe the different chemical quantities students were thinking about at different moments, because he found a bewildering variety of routes through just one problem. The problem happened to be about the composition of an oxide of nitrogen. A version of the network which describes the quantities is:

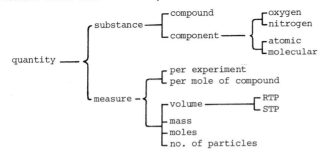

361

I hope you can begin to read it. One possible option is 'mass of atomic oxygen per mole of compound'; another is 'RTP volume of compound per experiment', and so on. There are 50 possibilities, of which nearly all could be traced in some student's solution.

The general point here, then, is about complexity. A fairly simple network allows one to represent a large number of interlinked choices, to think about their patterning, to ask whether (and why) there might be more of them, and so on. You can see how complexity develops by combining just the two notations 'bar' and 'bra' (or 'bracket'). Further, as the network spreads out to the right, choices become more and more delicate; that is, choices to the right are choices within choices. The choice RTP or STP only means anything in the environment of the previous choice 'volume'.

You will rightly object that the network says only what we already know, namely, the logic of combinations of quantities in problems about the composition of gases. The fact is that only after representing them explicitly like this was Harry Elliot able to see in his recorded interviews the presence of some of them, even though they were there all the time, and even though he knew his chemistry perfectly well.

The particular point here is about the representation of ideas with an existing and well known inner logic. This is always the easiest case to deal with, because one's knowledge of the relations can guide the construction of possible networks. Perhaps you would like to construct the network which allows the logical structures

        P AND Q
        P OR Q
        NOT(P AND Q)
        NOT(P OR Q)
        (NOT P) AND (NOT Q)
        (NOT P) OR (NOT Q)

If you turn to Kath Hart's paper, you will find mathematics problems described as patterns of mathematical features, and behaviours in stages described again as abilities to deal with patterns of mathematical features. It seems to me that the network notation could be at least a useful tool for handling such things.

Feelings and finiteness

Let me turn to a totally different kind of example, to make some rather different points. Joan Bliss and I had the problem of describing students' reactions to different learning situations. The two hardest aspects of the problem were, firstly, how to divide up and group things as tenuous as reported reactions, and secondly, when to stop making divisions and to admit that we could no longer distinguish things.

Our network looked like this (it looks like a simple tree, but it isn't really because terms are repeated):

Abbreviated net-work features   Examples of feelings

```
              ┌─ IP ──────────────┬ + 'You felt you could respect him.'
              │                   o 'I just didn't care what he did.'
              │                   └ - 'He really annoyed me.'
    ┌─ INV ───┤                    ┌ + 'I felt generally pleased & interested.'
    │         │           ┌─ GE ──┤ o 'I felt rather apathetic.'
    │         │           │        └ - 'It all seemed tedious - I was put off.'
    │         └─ IND ──────┤        ┌ + 'I felt fascinated and absorbed by it.'
    │                     └─ SP ───┤ o 'I felt relieved it was finished.'
    │                              └ - 'It was a complete waste of time.'
    │         ┌─ IP ──────────────┌ + 'I felt I was as good as anyone else.'
    │         │                   └ - 'I felt they were all much better than
    ├─ AS ────┤                                                          me.'
    │         └─ IND ─────────────┌ + 'I got more confident I could do it.'
    │                             └ - 'I didn't feel I was good enough to do
    │                                                                    it.'
    │                   ┌──had 'I felt, well I've got to do it.'
    │               ┌ ER┤
    │               │   └─free 'I felt I could do it in my own way.'
    │               │   ┌─oblig 'I felt I really ought to be getting it
    │               │   │                                            done.'
    │           ┌ IR┤
    │           │   └──want 'I wanted to work hard & understand it.'
    │           │                    ┌ + 'I felt reassured and relaxed.'
    │     ┌─ IND┤          ┌─ SEC ──┤ o 'I felt confused and bewildered.'
    │     │     │          │         └ - 'I really dreaded going.'
    │     │     │          │   ORD ┌ + 'I felt pleased & generally contented.'
    │     │     │          │       └ - 'I felt thoroughly fed up and upset.'
    └─ WS ┤     │        ┌ SAT┤
          │     │        │   INT ┌ + 'It was a thrill - I was really excited.'
          │     │        │       └ - 'I was in despair and totally miserable.'
          │     │        │            ┌ + 'I felt I was getting on top of it.'
          │     └──── SUC ┤
          │              └ - 'I felt frustrated & unable to get on.'
          │                                 ┌ + 'I felt they recognised it was good
          └─ IP──── ER ── SUC ┤                                             work.'
                             └ - 'I felt I deserved better marks.'
```

Abbreviátions: INV Involvement AS About oneself WS Within oneself
IP Interpersonal IND Individual ER Regulatory (external) IR Regula-
tory (internal) SEC Security SAT Satisfaction SUC Success   ORD
Ordinary INT Intense GEN General SP Specific + Positive o Null
- Negative

My general point here is that one immediately asks why there are just twenty-eight different finest divisions of types of reactions. Why no more? Is all of human sentiment to be caught in twenty-eight boxes? Of course not, with the consequence that students who said 'he really tried hard so that you knew he wanted you to learn' and 'he knew so much and always tried to explain' would probably both go in that first box (positive interpersonal involvement). What we did was to go on refining and dividing until we reached the point where, although further differences were surely there, we could not reliably tell them apart with the information we had. It is important here to recall the principle that meanings are contrasts: whether my two examples are the same is less important than that they are more the same than they are like any other defined possibility.

Of course I do not suppose that all feelings are well captured by a finite classification, and I have much respect for those who feel revulsion (negative   specific   individual involvement!)   at the attempt. My defence is simply that by saying how we did group them, we expose ourselves to criticism and so allow the possibility of improving our rather blunt insights. And I can tell you that constructing such a network is a painfully self-critical exercise, when the pathetic inadequacy of one's ideas becomes clear as they are made explicit.

My particular point (notice how I am keeping to my network for the paper!) is that feelings are an example of the kind of material where, unlike concepts belonging to a well known structure, one has essentially no idea about how they ought to be related and patterned. You will find it much easier to mount a fundamental attack on the very structure of the network of feelings than you will on that for relations amongst chemical quantities. Equally, producing any such scheme is very hard. Indeed, in this kind of case, the interest of the network is largely the way it chooses to organise the universe it is talking about, and changes tend to be fundamental rather than minor elaborations.

Processes

So far I have discussed dealing with something like 'single objects'. Let me turn to the problems of dealing with things which are inherently a pattern of pieces. My example will be a network devised by Farhan Mujib, also at Chelsea, to handle data on how students tackled some physics problems.

Part of his network looks like this:

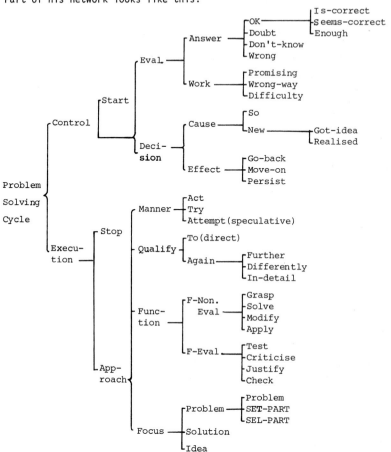

What does it buy him? A student's solution, as evidenced by his work, by observation, and by retrospective interview, gets boiled down to a code of pieces from the network. Some actual cycles from one student look like this:

```
START ACT TO GRASP SEL-PART
ENOUGH SO MOVE-ON ATTEMPT TO SOLVE PROBLEM
ENOUGH GOT-IDEA PERSIST TRY DIFFERENTLY GRASP PROBLEM
PROMISING SO PERSIST ATTEMPT FURTHER SOLVE PROBLEM
DIFFICULTY GOT-IDEA PERSIST FURTHER SOLVE PROBLEM
DOUBT SO PERSIST ATTEMPT TO MODIFY SOLUTION
PROMISING SO PERSIST TRY TO SOLVE PROBLEM
DIFFICULTY SO STOP
```

Let me say at once that the actual network is a little more elaborate, so that (for example) there are actually several kinds of 'difficulty' (those in the above case both being RUN OUT OF IDEAS). Equally, there are further distinctions, like those with 'OK', after 'DOUBT', 'WRONG', etc.

This lets me make a general point not advertised in my network prospectus: a point about handling things which are the same but different. ENOUGH is to be read, via the network, as a case of OK, as a case of attention to the ANSWER, as a case of EVALuation. That is, where divisions in a network become more delicate, the properties propagate back up the network. The result is that the actual data can be described at a level close to detail (the student judged he had enough) but later one can analyse the coded data from more general points of view (how often are there cycles which seem OK? What kinds of cycles come before and after them? And so on).

This is perhaps the most fundamental point of all. In short, how can one simultaneously keep in close touch with the complex actual detail of such data, and at the same time stand back and look at it more broadly?

Our solution at the moment is to use the telegraphic codes (like the example above) as an intermediary. The network is elaborated to the point where, viewed as a kind of generative grammar, it generates from its stock of most delicate terms a description in its own artificial language which is close enough to the data for one to judge how well it fits. Then, afterwards, the network is used to bring back all the implied meanings of each item.

I should mention that the obvious problem with the code above is that though one gets some idea of how the student's work flowed, one has no idea about what he actually did! In fact, Farhan Mujib's network does include such information, and so do his codes.

Computing on qualitative data

Let me now offend every sensitive soul here by saying that we have a computer program which can be told a network and some codes, can read and understand the codes (using the network) and can answer questions of the kind, 'How often does X occur with Y?' where X and Y are any combinations of network features. The program is written (in PASCAL) by Francois Grize of the University of Neuchatel, Switzerland.

We are still working on developing the program, and it is already clear that it needs modification so as to be able to be used sensibly and sensitively. At the same time it does promise to remove the burden (which we have found very great) of systematically counting and relating features present in data.

So what?

It may well seem to you that this is all an elaborate private game, tedious to play, and dangerous too since it fixes in amber what is far too subtle to be trapped so brutally. You may well be right, and it is certainly true that a network will accept boring and pointless analyses as happily, as interesting and perceptive ones.

Let me therefore merely list some of the kinds of problem where I think that such an approach, often in combination with others, might possibly pay off.

1. Describing examination questions.
    (The network for the content is rather easy; reflect that most exam boards categorise content just by syllabus section. The network for the skills needed in a question is proving very difficult.)

2. Describing APU (Assessment of Performance Unit) items.
    (Anyone familiar with the category descriptions produced by APU will see how they are clusters of patterns of features.)

3. Describing patterns of cognitive behaviours.
    (I have already mentioned those in Kath Hart's paper; the problem is of course analogous to that of describing what is involved in doing one of Michael Shayer's test items.)

4. Describing problem solving processes. (I have said enough already here.)

5. Describing interpersonal relationships (Turner, 1972).

6. Describing children's ideas and their structure (see Goëry Delacôte's paper).

There is much that remains unclear to all of those of us involved in the game. Amongst them are criteria for good networks and network features, criteria for trading off complexity and subtlety, ways to decide if a particular problem is worth the bother of such an approach, to mention only the most obvious. Let's hope we have some fun trying to get answers.

Discussion

The networks form a kind of 'decision tree' which when traversed gave meaning to each choice in that the other options had been rejected. Are there not occasions, when constructing a network, that it becomes difficult if not impossible to decide on a number of discrete categories? The network is not objective, but is a reflection of the analyst's perceptions. He could, therefore, include an 'undecidable' category, but it was suggested that by changing the choices to be made earlier in the network, the network could be modified so as to exclude the difficult choice altogether. Wouldn't a 'fuzzy' network be more useful in which, rather than discrete options, there was a continuous range of choices. The main point of the paper was that the use of a finite network allowed the researcher to describe the state of his work and gave him something, i.e. the network, to think with. This argued against the use of fuzzy networks by destroying the clarity.

SEQUENCING SCIENCE MATERIAL FOR PARTICULAR CLASSES

Gordon A.M. Cochaud (to whom further enquiries should be made) and

J.J. Thompson

Introduction

The problem being investigated is that of sequencing material to be learnt. In effect, by 'sequencing'we mean 'the pattern of starting points of a series of lessons'. We do not mean the deliberate selection of the actual content of each lesson, only the arrangement of that content, especially the starting point. My sequence is a series of first steps, and it is the first steps we are searching for. Whilst we have not solved this problem we believe we have got some indications of success, at least for science subjects in middle school. At the outset we reject the notions that:

1. empirical research will yield an optimum sequence that will be the best order of presentation regardless of the class of students, and

2. inherent in a logical structure of a topic there is hidden the best sequence for learning.

Nonetheless, in the situation where one has a class to teach and there is no possibility of individual tutoring the class has to be treated as a more or less homogeneous whole and an optimum approach determined. This does not imply that the optimum sequence for one class is the same as the optimum sequence for any other class. The second point we make is that raised by the question 'Just what sort of logic is applicable to research in the teaching context?'. The present research was not designed as a controlled experiment. Rather the data collecting was arranged deliberately to fit into normal classroom practice without undue interruptions of the lessons. The data provide evidence for applying inductive reasoning to the search for necessary antecedents to certain observables. Even so the method may be limited to the extent that the necessary antecedents may not be sufficient antecedents but at least one will be able to detect examples for which certain phenomona will not be subsequently observable. The method is illustrated by appropriate examples. We are not offering a proof that the method of induction is the most satisfactory method for a science based upon empiricism or that attempts by any other logic are futile.

Word Association Test

One of the purposes of the research is to enable the teacher to determine as precisely as possible the starting points for each new topic for each class. The Word Association Test (WAT) serves this purpose admirably:

1. an analysis of each test does give the teacher the light in which each class sees each new topic;

2. the test is quick to devise-taking only about five minutes;

3. each test is tailored for each new situation;

4. the test is a rapid group test taking about five minutes of class time;

5. the analysis for the purpose of planning lessons is rapid, only requires pencil and paper and there are no calculations;

6. no special skills are required for constructing or analysing the test;

7. the information obtained from the test is cumulative and can be used to pinpoint where individual students are failing to learn particular aspects of a topic.

In practice it turns out that there is more than enough information available; that the class is, in fine detail, composed of x different students who see each new topic slightly differently from one another. The WAT is constructed simply by taking a list of the new words one is hopeful of introducing and the words upon which it is hoped the students are going to build. A list of 20-30 seems sufficient in practice. When giving the test one offers an explanation to the class as to what you want them to do and why you want them to do the test. The exact form of the explanation will vary from class to class. We explain to the students that a response can be a single word or phrase, an equation, a quick sketch, a symbol or it can be a blank, that is no response comes to mind immediately. Whatever the response we want it to be the first thing that comes to their minds. We ask the class to try and concentrate on science if at all possible but they are not to give answers that they think we might want. The WAT is only of use if the answers are the students' own replies. There are no right or wrong answers. Each student lists down the left hand side of a piece of paper the numbers from 1 to however many there are on the test. By numbering the words on the list it is possible to keep the responses matching their stimuli. When ready, the teacher reads out the number and the stimulus word, pausing long enough for the students to write a short response (five seconds is usually adequate) then reads the next number and its stimulus. Stimuli must be clearly spoken because they are read out once only. At the end of the test we do not go back over stimuli unanswered at all.

WAT Validation

How valid is the word association test devised by an individual teacher? It is immediately apparent that each WAT has content validity because all of the stimuli were selected on the basis of having some direct bearing on the specific topic at hand. An interesting situation arises when we come to construct validity. What is constructed from each child's set of answers is a knowledge map (although this actually only needs to be done when diagnosing individual students). A knowledge map illustrates the apparent pattern in which the student retrieves, from long-term memory, the various pieces of information constituting a particular topic. The map is valid to the extent that it adequately represents whatever a student knows. This introduces the question of reproducibility of responses and, by implication, the stability of the inferred knowledge structure. The actual responses given by a student depend upon the exact context in which the stimuli were perceived. We have small samples and it is the differences between samples which we are going to capitalise upon in our teaching. At the individual level therefore we want some corroboration that the data from the WATs does yield reliable information and not just random noise. Eventually the validation comes from an examination of the data from several WATs for the same student pooled to construct a knowledge map. Based upon what the student is capable of retrieving from LTM (long-term memory) given certain stimuli we see obvious changes in the maps and hence changes in whatever the student knows and indeed, to a large extent, whatever the student is capable of learning in the next lesson. Our experimental data shows:

1. group data from the WAT is very useful information for lesson planning;

2. knowledge maps constructed from the WATs do show changes in the expected directions; that is, subject to certain restrictions the maps change in structure according to the sequence of presentation of material;

3. the knowledge maps are unique for each student at any point in time;

4. the patterns of changes are consistent across students.

For the remainder of this paper we will confine our attention to point 1, that is the differences between groups of students.

The advantage of determining the optimum approach to use for a class during the next lesson or so ought to be self-evident, especially in the situation where the teacher has not taught that class before or where the topic is one which is not just an extension of a previous similar topic. The analysis merely consists of categorising the responses to each of a number of stimuli and the result is such as is shown in table 1.

Table 1: Categories of responses to three stimuli by two classes (H and T) before any instruction on the topic of density

Stimulus	Response category	Class H	Class T	Class T'**
volume	sound/radio	4	3	0
	uncontained liquid	4	3	0
	*'---'	5	9	0
	objects	3	4	0
	units, cm^3, etc.	0	0	7
	other unique	6	2	10
space	fields, grass, etc.	7	0	0
	area	0	5	4
	empty, air	1	6	1
	stars, moon, etc.	0	7	3
	'---'	5	3	2
	volume	0	0	5
	other unique	9	1	2
mass	units	4	0	1
	weights	6	12	13
	volume	3	1	0
	'---'	4	5	2
	other unique	3	4	1

*'---' indicates that the student made no response at all

**after one week of instruction to most of class T

The most obvious observation is that stimuli do not always produce responses: that material taught (or at least presented as part of a logical sequence in class and recorded in the student's notebook) is not always incorporated into the student's knowledge structure immediately upon, or very soon after, presentation. Another obvious feature is the different responses to the same stimulus from different students. When the responses to pairs of stimuli are examined we find that most of the students exhibit different pairs of responses; extending this to multiplets of stimuli we soon reach the point where it is evident that every student has a demonstrably different view of a topic which involves the consideration of several items of information. In one very real sense we cannot hope to make our teaching presentation simultaneously suit exactly each student in the class. The best we can hope for is some acceptable optimum approach.

Now it may be argued that these differences are random or spurious. However 15 students did, during various times of the term, four WATs such that the first two were identical tests separated by one week of instruction, and the second two (different tests from the first two but again identical to each other) were separated by four days with no instruction between them. Table 2 shows for each student the number of identical responses on both of the first two tests (29 items) and the number of identical responses on the second pair of tests (30 items). One of the reasons for not giving a very long list of stimuli at the beginning and/or end of each lesson is to eliminate the effect of extraneous learning, that is, to ensure that the sequence of presentation of material is that of the lessons given in class because only in this manner will we be able to compare the presentation sequence with the subsumption sequence.

Table 2: Number of identical responses on two pairs of tests (class T)

Separation condition	Number of identical responses on pairs of tests separated as stated														
Instruction	7	16	10	3	9	7	8	8	6	10	10	9	9	7	5
No instruction	25	16	19	8	22	19	21	12	13	15	17	18	13	19	21

It will be noticed that in every case (except one) there were considerably less changes over the period in which there was no instruction than over the period during which there were two separate lessons. Indications of stability over longer periods of time may not be strictly comparable because the stimuli were not given under identical conditions - the WATs were slightly different. And in any case we would not expect the knowledge maps to remain stable over longer periods of time which included some appropriate instruction.

Some indication of the changes of group responses is given in table 3 wherein the responses to 'volume' are categorised.

Table 3:   Changes in group responses to 'volume'

Response Category	Timing of test with respect to period of instruction									
	Before		During		End of		+3 weeks		+15 weeks	
class	H	T	H	T	H	T	H	T	H	T
sound	4	3	0	1	0	0	0	1	1	-
liquids	4	3	6	1	2	0	3	0	5	-
containers	3	4	0	0	0	0	0	0	0	-
'---'	5	9	2	2	1	2	1	1	0	-
units	0	0	2	8	4	7	5	11	4	-
mass, density	0	0	1	8	4	7	6	1	6	-
rule	0	0	5	4	2	5	3	7	3	-
cube	1	1	1	0	4	1	2	2	1	-
other unique	5	2	4	0	4	2	2	1	4	-

If we classify the responses of individual students as either
relevant or irrelevant to the topic of density (the stimulus was
'volume') then we can see if the changes indicated by the WATs responses demonstrate learning. In order to indicate some sort of
permanency of response we compared the responses of individual students at the 'before' and '+3 weeks' conditions. Twenty-five students
changed from irrelevant to relevant responses, only two responses
changed from relevant to irrelevant and sixteen students' responses
did not change according to this categorisation. Currently other
teachers are replicating our method and we are also testing the predictive validity of the WATs by using knowledge maps to make
predictions of test scores by assessing whether or not individual
students would/not be able to solve certain problems.

Uses of the WAT

We turn now to the use to which the WAT data may be put in the
classroom situation. Referring to table 1 and the categories of
responses for class H we see that the responses to the stimulus word
'mass' were mostly relevant to the purpose in mind - to teach the
class about density. Most of the class are accounted for by students
associating 'mass' with 'volume, weight or a unit of mass'. However
the response to 'volume' and to 'space' indicate that the class in
general do not see volume as something to do with the taking up of
space and so they would not be able to grasp density as a measure of
how much substance/mass can be packed into a given volume/space.

To this end the entire first lesson was taken up by going over
some conservation of volume demonstrations emphasising the constancy

of the number of cubic centimetre for the same amount of water and later for the same amount of plasticine shown in different shapes. The next lesson was the measuring of the mass/weight and volume of different pieces of brass.

For class T the situation was rather different. 'Mass' was virtually tied to 'weight'; there being no mention of units at all. Almost half the class gave no response to 'volume' and 'space' was associated with the rather abstract notions of area, empty and nothing, as well as stars, moon and rockets. The next two lessons were spent examining the relationships between dimensionality and mass, volume and weight. About one third of the class had gone on a school trip and rather than start the work on density in their absence the week was spent on something of value to the learning of density with the rather dramatic effect on the responses as shown in table 1 - T' are class T who had these extra lessons.

For the remainder of this analysis we restrict ourselves to the data for 21 students from class T. The starting position for the work on density is that nearly all of these students (18) at least recognised the word 'density' and were able to produce some sort of response to it. Similarly for 'volume' & 'mass', with the added advantage that the responses to these two latter terms were generally quite relevant. To reinforce the relationship between volume and its units and to introduce the relationship between mass and its units a simple mass/volume conservation experiment was demonstrated. This also served to introduce the method of measuring volume, namely, by displacement in a measuring cylinder. The next step was the comparison between the mass and volume of several pieces of brass, after which the three rules were studied (density =, mass =, volume =) and their summary in the triangle noted: cover up any one $\frac{M}{D \times V}$ of M, V or D and the rule for its computation appears. A problem on each rule was gone through in class then the observations repeated using copper pieces, glass pieces and finally wood (held down with a skewer). The learning of the rules may have been by rote, however, for most of the class the terms involved in the rules were familiar and in the case of two of the terms their units as well.

At the end of the week of instruction 17 students had a relevant response to 'volume', 19 to 'mass' and 17 to 'density'; twelve students knew the three rules, 2 knew two rules and 5 one rule correctly - at least according to the WAT they were given at the end of the week.

One would have thought that as 16 students knew the rule for mass, and that for most of the class (mean verbal IQ 117) the words had relevant notions attached, we were ready to go on and attempt the work on displacement. It was on that basis that it was decided to extend the work to include loss of weight on sinking: the distinction between mass and weight can also be introduced in this manner too. Now displacement requires that the students see at least two sets of relationships - one set between mass/weight/units and another set between water/displacement/volume/units. A student was considered to know a relationship if her response to each element in a set was another element in the same set. On that basis 19 students knew the first set and 8 of these the second set too. Starting with weight the notion of upthrust was introduced by appealing to common-sense observations of holding things in an outstretched hand. We continued by weighing objects both in and out of water. Examination of the weight loss/volume data soon elicited the rule. Discussion of the explanation involved why things less dense than water do not sink, how it is that steel ships float and how to 'weigh' a ship. A problem sheet on the first three rules was handed out and the solutions gone over in the next class. The next lesson was an achievement test followed by a WAT. Sixteen students recalled the three rules correctly and another three two rules. This actually under-estimated what the students knew because the responses were rushed compared with the time available during the achievement test on which 20 students correctly wrote all three rules (that is, correctly stated the appropriate rule at the beginning of each problem). The rules were elicited in the WAT by using for example, 'mass equals' as the stimulus although in some cases the rule popped up when 'mass' was the stimulus. There were two displacement problems from the second week's work on the achievement test and three students (from the eight that were ready to attempt that section) got both problems correct.

Examination of the WAT responses indicated that very few students actually connected displacement with either mass or volume. The problem 'Why does a piece of wood float?' was set for homework and discussed in detail for the next lesson.

At the achievement test at the end of term 19 students knew all three rules and also got the two density problems correct. Ten students were able to work out correctly the two displacement problems. We are convinced that the WAT has a lot to offer to the classroom teacher. Currently we are examining the individual knowledge maps of these students for differences and similarities. Knowledge maps are constructed by making a digraph from the stimulus-response pairs. Each stimulus-response pair forms the nodes at the end of an arc with the direction of the arc being from stimulus to response. All knowledge is seen as discrete items of information and only the nodes of the digraph contain representations of items of information. The only relationship betwen the nodes is that of 'accessible from'. At this stage we feel that we have examined an insufficient number and variety of knowledge maps to be able to make reliable assertions.

Discussion

There was a lively debate following this paper, with the speaker maintaining the value of the knowledge maps derived from word associa- tion tests using the arguments of stimulus-response theory. Thus questions about the mental processes leading to associations, about the understanding of concepts, about behaviour-shaping, about the 'falsity' of making pupils respond to volume in different ways in different classes, about the long term stability of the associations, and the intensive properties of concepts were all turned aside with essentially the same reply: a concept is a set of rules, no more, and once the child learns the right responses to given stimuli in a given context, that is all that matters. Intensive properties, 'comprehen- sion' and mental processes are of no interest, at least in the context of the study reported here.

Other questions were raised about the ease of setting and scoring the tests. Cochaud explained that they were easier to set and score than conventional objective tests, the teacher only having to give key words in the topic he was proposing to teach. The knowledge maps them- selves were not important to the teacher. The first associations given by the child indicated something of the present state of a concept, and so aided the structuring of teaching material. Experience indicat- ed that whereas the first associated word may be non-scientific ini- tially, it tended to become more relevant during the teaching sequence, although a few children (divergent thinkers?) continued to produce quite inconsistent answers.

It was suggested that the absence of an association on the knowledge map suggested no relationship, while this was not necessarily the case. In Cochaud's experience it was the case, and when a map showed no connection, the child would fail to solve a problem that needed that relationship.

PSYCHOLOGICAL THEORIES AND RESEARCH METHODS RELATING TO PUPILS'
MENTAL STRUCTURES AS AIDS IN DESIGNING A CURRICULUM

Ronny F.A. Wierstra

Introduction

This paper deals with theories and research relating to pupils'
'mental structures'. The emphasis is on mental structures which
pupils may attain as a consequence of the learning tasks in one or
more units. In the PLON project[1] we gained experience in assessing
mental structures of a large group of pupils, within the context of
formative curriculum evaluation. This context demands that the
empirical data relating to pupils' mental structures should give indications in which way the tentative structure of the learning activities
('instructional structure') should be revised.

In sections 2 and 3 the concepts of instructional structure and
mental structure will be explained more fully. Finally, in section 4,
I shall discuss some recent techniques which enable us to operationalise facets of the hypothetical construct 'mental structure' and to
make it accessible for measurement and evaluation.

The instructional structure; 4 organisational principles

A curriculum-team makes many decisions about the selection,
sequencing and structuring of learning content and learning activities
of pupils. These decisions include the choice of learning content,
determining the extent of inductive versus deductive learning, the
amount of pupil experimentation and the amount of pupil control rather
than teacher control of the learning process. All of these are aspects
of what I call 'instructional structure' which should be specified by
the curriculum team. I think, at least the following organisational
principles[2] are important for providing links:

---

[1] PLON is a Dutch Curriculum development project for physics in
  secondary schools.
[2] I derive these principles on the one hand from my view of educational aims, on the other hand (probably most) from a number of
  general principles of learning.

1. The instructional structure should link up as much as possible
    with the subjective knowledge structure (mental structure) which
    is already possessed by the pupil.

    For instance: when dealing with the concept of voltage (poten-
    tial), the instruction should not leave out the fact that pupils
    associate voltage primarily with high voltage and danger and not,
    for example, with the voltage of a battery (this is what we found
    in our project);

2. The instruction should provide for 'integrative reconciliation'
    of learning experiences.

    This means that the instruction should illustrate explicitly how
    new meanings which the pupil learned compare and contrast with
    other previous meanings (especially more restricted versus more
    general meanings). Integrative reconcilation is needed in order
    to reconcile real or apparent inconsistencies.

    An elaboration of this concept with examples is given by
    Ausubel et al. (1978) and Novak (1977a);

3. The instructional structure should promote cross-references of
    learning content.

    We noticed in our project that after a unit on 'Electricity',
    pupils confused potential (tension) with electric current
    (strength of current). One can probably consolidate the speci-
    fic meaning of strength of current by relating it to the
    principle that electric current (strength) is the same every-
    where in a single circuit. So, we make a cross-reference between
    electrical circuit and strength of current;

4. The daily-life content which is brought up in the unit, should
    be able to evoke associations related to subject matter (in PLON:
    associations relating to physical concepts).

    For instance, at the end of a unit on electricity a number of
    pupils gave to the word short-circuiting the association:
    strength of current. After a unit about energy, the associa-
    tions with the terms dynamo and electricity consumption should
    include responses related to energy, e.g. energy production/
    energy generation.

These four principles - which are interdependent - should be used by
curriculum designers.

However, that is not the whole story: we also have to invent
research tools which enable us to investigate empirically which
concepts, in particular the organising links, need to be strengthened.
This demands first of all techniques for describing mental structures
of pupils.

The hypothetical construct 'mental structure'

The construct 'mental structure' refers to an organised network of interrelated concepts, which the pupil stores in his memory. It is difficult to give an exact definition of mental structure (generally referred to as 'cognitive' structure[1] in the literature).

Shavelson (1974, p.232) states: 'Cognitive structure is a hypothetical construct referring to the organisation (relationship) of concepts in memory.' Fenker (1975) speaks about the perceived organisation of the concepts in a topic area. The common core of the various descriptions is that a concept is never isolated in our memory, but is embedded in a network of associations. This embedding does not always follow strictly logical rules (not even in strictly discipline-centred instruction). Pupils have other associations too.

For this reason Schaefer (1979) makes a distinction between the 'logic core' of a concept (in physics teaching that which defines the concepts in a strict physical sense) on the one hand and the 'associative framework' of the concept on the other hand. The associative framework is the range of concepts with which this concept has relations which are not of a purely logical nature.

In PLON the concept associative framework is especially important because we do not teach strict discipline-centred physics, but try to do justice to relationships between physics and the environment. At the moment we try to explore the associative framework of pupils by measuring the semantic distance between concepts (see following section). Most researchers use these methods for other purposes. Preece (1978) for instance, is interested in investigating whether cognitive maps of pupils after instruction are similar to the cognitive maps of experts. This is definitely not our interest. We are interested in describing cognitive maps of pupils for the sake of revising the instructional structure, from the viewpoint of the four organisation-principles, mentioned earlier.

Techniques for assessment of mental structures within the framework of curriculum construction and evaluation

Methods are needed to assess mental structures in order to investigate which concepts require stronger organising links. Cognitive psychologists have made a start with the construction of models of mental (or cognitive) structure (e.g. Greeno, 1976; Posner, 1978) for use in instructional situations. In those models various types of relations (e.g. property, part-whole) are distinguished. Because of the complexity of these methods, most current research makes no

---

[1] I prefer the term mental structure, because not only cognitive, but also affective aspects play a part.

379

explicit distinction between kinds of relations but confines itself mainly to measuring (semantic) distances between concepts. After all, these methods appear to be promising enough.

Semantic distance (or its opposite, semantic proximity) has been defined operationally in a number of ways, and in studies of scientific concepts the word-association method of measuring semantic distance has been used most often. Pupils are presented with stimulus-concepts from physics lessons and have to respond with a number of associations for each concept.

Shavelson (1974) points out that it is important when using the word-association method to give pupils good instruction and also to define the context well, for instance, is the pupil allowed to give associations that are not directly treated or discussed in the physics lesson?

The semantic proximity between two stimulus concepts for a given individual is determined by the degree of overlap between the pair of response lists produced by that individual. The degree of overlap is generally expressed in the form of a 'relatedness coefficient', as defined by Garskof and Houston (1963). This measure permits differential weighting of associations so that this can reflect the greater salience of the earlier responses. By means of the word-association method (or another method: free recall, tree-construction, etc., see Preece 1978; Shavelson, 1974) one can calculate all inter-concept-distance data. From this data a number of different types of maps of cognitive structure can be produced, depending on the method of analysis (mostly multidimensional scaling, hierarchical cluster analysis or Waern's technique (Waern, 1972))and on the theory of semantic structure. Preece (1978) distinguishes between three kinds of cognitive map (spatial, hierarchical and graphic). It cannot be ignored that in a particular research situation some models appear to fit better than others; nevertheless, some researchers wonder whether the models are not actually more similar than had previously been thought.

With regard to the different methods of data collection, high correlations have been found between these methods, e.g. Henley (1969) found a correspondence between the word-association method and similarity rating[1]. Intriguing is the high correlation which Kintsch found between semantic distance (by means of word association) and reaction time (quoted in Preece, 1978). The correlations between the various methods provide some evidence that each method measures a substantial 'method-free' part of the cognitive structure. Other evidence is provided by findings that there is often a close

---

[1] This method asks pupils to rate directly the similarity of two concepts (on a 6-point scale for instance).

correspondence between the cognitive structure - measured by means of one of the above-mentioned methods - and a separate measurement of the content structure of written texts by the digraph method (e.g. Shavelson, 1972; Johnson, 1969).

In PLON we have some experience in revising the instructional structure of units on the basis of empirical data obtained by word-association tests and similarity ratings[1]. The pupils were presented with these instruments before and after a unit. The associations and the multidimensional scaling or cluster analysis of semantic distances provided useful information. We want to supplement these methods by asking the pupils for free definitions and by asking them to explain the relations which they perceive between stimulus-words.

Of course other methods are needed too for investigating the adequacy of the designed instructional structure. In PLON we also use:

- cognitive achievement test;

- learner reports;

- pupil questionnaire/interview.

With regard to learner reports, this method has been introduced by De Groot (1973, 1974). By learner report he understands a report produced by the pupil in which he reports learning experiences which are fundamental for him. The basic form of a learner report, as we use it, is:

I have learned (discovered, experienced) with regard to concept X

that (how........................,

or that (how)I....................

_____

[1] This method asks pupils to rate directly the similarity of two concepts (on a 6-point scale for instance).

INCLUSIVE THINKING WITH INCLUSIVE CONCEPTS

Gerhard Schaefer

In the last 15 years, many attempts have been made to integrate scientific subjects in school by interdisciplinary or even trans-disciplinary approaches. In all these endeavours one common aim is recognisable: the aim to re-combine disintegrated knowledge to achieve a more comprehensive understanding of our world. It is, in other words, a movement back from exclusive thinking to 'inclusive thinking' (Schaefer 1975, 1978a), which does not concentrate, with high precision, upon small sections of our life, but takes into consideration all essential interrelations with outside factors from other fields or disciplines. Inclusive thinking is thinking beyond a particular area of interest and includes a variety of aspects.

Thinking, in the Piagetian sense of operational thinking, means operating with concrete and abstract concepts. Hence there are at least two ways of achieving a higher inclusivity of thinking:

1. By increasing the total number of concepts in memory from different fields, disciplines or aspects, so extending the whole knowledge structure of the learner to a larger variety of sub-ject areas. (What in Germany is normally called 'Allgemeinbil-dung'.)

2. By developing single concepts with a high inclusive power.

The first way would proceed via an enlargment of the total system of knowledge, the second one via an improvement of its elements. Of course, these two processes, as in all systems, are interrelated with each other: the total volume of knowledge will normally affect the quality of individual concepts (by the linkages between the concepts), and conversely, the quality of particular concepts (especially those of a higher order of abstraction, the 'advance organisers' (Ausubel, 1960) or the 'cognitive bridges' (Novak, 1977a) will influence the characteristics of knowledge.

In figure 1 the second way is illustrated, which is the way followed in this paper. It will be shown, how both the interpersonal and the personal meaning of a single concept can be examined and in-fluenced by teaching in order to develop 'inclusive thinking'. The investigations are based upon the 'burr model' of concepts (Schaefer, 1978b, 1979), demonstrating three essential parts of a concept instead of two: the name (designation), the logic core (interpersonal, e.g. scientific meaning), and the associative framework (personal meaning).

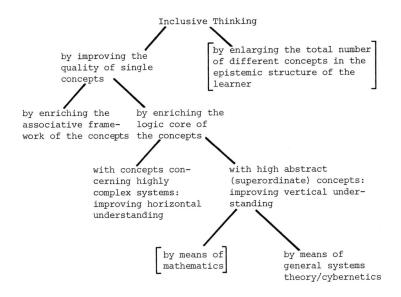

Figure 1: Strategy for the development of inclusive thinking

'Ecosytem' as an inclusive concept

The logic core, as it should be. Figure 2 demonstrates the pattern of logic relationships identifying the concept ecosystem. It is a representation of the interpersonal (international, scientific) meaning of the word 'ecosystem', i.e. a model of the logic core of the concept.

An adequate definition of an ecosystem, according to figure 2, would be:

An ecosystem is a sub-system of our biosphere composed of producers, consumers, decomposers, and abiotic factors, like a forest, a lake, a moor; it is able to maintain an ecological equilibrium (fluctuations between certain limits) over a certain period by means of self-reproduction of sub-units and self-regulation of the whole.

Although there is still some discussion among ecologists about the phenomenon of self-regulation being an essential criterion of an ecosystem or not, most ecologists today agree upon this criterion (Ellenberg, 1973; Odum, 1976). So the above definition can be taken

as an agreement among the scientific community of ecologists, and it
can be used as a measure for comprehension in a research project on
concept formation.

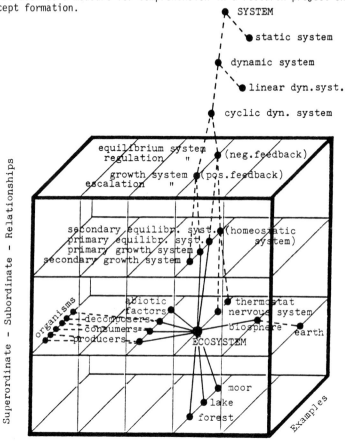

System - Part - Relationships

Figure 2: The logic core of the concept 'ecosystem'

Note that a full understanding of the concept can only be
achieved by also filling in the upper part of the vertical
axis (abstract concepts of general systems theory).
Otherwise the concept remains only partly understood.

Figure 2 demonstrates how the range-specific understanding of a particular ecosystem, say a lake, can be extended to a general understanding of ecosystems by comparing a lake with other examples of ecosystems. This understanding, however, although more general, is still rather 'range-specific' in respect to ecology. So the comparison of ecosystems with other, non-ecological self-regulating systems will yield a better understanding of the concept ecosystem on the next higher abstraction level, i.e. on the level of the concept 'equilibrium system' (regulation system). On this level it turns out that there are two distinct kinds of equilibrium systems: those with special information channels (homeostatic systems with indirect feed-back via 'messages', like nervous systems and most technical systems), and those without special information channels (systems with direct interaction of their parts, like chemical buffers, ecosystems). If ecosystems are misinterpreted as homeostatic systems, researchers will seek in vain for information channels, set points, regulators, etc. So the knowledge of the two different kinds of regulation system necessarily improves understanding of the concept 'ecosystem'. This kind of understanding by more generalised, abstract concepts is called by Greeno (1977) 'explicit' and by Schaefer (1978b, 1979) 'vertical' understanding (the latter according to the geometrical setup of figure 2, which is based upon the normal versions of 'higher' and 'lower' abstraction level).

'Equilibrium system', 'cyclic dynamic system', dynamic system', and finally 'system' therefore are continuous steps on the way to higher abstraction and to a higher degree of understanding of what an ecosystem is. They are 'advance organisers' as described by Ausubel (1960).

These abstract concepts of systems theory, however, can only be really effective in different fields of experience, if there is enough basic empirical knowledge in these fields which has been connected with them. So the concept of 'regulation cycle' has been shown to structure new ecological experience only if the linkage between ecology and cybernetics had been taught sufficiently (Eulefeld, Schaefer, 1974, English translation 1978, p.50). This again emphasises the marked influence associations have on thinking. The concept of 'regulation system' is able to link knowledge from physiology, ecology, chemistry, physics/technology, economics, sociology and psychology, as all these fields show examples of regulation that can be subsumed under this superordinate concept - provided the subsumption has been prepared by bringing those fields together in the associations of the students.

One way of teaching inclusive thinking is therefore to teach using superordinate concepts, 'subsumers' (Novak, 1977a),together with various examples from different subject areas. Textbooks in biology at schools and universities deal to a large extent with system/part relationships of biosystems (morphology, anatomy, physiology, genetics, etc.); superordinate/subordinate relationships are specified only on a rather low level of abstraction (see lower part of figure 2). Sections on system theory are lacking or rare. So the 'vertical understanding' of the students is hardly developed, especially when there is no obligation to study biology at the university together with mathematics. The author therefore, in the last 10 years, has published instructional devices under the heading 'cybernetic biology' in order to help the teacher to include more abstract levels into biology teaching (Schaefer, 1972, 1973; Eulefeld, Schaefer, 1974. English translation 1978; Bayrhuber, Schaefer 1978; Dylla, Schaefer, 1978). The evaluation of these curriculum units has proved the effect of cybernetic thinking on vertical understanding in biology and on the development of inclusive thinking by a rich pattern of associations to different subject areas.

The logic core, as it is. The analysis of definitions given by students at age 13/14 and 17/18 and by biology teachers yields an interesting insight into this knowledge structure with regard to the concept 'ecosystem'. Four kinds of analyses were carried out:

1. The qualitative nature of the definition.

2. The determination of the 'volume of the definition' (figure 2) composed of the number of levels occupied in each of the three dimenions by the definition.

3. The position of the definition within figure 2 (more above, more below, more right, more left, etc.).

4. The distribution of different content areas in the definition, compared with the categories found in free associations.

First results taken from schools in Northern Germany (Hamburg, Kiel and surroundings) are summarised in table 1. The table shows the following situation:

1. At age 13/14, about 75% of the students gave an incorrect or incomplete definition of an ecosystem. 41% of the students gave definitions which were of the associative kind and not logically structured. About 22% gave a partly correct definition, which was incomplete. None of the definitions was fully correct, but 5% were very close to being correct.

    At age 17/18, the situation has markedly changed: only 22% of the students gave an incorrect or incomplete answer. (It is surprising that 16% of the biology teachers in the sample also fell into this category.) The number of associative definitions dropped down to 17%, whereas the incomplete definitions increased to 41%. In this age group we found about 18% absolutely correct definitions (compared with the teachers, who gained 23% correct definitions).

386

Table 1: Formal evaluation of free definitions according to figure 2 showing percentages of population.

Categories of Evaluation	Population		
	age 13/14	age 17/18	Biol. teachers
Quality of Definition			
1. Tautological	0	0	0
2. Synonymic	3	0	0
3. Wrong	75	22	16
4. Negative	0	0	0
5. Associative	41	17	3.3
6. Incomplete	22	41	53
7. Partly wrong	0	31	10
8. Correct	0 (5)	18 (+25)	23 (+20)
Volume of Definition			
hori-zontal H 1	55	33	33
H 2	8	59	53
H 3	0	7	10
> H 3	0	0	0
verti-cal V 1	13	13	3.3
V 2	34	33	23
V 3	14	38	40
> V 3	1.5	16	33
examp-les E 1	33	10	10
E 2	20	29	27
E 3	8	38	27
> E 3	0	18	30
Position of Definition			
hori-zontal more right	9	59	47
medium	53	33	50
more left	0	10	7
verti-cal more above	28	49	63
medium	20	46	30
more below	16	21	7

Note: The sum of percentages in the upper block ('Quality of Definition') is greater than 100%, as the definitions are sometimes placed in more than one category. In the left column 13/14 year olds) the sum is, in the blocks 'Volume' and 'Position', less than 100%, as the missing definitions do not appear here.

2. In the horizontal dimension of the logic core we find a shift from the maximum being H 1 in the 13/14 age group (55%) towards the maximum being H 2 in the 17/18 age group (59%), which is also maintained by the teachers with 53%. Furthermore we find a marked increase of H 3: from 0% in 13/14 to 7% in 17/18, and to 10% in teachers. This means that the number of system-part-levels and so the degree of inclusive thinking in the horizontal dimension seems to rise the further someone studies.

3. In the vertical dimension of the logic core the maximum of the 13/14 year olds is in V 2 (two levels of abstraction) with 34% of all students. This maximum rises up to V 3 in the 17/18 year old group (38%), which is also maintained by the teachers (40%). The teachers distinguish themselves from the students by a rather high number with >V 3 (33%), which shows that with higher education the ability to move through different levels of abstraction grows visibly. This speaks for a growing ability for inclusive thinking in the vertical dimension in higher stages of education, an assumption which is also supported by point 6.

4. The number of examples in the definitions (examples in the strict sense as subordinated concepts) jumps from the maximum in E 1 (33% of the 13/14 year olds) to the maximum in B 3 (38% of the 17/18 year olds) and further increases to the maximum in >E 3 (30% of the teachers). This is surely to be seen in connection with the increase of the number of levels in the vertical dimension reported above, which leads inevitably to a broader spectrum of views, applications, specifications. It is symptomatic of inclusive thinking.

5. The position of the definitions within figure 2 spreads in the horizontal dimension from medium to the right end and left end. That means: More complex systems as well as more details (elements) of systems can be found in the definitions. This is obviously an effect of the biological system-part training prevailing in school and university curricula.

6. In all age groups the emphasis of the definitions in the vertical dimension lies in the upper (more abstract) region. Definitions mostly move on this level by using superordinate terms like 'system', 'process', 'science', etc. and then tend to remain on this level. There is an increase again through the ages from 28% to 49% to 63% and a growing differentiation towards the upper level in the teachers. This shows that high-order abstract terms are available in memory in the higher age groups,

which may function as advance organisers in inclusive thinking.

7. As figures 3 and 4 demonstrate, the distribution of content areas within the definitions is very similar to that of the free associations to the key-word ecosystem. This distribution will be analysed in the following section dealing with associations. One striking result gained from the definition tests should, however, be pointed out here: The distribution does not fit the 'standard definition' of ecosystem (see figure 2). It contains quite correct maxima in the biological and also formal field, but it is lacking equivalent values in the range of non-living nature (which is part of ecosystems!), such as economy (which is also an essential factor influencing ecosystems), and environmental affairs (which cannot, although having a political side, be detached from the scientific concept of ecosystem).

Points 1 to 7 of these investigations, carried out in West Germany, correspond to similar results gained in the Philippines in February 1979. These results will be published in a cross-cultural study on concept formation at a later stage.

The associative framework, as it should be. A hopeful approach to inclusive thinking can certainly be the interlinkage of associations from different subject areas on a non-logic, non-systematic level. People will use advance organisers and logic relationships as long as they are moving in a 'logic world' (e.g. world of science, world of technology). But there are plenty of examples showing that people forget about scientific, logic relationships and fall back to associative behaviour when moving in a 'non-logic' (that means: non-systematic, not purposely structured) world which is predominant in parts of our daily life (family, friendship, sports, hobby, etc.). Preparing students for life and not only for specific professions (the major aim of primary and secondary school teaching) would mean teaching towards inclusive thinking for both types of life situations, the 'logic' and the 'non-logic' one.

If we are going to make a concept associable to all fields of everyday life where it may be important, we have to take care that its associative framework covers all these fields to an adequate degree.

The concept ecosystem seems important in at least the following areas:

1. Living nature (biology, ecology);

2. Non-living nature (physics, chemistry, geology, etc.);

3. Environmental affairs (environmental policy, pollution, preservation of nature, etc.);

4. Agriculture, horticulture;

5. Science (terminology, research, university, etc.);

6. Formal disciplines (mathematics, systems theory);

7. Economies (industry, commerce, resources, structure of society, etc.);

8. School (teaching events in connection with ecosystem).

So we have to expect a spectrum of associations in connection with the term 'ecosystem' which contains to some degree associations from all these 8 categories. In the following section empirical investigations will throw light upon this theoretical expectation.

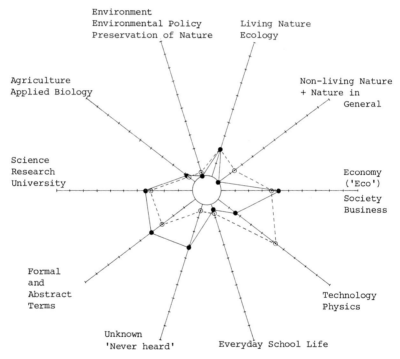

Figure 3:   Distribution of free associations (---) and elements of free definitions (—) upon the key-word ECOSYSTEM. Gymnasium Hamburg. One mark means 5%. 12/13 year olds, before instruction on 'ecosystem'.

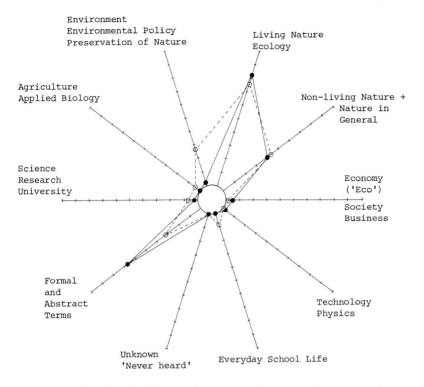

Figure 4: Distribution of free associations (---) and elements
of free definitions (——) upon the key-word
ECOSYSTEM. Gymnasium Hamburg. One mark means 5%.
17/18 year olds, before special course in ecology.

The associative framework, as it is. In the last ten years, investigations on free associations and free definitions of various biological
concepts have been carried out in West Germany. The investigations
have been extended to Israel and to the Philippines. The total number
of students tested in the age group 13/14 years is now 206, in the
age group 17/18 years 163, and 52 biology teachers have also been
tested. A rather clear picture about the distribution of associations
and definitions relating to the concept 'ecosystem' is emerging for
these groups, which is represented by two selected examples of classes
(same school, same teacher) and by a teacher group (figures 3,4 and 5).

The figures demonstrate general results we find in the West German and also Philippine populations so far examined:

1. There is a marked correlation between the distribution of free associations and the distribution of free definition elements. The correlation coefficient in the total population examined up to now is between + 0.7 and + 0.8.

2. The distribution of free associations does not cover all 8 expected categories to a satisfactory extent.

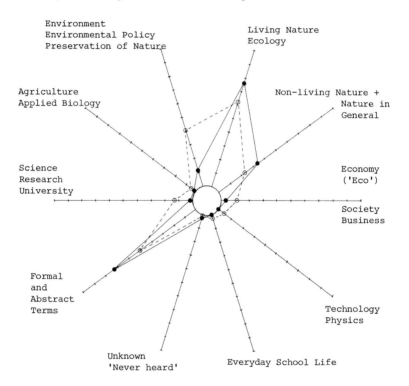

Figure 5: Distribution of free associations (---) and elements of free definitions (——) upon the key-word ECOSYSTEM, given by Biology Teachers (n = 52). One mark means 5%.

392

3. There is a clear deficiency in the associative framework of grown-ups (17/18 year olds and biology teachers, figure 4 and 5) in respect to agriculture, economy, technology. It is surprising to see that the younger students (13/14 year olds, figure 3), although to a great extent not yet knowing what an ecosystem 'is' (see definitions, category 'Unknown'), associate with this word many more elements from agriculture, economy, and technology/physics. It seems, as if school and university, by training a narrow scientific concept of ecosystem, 'spoil' the associative framework of this word.

4. In all cases the associative framework of the subjects contains two distinct maxima: one in the category 'living nature', the other in the category 'formal and abstract terms'. Whereas the first one is not surprising, the latter was unexpected, especially in the younger age group (12/13). The individual associations and definitions show that this maximum is induced by the keyword 'systems' which seems to provoke a great number of abstract terms.

These results may cause some reflections among teachers about the type of environmental education they are practising in school. The deficiencies pointed out in 3 should make them think about including more concrete examples and tasks from the fields of applied ecology into teaching, if they really want to develop an 'inclusive' concept of an ecosystem.

Logic core, associative framework, and action

As long as we regard concepts as having an affective component which is included in the associative framework influencing the actions of a person, we avoid the mistake of a purely cognitive view of concept learning. Interviews with 20 students whose definitions and associations related to 'ecosystem' had been examined, showed that the cognitive training of the logic core had an effect on students' actions (as anticipated by them) only through the 'filter' of the associative framework. The logic core of the concept 'ecosystem' was memorised and used in such situations where it was associated with the situation in some way. Otherwise it was not remembered at all. Furthermore, it turned out that emotions connected with the associations were determining to a great extent the anticipated actions. So the knowledge of the word 'system' and the understanding of its scientific meaning did not allow one to make any prediction as to what the student would do with systems in practical life. But the analysis of free associations revealed two different types of reaction to the word: one student associated with 'system' the terms 'entity' and 'life'. Asked about his possible future actions in respect to systems, he answered in the sense of 'positive engagement for scientific ecology'. That means: the concept 'system' (with ecosystem) was associated with positive feelings, which brought about pleasant associations (or vice versa) and could be recognised. So a prediction in the direction 'positive engagement...' was possible and was later confirmed in the interview.

The opposite was true with another student, who associated 'mathematics', 'abstraction', 'dead'. The prediction concluded from his associations was: negative attitude towards systems, general antipathy against formalisation. The interview again confirmed this expectation. The student rejected any systematic analysis of nature in the way science operates; he was a strong opponent of science and promised 'never to become a scientist'. So the free associations seem to allow some assessment of future actions on the emotional level. The findings by the method of interviews have, of course, to be confirmed by the study of real actions in life instead of only anticipated ones. These studies are being carried out. Some of the data presently available are illustrated in figure 6. This figure gives a picture of possible relationships between the logic core of 'ecosystem' and the field of everyday actions. It also shows the high significance of free associations with respect to the assessment of future impulses originating from concepts. One highly important impulse found in the interviews was: reflection upon the epistemic structure in oneself. Any controversion in actions or feelings may lead back (see reflected arrow in figure 6) to the logic core and clarify the conceptual situation before acting. This kind of 'action' is an internalised one and receives growing importance in our complicated and controversial, pluralistic world.

Further research and curriculum development have to prove to what degree concepts like 'ecosystem' learned in an inclusive way are able to determine man's actions in everyday and scientific life.

The author predicts that through this kind of learning it will become possible to develop a new 'ecology of mind' (Bateson, 1972), which should continue the present ecological movement to an 'inside ecology'.

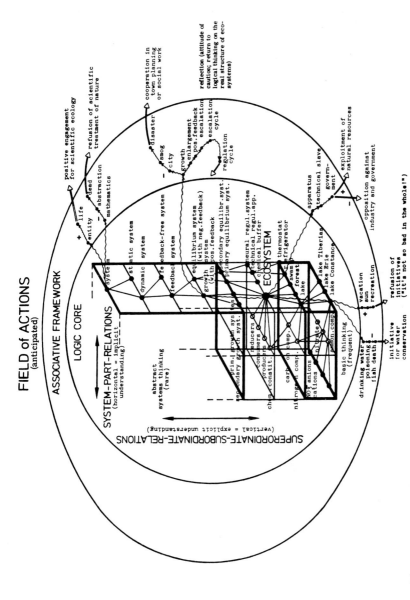

Figure 5: <u>Possible influences of a concept on human behaviour, demonstrated with the concept ECOSYSTEM.</u>

395

Discussion

Much of the discussion centred around the use of free word association studies, one speaker reporting that word associations and digraph analysis gave very similar results. Questions were raised about the origin of responses - did they simply measure acquired knowledge, or could they really be used to explore the extent of the child's concept elaboration? What difference did it make if the child had time for reflection on his answers? It was agreed that a free association test is not all that free, especially after the first word, and for this reason the tests were administered rapidly, to give little time for reflection. Sometimes the first word association seemed to owe more to similarity of word sound than to concept association (e.g. ecosystem - economy).

One person claimed that the logical extent of a concept could not be tabled by free association, since semantic, structural definitions must be explored. However, the reply that the 'volume' of a definition could be assessed from the prepared logic core diagram, or that the number of subordinate and superordinate relations could be counted, was met with a criticism that the relationships between concepts were being reduced to 'mere' measurement and counting.

Schaefer explained the value of his system in terms of the association of scientific concepts with social and political ones. The raw material for thinking depends on associations - some things are selected, others are rejected, and if we are aware of, and can foster, certain links then maybe the engineer building an autobahn will be more likely to take account of ecological and social aspects of his work. Definitions learned in science lessons do not include political aspects - associations do, and this is an essential difference between free association and 'logical thinking'.

The Research — Practitioner Interface in Science and Mathematics Education

HANS VAN AALST

Summary

The general theme of this paper is the role of cognitive development studies in science teaching and in science curriculum development.
The main focus is on secondary school teaching, because the author's
experience has been mainly in that area. The paper is divided into
four parts.

The first part includes some comments on the nature of research
and the work of teachers and those concerned with curriculum-innovation.
There is a great gap between researchers and practitioners because of
the nature of their respective tasks, aims and approaches to their
work. Where practitioners and researchers do meet is in their involvement with educational innovation. However, innovations need to be
recognised or approved by those who will have to put them into practice.
Before new ideas become fully accepted they have often undergone considerable modification. Therefore, the research-practitioner interface exists only in specific contexts of educational change.

The second part highlights some issues relating to adaptive education. If education is adaptive, pupils will not drop out on the basis
of failure to achieve predetermined uniform outcomes. Whereas some
cognitive development studies suggest that content which cannot be
mastered by the majority of pupils be dropped, the author believes that
more differentiated decisions should be reached on the basis of the
acceptance of qualitatively different levels of outcomes and that
teaching procedures should be based on these differences. Some
specific remarks are devoted to the concept of 'alternative frameworks'
- conceptions which pupils tend to apply spontaneously to tasks. Such
frameworks, which stem from natural (incidental) learning may be quite
robust. It may well be that special teaching and learning strategies
are required to deal with such stable alternative frameworks.

The third part contains an analysis of the differences between
'naive' learning about the physical world in the out-of-school environment and learning through school-science.

On the basis of this analysis an attempt is made to find out whether the development of 'common-sense' understanding of the physical world interacts with pupils' learning of the 'productive' ways of thinking which are characteristic for skilled scientists, and if so, to what extent. As a starting point for discussions about these different approaches to cognitive growth a sequence of goals for science education is proposed, ranging from 'functional everyday skills' to 'functional productive skills'.

The last part of the paper proposes kinds of work which might stimulate researchers and practitioners to meet more frequently. Four suggestions are given:

a. good reviews of empirical studies, which are not classified according to theoretical streams of research concepts but which use concrete pedagogical contexts as their organising principle;

b. writings that illuminate through personal experience;

c. so-called 'local theories', limited to specific instrumental situations, and

d. holistic descriptions of objectives, which avoid the separation of content and method.

Foreword

My experience with cognitive development research and educational innovation is rather restricted. It is coloured by developments in the Netherlands in the field of science education, by my own teaching experience and especially by my full-time involvement since 1971 with the Physics Curriculum Development Project for General Secondary Education (PLON).[1] This is why I shall concentrate in this paper on secondary education. Science education in primary schools is

---

1. PLON = Projekt Leerpakket Ontwikkeling Natuurkunde (Physics Curriculum Development Project for General Secondary Education). The general purpose of the project is to modernise and update physics teaching and the physics curriculum in secondary schools in the Netherlands. The materials being developed are for use with pupils aged 12 to 17 at schools providing tuition at the following levels: intermediate general (MAVO), higher general (HAVO) and pre-university (VWO). The project has been accommodated in the premises of the Teacher Training and Educational Research Group of the Physics Department of the State University of Utrecht.

comparatively rare in the Netherlands;[2] physics is not taught to pupils below the age of 13, the stage at which PLON begins.

However, the age range of 7 - 12 is important for cognitive growth, because during this period fairly rapid changes in levels of thinking occur.[3] In fact it might well be that discussions about cognitive development research and science education should concentrate on the 7 - 12 age range rather than on the 13 - 18 age range.

The research-practitioner interface

The general theme of this paper is the 'interface' between cognitive development research on the one hand and science teaching in schools and science curriculum development on the other hand.

As I sat thinking about this theme I began to ask myself if there really was an interface. Is there really an interlinking mechanism? Let us first consider what is meant by the terms 'practitioners' and 'researchers'. By practitioners I mean the people who have direct responsibility for the quality of school-teaching. This group includes most of the persons involved in curriculum development and teacher-training, administrators and some curriculum-evaluators.

In a sense practitioners can be said 'to make the best of it'. They do what they can when they can. They have their own peculiar reactions to particular, often complex situations; they take all kinds of subjective decisions, not all of which are really logical; they are tempted to adopt easy, short-term solutions for problems; quite often their action is inconsistent, revealing inner conflicts. Although this description is, of course, rather too rough and ready, I think it reveals some of the general characteristics of practitioners.

And what about researchers? They are chiefly concerned with the many facets of research and this is reflected in their responsibility for conceptual structures, theoretical models, methodology and so on. Therefore, researchers go about things in a different way from practitioners: in fact they search for problems, and having found a solution they look for alternative solutions; they act according to generally accepted methodologies in simplified situations, they reason logically and aim to produce objective generalisations.

---

2. It was only last year that a project for science education for 5 to 12 year olds started under the auspices and guidance of the Foundation for Curriculum Development (Stichting voor de Leerplan Ontwikkeling), Enschede. Project 3213: Natuuronderwijs voor de Basisschool.

3. cf. Ausubel et al. (1978) p.230, 243; Klausmeyer & Allen (1978).

We can say therefore that researchers and practitioners differ completely because of the nature of their respective tasks, aims and approaches to their work. Can one imagine a greater gap?

Interlinking requires commitment to innovation. Practitioners and researchers meet in their concern with educational innovation. Is it not true that the concluding section of research studies often deals with 'implications for education' (although the authors already have their own plans as well)? And, is it not the desire and need for change and improvement which makes educationalists want to find out about the latest developments in research? However, as we have seen, there is a mismatch between research and practice, which is of a rather fundamental character. Most questions which practititoners ask are not really research questions. Research perceives a problem from very specific standpoints. Practititoners may judge from several stand-points, taking an eclectic position. But one can hardly expect the practitioner to test every theory against evidence. The 'art' of the scholarly practitioner is that he can change his standpoint while looking at a specific aspect of reality. And in the end there is always a kind of magic involved in synthesising constraints coming from different 'schools' for the purpose of creating practical solu-tions to a concrete problem (Carpay, 1975).

There is always a struggle between scientific justification and concrete decision making. Whether a research-outcome is 'good' is not solely a matter of conceptual, theoretical completeness and validity. There is another dimension, which can be called 'legitimisation': reasoning needs to be complemented by recognition or approval on the part of those concerned. The process of legitimisation seems to be very complex. 'Irrational' arguments play a role here. Innovations always cause a disturbance and therefore encounter opposition. Also, innovations which are suggested as improvements might, from another point of view, be considered as the opposite and what position one adopts is a matter of value-judgement. Also an innovatory theme is not static; it is specified during the process of implementation and a variety of specifications arise, which are adapted to personal values, norms, priorities and contextual conditions. Too low a degree of explicitness beforehand leads to confusion, lack of clarity and frustration (van Aalst, Ebbens, 1979). But it is important to be aware of the fact that ideas often change quite considerably during the process of their legitimisation in practical situations.

To sum up then, the interface between research and practice involves personal commitment to educational change and educational im-provement. Consequently, discussing 'the' interface is useless unless one specifies a context of specific commitments to educational change.

400

The issues in this paper. Cognitive development studies provide knowledge about how children develop, about the kind of things which they
are likely to be able to grasp and the kind of things which they might
not be able to learn meaningfully. What kind of innovations are
linked with such studies?

There are four innovatory themes, connected with cognitive development, to which I feel personally committed:

a.   Adaptive education - how are we to make teaching more adaptive?

b.   Individual differences - how are we to deal with these in
     programme development?

c.   The question of 'science' - how are we to make 'science' more
     relevant to daily life reasoning?

d.   The long term aspects of cognitive growth - how are we to improve
     the quality of long term learning-outcomes? What kinds of early
     experiences are most useful for later learning?

Each of these issues would demand a paper in itself; in this paper I [4]
shall concentrate on adaptive education and the question of 'science'.

How are we to make teaching more adaptive?

Many teachers use a teaching procedure where the physics in the
textbook in fact dictates the teaching scheme. After teaching a chapter these teachers proceed to teach the following chapter. A teacher
who uses the textbook as the main check for progress certainly knows
that not all pupils have understood his teaching. But this is not seen
as the problem per se.These pupils might still have a chance to learn
as they do their homework or when the teacher goes over the new point
in the next lesson. If pupils still fail to understand they will get
a low mark on the test, and if this happens again and again they are
put into a lower stream or have to repeat the year.

A strategy of teaching where pupils drop out on the basis of
failure to achieve predetermined uniform outcomes is called a selective
mode of teaching. Of course, such a mode of teaching is related to
the general model of the educational 'enterprise' which one has in
mind. A school system which does not care about having a high percentage of failues will certainly permit a selective mode of teaching.
But most school systems nowadays try to avoid failures - at least up
to the age of 15, and propagate an adaptive model.

---

4. A draft of this paper included preliminary exercises relating to
each of the four issues, but for reasons of time and space a selection
has been made here.

The adaptive model requires specific forms of school organisation, as well as specific teaching strategies.

One approach is exemplified in the 'Learning for Mastery Strategy' of Bloom, Block, Anderson and their followers (Block, 1971; Block, Anderson, 1975). Bloom et al. offers as an explanation of 'failure' in education the lack of prerequisite knowledge and their adage is: check initial knowledge and correct (if necessary) before proceeding with your teaching. Teaching does not proceed until each pupil has mastered an acceptable number (e.g. 80%) of goals out of a given number of goals for a teaching unit. One of the main teaching-devices is time. If some of the children are allowed to spend more time on the tasks given, they will master them. One claim of the 'Learning for Mastery Strategy' is that it has a motivating effect on children because they always have the feeling that they are able to master the tasks set. As we know, the 'Learning for Mastery Strategy' is successful in relation to most down-to-earth objectives of education, perhaps mainly because it forces teachers to be aware of and to react to failures in pupils' understanding (van Aalst, Wierstra, 1978).

The problem of how to reduce the number of failures is also encountered in articles from the field of cognitive development studies. In these studies one tries to find out which content is unlikely to be learned adequately at different age-levels. For example: Shayer (1978c) concluded from his research that certain elements of learning tasks in the Nuffield Combined Science Course had not been mastered by the majority of pupils. He provides evidence to support the hypothesis that non-mastery is related to failure in Piaget's formal thinking tasks. His main criticism is that in schools which have a broad ability-distribution, many groups of pupils do not master basic concepts, yet these basic concepts determine the teaching sequence of the sections. As a result the pupils do not get the feeling that the course hangs together.

> 'A series of excursions half way up the cliffs surrounding
> what would be interesting territory, if it were ever
> reached, is no use to anyone.'

Shayer thinks that the content selected for teaching should be radically different from the content traditionally used and suggests selecting a set of minimum objectives which are attainable by the pupils at the age at which they meet them and are interconnected in a logical sequence so that the pupil experiences a sense of increasing mastery. It is interesting to note that this is essentially the argument of those who advocate the 'Learning for Mastery Strategy'.

Lock (1979) reacted to Shayer's article and argued that it is not necessary for all pupils to attain everything straight away. Some will succeed when they try again, possibly within a spiral syllabus, and there is no need for everyone to reach the highest summit:

'With regard to Section 6 (biology content) and the understanding of controls as an objective, I feel that many teachers
would be pleased with 20 to 30 percent of pupils at this stage
(12+) gaining this objective and would think this sufficient
justification for inclusion of this experiment in the course.'
(...) 'Finally, I believe all learning experiences are, to
use Shayer's analogy, a series of excursions up the cliffs
and in many cases the top is reached long after the experience.'

Shayer, who refers to Piagetian levels, argues that children who
are not formal thinkers cannot master tasks which require formal
thinking. His conclusion is that such tasks should be left out of the
course.

Lock argues: do not leave this content out of the course, for
pupils will learn something useful from it, albeit not of 'final'
quality. I find this view interesting because I think that Lock in
fact accepts at a given moment of the course different levels of
understanding. He does not clarify which levels, and he is also not
very specific about the question of how to deal with these different
levels as teaching proceeds; he just leaves us with: a 'spiral
syllabus' and 'a number of attempts'. But the interesting difference
between my interpretation of Lock's view and the 'Learning for
Mastery Strategy' is that Lock accepts non-uniform outcomes at a given
moment in the course.

In fact, one encounters qualitatively different outcomes here,
and not just quantitative differences in the number of correct
performances on given test items.

What I am trying to make clear here is that results of cognitive
development studies can be regarded as indicators to ways of avoiding
quantitative failure, if that part of the content which is likely to
be too difficult is dropped. But, on the other hand, these studies
can also be seen as indicating qualitatively different levels of understanding, on the basis of which one might try to improve the teaching-
learning process. This means that one does not adhere to uniform
outcomes, but accepts to a certain extent qualitatively different
outcomes within one class.

But what kind of qualitatively different outcomes can one expect?
Many attempts have been made in the last twenty years to specify such
differences in terms of Piagetian levels. Driver and Easley (1978)
comment on Piaget's investigations in relation to concept development
in the physical sciences during adolescence. They advise caution in
the classification of pupils according to Piagetian stages in order to
prescribe or limit the way in which they should be taught. The
reasons for their cautious approach stem from indications that context
and content in fact have primacy over structural characteristics of
problem solving. Also, Karplus reports that whether or not a subject

403

will give evidence of formal reasoning depends heavily on the familiarity and the complexity of the context as well as on certain details of the reasoning task (Karplus, 1978b).

Mr. and Mrs. van Hiele (1957, 1973) proposed a model of learning which clarifies some of the content-dependency of pupils' reasoning. The van Hieles distinguish three levels of thinking which reflect qualitative differences between individual pupils. In their view different rates of progress in classroom learning can be interpreted as discontinuities between the three levels of the learning process.

1. The basic level (grondnivo). Here children are addressed in terms of their knowledge of objects, and an appeal is made to skills which are basic for the first level. The basic level is characterised in a negative sense, because no argumentation is possible. The transition from the basic level to the first level is characterised by the focussing of attention on a specific context. In physics teaching the focus is on the context of physics.

2. The first thinking-level. Now experiences are placed in a network of relationships, and on the basis of that network, argumentation is possible.

3. The second thinking-level. At the first level generalised experiences (concepts, rules, principles) are described, whereas at the second level such rules are explained. This means that a model (line of thought, image) is created which summarises the rules in terms of their logical connection. On the second level reasoning occurs about the structure of the first-level-network.

One of the main differences between the views of the van Hieles and Piaget becomes apparent if one compares the nature of van Hieles' levels with Piaget's stages. Van Hiele (1973b) showed that in terms of his levels there are large differences between different Piaget tasks. With some subjects (e.g. the concept of number, 'floating' in relation to Archimedes' principle) the Piaget stages are far apart in terms of thinking-levels, while other subjects (part-whole-relation) one cue-experience may be sufficient to raise a child's level of thinking. Thus van Hiele makes the point that Piaget's stages are suitable for pinpointing weaknesses in a programme, but that we need more precise knowledge about learning-processes in a content-area, if we want to improve teaching-learning methods.

I would suggest that in addition to content, 'instructional context' influences pupil's reasoning. By 'instructional context' I mean variables like classroom climate as well as task-variables such as clarified sequences, meaning of tasks, etc. It makes a big difference whether you work on your own or work in a situation where there are time-limits and checks. There is a difference between answering a question from somebody who really wants to know something and answering a question which has been asked to check whether you understand a topic. There is a difference between responding to a task in order to solve a problem and responding in order to keep busy (Elshout-Mohr, 1977). Stimulating suggestions for the matching of content and environment to individual children have been given by Harlen et al. (1977).

In summing up we can say that Piaget's stages are suitable for pinpointing weaknesses in a programme, but that it is too rigorous a conclusion at the moment to delete from junior science courses all topics that require formal thinking to understand them. We need more differentiated knowledge before we can make such rigorous decisions. For the improvement of teaching and learning we need to work out more precise and differentiated teaching-learning procedures.

Alternative frameworks. A useful starting point for the development of more differentiated instruction seems to be a study of conceptions which pupils tend to apply spontaneously to tasks. (Vegting, 1977; Driver, Easley, 1978). Driver and Easley introduce the term 'alternative framework' to indicate such spontaneous conceptions that are really qualitatively different. These authors conclude from several studies that pupils' pre-instructional ideas may remain after instruction, with classroom words imposed, or the new and old ideas may co-exist. An example of this is given by Viennot (1977) who shows how in spontaneous reasoning in elementary dynamics a linear relation between force and velocity is very often assumed, rather that one between force and acceleration. She shows also that such reasoning is highly robust and that it outlives teaching which contradicts it. Driver (1973), quoted in Driver and Easley (1978), found that counter-examples and conflicting evidence did not in themselves induce a change in pupils' thinking, and at times produced only confusion. And Ausubel suggest that instruction which ignores pre-conceptions rather than taking them into account is likely to make misconceptions more elaborate and stable instead of extinguishing them (Ausubel et al., 1978).

The idea that cognitive entering characteristics not only limit the chance of achieving an objective but also increase the chances of getting things wrong is related to the idea that the child himself plays an active role in learning. What the learner believes or thinks, together with his knowledge of the world and his analysis of the context, determine the meaning he assigns to (learning-) tasks (e.g. in an example given later, a boy named Fred, attempts to relate the heating of a room by convection to 'smoke', something which was familiar to him). Since existing knowledge is not just a pre-requisite, but an active agent in a new learning process, it is important to know what natural cognitive reactions the student makes to a new lesson.

However, it seems to me that a distinction should be made between children's dynamic reactions to tasks and the kind of thinking which is more stable in young children. The first are elements of the teaching process. If a teacher listens carefully to his pupils he can use these ideas for teaching-progression by giving the ideas back to the pupil and discussing them. Also, small group work by pupils is efficient as a means of teaching here (Barnes, Todd, 1977).

By allowing pupils' frames rather than teachers' frames to determine the progress of discussion, Barnes and Todd observed changes in the nature of learning, because pupils were required to negotiate their own criteria of relevance and truth. Barnes and Todd suggest that the progress they observe may stem from a better understanding of language among the children themselves, because of the greater similarity of their semantic structures, which in turn determines the meaning and relevance they assign to what is said in a discussion.

It seems to me that studies for 'alternative frameworks' should be done in some kind of pedagogical context. Methods such as the directive or the non-directive interview (Tiberghien, Delacôte, 1978) and the clinical interview are in fact rather 'static' approaches. What they do show is the surprising range of qualitatively different frameworks children apply to tasks, and this is a major contribution. But we do not learn from such studies how stable these frameworks are, i.e. how resistant they are to extinction by a given teaching-method.

Let us take an example. Tiberghien and Delacôte (1978) give an account of how an 11½ year old boy - called Frederique - tried to explain how a radiator heats an entire room. Fred:

'But heat comes out of the radiator; that's just like smoke, smoke which comes out and fills the whole room, and it's the same with the radiator. It's the same with the radiator, it's smoke you can't see, it fills the whole room.'[5]

Suppose we asked teachers how they would react to such a statement. I suppose most teachers would say:

'Clearly Fred doesn't understand that this is a case of convection, so I shall have to explain it. I would get him to look at the water-model of convection, which shows that water starts to flow if heated at an appropriate spot, and then I would show him that the air in a heated room flows too. I would demonstrate this to him with the help of a paper spiral on a needle or with a test flame.'

---

5. The original French quote was: 'La chaleur s'en va du radiateur, c'est comme de la fumée, de la fumée, de la fumée par exemple qui s'en va et que ça envahit toute la pièce, alors le radiateur c'est pareil. Alors le radiateur c'est pareil c'est de la fumée qu'on ne voit pas ça envahit toute la pièce.'

But there might also be a teacher who reacts as follows:

'Fred is well aware that the entire room is heated by
the radiator. When he is asked to explain this, he searches
for words to express what he experiences: that heat spreads
around the room. He finds a word for it: "smoke". Now, I
would try to make it clear to Fred that I do not understand
"just like smoke" in this context and ask him what he means
by it. Perhaps I would discuss some other experiences Fred
might have had with air circulation. I hope that Fred and
I will agree that "just like smoke" is no longer adequate to
describe the situation and that Fred will be happy to accept
his new understanding together with the more appropriate term
convection.'

This teacher thinks that Fred was intuitively aware of the fact
that heat was transferred from the radiator to the air and that he
tried to find a word for the 'spreading out', because he could not
give an adequate description of the air flow. In terms of the van
Hiele model, this teacher tries to 'raise' Fred's thinking from the
basic level to the (descriptive) first level.

The interpretation by Tiberghien and Delacôte is a little different. They suggest that Fred imagines that the radiator gives off an
invisible concrete substance 'heat' and uses words like 'smoke',
'steam' or even 'air' to designate the substance.[6] They in fact
suggest that Fred has a rather stable idea of heat which he applies to
this task.

Which of the given interpretations of Fred's statement is true
should be investigated by further questioning; this is a common
method in developmental research. A good example is given by
Nussbaum and Novak (1976). However, for practical purposes it would
be more appropriate to create instructional activities, which take
the different interpretations into account and to investigate in
detail the learning processes which occur. Such a methodology would
illuminate how important a particular alternate framework might be in
the light of a given pedagogical context.

---

6. The idea of an 'evaporating' substance was reported by one of my
team members in connection with electricity: a group of 14 year old
children concluded from their experiment that the longer a resistance
wire was in a circuit the lower the current in that circuit. Their
explanation was: 'that's obvious, the longer the wire, the better the
current can evaporate'. They proved their statement by taking a plastic insulated wire (which was - fortunately for their 'proof' - not a
resistance wire), replacing the blank wire by the plastic covered wire
and showing their teacher that in this case the current was very high
indeed, because the current could no longer evaporate (Private communication of C.A.S. Groen [PLON]).

<u>Teaching and alternative frameworks</u>. If the kind of thinking about
the radiator as revealed by Tiberghien and Delacôte is stable in young
children, then there is good reason to believe that the way of teaching which I suggested most teachers might use is quite inadequate. The
demonstration of flowing water or flowing air will and can be accepted
by the pupils, but they will not attribute appropriate meaning to it
in the context of the problem offered.

Their thinking goes something like this:

'I realise that air is constantly flowing, but what
happens with the heat that comes from the radiator?'

These children will learn the new ideas, but these ideas will co-exist
with the old ideas.

How can we prevent misconceptions arising from a mismatch of
instructional tasks and natural frameworks? First of all we shall
have to adopt new strategies of teaching and secondly change some of
our aims in science education. I will come back to this last point
in the next section. I will now elaborate a little on strategies of
teaching by discussing a model of teaching and learning where children's
own frameworks are taken seriously.

Ten Voorde (1977) did some research in connection with a chemistry
course which was based on small group discussions as well as on teacher-
group discussions. Protocol analysis revealed that the collective
formation of language and of opinion lends itself to analysis and
therefore to description. Described regularities turn out to be
explicable in terms of a <u>discussion</u> model according to which everyone
takes part in the discuss<u>ion on the</u> basis of his own experiences,
background and expectations. But the shape of the dialogue is defined
by people understanding or failing to understand others or by understanding only parts of what is being said. Thus understanding regu-
lates the progress of the discussion. Because the discussion progresses, group productivity is possible.

Ten Voorde based his research on the model of learning proposed
by Mr. and Mrs. van Hiele (1957), mentioned before. According to Ten
Voorde, level raising can be recognised as a change in frame of
reference. Children must discover the new frame of reference. In
the old, familiar world of language, variations arise because certain
questions cannot be answered adequately. The fact that crisis-like
situations arise in a learning group infers a state of insecurity.
Transition from the first thinking level to the second thinking level
by way of Ten Voorde's productive group discussions makes pupils aware
of their <u>freedom to choose</u> a model according to their own point of view,
but at the same time it implies that pupils have the strength of mind
to hold on to a chosen viewpoint or to choose another instead. This
experience is seen as essential for the type of education which aims
at producing literate scientists. Ten Voorde and his colleagues put

emphasis on the learning process of <u>teachers</u> themselves during the period of developmental work. Adults need a very specific skill if they are to understand children's alternate framework in such a way that 'fair' discussions become possible. It appeared to be very difficult for teachers to discuss the transition from the basic level to the first level. This is because adults are no longer able to picture to themselves what the basic level is. Thinking operations are largely unconscious operations and adults very often cannot remember how they saw a problem in their childhood. Learning often involves forgetting a formerly held view. For example, as soon as you have learned how to solve a problem it is very difficult to remember how you saw the problem before you learned how to solve it. Ten Voorde reports that even teachers who discovered the basic level in the course of a 'de-dogmatising' process showed gaps in their understanding of pupils.

Ten Voorde et al. undoubtedly made an attempt to handle children's alternative frameworks in an intellectual honest way. My only criticism would be that in some content-areas such an approach might be quite useful while in others more straightforward teaching might be more effective. Here again we see how important it is to know how stable children's alternative frameworks are. Less stable frameworks permit more straightforward teaching.

My conclusion is that if we want to follow the line of adaptive education where different levels of outcomes are accepted to a certain extent - and there is good reason to do this - we must work at the teaching and learning of a specific piece of content in a specified context for a given group of pupils in a specified instructional environment. Because we have so little precise knowledge about which activities match different ways of thinking, this will demand quite a lot of opportunistic ingenuity on the spot.

How are we to make 'science' more relevant for daily life reasoning?

The development of 'thinking' has always been a basic theme in cognitive development psychology. Some educationalists emphasised that 'learning to think' was the sole aim of education (Furth, Wachs, 1974; Renner et al., 1978). In their view education should enable pupils to cope with mathematical and scientific reasoning generally, and should encourage the development of attitudes and intellectual skills. However, scientific reasoning is not in itself an adequate way of thinking in daily life situations, it is not a major component of intelligent actions in daily life.

What I am trying to express here is nicely illustrated by what a physics teacher said about the relevance of physics teaching for the present generation of school children (CSSE, 1978):

'In recent years I've wondered if you could justify it
(physics). Earlier I would have said that physics was a
part of cultural knowledge, something enormously practical, like all sciences having something philosophical
to offer the public, an intellectual integrity which could
carry over into politics and society.

Now I don't know. We live in a technological society so it
is necessary to propagate information to some parts of the
society. But for the general person in high school who
will eventually go into business or become a homemarker,
they really don't need to know about physics, except in a
very superficial way. If you want a kid to know how to
change a tyre, you teach him about levers...I'm a good
sailor and I apply my knowledge of physics, but other
people are better sailors and have no physics background.'

The same point arises in the research field in a very cleverly argued
paper by Neisser (1976) about general, academic and artificial intelligence. I quote Neisser:

'Intelligent behaviour in real settings often involves
actions that satisfy a variety of motives at once - practical and interpersonal ones, for example - because opportunities
to satisfy them appear simultaneously. It is often accompanied
by emotions and feelings as is appropriate in situations that
involve other people. Moreover, it provides continual opportunities for cognitive growth of many kinds, because most
situations turn out to have facets of which we were formerly
unaware.

All this is different in school. We are expected to leave
our life situations at the door, as it were, and to solve
problems that other people have set. Notice also that problems on school tests are supposed to be "fair" - that is, all
the information needed to solve them is typically given from
the beginning. The pupil does not find out anything as he
goes along that might have been otherwise. I will call problems of this kind "puzzles", because they are so different
from the problems of ordinary human life. To solve "puzzles"
like this requires particular skills, often skills of a high
order. It is appropriate to call them academic skills.'

Neisser is not trying to suggest that 'academic skills' have no use out
of school. His point is that certain aspects of intelligent behaviour
in natural situations are not part of academic intelligence, although
perhaps only in the ideal case.

'Academic people tend to over-estimate their own abilities.
The existing evidence does not suggest that they are markedly
more successful than the unintelligent in the conduct of their
affairs or of the affairs of others.'

Neisser also thinks that the learning of complex problem-solving has little meaning for an increasing understanding of the world itself.

Now, how does this relate to cognitive development research and to science teaching?

Firstly, it seems to me that we should be very much aware of what we mean by cognitive development. If it is defined as a child's increasing capacity to make sense of the world, then the kind of thinking used in the natural science is only one possible way in which aspects and phenomena of the world are encountered. Not only is this kind of thinking limited to physical aspects of that world but its 'academic' character is a limiting feature also. It might well be that attempts to reconcile stable 'alternate frameworks', which stem from natural experiences, as I have already indicated, with scientific frameworks are doomed to fail, because the differences between these frameworks are so fundamental.

For example, as Viennot (1977) has shown, the intuitive scheme ($F = mv$) deals without contradiction with most situations encountered in daily life. Thus for most children there is very little functional need to learn $F = ma$. If scientific frameworks are the major criteria for selecting and organising school science activities, we are faced with conflicts between science lessons and daily life which might go beyond pupils' understanding.

The role of formal schooling in the process of making sense of the world has been discussed by Bruner (1966).

As Bruner pointed out, the important thing about school nowadays is that it is removed from the immediate context of socially relevant action. The pupil is removed from the task-context in which learning occurs directly and where the situation carries the meaning of what is being learned (as is the case in native cultures). This disengagement makes learning an act in itself. According to this view, the school can be said to offer special possibilities because it is not closely bound up with natural surroundings and natural attitudes. People who view schools in this light see their purpose as being to help children to learn important things about our culture which they would not learn otherwise.

The work of Bernstein (1971b) revealed that schools socialise pupils into knowledge frames which discourage connections with everyday reality.

'Such framing also makes educational knowledge something that is not ordinary or mundane, but something esoteric which gives a special significance to those who possess it.'(...) 'As you get older, you become increasingly different from others.' (Bernstein, 1971a)

411

What Bernstein is really questioning is whether our traditional
aims of science teaching ('think scientifically') are adequate any
longer. He suggests that everyday realities be included in education.
I tend to agree with him, but at the same time I feel that to do this
could be to strike at the very roots of what we have come to regard
as 'science teaching'. There are fundamental differences between
school knowledge and the everyday community knowledge of the pupil,
his family and his peer group.

The latter type of knowledge is known as common-sense knowledge.
Now, one reason why I tend to agree with Bernstein is not directly
related to my attitude about the aims of science education (for example:
the aim that the pupil should be able to use scientific reasoning in
everyday situations), but rather to the fact that so many interactions
between pupils and teachers, which are normally judged to be ineffective for classroom learning can be explained as natural social interaction - as common-sense behaviour, and pupils who use scientifically
valid arguments in normal social discussions tend to become isolated
from the group as a whole.

It seems to me that a 'fair' way of introducing everyday realities into the class would mean that common-sense reasoning and
scientific reasoning should both have a place, so that their respective
weaknesses and strengths could be shown. Our preference for science,
which is only natural because we are scientists, is not in itself a
good reason for accepting scientific reasoning as the major framework
for science teaching.

Common-sense knowledge. I propose to analyse some of the features
which distinguish common-sense knowledge from scientific knowledge. I
shall follow Schutz and Luckman (1974) and Singer (1975)[7].

One of the most important characteristics of common-sense thinking
seems to be its self-evident character. We live in the security and
acceptance of reality. There are plenty of examples of this in the
classroom, e.g.

teacher: *'Can you suggest a reason why ice floats on water?'*

pupil: *'It just floats, that's all, what else can I say?'*

Barnes and Todd (1977) offer many examples of accepted realities which
are not subject to any doubts. The fact that natural knowledge is
self-evident does not mean that it is a reflection of reality. There
are interpretations. Interpretations are subjective but are not consciously felt to be subjective. Awareness of the fact that knowledge
is an interpretation of reality is not felt. Nothing is more opposed

---

7. Singer (1975) refers to Piaget (1964); Holzmer (1968); Young (Ed.)
(1971); Wright (1971); Schutz, Luckmann (1974), and others.

to the natural attitude than scientific and philosophical doubts that reality is not as it seems to be, or that reality could be other than it is now.

There is also no need for explanations in common-sense thinking. Particular phenomena are not related to situational or environmental influences. For example, pupils seeing a 'broken' pencil in water do not look at it from a different angle, nor do they change the position of the pencil to see what happens. The self-evident character of phenomena leads also to the idea that knowledge is intersubjective: what we perceive is what others can perceive also, and this is true of the perception of events as well as of motives for actions. This is why children find it very difficult to explain to their teachers why they are doing something. 'That's obvious - can't you see for yourself?' For them their motives are inherent in the action!

Finally, the self-evident character of knowledge relates to the idea that the world remains the same. Reality is stable and events repeat themselves. This idea is also related to the second major feature of common-sense thinking: its pragmatic character. The way in which we perceive objects, people and phenomena is determined to a great extent by what we can or should do. This orientation towards action is made possible by the implicit value and 'receipts for behaviour' which are inherent in common-sense knowledge. Common-sense knowledge does not only tell us what the world is like, it also tells us how it should be.

If we accept that common-sense knowledge is pragmatic and self-evident, we see how it contrasts with the system of science teaching whereby we try to stimulate pupils to set problems, to think about explanations and to create alternative explanations. Knowing and acting tend to be separate entities. I think that for many pupils the gap between this kind of school science teaching and common-sense knowledge is too big. Adolescents seek social acceptance; there is an increasing age clannishness. If an individual wishes to be accepted by his equals he must abide by their standards, or he will be an outsider. I think this puts serious limitations on school science teaching and especially on the development of scientific thinking. In an informal classroom environment common-sense thinking plays a role. A classroom climate that accepts common-sense ideas on the one hand and stimulates cognitive development in the direction given by scientific reasoning on the other constitutes one of the major challenges we are facing.

The ideas expressed here are in line with Frey's paper about priorities in science education research. Frey (1977):

'I assume that pupils' individual desires for information, their actual living conditions, parallel learning experiences and need for articulation are just as important elements of 'suitability' as the ability of topics and methods to be taught and learned.'

In a comment on Frey, Steiner (1977) does agree that it is important to put science education into the broader spectrum which is
determined by the interaction with society and the needs (assumed or
real) of the individual that follow therefrom.

> 'However, there is no substitute for the intellectual
> instruments science gives us, nor is there a replacement
> for the experience one gains while working within a
> science.'

and:

> 'One has to search for a dialectic solution for the exist-
> ing contradictions between the sciences and their specific
> methods and results on the one hand, and the social con-
> cerns on the other.'

This quotation brings us back to the aims of science education. I
think there are good reasons for establishing a hierarchy of goals in
science education, which have relevance for real-life situations, the
sequence being dictated by the decreasing importance of goals for
various groups of pupils and by an increasing complexity of intelligence skills. Once we have delineated such a hierarchy, we are in a
better position to judge different approaches to cognitive growth.
As starting points for discussions I propose the following sequence:

a. <u>functional everyday skills</u>:

understanding instructions for the use of technical apparatus;
ability to - read meters;
          - repair electric plugs;
          - give names to certain natural phenomena and
            technical apparatus;
etc.

b. <u>functional recognition skills</u>:

understanding popular scientific/newspaper explanations of
     technical and natural phenomena;
ability to classify certain phenomena according to the principles
     involved;
ability to judge soundness of reasoning in advertisements;
etc.

c. <u>functional understanding skills</u>:

understanding an experiment;
ability to - explain the working of apparatus or natural
          phenomena;
          - follow scientific argumentation about familiar
           situations;
etc.

d.   functional productive skills:

    ability to - transform a situation into a science problem;
                 - set up an experiment;
                 - hypothesise from data;
                 - write an article or a report;
                 - criticise an article;
    etc.

Cognitive development studies and practitioners

The first paragraphs of this paper stressed the notion that researchers and practitioners might meet if they committed themselves to specific educational innovations. It has been argued that such innovations are defined during the 'enterprise of legitimisation' by those concerned. Then, I discussed two innovations which seem to be related to cognitive development studies: adaptive education and the introduction of functional everyday reasoning into the school curriculum.

To conclude I would like to make some other suggestions about the kind of work which might stimulate researchers and practitioners to meet more frequently.

First of all, the availability of good reviews of the available empirical studies would facilitate practical work. We do not have a rich archive of studies and catalogued accounts of teaching-learning practice recording what happened and how well it happened. So far, most reviews have classified studies according to theoretical streams or according to specific theoretical concepts such as the concepts of the 'advance organiser', or the concept of 'formal thought'. For judging applicability, we need studies and reviews of such studies which depart from concrete pedagogical contexts. For example, which approaches to the learning of density have been studied for the 13 to 15 age group? What kinds of tests have been developed and what kinds of learning processes occurred? Which qualitative levels of outcomes could be distinguished in relation to certain types of tasks? There is a need for careful didactical analysis and long term observation and experiments in normal school classes. Such studies might begin in areas that are acknowledged to have high levels of 'failure'. These may be identified by procedures such as Johnstone and his colleagues used in Scotland for determining areas of science knowledge as ones of general difficulty. (Johnstone and Mughol, 1976; Johnstone, MacDonald and Webb, 1977.) Also Shayer's work on the analysis of science curricula for Piagetian level of demand provides useful information as to which normal school tasks give rise to difficulties (Shayer, 1978c). Also valuable information about difficulties in learning-processes is often revealed in talks with experienced teachers.

Elvin (1977) argues in favour of greater recognition for writing that illuminates through personal experience. These personal writings contain direct and personal expression of experience, imaginatively realised. These writings can be of very great importance, because they make the dry bones of research live. Some of these writings contain a research element, although it could not really be described as research. There may have been some fact finding, some investigations of situations, but the purpose is not so much to establish objective generalisations as to illuminate through experience. Examples can be found sometimes in journals for teachers such as the School Science Review.

With respect to research studies, I think we should not expect too much from general theories, as has been pointed out before. I would like to advocate 'local' theories, which are quite specific, limited both in time and place, in specific instructional situations and limited to specific groups of pupils (c.f. Snow, 1977). For example, are we ready for a seminar on the teaching and learning of heat in the context of energy transfer, for pupils aged 11-13 with an approach resembling Karplus' learning cycle (Karplus & Lawson, 1974)?

RESPONSE by Wynne Harlen

There are many points in this paper with which I find myself in agreement but none more so than the statement that the age range 7 - 12 years is perhaps a better basis for discussions about cognitive development and science education than the 13 - 18 age range.

It is striking how the same generalisations about the application of cognitive development research to science education seem to emerge from work with both younger and older pupils; the nature of cognitive functioning and the nature of science teaching may differ, but the relationship between the two does not differ to anything like the same extent. So much knowledge seems to be hard won from research in the 13 - 18 age range that is identical with what has been learned for the younger pupils, and learned much more easily, for it seems so obvious. There are several examples in this paper which I will mention briefly, and, I hope, without giving the impression that the practical problems to which they are related have been solved at the younger age level.

The first example appears where the 'instructional context' is recognised as influencing pupils' reasoning and it is explicitly stated that this phrase includes the way an activity is conducted, the class management and the teacher's role. I would like to return to this later, as it seems to be a central issue, but for the moment simply point out that this is a finding which you don't have to look for when working with young pupils, it forces itself upon you. If you work with 8, 9, 10 year olds you get nowhere unless you pay attention to social and organisational matching as well as the matching of cognitive demand - the latter is just no use without the former. A second example concerns the role of language, e.g. the different interpretations of Fred's explanation of how a radiator heats a whole room illustrates the problem of communication. Children can only explain things in terms of what is familiar to them and it is difficult to distinguish metaphorical use of words, when one idea is used to explain another, from the confusion of the two concepts. Even young children use words metaphorically, though they can less easily understand other people's metaphorical explanations. It seems that a large part of education in science is a matter of persuading pupils to transfer from their individual metaphorical images or models to ones which adults use and are more widely understood and applicable.

This issue is closely related to the third example of a point made in this paper which would seem almost too obvious had the context been the discussion of the younger age group - the need to find out about the child's preconceptions, rather than ignoring them, before attempting to remove misconceptions. What follows from this, as van Aalst so rightly says, is that teachers have to learn how to understand the pupils' point of view, how to gain access to their kind of preconceptions. This is a skill which not all teachers have. From evaluating work with younger children it has become quite clear that whatever the content, certain objectives are not likely to be achieved unless certain methods and organisations are used. The converse is not true - the right methods are not enough on their own whatever the content, but it is certainly not enough to have a list of content, nor to have the content and methods separately spelled out. What is required is some indication of how the two are to be articulated. To do this, however, and yet maintain a respect for individual differences requires a balance between prescription and licence which is rarely struck.

Many more examples could be given both from this paper and elsewhere of the common concerns at all ages. For instance, the importance of teacher-pupil relationships avoiding the 'assault on the ego' of a pupil, which Novak has mentioned. Perhaps the point does not have to be laboured further. Instead we could ask what use can be made of the fact that issues are shared? Are there, for example, insights at one age which can be used at another, or ideas for addressing problems which could be applied at other age levels? Possibly the interconnection between the four themes which are treated separately in the four parts of this paper is one such topic. It would have been to its advantage had this paper included a discussion of the way these four themes have to be orchestrated in science education. To treat them separately is to adopt the position of the researcher, who has the luxury of choosing his problems and how he treats them; the educator has his problems selected for him and cannot treat them separately when in practice they interact.

Whilst sounding a slightly discordant note I will make my other main criticism of this paper. Despite all that there is to agree with, it is right at the beginning where I disagree with a sentence which talks of the interface between cognitive development research and science teaching in schools and curriculum development. Of course science teaching in schools and curriculum development cannot be parcelled together like this as if they were the same. There are three interfaces to consider not one; the interface between cognitive development research and science teaching, between cognitive development research and curriculum development and between curriculum development and science teaching. All these are very large topics and we would not expect them to be treated in a single paper - a whole conference on each is nearer to being adequate - but the acknowledgement of the distinction is important to avoid over-simplification.

I would like now to return to the problem of matching content and methods to pupils' development. This problem is at the centre of the interface between research and curriculum development. It is characterised by van Aalst in terms of the different reactions of practitioners and researchers. The practitioner's reaction is to blame failure on the level of cognitive demand of the tasks and to avoid failure in the pupils by avoiding these tasks. In view of the fact, already mentioned, that cognitive demand is not the only aspect to be considered in matching, we could ask whether the practitioner may be in error in blaming failure on the task; perhaps, if it were presented differently, linked to other work or to a problem of concern to the pupil, pursued in groups, through practical work or discussion - a whole range of variations could be tried - the failure might be avoided. The practitioner judges from the results, we are told, whilst it would seem that the researcher knows a priori that the task cannot be completed successfully. It is implied that he has some information about the pupils other than the result of having tried this sort of task with these sorts of pupils before. Could not the researcher be guilty of a different error, of thinking that he can know the pupils' developmental readiness for this particular task by virtue of having some general information about their cognitive level? If we accept - as I think we must - that there is more to matching than consideration of cognitive development alone, then I think we must reject both the premature rejection of the task by the practitioner and also the assumption of the researcher that there is a level of functioning which is independent of context and of methods of teaching. I am not arguing for abandoning description of task demands and of pupils in terms of cognitive development levels, but only for a much more circumspect view of them. They are useful as general guidelines but can never be very precise because pupils' ideas can only be assessed within the influence and limitation of particular contexts - and moreover their ideas are constantly changing - and the demands of a certain task will appear different to pupils with different past experiences in different conditions of learning and with different teacher mediation.

All the discussion of the effect of the 'instructional context' on pupils' reasoning seems to be in terms of a negative influence, that is, that lack of attention to variables of the learning environment tends to lower performance and sometimes prevents the pupils operating at the level of which they are supposedly capable. But could there not be something reciprocal here - is it possible that a very good match of contextual variables could make up for a poor match

of the cognitive level of the task? To jump in to answer this question
one way or the other would be to fall again into the error of assuming
that we know what a child is capable of doing in a particular set of
circumstances without having tried it in those circumstances. Profess-
or Lovell brought out clearly in his paper the point that the content
and context of a task affect performance on it. He has also given
clues through his own work that the range of influence may be limited,
that there are formal operational tasks which 10 year olds cannot
tackle successfully. These arguments and research findings seem to
point to a middle-of-the-road position, that the manipulation of the
instructional context can both depress and elevate performance within
a certain range, which is perhaps wider than has been acknowledged
before. The increased width is due partly to this appreciation of the
effect of variables of the learning environment and partly because of
uncertainty about what the reasoning capacity of any pupil actually
is, since measurements of this are themselves context-dependent. The
success of individual tuition on pupils who fail to learn in normal
large classes must surely bear this out.

We must now return to the interfaces between research and teaching
and between research and curriculum development and ask where all this
leaves the teacher. To my mind it is at the interface between research
and curriculum development that the broad limits to the range of cognitive demand of tasks should be worked out for a particular group of
pupils. At the interface between cognitive development and teaching
the finer details of matching to individual pupils should be clarified.
As we have seen, this cannot be by prescribing what will match in any
particular case, since this is subject to so many uncertainties that
it is unknown. But it can be by adopting a strategy of gathering the
necessary information about pupils' present understandings, interests
and preferred ways of working and adapting the learning environment,
including the teacher's own intervention to optimise the pupil's level
of performance. Teacher education to understand and adopt such a
strategy is an essential feature of the curriculum development-teaching
interface.

So far most of the points I have mentioned arise directly
from the first part of van Aalst's paper and I must turn now to the
other three parts. This can be done more briefly since many points
link back to what has already been mentioned. For example, the difference between 'everyday knowledge' and 'school knowledge' could be
regarded as the difference between the pupils' metaphors or models
and the more widely accepted ones of school science. To bridge the gap
we must start from the pupils' view of things. Clearly we fail to do
this at the secondary level for many pupils. But I think it would be
wrong to deplore totally that there is a difference between 'natural'
or everyday knowledge of phenomena and the understanding which comes
from the application of scientific curiosity and processes. None of
us goes about questioning everything all the time and we do not expect
school pupils to do this either. Part of life is working with this
natural knowledge - switching on the light or the television without

worrying about how it works. Part of life is also questioning ourselves about how things work, for without this we would be slaves rather
than masters of our environment. We have to learn when it is appropriate to question and when to accept and we cannot blame our pupils
if their science teaching doesn't exactly convey the message that
science lessons are a time for questioning.

A more important point, given less emphasis in this section, is
the problem of relative emphasis on process and content. Again the
earlier discussion is relevant. Research has been used to show that
reasoning power is dependent on content and context, so the reasoning
processes learned in a school context may not necessarily be applied
in other contexts. (This should be no surprise, however, since there
are plenty of examples in adults of contrasts between 'professional'
and 'everyday' behaviour - from safety officers whose homes are a
series of accidents waiting to happen, to educationists who cannot
relate to their own children.) This suggests that careful thought
needs to be given to the combination of processes, content and contexts which are embodied in science curricula.   Van Aalst's list
is clearly an attempt to do this and deserves much more detailed
discussion than can be given here.

Throughout the latter part of the paper there is much which
relates to the interface between cognitive research and curriculum
development. An underlying issue is the distinction to be made between education, cognitive development and concept development.
Van Aalst contrasts the view of Davydov, that education should get
ahead of cognitive development, with that of the Piagetian researchers,
that it should follow cognitive development. Working in classrooms
with young children shows that neither of these is correct, of course.
The dangers of both were, to my mind, beautifully caught in these
words from 'Children and their Primary Schools':

'There has to be the right mixture of the familiar and the
novel, the right match to the stage of learning the child
has reached. If the material is too familiar or the learning skills too easy the children will become inattentive
and bored. If too great maturity is demanded of them, they
fall back on half-remembered formulae and become concerned
only to give the reply the teacher wants.'

Thus in conclusion I am returning to my earlier theme that there
is much that we can learn from work with young pupils which can be
applied to the older ones. What teachers at all levels require is a
strategy for finding the right size of step which a pupil can take from
his present position and for adapting the learning context so that the
step can be taken successfully. Then learning is cognitive development
and not something which can be distinguished from it.

Discussion

The discussion centred on three main issues:

- the specification of objectives by curriculum planners, as against the development of holistic 'three dimensional' goals;
- problems relating to the influence of teacher and researcher on one another; and
- the relative merits of local theories and general theories of education for the teacher and for the researcher.

Objectives. In his paper, van Aalst suggested that the practice of curriculum designers specifying objectives of their courses did not adequately allow for the wide differences in pupils' frameworks of understanding. He proposed, rather, that holistic goals which took more account of the process of learning and of the experience of teachers than of specified outcomes were more appropriate. This position was questioned, pleas being made for the value of specific curriculum objectives on the grounds that,

a. they provided necessary guidance for those who had to write textbooks for national curricula;

b. they established the standards of a course.

Van Aalst accepted that such objectives did have a place, but he expanded his description of holistic goals, giving as an example 'understand the concept of a closed circuit by making a doll's house with two bulbs in the bathroom which are safe...by doing specified experiments...', followed up with accounts of teachers' actual experience and examples of pupil-teacher interaction.

Van Aalst was asked whether he did not believe that we were all working within one framework of science, and whether this allowed for alternative routes to the goals. Personally, he felt that one should accept very different qualitative outcomes from different pupils, although he recognised this as a political issue.

Teacher-researcher relations. One person expressed the hope that by working closely together, teachers would learn to reflect on their practice in the light of research results, and researchers would learn to relate their research more directly to the teachers' problems.

Van Aalst doubted that this would work, since researchers and practitioners each have different sets of internal rules - but at least they might learn to understand something of one another's rules.

One proposal was that researchers should involve teachers more directly in research work, but another questioned whether there was even any need for a research-practitioner interface. In other disciplines the functions are often quite separate. An experience of some 20 teachers and researchers working together was quoted. Tensions arose because of the different aims of the two groups, with teachers claiming that the researchers' presence inhibited their practice, and that the researchers failed to understand the constraints under which they worked.

The role of theory. This aspect of the discussion was opened by a strong plea to give more direct consideration to the need of the teacher. Our theories are too big and too general to be usable in the classroom. The teacher 'needs the metaphors to be written down ' - small theories, not big ones.

Other speakers expanded on this, making the point that the more local you are, the more difficult it is to use theories. There is a need for general theories which can be adapted to each special case. But is there any satisfactory general theory of learning? Van Aalst had suggested that maybe there was not, but others questioned this. While one pointed to the progress that had been made during the Seminar in seeking out the common ground in the Piagetian and Ausubelian frameworks, another queried the need for unification of educational theory. After all, we are prepared to accept side by side diverse views of the nature of science - why not of educational processes also?

A parallel was drawn between agricultural research and educational research. Both are practitioner-oriented, but still yield many fruitful areas for the pure researcher.

Wynne Harlen believed that teachers would not use theories if they could not see their relevance, but by using local theories they learn, and then maybe they will look for more general ones. Others, however, suggested that local theories were often the untested beliefs of the practitioner. If such concretised local theories could not be generalised, then communication between teachers, and between teachers and researchers would fail.

Van Aalst emphasised that the process of putting the practitioner/ researcher commitments into reality is long and complex, and the need for continuous dialogue must be recognised.

The overall tone of the discussion may be seen as rather depressing for the researcher, if that researcher is concerned about the impact of his findings on classroom practice. The story so far seems to be that local theories are often little more than crystallised prejudice, while general theories - even if accepted by the research establishment - fail to provide teachers with the sort of detailed guidance that they need. In very few curriculum development/research projects does the sort of dialogue proposed by van Aalst actually occur.

The Future

RICHARD KEMPA

Introduction

As the title of this paper indicates, I propose to concern myself
with some issues which, in my view, require the attention of science
educationists and mathematics educationists in the not-too-distant
future and which are likely to have a major impact upon the way in
which we design and conduct education in these two fields. Naturally,
any attempt to point to areas which should (and so far have not)
attracted attention by the researcher places one in a vulnerable
position: one exposes one's own value judgements which need not
necessarily be shared by one's colleagues; also, one places oneself
in the role of a prophet - and we all know of the dangers associated
with that.

The major focal point of the Seminar so far has been the discussion of theories and empirical facets of cognitive development, and
within that framework, the exploration of Piaget's theories in particular, with reference to science and mathematics education. It is
fair to say that Piagetian ideas have become so much part of our
thinking and language in education, that it is difficult to imagine
how we could ever make decisions about the design of education without
these ideas and recourse to them. Yet, as we are aware, this reliance
on Piagetian ideas and theories is not without its critics.

A recent article in Science Education, for example, seeks to
explore alternatives to Piagetian models (Novak, 1977c). Whatever
the merits of particular alternatives may be judged to be, the
existence of these alternatives provides us with an apt reminder that
the Piagetian theory is a model; it is essentially a scientific
model and, as such, is subject to change, modification and, at
least potentially, also subject to being supplanted by alternative
models. Therefore, in talking about future developments and new
directions in cognitive psychology research and innovation, the
possibility of alternative approaches or different priorities cannot
be ruled out ex cathedra, but has to be seriously considered.

It is fair to claim that the overriding justification for our
concentration on and concern with Piagetian type studies has been
and still is that we expect the findings to be of direct usefulness

and applicability in educational decision-making, especially decisions concerning the basic question 'When can what be learned by whom and in what form?'. Research findings which attempt to provide information about this general issue are bound to be 'normative' in character. This is to say that the pronouncements derived from them are stated in the form of general rules, sometimes with minor or major caveats. Nevertheless, the very essence of the rules is that they are normative in the sense that they describe (or seek to describe) fairly global characteristics of a population (of specified age, in a specified educational setting, for example), or of sub-populations. If one looks at the global impact of Piagetian research findings, the normative nature of the latter becomes strongly apparent. Rules such as:

> 'Pupils at the age of 13+ are at the verge of the transition from the concrete to the formal reasoning phase',

or

> 'Even at the age of 16, only 20% of the population can be said to have developed formal reasoning abilities',

exemplify the normativeness of many of our research findings.

Without doubt, 'rules' of this type already have a distinct influence on many of our educational practices. Indeed, their importance for certain types of curriculum development work is beyond question. Nevertheless, the normative character of the rules and their apparent simplicity also leads to certain dangers arising from their uncritical application. The greatest one of these is undue 'reductionism' (by which is meant the reduction of a complex interactive system into a relatively simple set of rules or simple relationships). This has tended to be overdone, so much so that the view is widely held that all decision-making concerning 'what to teach, when and how' becomes simply a matter of assessing the intellectual demand of the subject matter and the intellectual capabilities of students, and then 'matching' the two.

Whilst this procedure is now an important aspect* of our decision-making about instructional procedures and processes, it is merely one dimension of the complex network which teaching/learning situations constitute. Thus it is not inappropriate that attention should be paid to other dimensions also. One such dimension is that of cognitive styles, and it is to this that I wish to address myself in particular.

---

*There can, incidentally, be much debate about whether the assessments that are stipulated really can be carried out with high validity/reliability.

Cognitive styles - some general comments

The concept of cognitive style itself may require a brief explanation. The concept is strongly associated with and arises from the area of psychology known as psychological differentiation. By this is meant in the broad sense that differences exist between different individuals in relation to their psychological functioning and that, where such psychological functioning appears to take place in stable or relatively stable modes, stylistic qualities may be ascribed to it.

The literature on 'individual differences' is extensive, and so only a few references can be given here from which the reader can advance more deeply into the field (Witkin et al., 1974; Messick, 1976). Such literature is, on the whole, more concerned with the precise identification of the dimensions of individual differences and their measurement, rather than with establishing qualitatively that such differences exist. The latter is hardly a major problem for, as Bruner (1966) and Cronbach (1977) have discussed, the range of individual differences in actual classrooms is one of the most striking phenomena open to observation by the teacher and researcher. Research into individual differences is very closely connected with the names of H.A. Witkin, J. Kagan, D.R. Goodenough, and S. Messick and their respective co-workers. Their work and that of others in the field has led to the identification of several dimensions of individual differences which have by now become accepted as 'cognitive styles'. A detailed summary of the various style dimensions was given in 1970 by Messick. More recent reviews deal with selected cognitive styles, especially that of field dependence/field independence (Witkin, Moore, Goodenough, Cox, 1977; Goodenough, 1976).

Research into the educational applications and implications of such differences is still very much in its infancy, despite the fact that the field of differential psychology has become increasingly popular as a focus of educational research. Nevertheless, in the light of findings made so far, there can be hardly any doubt about the potential importance of individual differences as factors in learning and mental functioning. For this reason, I am advocating here that attention be given by science and mathematics education researchers to this field, in relation to science and mathematics learning.

It is appropriate at this juncture to point to some essential characteristics of cognitive styles.

i) First, cognitive styles relate to the _form_ in which cognitive activities are performed, rather than to their content. Thus, they are concerned with the process of perception, mental transformation, learning, problem-solving, etc.

In so far as cognitive styles are independent of the content of a mental activity, they should cut across the traditional subject boundaries, although the possibility of subject-specific styles has been acknowledged (Kempa, Dubé, 1973)

ii) Cognitive styles represent relatively stable features of cognitive functioning; by stability here is meant stability over time. Researches, (e.g. by Witkin et al, 1967) suggest that this stability extends not merely over weeks and months, but over years. Thus, any educational implications which may be attributed to cognitive styles, would have long-term validity.

iii) Cognitive styles appear as bipolarities, with opposite characteristics at the two extremes of a bipolarity. It has been suggested that this feature distinguishes cognitive styles from intelligence and other ability-related dimensions (Witkin et al., 1977). This also removes the 'value assignment' from the cognitive styles field as each end of the bipolarity of a particular style may be deemed to be advantageous under certain circumstances (no such situation exists in relation to an ability-related characteristic: to have less of it is invariably worse than to have more of it, as Witkin et al. aptly observe). A full discussion of the issue of 'good' or 'bad' in connection with cognitive styles has been given by Witkin, Oltman, Raskin, Karp (1971).

In the following section of this paper, a review is presented of some of the findings from research into individual differences which may be deemed to have a direct bearing on aspects of mathematics and science learning and teaching. Two cautionary notes have to be made first. One is that a review like this must of necessity be selective in terms of the material included in it. It would thus be wrong to attribute any degree of comprehensiveness to the exploration of the cognitive styles theme in relation to science and mathematics education. The other cautionary note, probably more important than the first, concerns the transferability of the findings from research into individual differences to the area of science/mathematics learning. One must immediately voice a warning that transferability on what may appear grounds of logic or commonsense, should not be taken for granted - the uncritical application and transfer of Piagetian notions to areas such as science learning, which has in the past been so prominent, should underline this warning. Nevertheless, some speculation about the transferability of findings from the individual differences field to science/mathematics education may well be justified if only to stress the importance of this area and to point forward to potentially profitable research questions.

Some cognitive styles and their implications for science education

Three cognitive styles, well established through general researches, are considered in the following, in relation to science learning and teaching. They are: field dependence/field independence, categorisation styles, and reflectivity/impulsivity. It should be noted in passing that the literature reveals some debate as to whether cognitive styles should be considered to be 'cognitive characteristics' of students, or whether they represent 'personality dimensions'. In the opinion of the author, such debate is fruitless or, at best, of academic value only. In as much as cognitive styles have a bearing on students' intellectual functioning, or are rationalised descriptions thereof, they must be included in the cognitive psychology field.

Field dependence/field independence.

This has probably been the subject of more investigations than any other cognitive style. Essentially, this stylistic characteristic concerns the perception of items of physical reality or items of information. What is at issue is basically the extent to which an individual's perception of an item of information in a complex field is dominated by the information in the field itself. For example, one may consider a simple geometric figure embedded in a complex figure and ask how difficult or easy an individual finds it to locate the simple figure within the complex one. A person who manages to accomplish tasks of this nature with no difficulties is said to be 'field independent' in his perception, whereas the person encountering difficulties is 'field dependent'. Thus, it may be said in general terms that the cognitive style of field dependence/field independence is concerned with the extent to which a person perceives information analytically, or the extent to which he tends to attend to information 'globally'.

Concerning the effect of this cognitive style on learning behaviour, reference may initially be made to a conclusion reached by Goodenough (1976) in a recent review. According to this, in typical concept-attainment problems where stimuli composed of a number of attributes are used, field dependent subjects are dominated by the salient (most noticeable) attribute of the stimulus and tend to ignore the non-salient cues in constructing hypotheses about the concept. By contrast, a field independent person tends to sample more fully the range of attributes and treat these more objectively for concept identification than his field dependent counterpart.

Experimental evidence of how the two contrasting behaviours affect concept attainment as such, is still scant and there is certainly no evidence available as yet about how the attainment of science concepts is affected by field dependence and field independence. Nevertheless, it does not seem unreasonable to predict that the two groups should perform differently when confronted with concept learning tasks under different instructional conditions. Field dependent persons, for example, might well be expected to do better in 'normal' concept learning situations where the distinction between relevant and irrelevant cues (with respect to the concept to be learned) is not immediately obvious, especially when salient cues happen to be irrelevant. Several general studies have indeed indicated that this expectation is fulfilled: field independent subjects tend to be better at concept attainment than field dependent ones (e.g., Davis, Klausmeyer, 1970; Helgeson, 1971; Lane, Evans, 1972).

The apparent superiority of field independent persons in concept attainment tasks, discussed so far, emerges as the consequence of the field independent person being less prone to fix his attention to particular, salient cues than the field dependent learner. In a wider interpretation, this phenomenon is essentially a phenomenon concerning the perception of information. One must recognise, of course, that perceptional behaviours, as they correspond to field dependence and field independence, respectively, will manifest themselves not only in 'intellectual' tasks, but also in genuine 'perceptual' situations, such as observational tasks in science learning. (Indeed, the early work on field dependence/field independence relied entirely on measuring the extent to which a person's perception in the visual sense is affected by a surrounding frame work.)

Several years back, we reported that different modes of task orientation resulted in different observational attainment in the context of practical chemistry (Kempa, Ward, 1975). The modes of task orientation investigated by us, were:

a)   an open-ended mode in which observational tasks have to be accomplished in the absence of any form of cueing;

b)   a method of partial direction in which students receive cueing of some, but not all observations to be made;

c)   a check-list approach in which students are required to carry out observational tasks with reference to a comprehensive schedule listing all possible observations (thus providing extensive cueing).

The observational tasks embraced the most common areas in which visual observations have to be made in chemistry, viz. changes in colour; changes involving the formation or disappearance of solids; changes involving the liberation of gases; and temperature changes resulting from the absorption or evolution of heat during a reaction.   The details of the study have been given elsewhere (Ward, 1973). For the present purpose, reference need only be made to the observational attainment scores achieved by students in different academic ability groups, on the various modes of task definition.   These are given in Table 1. What is of interest here, apart from the fact that the mode of task definition bears strongly on observational attainment, is the complete absence of any influence on the observational scores of students' academic achievement in chemistry. At the time of first presenting our data, we accepted readily (and logically) that observational abilities in the context of laboratory work in chemistry are not primarily 'intellectual' in character, but predominantly 'perceptual' in nature.

Table 1: Observational attainment scores for different modes of task orientation, for students in different achievement groups.*

Treatment mode	Observational mean score for		
	Top Group*	Middle Group*	Bottom Group*
Open-ended	20.6	19.9	20.1
Partial direction	17.3	20.0	16.3
Check-list	23.6	22.6	21.0
Total	20.2	20.8	19.2

Total N = 126

*The allocation of students to the three achievement groups was based on their performance in a chemistry achievement test, using the following criteria: Top group, score > 12; middle group, score 8 - 12; bottom group, score < 8; max. possible score: 20.

Since then, this work has been considerably extended and refined and we have included selected cognitive styles among the variables examined as potential influences upon observational attainment. With reference to field dependence/field independence we find distinct correlations to exist between observational attainment and scores on a complex 'hidden figures test' developed for the purpose of assessing degrees of field independence. Table 2 indicates (i) that field independent persons achieve on the whole better observational scores and (ii) that in the partial direction mode of task orientation, they are significantly less influenced and biased by the cueing provided than are the field dependent persons. It should be noted here that, in the latter case, observational attainment refers to the detection and perception of non-cued observations, not that of the observations for which cues had been provided. The work is still in progress and therefore it would be premature to quote extensive data before they have been fully checked and evaluated. Nevertheless, in common with the findings of other authors, our results indicate clearly the important effect which cognitive styles orientation can and does have on attainment and performance in both the intellectual and the perceptual domain. If, as may be suggested in the light of experimental findings to date, persons' concept attainment and observational behaviour are significantly affected by the extent of their field dependence, the effect of such trait on science learning should receive urgent and detailed attention.

Table 2: <u>Observational attainment scores for different modes of task orientation, in relation to hidden figures test scores.</u>

(Standard deviations in brackets; total N = 456)

Hidden figures test score group	Open-ended	Partial direction	Check-list
High	26.00 (3.29)	25.80 (3.63)	28.30 (3.16)
Intermediate	23.95 (3.70)	24.57 (3.06)	27.57 (3.47)
Low	22.59 (3.73)	24.13 (3.04)	27.10 (3.39)

Significance test for HFT levels: $p < 0.01$.

It is of course not simply with learning behaviour that we are concerned. Findings about students' and pupils' learning behaviours should, if at all possible, be translated into meaningful decisions about the design of teaching and instructional procedures. Therefore, it is appropriate to look at this aspect also in this brief discussion of field dependence/field independence. Unfortunately, we have as yet available little evidence as to how different methods of teaching interact with different cognitive styles. Indeed, the complexity of undertaking controlled experimentation into such interactions in the natural setting of a school makes it unlikely that evidence of a generalisable nature will readily be forthcoming. Nevertheless, some speculation is justified here, against the background of findings from a limited, but important range of studies.

430

Science education, possibly more so than any other branch of education, has strongly advocated the notion of 'learning by discovery' or 'enquiry learning'. Without wishing to discuss the pros and cons of this instructional approach, one may argue that effective learning under such conditions of 'enquiry learning' requires the learner to organise the experiences with which he is presented and to arrive at some meaningful cognitive structure on the basis of such experiences. If this view is accepted, it would follow that persons whose cognitive style tends to the field independent or articulated end of the field dependence/field independence spectrum should find 'learning by discovery' an easier and more effective educational procedure than field dependent persons. This hypothesis is justified basically because field independent persons possess the ability to structure information from a learning experience more effectively and readily than field dependent persons.

Some evidence for this is presented by a recent study by Satterly and Telfer (to be published) in which the relationships between field dependence/independence and the effectiveness of Ausubelian type advance organisers was examined. The key issue of this study, in relation to the present argument, was the expectation that advance organisers would enhance the performance of field dependent, though not field independent subjects, in coding tasks requiring more than simple rote-learning. This should be so because (a) advance organisers are essentially an aid to the structuring of materials in the learner's mind, and (b) field dependent persons display far more limited structuring ability than do field independent persons.

The subject of Satterly and Telfer's study was word structure, and their experimental treatment used (a) lessons on word structure and (b) similar lessons but involving advance organiser plus reference at particular points during the lessons to the key ideas presented in the advance organiser. Their findings are summarised semi-quantitatively by Figure 1 which compares the two treatments.

It is seen that, first, in the absence of advance organisation, field independent learners accomplish the learning task significantly better than their field dependent counterparts, with 'intermediate' subjects coming in between the two groups. Second, the use of advance organisers with intermittent reinforcement (Treatment b) enhances the score of the field dependent learners, but has no significant influence on the scores of the field independent group. It is thus clear that the field dependence/field independence cognitive style is an educationally important characteristic which has a significant bearing on learning and on the effectiveness of different instructional strategies for different pupils.

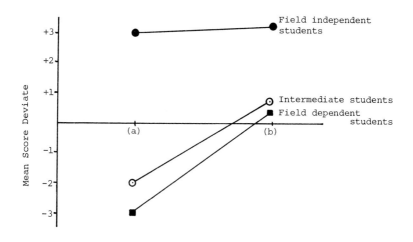

Figure 1:   Field dependence/field independence style and
the effectiveness of advance organisers (after:
Satterly and Telfer). (a) = control treatment
(no advance organiser); (b) = treatment involving advance organisers plus reference to
advance organisers during learning sequence.

It may be opportune here to mention that at Keele we are currently in the process of investigating how cognitive styles interact with
learning based on a discovery and expository approach, respectively.
In the initial phase, we have been using coding exercises and simple
mathematical tasks of the type used by previous workers for investigations into discovery and expository teaching (Guthrie, 1967;
Haslerud, Meyers, 1958). We are now in the process of extending this
work to actual science learning situations. Again, a key variable in
our study is the field dependence/field independence style.

Categorisation styles

A further cognitive styles characteristic of potential interest
in science education is that relating to conceptual categorisation.
Conceptual categorisation is a common task in science learning where
the learner is required or expected to analyse sets of evidence and
observations, to recognise relationships and make abstractions of
rules or generalisations that go beyond the evidence before him.
Essentially, any act of hypothesis formulation made on the basis of

e.g., laboratory-based observations, requires such categorisations to be made. Generally, the categorisations which we expect are of an analytic-inferential mode in which some superordinate concept is abstracted or invoked. (There are, of course, different degrees of abstraction possible for science concepts, as has been suggested by Kempa, Hodgson, 1976.)

In consequence, individual differences in categorisation behaviour must be a further dimension of relevance to science education. As in the case of the field dependence/independence style, categorisation styles have not so far been explored in relation to science teaching and learning. The main information about individual differences in categorisation behaviour derives from the work by Kagan et al. (1963) and Sigel (1967). These workers recognised three main types of categorisation behaviour:

i)   Tendency to group together objects or events on the basis of features establishing a relational link between them.

ii) Tendency to group together objects or events on the basis of common characteristics which are directly discernable.

iii) Tendency to group together objects or events on the basis of superordinate features which are not directly discernable, but are inferred.

The test situations whereby students' leanings towards these different modes of categorisation are established, generally involve simple classification tasks whereby from an array of three or more pictures, students are required to select two or more on the basis of 'what they have in common or what links them' and to state the reasons for their choice. For example, given a triad of pictures representing, respectively, an upright-standing person, a watch and a ruler, a student may place together the person and the watch on the grounds that 'the man can wear the watch' (relational); or he can place together watch and ruler 'because they have numbers' (descriptive of a common discernable characteristic); alternatively, ruler and watch may be placed together because they are measuring instruments (inferential use of a superordinate concept).

It is reasonable to suggest that students whose leaning in conceptual categorisation tends towards modes (i) and (ii) indicated above, may on the whole be less successful in typical science learning situations than students who tend towards the inferential mode of conceptual categorisation. This again is an area which merits attention, particularly since Kagan and co-workers have suggested that there may be an age-related progression from modes (i) to (iii). If this is the case, it may well be that this development runs parallel to the Piagetian type of development, but this aspect has, to my knowledge, not so far been examined. However, the possibility that failure in concept attainment tasks may be attributable to cognitive styles influences,

433

rather than to non-progression to particular Piagetian developmental stages, cannot automatically be ruled out. On the contrary it would seem to be a field for considerable research involvement in the future.

Reflectivity - Impulsivity

This is the third cognitive styles dimension to which I wish to make reference, again because of its potential importance in the context of science teaching. As has already been indicated, science learning as we understand it in its contemporary setting, attaches much importance to the student's participation in the 'process of science': he is expected to analyse information, organise it conceptually and form hypotheses or generalisations.

Following the findings by Kagan and co-workers (1964, 1966) that some individuals are by nature more reflective than others (the latter appearing impulsive by comparison) in their thinking habits, we may predict that such differences should affect individuals' success in science learning situations. An 'impulsive' thinker would tend to be non-analytic in his reasoning because of a tendency to focus on an immediately obvious relationship to be discerned from a range of stimuli. He would adhere relatively firmly to this initial relationship and lack the flexibility in thinking style to consider also alternative hypotheses and relationships. In other words: an impulsive learner may well tend to 'jump to conclusions' without adequate prior reflection of alternative solutions or of all available information, unless he is restrained from so doing. This would apply not only to genuine learning situations, but also to problem-solving situations of the type encountered, for example in examinations.

Again, one may predict that students of similar ability, but different leanings towards reflectivity or impulsivity, should perform differently in situations involving discovery learning and reception learning, respectively. No direct evidence has so far been produced in support of this notion, and therefore the argument must remain a speculative one at the moment.

One area where we suspect degrees of impulsivity and reflectivity to have a significant effect and which is currently being investigated by Ward (mentioned previously in connection with the study of observational attainment), is concerned with the interpretation of observations made under actual practical conditions. Such observations, as we managed to establish previously, are frequently incomplete, because of the student's failure to notice particular phenomena, or they contain excessive information, often of an illusory nature because the student thought to observe certain phenomena which, in reality, could not have been observed.

The consequence is that subsequent interpretations of observations cannot always be made against the background of fully correct sets of observations. What we have noticed, especially in cases where excessive information is available to the student which is contradictory within itself, is that different students tend to behave entirely differently: some form hypotheses or draw conclusions on the basis of the first piece of evidence which they meet and adhere firmly to their initial position, notwithstanding subsequent evidence which conflicts with the first; other students, although also forming the initial hypotheses, adhere far less rigidly to them and modify them in the light of subsequent information. We have not as yet been able to relate this behaviour to an accepted measure of reflectivity/impulsivity, but hope to be able to do so before long. Our hunch is that there may well be a significant relationship!

Concluding comments

My brief for this contribution was to look ahead and suggest how and in what areas progress might be made in our understanding of the complexity of the learning process, especially in so far as it relates to science and mathematics learning. I make no apologies for departing from what has been the main theme of the Seminar: that of cognitive developmental psychology. Instead, I have attempted to draw into our field of vision another area of psychology which, to me, is not only interesting, but also potentially important.

It is an area which for those concerned with science education and mathematics education presents a major challenge, no less so - I believe - than did Piaget's work before it began to be systematically explored in its significance for and application to science and mathematics education. How much fruit this exploration has borne, is evident to all of us: there can be few teachers not aware of the importance of Piagetian findings in relation to the practice of education, and the incorporation of these findings in actual curriculum projects highlights their importance in the educational context. We owe a major debt of gratitude to those who pioneered this exploration, foremost among them Professor Kenneth Lovell.

It would be wrong, though, not to recognise that the Piagetian model relates to only one aspect of pupils' and students' cognitive functioning. Certainly, the stage theory of Piaget in its exploration within the science/mathematics education field, has provided us with a most useful tool to decide about when pupils and students are likely to be 'ready' intellectually to engage in particular forms of learning. Where I now see the extension and development from here is basically concerned with styles of learning; it relates to the many modes of intellectual and cognitive functioning which are prevalent in individuals and which affect the way and manner in which they interact with and benefit from the learning experiences with which we provide and confront students and pupils. To attend to these matters now seems to me to be a natural development from Piaget's work.

RESPONSE by J. Keri Davies

Professor Kempa declared in his opening remarks that his concern
would be with issues likely to have a major impact upon the way in
which 'we' (whoever 'we' are) design and conduct education in the
curriculum areas of science and mathematics. Presumably the 'we' he
has in mind will not be those restricted to the membership of this
Seminar but includes other researchers, curriculum developers, policy
makers, institutional curriculum planners, and teachers. I detect
that he is seeking wide attention for his ideas because there is more
than a hint that they may be applicable in the learning of science and
mathematics.

I think few of us would disagree with what I took to be a warning
about accepting Piagetian ideas uncritically, which appeared to re-
enforce Lovell's wise counsel: '...it is important that when we are
discussing developmental theories we remember their differing bases
and the possible practical outcomes. This is especially true when
dealing with teachers.' Kempa reminded us of the evolving and changing
nature of Piagetian theory, a point which has not eluded Piaget himself
as Lovell reminded us in his paper: 'It is necessary to say this for
oftimes it is forgotten that Piaget himself says that he is his own
chief revisionist'. Kempa has also indicated the problems inherent
in any expectancy from the outcomes of Piagetian-type researches,
their direct usefulness and applicability in educational decision-
making, and their influence on curriculum development and classroom
practice.

Here it may be as well to point out that researchers probably need
no reminder of the dangers of the uncritical acceptance of theories
and/or the outcomes of research; criticism is a tool in trade of the
researcher. However, the teacher, whose orders of concern are different (not less or more important) from the researcher, will have gained
their understanding (or more often their misunderstanding) of Piagetian
ideas from harsh distillates crudely administered on initial teacher
training programmes and/or in-service courses. There are exceptions,
but few teachers will be as aware or as informed as they might be to
make maximum use of Piagetian ideas or any other areas of cognitive
psychology within the context of the classroom. As this stage I will
note this as a problem and return to it later in my comments.

The major content of Kempa's paper is devoted to his review of
'Cognitive Styles' and an outline of their possible implications for
science education. He admits to a departure from the main theme of
the Seminar but concludes that much of the work basically concerned
with styles of learning is a natural development from Piaget's work.
In much of what he has suggested I would want to challenge very little,
except perhaps for the observation that I had expected him to have
been a little more speculative on a wider front rather than the restricted one presented - unless of course all the answers lie in this
direction!

Within the field of 'Cognitive Styles' he has made interesting speculations and suggested lines of exploration and even declared the odd hunch. Perhaps these lines of research could be helpful to a number of concerns that have been identified by curriculum researchers for some time. When reading Kempa's paper I was reminded of Caswell's warning given in the middle 1960s on discussions about the concept of 'structure' in respect of the organisation of learning: 'There are many ways or organising knowledge. What may be most useful to one person in a particular situation may be of little use to another in a different situation'. (Caswell, 1965) Although Caswell was making a slightly different point it does seem to me that the concept of 'cognitive styles' might be a useful one for the curriculum designer. Certainly it should be useful if, as has been argued, when looking for 'curriculum organisers',strategies of individual learning could provide the major focus. This was argued by Herrick as far back as 1950.

Throughout his paper Kempa provides an emphasis on identifying new avenues for research and it is not surprising that he should become explicit and suggest his own area of interest and expertise as a potentially fruitful one. A position which no doubt can be justified. After all he was honest enough to state at the beginning of his paper that he would expose his own value judgements. Others will have different priorities for research and provided they have the motivation and/or the funds, their priorities can be pursued in cognitive psychology whether or not they are relevant to science or mathematics education.

However, there are other issues in Kempa's paper upon which I wish to pass comment. These issues I think are more implicit than explicit but deserve attention. One can perceive in the paper (and this may be where I am at fault as they are my perceptions and may not be his intentions) a desire to provide knowledge in cognitive psychology that will be functional in an educational context - be that context in a classroom or laboratory learning situation, designing curricula, assessing pupil learning and the like. These desires point to a number of problems relevant to contemporary and future concerns - not the least being the one I noted earlier about how the practitioners (the teachers as curriculum implementers) acquire and apply knowledge for their professional tasks.

The bulk of research in teaching and learning (including cognitive psychology) employs the objectifying language of empirical science and there is an attempt to formulate, for example, empirical structures of cognitive processes. Here the empirical approach is hard at work providing findings that are either inaccessible to many educational practitioners in classrooms, or if accessible, incomprehensible because of the language used, or if understood do not represent reality as the practitioner understands it.

437

There are signs that contrasting, complementary, or alternative
research strategies are emerging which might draw upon 'reality'
through interpretive analysis as, for example, in ethnomethodology or
phenomenology. If we are pragmatic and eclectic, and not so ideo-
logically committed to research strategies that are mutually exclusive
of alternatives, we might be able to develop a reasonable set of
theoretical positions to guide research in cognitive psychology which
is relevant to science and mathematical education. Relevant in the
sense that the theories and outcomes of research may not be only
comprehensible to the researcher but understandable to the teacher
and curriculum developer and also applicable by them.

However, as soon as one considers applicability one runs into a
difficult problem which is not a new one: although psychology
abounds with theories of learning and development, these theories are
descriptive rather than prescriptive. In this respect psychology
does not have a recognisable theory of instruction apart from the
brave attempts of Bruner (1963, 1966). There is still a gap between
the descriptive theories based on normative data - with their attend-
ant dangers in 'application' as Kempa and Lovell have warned us - and
prescriptive theories which are for action. We have theories of
cognitive psychology: how near are we to developing theories for
cognitive development? This is not just a semantic problem. Education is not conducted on a value free basis on neutral theories of
education. Educational theories are by their very nature value
loaded and one should not be surprised to learn that schooling is
prescriptive. When one examines closely attempts at theorising about
the curriculum, each theory turns out to be for curriculum not of
curriculum (Davies, 1978).

I am suggesting that it may be useful for us to begin to think
more constructively about a practice theory (see Greenwood, 1961) in
cognitive psychology particularly if we are to attempt to pay attention to the ideas of Kempa and others. This may be an area of useful
speculation in the future.

Let me give one example to clarify my point. If the question is
asked: How can cognitive psychology inform decision-making in
education? And this question is placed in the specific context of
the policy decisions that are to be made by the Association for Science
Education (1979) in respect of its recently issued consultative document: Alternatives for Science Education. I wonder if a coherent and
cohesive statement for prescribed action could be given?

To summarise: I see the issues for the future not only ones that
might be called pure research of an empirical kind, but the emergence
of alternative research strategies that will be complementary. I see
the need for thought and speculation to be given for the development
of metatheories on the one hand to relate different forms of theorising
but also attempts should be made to formulate practice theories for
the guidance of educational practitioners.

If my response has been slightly different from what might have been expected, I would justify in two ways -

1. If Kempa can deviate from the main theme of the Seminar, then I claim the same privilege!

2. More probably the justification lies in the fact that I may have a different cognitive style from everyone else!

Discussion

The final session of the Seminar provided an opportunity to identify the salient issues of theory and methodology for the future through reflection on the different sorts of work that had been reported throughout the week, recognition of the common strands uniting the various studies, and speculation about how findings in cognitive developmental psychology may be of most use to science and mathematics education.

Kempa introduced a discussion of cognitive styles to the Seminar. In this discussion he defended his emphasis on this single theme rather than a broader scheme of issues by arguing that this was an important aspect of the learning behaviour of the individual student that had been neglected, and that it provided an alternative descriptive framework that takes account of the predispositions that students may have towards different modes of thinking. He did not see this, however, as mutually exclusive or competitive with other frameworks such as those of Piaget and Ausubel, which he also regarded as descriptive and not explanatory.

There was very little discussion of the alternative approaches of Ausubel or the skills integrationists referred to in the first session of the Seminar and only brief mention of the application of Gagné's learning hierarchies. Kempa expressed some doubts about the Piagetian model; he claimed that it had been accepted by many teachers as if it were a set of established rules, that its use had provided normative group measures which could lead to neglect of individual differences, and that there were low correlations between pupils' performances on tasks requiring the same level of thought process in different contexts. This was challenged from the floor by the assertion that Piagetian-based work had emphasised and not disguised individual differences; it was claimed that it had described the situation by demonstrating that the variation among children in the same year was very great in comparison with the difference between one year and another, but such work did not purport to tell us how to teach. The low number of studies that have examined the mismatch between existing science teaching routines and pupils' learning capabilities was commented upon.

A persisting theme of the discussion was the appropriate scope (i.e. 'local' or 'general') of theories upon which work on cognitive development in relation to science and mathematics education should be based. Kempa saw himself as a practitioner who was looking for a theory of instruction that rested upon a framework deriving not only from cognitive development theories but also from other areas of psychology and from sociology. Such a theory would inform instructional decision-making. He was sceptical of 'local' theories because they risked being little more than sets of long-held value judgements.

Several speakers from the floor suggested that 'local' and limited theories might well be valuable for some purposes; throughout the Seminar, it was suggested, there had been discussions of various theories and their advantages and disadvantages but no comparable clarification of the categories of problems to which they were applicable. If different studies have different purposes, then they will probably require different sorts of theories and different methodologies. One questioner asked whether those concerned with cognitive psychology, as applied to education, were involved in a science, i.e. a theory building exercise studied for its own sake, or a technology, i.e. concerned with using theory to solve a problem. It was suggested that the theories with which we are dealing are at a stage comparable with that of medical theories of two hundred years ago; furthermore, we are constrained not only by the diversity of approaches to cognitive psychology but by the even greater variety of other disciplines that impinge on education.

As well as the uncertainties about the roles of sophisticated theories as opposed to local, piecemeal approaches, some concern about the impact on teachers of these theoretical perspectives was expressed. If developments in this area were to fulfil the function of aiding teachers' and others' decision-making, then new patterns of communication, if not new forms of theorising, might have to be developed and we shall have to explore the reasons why teachers for the most part reject educational research and its findings. It was suggested that more attention should be paid to a mediation process whereby the theoretical developments are marked out in such a way as to show how they lead back to the practical problems of the classroom; theories must not only be understood by researchers but must be comprehensible to teachers and curriculum developers.

There was some discussion and some disagreement about the relationship between the dimension of cognitive style exemplified by Kempa (field dependence/field independence) and I.Q. Various studies were cited where the findings suggested that I.Q. and field independence were correlated very closely, only moderately or not at all. Several questions were asked about the report of findings relating this cognitive style with the effectiveness of advance organisers and the inferences that might be drawn about the different instructional strategies for different pupils. For example, would the lack of influence of advance organisers on the attainment of field independent students be explained by a ceiling effect since their attainment was already very high? Could the findings be explained by field independent students already having the advance organisers before instruction rather than by not needing them? Does the research distinguish sufficiently between 'necessary' and 'sufficient' conditions for learning?

Some general unease was also expressed about the aptitude-treatment interaction (A.T.I.) approach implied by the concern to use cognitive styles as a basis for a local theory of instruction; it was pointed out that the avid proponents of A.T.I. in the sixties and early seventies had now lost confidence in this approach. As rapporteurs we were rather surprised that this part of the discussion did not develop further; our general impression was that very few strong views on the value of the cognitive styles approach were expressed during the session.

A number of other issues were neglected that we had predicted would come up in discussion - issues that had formed salient features of a variety of sessions throughout the week. For example, there was little comment on questions of what we might term the 'maths-science interface', or on relationships between the conceptual frameworks and language, or on the need and possibilities for more classroom-based research (although the last of these was strongly implied in some of the comments).

References

AALST, H.F. van, WIERSTRA, R.A.F. (1978) *Het ontwikkelen van een leergang op basis van mastery learning principles - enkele aantekeningen,* Utrecht, Rijks Universiteit Utrecht.

AALST, H.F. van, EBBENS, S. (1979) *Het projekt leerpakket ontwikkeling* in *Leerplanontwikkeling in Nederland Natuurkunde,* Zeist, NCSV.

ANDELFINGER, B. (1979a) *Zur Lage: Schulmathematik, Standort und Perspektiven,* Freiburg, Herder.

ANDELFINGER, B. (1979b) *Zur Sache: Schulmathematik, Wege und Chancen,* Freiburg, Herder.

ANDERSON, J.A. (1977) Neural models with cognitive implications in Laberge, D., Samuels, S.F. (Eds.), *Basic process in reading: perception and comprehension,* Hillsdale, New Jersey, Lawrence Erlbaum Associates.

ANDERSON, J.R. (1978) Arguments concerning representations for mental imagery, *Psychological Review,* 85, 249.

ANDERSON, R.C., BIDDLE, W.B. (1975) On asking people questions about what they are reading in Bower, G.H. (Ed.), *The Psychology of Learning and Motivation, Vol.9,* New York, Academic Press.

ANDERSON, R.C., SPIRO, R.J., MONTAGUE, W.E. (1977) *Schooling and the acquisition of knowledge,* Hillsdale, N.J., Erlbaum.

ANKNEY, P.H., JOYCE, L.K. (1975) The development of a Piagetian paper-and-pencil test for assessing concrete operational reasoning, *Dissertation Abstracts International,* 35, 5947-A.

ARCHENHOLD, W.F. (1975) *A study of the understanding by sixth-form students of the concept of potential in physics,* M. Phil. thesis, University of Leeds.

ASSOCIATION FOR SCIENCE EDUCATION (1979) *Alternatives for science education: a consultative document,* Hatfield, England, Association for Science Education.

442

ASSOCIATION OF TEACHERS OF MATHEMATICS (1973) *Focus on teaching,* (Section on 'Investigating children's difficulties'), Association of Teachers of Mathematics, Nelson, England.

AUBLE, P.M., FRANKS, J.J. (1978) The effects of effort towards comprehension on recall, *Memory and Cognition,* 6, 20-25.

AUSUBEL, D.P. (1960) The use of advance organizers in the learning and retention of meaningful verbal material, *Journal of Educational Psychology,* 51, 267-272.

AUSUBEL, D.P. (1963) *The psychology of meaningful verbal learning,* New York, Grune and Stratton.

AUSUBEL, D.P. (1968) *Educational psychology: a cognitive view,* New York, Holt, Rinehart and Winston.

AUSUBEL, D.P., ROBINSON, F.G. (1969) *School learning,* New York, Holt, Rinehart and Winston.

AUSUBEL, D.P. (1978) In defense of advance organizers: a reply to critics, *Review of Educational Research,* 48, 251-258.

AUSUBEL, D.P., NOVAK, J.D., HANESIAN, H. (1978) *Educational psychology: a cognitive view,* 2nd ed., New York, Holt, Rinehart and Winston.

BADY, R.J. (1978) Methodological issues in formal operations research: what does it mean to be formal? *Science Education,* 62, 233-239.

BARNES, D., TODD, F. (1977) *Communication and learning in small groups,* London, Routledge and Kegan Paul.

BART, W.M. (1971) The factor structure of formal operations, *British Journal of Educational Psychology,* 41, 70-77.

BATESON, G. (1972) *Steps to an ecology of mind,* New York, Ballentine Books.

BAYRHUBER, H., SCHAEFER, G. (1978) *Kybernetische Biologie,* Köln, Aulis.

BEARD, R.M. (1962) Children's reasoning: a repetition of some of Piaget's experiments by members of the A.T.M. *Mathematics Teaching,* 21, 33-39.

BEARD, R.M. (1963) The order of concept development studies in two fields (I and II), *Educational Review,* 15 (1962-63) 105-17 and 228-237.

BEARD, R.M. (1964) Further studies in concept development, *Educational Review,* 17 (1964-65), 41-58.

BELBIN, E. (1979) Applicable psychology and some national problems, *British Journal of Psychology*, 70(2), 187-197.

BELL, A.W. (1976) *The learning of general mathematical strategies,* Shell Centre for Mathematical Education, University of Nottingham.

BELL, A.W. (1979) The learning of process aspects of mathematics, *Educational Studies in Mathematics,* 10.

BELL, A.W., ROOKE, D.J., WIGLEY, A.R. (1979) *The South Nottinghamshire project, 13-16 material* (unpublished), Shell Centre for Mathematical Education, University of Nottingham.

BELL, D., HUGHES, E.R., ROGERS, J. (1975) *Area, weight and volume: monitoring and encouraging children's conceptual development,* Nelson for the Schools Council.

BERNSTEIN, B. (1971a) *On the classification and framing of educational knowledge* in Young, M.F.D. (Ed.) (1971), *Knowledge and control,* Collier MacMillan.

BERNSTEIN, B. (1971b) *Theoretical studies towards a sociology of language* in *Class, codes and control, Vol.1,* London, Routledge and Kegan Paul.

BLAKE, A. (1978) *The predictive validity of written tests of Piagetian developmental level,* Riverina College of Advanced Technology, Australia.

BLOCK, J.H. (Ed.) (1971) *Mastery learning, theory and practice,* New York, Holt, Rinehart and Winston.

BLOCK, J.H., ANDERSON, L.W. (1975) *Mastery learning in classroom instruction,* New York, Macmillan.

BLOOM, B.S. (1968) Learning for mastery, *UCLA Evaluation Comment,* 1 (2), 1.

BLOOM, B.S. (1976) *Human characteristics and school learning,* New York, McGraw Hill.

BOGDEN, C.A. (1977) *The use of concept mapping as a possible strategy for instructional design and evaluation in college genetics,* M.S. thesis, Cornell University.

BRAINERD, C. (1978) Cognitive-developmental theory, *Behavioural and Brain Sciences,* 2, 173-213.

BROWN, A.L., DELOACHE, J.S. (1978) Skills, plans and self regulation in Siegler, R.S. (Ed.), *Children's thinking. What develops?* Hillsdale, N.J., Erlbaum.

BROWN, G., DESFORGES, C. (1977) Piagetian psychology and education: time for revision, *British Journal of Educational Psychology,* 47, 7-17.

BRUMBY, M.N. (1979) *Students' perceptions and learning styles associated with the concept of evolution by natural selection,* Ph.D thesis, University of Surrey.

BRUNER, J.S. (1963) Needed: a theory of instruction, *Educational Leadership,* 20(8).

BRUNER, J.S. (1966) *Toward a theory of instruction,* Cambridge Mass., Harvard University Press.

BRUNER, J.S. (1966) On cognitive growth in Bruner, J.S., Greenfield, P.M., Oliver, R.R. (Eds.), *Studies in cognitive growth,* 1-67, New York, John Wiley.

BRUNER, J.S. (1972) Nature and uses of immaturity, *American Psychologist,* 27(8), 1-28.

BURT, C. (1919) The development of reasoning in school children, *Journal of Experimental Pedagogy,* 5, 68-77, 121-127.

BURTON, W.H., KIMBALL, R.B., KING, R.L. (1960) *Education for effective thinking,* New York, Century, Croft.

CALVERT, B. (1958) *Non-verbal test, D.H.,* National Foundation for Educational Research, Slough, Bucks.

CAMPBELL, D.T., STANLEY, J.C. (1963) Experimental and quasi-experimental designs for research on teaching in Gage, N.L., *Handbook of Research in Teaching,* Rand McNally.

CARPAY, J.A.H., BOL, E. (1974) *Engels in het basisonderwijs,* 's Hertogenbosch.

CARROLL, J.B. (1963) A model for school learning, *Teachers College Record,* 64, 723-33.

CASE, R. (1975) Gearing the demands of instruction to the developmental capacities of the learner, *Review of Educational Research,* 45, 59-87.

CASTALDI, P. (1975) *A summary of cognitive educational research done in introductory science courses at Cornell university and a study of the effects of tutoring made and learner's conceptual abilities on learning efficiency in introductory college,* Ph.D. thesis, Cornell University.

445

CASWELL, H.L. (1965) Difficulties in defining the structure of the curriculum in Passow, A.H. (Ed.), *Curriculum crossroads,* New York, Teachers College, Columbia University Press.

CHAMPAGNE, A.B., KLOPFER, L.E., DeSENA, A.T., SQUIRES, D.A. (1978) *Student knowledge structure representations: relations to science content structure and changes through instruction,* Unpublished document. Learning Research and Development Centre, University of Pittsburg.

CHASE, W.G., SIMON, H.A. (1973) The mind's eye in chess in Chase, W.G. (Ed.), *Visual information processes,* London, Academic Press.

CHEN, H.H. (1979) *Relevance of Gowin's structure of knowledge and Ausubel's learning theory to methods for improving physics laboratory instruction,* Ph.D. thesis, Cornell University.

CHI, M.J.H. (1978) Knowledge structures and memory developments in Siegler, R.S. (Ed.), *Children's thinking. What develops?* Hillsdale, N.J., Erlbaum.

CHILD, D. (1970) *The essentials of factor analysis,* London, Holt, Rinehart and Winston.

CLOUTIER, R., GOLDSCHMID, M. (1976) Individual differences in the development of formal reasoning, *Child Development,* 47, 1097-1102.

COHEN, G. (1977) *The psychology of cognition,* London, Academic Press.

COLE, M., SCRIBNER, S. (1974) *Culture and thought: a psychological introduction,* New York, John Wiley and Sons, Inc.

COLEMAN, J.C. (1970) The study of adolescent development using a sentence-completion method, *British Journal of Educational Psychology,* 40, 27-34.

COLEMAN, J.C. (1974) *Relationships in adolescence,* London, Routledge and Kegan Paul.

COLEMAN, J.C. (1978) Current contradictions in adolescent theory, *Journal of Youth and Adolescence,* 7 (1),1-11.

COLLIS, K. (1975) *The development of formal reasoning,* University of Newcastle, Australia.

COULSON, E.H. (1966) Aims and ideas in Nuffield chemistry project, *Education in Chemistry,* 3, 229-232.

CRAIG, F.I.M. (1973) A 'Levels of analysis' view of memory in Piner, P., Frames, I., Alloway, T.M. (Eds.), *Communication and affect: language and thought*, London, Academic Press.

CRONBACH, L.J. (1963, 1977) *Educational psychology*, New York, Harcourt, Brace Jovanovich.

CRUTCHFIELD, R.S., COVINGTON, M.W. (1963) *The facilitation of creative thinking and problem solving in school children*, Symposium paper, American Association for the Advancement of Science, Cleveland.

CSSE (1978) *Case studies in science education*, University of Illinois.

DAHLGREN, L.O., MARTON, F. (1978) Student conceptions of subject matter, *Studies in Higher Education*, 3(1), 25-35.

DASEN, P.R., NGINI, L., LAVALLEE, M. (1979) Cross-cultural training studies of concrete operations in Eckensberger, L., Lonner, W., Poortinga, Y.H. (Eds.), *Cross-cultural contributions to psychology*, Lisse, Netherlands, Swets and Zeitlinger.

DAVIES, J.K. (1978) *Seminar paper no.3: Curriculum theorising*, Department of Education, University of Stirling.

DAVIS, J.K., KLAUSMEIER, H.J. (1970) Cognitive style and concept identification as a function of complexity and training procedures, *Journal of Educational Psychology*, 61, 423-430.

DAVIS, R.B., JOKUSCH, E., McKNIGHT, C. (1978) Cognitive processes in learning algebra, *Journal of Children's Mathematical Behaviour*, 2, 1-320.

DAVIS,R.B.(1979) *The formulations of Karplus, Piaget, and the Madison project*, The Curriculum Laboratory, University of Illinois.

DEADMAN, J.A. (1976) *The structure and development of concepts associated with the topic of evolution in secondary schoolboys*, Ph.D. thesis, University of London.

DEPARTMENT OF EDUCATION AND SCIENCE (1970) *Statistics of Education*, 2, London, H.M.S.O.

DELUCCA, R.P. (1977) Measurement of logical thinking: an electronic equivalent of Piaget's first chemical experiment, *Journal of Research in Science Teaching*, 14, 539-544.

DE VRIES, R. (1978) Early education and Piagetian theory in Gallagher, J.N., Easley, J.A. (Eds.), *Knowledge and development*, Vol.2, London, Plenum.

DIENES, Z.P. (1978) Learning mathematics in Wain, G.T., *Mathematical education*, London, Van Nostrand Reinhold.

DONALDSON, M. (1978) *Children's minds*, Fontana/Collins.

DORAN, R.L. (1972) Misconceptions of science concepts, *Journal of Research in Science Teaching*, 9(2), 127-137.

DORMOLEN VAN, J. (1978) *Didaktik der Mathematik*, Braunschweig.

DOUVAN, E., ADELSON, J. (1966) *The adolescent experience*, Wiley.

DOYLE, J.D., LUNETTA, V.N. (1977) Piaget in perspective, *School Science and Mathematics*, 78, 475-480.

DRESSEL, P.L., MAYHEW, L.B. (1954) *General education: explorations in evaluation*, The final report of the cooperative study of evaluation in general education, Washington D.C., American Council on Education.

DREYFUS, A., EGGLESTON, J.F. (1979) Classroom transactions of student-teachers of science, *European Journal of Science Education*, 3, 315-325.

DRIVER, R. (1973) *The representation of conceptual frameworks in young adolescent science students*, Ph.D. thesis, University of Illinois.

DRIVER, R. *Between observation and interpretation: a study of pupil activity in the learning of mechanics*, To be published.

DRIVER, R., EASLEY, J. (1978) Pupils and paradigms: a review of literature related to concept development in adolescent science students, *Studies in Science Education*, 5, 61-84.

DUNKIN, M.J., BIDDLE, B.J. (1974) *The study of teaching*, New York, Holt, Rinehart and Winston.

DYLLA, K., SCHAEFER, G. (1978) *Tiere sind anders*, Köln, Aulis.

EASLEY, J.A. (1978) Four decades of conservation research: what do they mean for mathematics education? in Gallagher, J.M., Easley, J.A. (Eds.) *Knowledge and development*, Vol.2, London, Plenum.

EGGLESTON, J.F., GALTON, M., JONES, M.E. (1975) *A science teaching observation schedule* (Schools Council Research Studies), Macmillan Education.

ELKIND, D. (1961) Children's discovery of the conservation of mass, weight and volume: Piaget replication study II, *Journal of General Psychology*, 98(2), 279-287.

ELLENBERG, H. (Ed.) (1973) Ökosystemforschung, Heidelberg, Springer.

ELSHOUT-MOHR, M. (1977) De theorie van het cotnitieve leren en de praktijk van het kenniswerven, *Pedagogische Studien*, 54, 280-281.

ELVIN, L. (1977) *The place of commonsense in educational thought*, London, George Allen and Unwin.

ENNIS, R.H. (1962) A concept of critical thinking, *Harvard Educational Review*, 32, 81-111.

ENNIS, R.H. (1975) Children's ability to handle Piaget's propositional logic: a conceptual critique, *Revue of Educational Research*, 45(1), 1-41.

ENNIS, R.H. (1976) An alternative to Piaget's conceptualization of logical competence, *Child Development*, 47, 903-919.

ERDELYI, M.H., FINKELSTEIN, S. (1976) Coding modality vs input modality in hypermnesia: is a rose a rose a rose? *Cognition*, 4, 311-319.

ERIKSON, E.H. (1965) *Childhood and society*, Hogarth Press.

ERLANWANGER, S. (1975) Case studies of children's conceptions of mathematics : part I, *Journal of Children's Mathematical Behaviour*, 1, 157-283.

ESTES, W.K. (1950) Toward a statistical theory of learning, *Psychological Review*, 57, 94-107.

ESTES, W.K. (1978) *Handbook of learning and cognitive processes, Vol.5, Human information processing*, New York, John Wiley & Sons.

EULEFELD, C., SCHAEFER, G. (1974) *Biologisches Gleichgewicht*, Köln, Aulis.

EYSENCK, M.W. (1978) Levels of processing: a critique, *British Journal of Psychology*, 69, 157-169.

FELDMAN, C.F. (1977) Two functions of language, *Harvard Educational Review*, 17, 282.

FENKER, R.M. (1975) The organization of conceptual materials: a methodology for measuring ideal and actual cognitive structures, *Instructional Science*, 4, 33-57.

FOGELMAN, K.R. (1969) Difficulties of using Piagetian tests in the classroom, *Educational Research*, 12, 36-40.

FRASE, L.T. (1967) Learning from prose material: length of passage, knowledge of results and position of question, *Journal of Educational Psychology*, 58, 266-272.

FRASER, B.J. (1977) *Review of research on ASEP*, Curriculum Development Centre, Macquarie University.

FREDERIKSEN, C.H. (1975) Acquisition of semantic information from discourse: effects of repeated exposures, *Journal of Verbal Learning and Verbal Behaviour*, 14, 158-169.

FREY, K. (1977) *Methodology and main areas of research in science education* in Frey, K. et al. (Eds.) (1977) *Research in science education in Europe*, Amsterdam, Swetz & Zeitlinger.

FUCHS, R. (1978) Einzelfallstudien von Legastheniker-Schicksalen und ihre Deutung im Lichte eines Regelkreiskonzepts der Lernstörung, *Zur Lage der Legasthenieforschung*, Kommission für Erziehungswissenschaft, Mitteilungen 1, Deutsche Forschungsgemeinschaft, 119-137.

FURTH, H.G., WACHS, H. (1974) *Thinking goes to school, Piaget's theory in practice*, Oxford University Press.

GAGNÉ, R.M. (1965, 1970, 1977) *The conditions of learning*, New York, Holt, Rinehart and Winston.

GAGNÉ, R.M., WHITE, R.T. (1978) Memory structures and learning outcomes, *Review of Educational Research*, 48, 187-222.

GALTON, M., EGGLESTON, J. (1979) Some characteristics of effective science teaching, *European Journal of Science Education*, 1, 75-86.

GALVIN, W.P., BELL, A.W.(1977) *Aspects of difficulties in the solution of problems involving the formation of equations*, Shell Centre for Mathematical Education, University of Nottingham.

GARSKOF, B.E., HOUSTON, J.P. (1963) Measurement of verbal relatedness: an ideographic approach, *Psychological Review*, 70, 277-288.

GEORGE, K.D. (1967) A comparison of critical thinking abilities of science and nonscience majors, *Science Education*, 51, 11-18.

GIBSON, C., ABELSON, R.P. (1965) The subjective use of inductive evidence, *Journal of Personal and Social Psychology*, 2, 301-310.

GLICK, J. (1969) Culture and cognition: some theoretical and methodological concerns in Spindler, C.D. (Ed.), *Education and cultural processes*, New York, Holt, Rinehart and Winston.

GOODENOUGH, D.R. (1976) The role of individual differences in field dependence as a factor in learning and memory, *Psychological Bulletin,* 83, 675.

GOODNOW, J.J. (1976) The nature of intelligent behaviour: questions raised by cross-cultural studies in Resnick, L.B. (Ed.), *The nature of intelligence,* Hillsdale, N.J., Erlbaum.

GOWIN, D. Bob, (1978) *The domain of education,* Unpublished manuscript, Cornell University.

GRAY, W.M. (1976) The factor structure of concrete and formal operations: a confirmation of Piaget in Modgil, S., Modgil, C.(Eds.), *Piagetian research, Vol.4,* Slough, Berks, N.F.E.R.

GREENO, J.G. (1976) Cognitive objectives of instruction: theory of knowledge for solving problems and answering questions in Klahr, D. (Ed.), *Cognition and instruction,* Hillsdale, N.J., Erlbaum.

GREENO, J.G. (1977) *Analysis of understanding in problem solving* in *Developmental models of thinking,* Kiel, IPN.

GREENWOOD, E. (1961) *The practice of science and the science of practice* in Bennis, W.G., Benne, K.D., Chin, R. (Eds.), *The planning of change,* New York, Holt, Rinehart and Winston, 1st ed. (N.B. This paper is not included in the 1970 2nd edition.)

GROOT, A.D. de (1973) Categories of educational objectives and effect measures: a new approach discussed in the context of second-language learning, *RITP-Memorandum nr.036.* Amsterdam.

GROOT, A.D. de (1974) Over fundamentele ervaringen: prolegomena tot een analyse van gesprekken met schakers (in Dutch), *Pedagogische studiën,* 51, 329-349.

GUTHRIE, J.T. (1967) Expository instruction versus a discovery method, *Journal of Educational Psychology,* 58, 45-49.

HACHETTE (Ed.) (1978) Quelques remarques sur les notions de chaleur et de conductibilité thermique, *Sciences Physiques,* 5eme, livre du professeur, 156 Paris.

HALFORD, G.S. (1978a) Towards a working model of Piaget's stages in Keats, J.A., Collis, K.F., Halford, G.S. (Eds.) *Cognitive development,* New York, Wiley.

HALFORD, G.S. (1978b) An approach to the definition of cognitive developmental stages in school mathematics, *British Journal of Educational Psychology,* 48, 298-314.

HAMMOND, J., RAVEN, R.J. (1973) The effects of a structured learning sequence on the achievement of compensatory tasks, *Journal of Research in Science Teaching,* 10(3), 257-262.

HARARY, F., NORMAN, R.Z., CARTWRIGHT, D. (1965) *Structural models,* New York, John Wiley and Sons.

HARLEN, W., DARWIN, Sr. A., MURPHY, M. (1977) *Match and mismatch: raising questions/finding answers,* Edinburgh, Oliver and Boyd.

HARRÉ, R., SECORD, P.F. (1972) *The explanation of social behaviour,* Oxford, Blackwell.

HART, K. (1978) Mistakes in mathematics, *Mathematics Teaching,* 85, 38-40.

HASLERUD, G.M., MEYERS, S. (1958) The transfer value of given and individually derived principles, *Journal of Educational Psychology,* 49, 293-298.

HAUSER, S.T. (1976) Loevinger's model and measure of ego development: a critical review, *Psychological Bulletin,* 83 (5),928-955.

HEAD, J. (1979a) Personality and the pursuit of science, *Studies in Science Education,* 6, 23-44.

HEAD, J. (1979b) A model to link personality characteristics to a preference for science, To be published.

HELGESON, R.L. (1971) An investigation of concept learning as a function of cognitive style, stimulus characteristics and training procedure, *Dissertation Abstracts International,* 31, 4995B.

HENLE, M. (1962) On the relation between logic and thinking, *Psychological Review,* 69, 366-378.

HENLEY, N.M. (1969) A psychological study of the semantics of animal terms, *Journal of Verbal Learning and Verbal Behaviour,* 8, 176-184.

HERRICK, V.E. (1950) The concept of curriculum design in Herrick, V.E., Tyler, R. (Eds.), *Toward improved curriculum theory,* Chicago, University of Chicago Press.

HEWETSON, V.P. (1975) *The concept of surface area/volume ratio and related issues in biology,* M.A. dissertation, University of Leeds.

HIELE, P.M. van, (1973a) Nawoord, Mary Sime, *Zoals een kind het ziet,* Purmerend, Muusses.

HIELE, P.M. van, (1973b) *Begrip en Inzicht,* Purmerend, Muusses.

HIELE-GELDOF, D. (1957) *De didaktiek van de meetkunde in de eerste klas van het VHMO,* Dissertatie, Rijks Universiteit Utrecht.

HOOPER, F., DIHOFF, R.E. (1975) *Multidimensional scaling of Piagetian task performance,* Madison, Wisconsin Research and Development Centre for Cognitive Learning.

HOOPER, F., SIPPLE, T.S. (1975) *An investigation of matrix task, classificatory and seriation abilities,* Madison, Wisconsin Research and Development Centre for Cognitive Learning.

HUGHES, E.R. (1979) *Conceptual powers of children: an approach through mathematics and science* (Schools Council Research Studies) Macmillan Education.

HUGHES, M.M. (1965) *A four-year longitudinal study of the growth of logical thinking in a group of secondary modern schoolboys,* M.A. thesis, University of Leeds.

HUTTENLOCHER, J. (1968) Constructing spatial images: a strategy in reasoning, *Psychological Review,* 75, 550-560.

HUTTENLOCHER, J., BURKE, D. (1976) Why does memory span increase with age? *Cognitive Psychology,* 8, 1-31.

HYDE, D.M.G. (1970) *Piaget and conceptual development,* Holt, Rinehart and Winston.

INGLE, R.B., SHAYER, M. (1971) Conceptual demands in Nuffield O-level chemistry, *Education in Chemistry,* September 1971, 182-183.

INHELDER, B., PIAGET, J. (1958) *The growth of logical thinking from childhood to adolescence,* London, Routledge and Kegan Paul.

INHELDER, B., PIAGET, J. (1964) *The early growth of logic in the child,* London, Routledge and Kegan Paul.

JANVIER, C. (1978) *The interpretation of complex cartesian graphs representing situations: studies and teaching experiments,* Shell Centre for Mathematical Education, University of Nottingham.

JEARSAIN, D., ANDREANI, J., HALBWACHS, F. et al. (1978) Initiation à l'étude de la température et de la chaleur en classe de cinquième, *Bulletin de l'Union des Physiciens,* 604, 1013-1035.

JOHNSON, M., Jr. (1967) Definitions and models in curriculum theory, *Educational Theory,* 17(2), 127-140.

JOHNSON, P.E. (1969) On the communication of concepts in science, *Journal of Educational Psychology,* 60, 32-40.

JOHNSON, C.J. (1976) *The investigation of cognitive structure by directed graph analysis of essays,* Unpublished M.Sc. thesis, U.E.A. Norwich.

JOHNSON-LAIRD, P.N., WASON, P.C. (Eds.) (1977) *Thinking,* London, Cambridge University Press.

JOHNSTONE, A.H., MACDONALD, J.J., WEBB, G. (1977) A thermodynamic approach to chemical equilibrium, *Physics Education,* 12 (4), 248-251.

JOHNSTONE, A.H., MUGHOL, A.R. (1976) Concepts of physics at secondary level, *Physics Education,* Nov. 1976, 466-469.

JOINT MATRICULATION BOARD (1972) *Regulations and syllabuses, Physics Advanced,* Manchester, Joint Matriculation Board.

JUNGWIRTH, E. (1971) Taxonomy-learning of BSCS pupils, *Australian Science Teachers Journal,* 17, 80-82.

KAGAN, J., MOSS, H.A., SIGEL, I.E. (1963) Psychological significance of styles of thinking *in* Wright, J.C., Kagan, J. (Eds.), *Basic cognitive processes in children, Monograph of the Society for Research into Child Development,* 28, 73-112.

KAGAN, J., ROSMAN, B.L., DAY, D., ALBERT, J., PHILLIPS, W. (1964) Information processing in the child: significance of analytic and reflective attitudes, *Psychological Monographs,* 78, 1.

KAGAN, J. (1966) Developmental studies in reflection and analysis *in* Kidd, A.H., Rivoire, J.E. (Eds.), *Perceptual development in children,* New York, International Universities Press.

KARMILOFF-SMITH, A., INHELDER, B. (1975) If you want to get ahead, get a theory, *Cognition,* 3, 195-212.

KARPLUS, E., KARPLUS, R., WOLLMAN, W. (1973) *Intellectual development beyond elementary school IV: ratio,* Lawrence Hall of Science, Berkeley, California.

KARPLUS, E.F., KARPLUS, R., WOLLMAN, W. (1974) Intellectual development beyond elementary school IV: ratio, the influence of cognitive style, *School Science and Mathematics,* 74, 476-482.

KARPLUS, R., KARPLUS, E., FORMISANO, M., PAULSEN, A-C. (1975) Proportional reasoning and control of variables in seven countries, *Advancing education through science oriented programs, Report 1D - 65.*

KARPLUS, R. (1978a) *Education and formal thought,* Paper presented at the Eighth Annual Symposium of the Jean Piaget Society, Pennsylvania, May 18-20.

KARPLUS, R. (1978b) The Intellectual Development Project at the Lawrence Hall of Science, *Studies in Science Education,* 5, 111-113.

KARPLUS, R., LAWSON, C.A., (Eds.) (1974) *SCIS Teacher's handbook,* Berkeley, University of California.

KASTRINOS, W. (1962) Interpretation of data in science teaching, *School Science and Mathematics,* 696-703.

KELLEY, H.H. (1972) *Causal schemata and the attribution process,* New York, General Learning Press.

KELLY, A. (1976) Women in science: a bibliographic review, *The Durham Research Review,* 7(36), 1092-1108.

KEMPA, R.F., DUBÉ, G.E. (1973) Cognitive preference orientations in students of chemistry, *British Journal of Educational Psychology,* 43, 279-288.

KEMPA, R.F., WARD, J.E. (1975) The effect of different modes of task orientation on observational attainment in practical chemistry, *Journal of Research in Science Teaching,* 12, 69-76.

KEMPA, R.F., HODGSON, G.H. (1976) Levels of concept acquisition and concept maturation in students of chemistry, *British Journal of Educational Psychology,* 46, 253-260.

KINTSCH, W. (1974) *The representation of meaning in memory,* Hillsdale, N.J., Erlbaum.

KLAHR, D., WALLACE, J.G. (1976) *Cognitive development: an information processing view,* Hillsdale, N.J., Erlbaum.

KLAHR, D., SIEGLER, R.S. (1978) The representation of children's knowledge in Reese, H.W., Lipsett, L.P. (Eds.), *Advances in child development and behaviour,* London, Academic Press.

KLAUSMEIER, H.J., GHATALA, E.S., FRAYER, D.A. (1974) *Conceptual learning and development: a cognitive view,* New York, Academic Press.

KLAUSMEIER, H.J. (1977) Educational experience and cognitive development, *Educational Psychologist,* 12, 179-197.

KLAUSMEIER, H.J., ALLEN, P.S. (1978) *Cognitive development of children and youth, a longitudinal study,* New York, Academic Press.

KLEINE, K., SALTZ, E. (1976) Specifying the mechanisms in a level of processing approach to memory, *Journal of Experimental Psychology: Hum. Learn. Mem.2*, 671-679.

KOBASIGAWA, A. (1977) Retrieval strategies in the development of memory i̲n̲ Kail, R.V., Hagen, J.W. (Eds.), *Perspectives on the development of memory and cognition*, Hillsdale, N.J., Erlbaum.

KOHL, H. (1974) *Mathematics, writing and games in the open classroom*, New York, New York Review Book (NYR 109).

KORNADT, H.-J̲. (1975) *Lehrziele, Schulleistung und Leistungsbeurteilung*, Düsseldorf, Schwann.

KRUTETSKII, V.A. (1976) *The psychology of mathematical abilities in schoolchildren*, University of Chicago.

KUHN, D. (1977) Conditional reasoning in children, *Developmental Psychology*, 1̲3̲, 342-353.

KUHN, D., BRANNOCK, J. (1977) Development of the isolation of variables scheme in experimental and 'natural experiment' contexts, *Developmental Psychology*, 1̲3̲, 9-14.

KUHN, D. (1979) The relevance of Piaget's stage of formal operations in the study of adult cognition, *The Genetic Epistemologist*, February, 1-3.

KUHN, D.E., ANGELEV, J. (1976) An experimental study of the development of formal operational thought, *Child Development*, 4̲7̲, 697-706.

KUHN, D.J. (1967) *A study of varying modes of topical presentation in elementary college biology to determine the effect of advance organizers in knowledge*, Ph.D. thesis, Purdue University.

KUHN, T.S. (1962, 1970) *The structure of scientific revolutions*, International Encyclopedia of Unified Sciences, 2nd ed., enlarged Vols. 1 and 2: Foundations of the Unity of Science, Vol. 2, No.2,Chicago, University of Chicago Press.

LAKATOS, I. (1976) Falsification and the methodology of scientific research programmes i̲n̲ Lakatos, I., Musgrave, A. (Eds.) *Criticism and the growth of knowledge*, Aberdeen, Cambridge University Press.

LANE, S.H., EVANS, S.H. (1972) *Some aspects of individual differences in schematic concept formation* (Technical Memorandum), Aberdeen Proving Ground Maryland, U.S. Army Human Engineering Laboratory.

LAWSON, A.E., NORDLAND, F.H., DEVITO, A. (1974) Piagetian formal operational tasks: a crossover study of learning effect and reliability, *Science Education*, 5̲8̲(2), 267-76.

LAWSON, A.E., RENNER, J.W. (1974) A quantitative analysis of responses to Piagetian tasks and its implications for curriculum, *Science Education,* 58(4), 545-559.

LAWSON, A.E. (1975) Sex differences in concrete and formal reasoning ability as measured by manipulative tasks and written tasks, *Science Education,* 59(3), 397-405.

LAWSON, A.E., BLAKE, A.J.D., NORDLAND, F.H. (1975) Training effects and generalisation of the ability to control variables in high school biology students, *Science Education,* 59(3), 387-396.

LAWSON, A.E., RENNER, J.W. (1975) Relationships of science subject matter and developmental levels of learners, *Journal of Research in Science Teaching,* 12(4), 347-358.

LAWSON, A.E., NORDLAND, F.H. (1976) The factor structure of some Piagetian tasks, *Journal of Research in Science Teaching,* 13, 461-466.

LAWSON, A.E., WOLLMAN, W.T. (1976) Encouraging the transition from concrete to formal cognitive functioning, *Journal of Research in Science Teaching,* 13(5), 413-430.

LAWSON, A.E. (1978) The development and validation of a classroom test of formal reasoning, *Journal of Research in Science Teaching,* 15, 11-24.

LAWSON, A.E., KARPLUS, R., ADI, H. (1978) The acquisition of propositional logic and formal operational schemata during the secondary school years, *Journal of Research in Science Teaching,* 15(6), 465-478.

LAWSON, C.A. (1969) *So little done - so much to do,* S.C.I.S. booklet, Berkeley, California, Regents of the University of California.

LEAPFROGS (1975) *Action Books, Link Books, Treatments,* Leapfrogs, Coldharbour, Newton St. Cyres, Exeter.

LEWIS, D.G. (1967) *Statistical methods in education,* London, University of London Press.

LIEBEN, L.S. (1977) Memory in the context of cognitive development: the cognitive approach in Kail, R.V., Hagen, J.W. (Eds.), *Perspectives on the development of memory and cognition,* Hillsdale, N.J., Erlbaum.

LINDSAY, P.H., NORMAN, D.A. (1976) *Human information processing,* London, Academic Press.

LINN, M.C. (1978) Influence of cognitive style and training on tasks requiring the separation of variables schema, *Child Development*, 49, 874-877.

LIU, A. (1978) A direct proof of Pick's theorem, *Crux mathematicorum*, 4, 242-244.

LOCK, R.J. (1979) Nuffield Combined Science: do pupils understand it? *The School Science Review*, 60 (212) 584-585.

LOEVINGER, J. et al. (1970) *Measuring ego development*, San Francisco, Jossey-Bass.

LOEVINGER, J. (1976) *Ego development: conception and theories*, San Francisco, Jossey-Bass.

LONGEOT, F. (1969) Psychologie différentielle et théorie opératoire de l'intelligence in Dunod (Ed.), *Coll. Sciences du Comportement*, Paris.

LONGEOT, F. (1974) Echelle de développement de la pensée logique, E.P.L. Manuel d' instructions, *Ed. Scientifiques et Psychotechniques*, Issy-les-Moulineaux.

LOVELL, K., OGILVIE, E. (1960) A study of the conservation of substance in the junior school child, *British Journal of Educational Psychology*, 30(2), 109-118.

LOVELL, K., OGILVIE, E. (1961a) A study of the conservation of weight in the junior school child, *British Journal of Educational Psychology*, 31(2), 138-144.

LOVELL, K., OGILVIE, E. (1961b) The growth of the concept of volume in junior school children, *Journal of Child Psychology and Psychiatry and Allied Disciplines*, 2(2), 118-126.

LOVELL, K., BUTTERWORTH, I.B. (1966) Abilities underlying the understanding of proportionality, *Mathematics Teaching*, 37, 5-9.

LOVELL, K., SHIELDS, J.B. (1967) Some aspects of a study of the gifted child, *British Journal of Educational Psychology*, 37, 201-208.

LOVELL, K. (1974) Intellectual growth and understanding science, *Studies in Science Education*, 1, 1-19.

LOVELL, K. (1977) Logic and life style, *New Horizons*, November, 17-22, Hong Kong.

LOVELL, K. (1979) Some aspects of the work of Piaget in perspective in Floyd, A. (Ed.) *Cognitive development in the school years*, London, Croom Helm.

LOWENTHAL, F. (1977) Games, graphs and the logic of language acquisition, *Communication and Cognition,* 10(2), 47-52.

LOWENTHAL, F. (1978) Logic of natural language and games at primary school, *Revue de Phonétique Appliquée,* 46-47, 133-140. (Proceedings of the first Mons Conference on Language and Language Acquisition, 1977.)

LOWENTHAL, F. (1979) Hypothetico-deductive reasoning at the age of 8. Clinical observations, *Proceedings of the 1979 symposium organised by Communication and Cognition on 'Theory of knowledge and science policy'.*

LOWENTHAL, F. *Games, logic and cognitive development: a longitudinal study of classroom situations.* To be published.

LOWENTHAL, F., SEVERS, R. (1979) Langage, jeu et activité mathématique. Un essai à l'école primaire, *Educational Studies in Mathematics,* 10, 245-262.

LOWENTHAL, F., SEVERS, R. *Inductive and axiomatic reasoning at elementary school level.* To be published.

LUNZER, E.A. (1973) *Formal reasoning: a re-appraisal,* Psychology of Mathematics Education Paper, No.3, Chelsea College, London.

LUNZER, E.A. (1978) Formal reasoning: a re-appraisal in Floyd, A.(Ed.) *Cognitive development in the school years,* London, Croom Helm.

LUNZER, E.A., GARDNER, K. (1979) *The effective use of reading,* London, Heinemann.

LURIA, A.R. (1976) *Cognitive development,* Harvard University Press.

LYBECK, L. (1977) Research in Science Education: Sweden in Frey, K., Blänsdorf, K., Kapune, T., Schaefer, G., Archenhold, F. (Eds.) (1977), *Research in science education in Europe. Perspectives, structural problems and documentation 1976.* Report of a Cooperative Study and a European Contact Workshop organised by the Council of Europe and the Institute for Science Education - Federal Republic of Germany (Kiel), Amsterdam and Lisse, Swets & Zeitlinger.

LYBECK, L. (1978a) A research approach into science education at Göteborg. Paper presented at the Joint ICMI/ICPE/CTS/UNESCO/IDM conference on 'Cooperation between Science Teachers and Mathematics Teachers', September 17-23, 1978. Institut für Didaktik der Màthematic, Bielefeld, FRG. *Reports from the Institute of Education,* University of Göteborg, No.71.

LYBECK, L. (1978b) Studies of mathematics in the teaching of science in Göteborg. Paper presented at the Joint ICMI/ICPE/CTS/UNESCO/ IDM conference on 'Cooperation between Science Teachers and Mathematics Teachers', September 17-23, 1978. Institut für Didaktik der Mathematik, Bielefeld, FRG. *Reports from the Institute of Education,* University of Göteborg, No.72.

LYBECK, L. (1979a) A research approach to science education at Göteborg, *The European Journal of Science Education,* 1(1), 119-124.

LYBECK, L. (1979b) Studien über Mathematik im Naturwissenschaflichen Unterricht in Göteborg, *physica didactica,* Zeitschrift für Didaktik und Methodik der Physik, 6(1), 25-55. Bad Salzdetfurth/ Hildesheim, FRG, Didaktischer Dienst.

MARCIA, J.E. (1966) Development and validation of ego identity status, *Journal of Personality and Social Psychology,* 3 (5),551-558.

MARCIA, J.E. (1976) *Studies in ego identity.* Unpublished monograph.

MARKLE, S.M., TIEMANN, P.W. (1970) Behavioural analysis of cognitive content, *Educational Technology,* 10(1), 40-45.

MARKMAN, E.M., SIEBERT, J. (1976) Classes and collections: internal organisation and resulting holistic properties, *Cognitive Psychology,* 7, 548-559.

MARTIN, M. (1972) *Concepts of science education: a philosophical analysis,* San Francisco, Scott, Freeman & Co.

MASEY, N.B. (1965) *Patterns for the teaching of science,* Toronto, MacMillan Co. of Canada.

MATALON, B. (1962) Étude génétique de l'implication in Beth, E.W.(Ed.), *Implication, formalisation et logique naturelle: études d'epistemologie génétique,* 16, 69-93, Paris, Presses Universitaires de France.

MAYER, W.V. (1974) *The unreal school in the real world,* B.S.C.S. Newsletter No.54, Boulder, Colorado, Biological Sciences Curriculum Study.

MAYER, R.E., GREENO, J.G. (1972) Structural differences between learning outcomes produced by different instructional methods, *Journal of Educational Psychology,* 63(2), 165-173.

MAYER, R.E. (1975) Information processing variables in learning to solve problems, *Review of Educational Research,* 45, 525-541.

MESSICK, S. (1970) The criterion problem in the evaluation of instruction: assessing possible, not just intended outcomes in Wittrock, M.C., Wiley, D.E. (Eds.), *The evaluation of instruction: issues and problems,* Chicago, 183-202.

MESSICK, S. (Ed.) (1976) *Individuality in learning: implications of cognitive style and creativity for human development,* San Francisco, Jossey-Bass.

MILKENT, M.M. (1977) It's time we started paying attention to what students don't know. *Science Education,* 61(3), 409-413.

MODGIL, S. (1974) *Piagetian research; a handbook of recent studies,* Slough, N.F.E.R.

MOREIRA, M.A. (1979) Concept maps as tools for teaching, *Journal of College Science Teaching,* 8(5), 283-286.

MORGAN, J. (1977) *Affective consequence for the teaching and learning of mathematics of an individualised learning program,* Department of Education, University of Stirling.

NAEGELE, C.J. (1974) *An evaluation of student attitudes, achievement, and learning efficiency in various modes of an individualised, self-paced learning program in introductory college physics,* Ph.D. thesis, Cornell University.

NEISSER, U. (1976) *General, academic and artificial intelligence* in Resnick, L.B. (Ed.) (1976), *The nature of intelligence,* New York, John Wiley & Sons.

NEWELL, A., SIMON, H.A. (1972) *Human problem solving,* Englewood Cliffs, N.J., Prentice Hall.

N.F.E.R. (1979) *Science reasoning tasks,* Slough, N.F.E.R.

NIE-SRCD (1978) NIE-SRCD conference on future research on adolescent reasoning, Berkeley, California.

NITSCH, K.E. (1977) *Structuring decontextualised forms of knowledge,* Ph.D. thesis, Vanderbilt University reported in Bransford, J.D. *Human cognition,* 1979, Belmont, Wadsworth.

NOELTING, G. (1976) Stages and mechanisms in the development of the concept of proportion in the child and adolescent in Poulsen, M.A. (Ed.), *Piagetian theory and the helping professions 5th annual conference,* Los Angeles, California.

NOELTING, G. (1978) *The development of four mathematical concepts in the child and adolescent: ratio, fraction, chance and geometric proportion,* Meeting of the Canadian Association for Mathematical Education, Kingston (Ontario).

NORDLAND, F.H., LAWSON, A.E., KAHLE, J.B. (1974) A study of levels of concrete and formal ability in disadvantaged junior and senior high school students, *Science Education,* 58(4), 569-575.

NOVAK, J.D. (1958) An experimental comparison of a conventional and a project centered method of teaching a college general botany course, *Journal of Experimental Education,* 26, 217-230.

NOVAK, J.D., RING, D.R., TAMIR, P. (1971) Interpretation of research findings in terms of Ausubel's theory and implications for science education, *Science Education,* 55(4), 483-526.

NOVAK, J.D. (1977a) *A theory of education,* Ithaca, Cornell University Press.

NOVAK, J.D. (1977b) Epicycles and Homocentric earth: or what is wrong with stages of cognitive development? *Science Education,* 61(3), 393-395.

NOVAK, J.D. (1977c) An alternative to Piagetian psychology for science and mathematics education, *Science Education,* 61(4), 453-477 (1977) also in *Studies in Science Education,* 5, 1-30 (1978).

NUFFIELD ADVANCED PHYSICS (1971) *Teachers' handbook,* London, Penguin Books/Longman Group.

NUFFIELD SECONDARY SCIENCE PROJECT (1970) *Teacher's Guide,* London, Longman Group.

NUSSBAUM, J., NOVAK, J.D. (1976) An assessment of children's concepts of earth utilizing structured interviews, *Science Education,* 60, 535-550.

NUSSBAUM, J. (1979) Children's conception of the earth as a cosmic body: a cross age study, *Science Education,* 63(1), 83-93.

NUSSBAUM, J., NOVICK, S. (1979) *Physical phenomena and pupils' misconceptions.* Unpublished Study, Israel Science Teaching Centre, The Hebrew University of Jerusalem, Jerusalem, Israel.

O'BRIEN, T.C. (1972) Logical thinking in adolescents, *Educational studies in mathematics,* 4, 401-428.

ODUM, H.T., ODUM, E.C. (1976) *Energy basis for man and nature,* New York, McGraw Hill.

OGBORN, J. (1977) *Small group teaching in undergraduate science,* London, Heinemann.

OHUCHE, R.O., PEARSON, R.E. (1974) Piaget and Africa: a survey of research involving conservation and classification in Africa in *The development of science and mathematics concepts in young children in African countries,* Nairobi, Unesco/UNICEF, Reprinted in *Piagetian Research,* Vol.8 (Eds. Modgil, S. and Modgil C.), Slough, Berks, N.F.E.R., 1976.

OGUNLADE, J.O. (1973) Family government and educational attainment of some school children in Western Nigeria, *West African Journal of Education,* XVII(3), 429-433.

OKEKE, E.A.C. (1976) *A study of the understanding in Nigerian school certificate biology candidates of the concepts of reproduction, transport mechanisms and growth,* Ph.D. thesis, University of Leeds.

OLSON, D.R. (1970) *Cognitive development,* London, Academic Press.

ORMEROD, M.B., DUCKWORTH, O. (1975) *Pupils' attitudes to science: a review of research,* Slough, N.F.E.R.

ORTON, A. (1970) *A cross-sectional study of the development of the mathematical concept of a function in secondary schoolchildren of average and above average ability,* M.Ed. thesis, University of Leeds.

OSBORNE, R.J., GILBERT, J.K. (1979) *An approach to student understanding of basic concepts in science,* Guildford, I.E.T., University of Surrey.

PARIS, S.G., LINDAUER, B.K. (1977) Constructive aspects of children's comprehension and memory in Kail, R.V., Hagen, J.W. (Eds.), *Perspectives on the development of memory and cognition,* Hillsdale, N.J., Erlbaum.

PARSONS, C. (1960) Inhelder and Piaget's growth of logical thinking: a logician's viewpoint, *British Journal of Psychology,* 51 (1), 75-84.

PASCUAL-LEONE, J. (1970) Mathematical model for the transition rule in Piaget's developmental stages, *Acta Psychologica,* 32, 301-345.

PASCUAL-LEONE, J. (1978) Piagetian theory and neo-Piagetian analysis as psychological guides to education in Gallagher, J.N., Easley, J.A. (Eds.), *Knowledge and development Vol.2,* London, Plenum.

PEEL, E.A. (1971) *The nature of adolescent judgment,* London, Staples Press.

PELLA, M.O., BILLEH, V.Y. (1972) Relationship between mental maturity, ability level and level of understanding in three categories of science concepts, *Science Education,* 56, 5-15.

PIAGET, J., INHELDER, B. (1956) *The child's conception of space,* London, Routledge and Kegan Paul.

PIAGET, J., INHELDER, B., SZEMINSKA, A. (1960) *The child's conception of geometry,* London, Routledge and Kegan Paul.

PIAGET, J., INHELDER, B. (1966) *La psychologie de l'enfant,* Paris, Presses Universitaires de France.

PIAGET, J., INHELDER, B. (1967) *The child's conception of space,* London, Routledge and Kegan Paul.

PIAGET, J. (1969) *Science of education and the psychology of the child,* (Trans. D. Coltman), London, Longman.

PIAGET, J. (1970) Piaget's theory in Mussen, P. (Ed.), *Manual of Child Psychology, Vol.1.,* London, Wiley.

PIAGET, J. (1972) *The principles of genetic epistemology,* New York, Basic Books.

PIAGET, J., INHELDER, B. (1973) *Memory and intelligence,* London, Routledge and Kegan Paul.

PIAGET, J., INHELDER, B. (1974) *The child's construction of quantities,* London, Routledge and Kegan Paul.

PIAGET, J. (1975) *L'équilibration des structures cognitives: problème central du dévelopment,* Paris: Presses Universitaires de France (Trans. Rosin, A. (1977) *The development of thought,*New York, Viking).

PIAGET, J., INHELDER, B. (1975) *The origin of the idea of chance in children,* London, Routledge and Kegan Paul.

PIAGET, J. (1976) On correspondences and morphisms, *The Genetic Epistemologist,* May.

PIAGET, J. (1977) *The grasp of consciousness,* London, Routledge and Kegan Paul.

PINES, A.L. (1977) *Science concept learning in children: the effect of prior knowledge on resulting cognitive structure subsequent to A-T instruction,* Ph.D. thesis, Department of Education, Cornell University.

PINES, A.L., NOVAK, J.D., POSNER, G.J., VAN KIRK, J. (1978) The clinical interview: a method for evaluating cognitive structures, *Curriculum Series Research Report No.6,* Department of Education, Cornell University.

PLUNKETT, S.P.O. (1979) Diagrams, *Mathematical Education for Teaching,* 3 (4),3-15.

POOLE, H.E. (1968) The effect of urbanisation upon scientific concept attainment among the Hausa children of Northern Nigeria, *British Journal of Educational Psychology,* 38(1), 57-63.

POSNER, G.J. (1978) Tools for curriculum research and development: potential contributes from cognitive science, *Curriculum Inquiry,* 8(4), 311-340.

POSTIC, M. (1977) *Observation et formation des enseignants,* Paris, P.U.F.

POWER, C. (1977) A critical review of science classroom interaction studies, *Studies in Science Education,* 4, 1-30.

PREECE, P.F.W. (1978) Exploration of semantic space: review of research in the organization of scientific concepts in semantic memory, *Science Education,* 62(4), 547-562.

PRINGLE, J.W.S. (1963) *The two biologies,* Oxford University Press.

RAVEN, R.J. (1967) The development of the concept of momentum in primary school children, *Journal of Research in Science Teaching,* 5, 216-223.

RAVEN, R.J. (1972) The development of the concept of acceleration in elementary school children, *Journal of Research in Science Teaching,* 9, 201-206.

RAVEN, R.J. (1973) The development of a test of Piaget's logical operations, *Science Education,* 57(3), 377-385.

RAVEN, R.J. (1974) Programming Piaget's logical operations for science inquiry and concept attainment, *Journal of Research in Science Teaching,* 11(3), 251-261.

RAVEN, R.J., GUERIN, R. (1975) Quasi-simplex analysis of Piaget's operative structures and stages, *Science Education,* 59(2), 273-281.

REDER, L.M. (1978) *Comprehension and retention of prose: a literature review,* Technical Report No.108, Centre for Study of Reading, University of Illinois, Illinois 61820.

RENNER, J.W. et al. (1976) *Research teaching and learning with the Piaget model,* Norman, University of Oklahoma Press.

RENNER, J.W., GRANT, R.M., SUTHERLAND, J. (1978) Content and concrete thought, *Science Education,* 62(2), 215-221.

RIESMAN, F. (1962) *The culturally deprived child,* New York, Harper and Row.

ROBERTSON, W.W., RICHARDSON, E. (1975) The development of some physical science concepts in secondary school students, *Journal of Research in Science Teaching,* 12(4), 319-329.

ROBINSON, F.P. (1946) *Effective reading,* New York, Harper and Row.

ROHWER, W.D., DEMPSTER, F.N. (1977) Memory development and educational processes *in* Kail, R.V., Hagen, J.W. (Eds.), *Perspectives on the development of memory and cognition,* Hillsdale, N.J., Erlbaum.

ROSENBERG, M. (1965) *Society and the adolescent self-image,* New Jersey, Princeton University Press.

ROSENSHINE, B., FORST, N. (1973) The use of direct observation to study teaching *in* Travers, R.W. (Ed.), *Second handbook of research in teaching,* Chicago, Rand McNally.

ROSS, R.J. (1973) Some empirical parameters of formal thinking, *Journal of Youth and Adolescence,* 2, 167-177.

ROWELL, J.A., DAWSON, C.J. (1977a) Teaching about floating and sinking: an attempt to link cognitive psychology with classroom practice, *Science Education,* 61(2), 245-253.

ROWELL, J.A., DAWSON, C.J. (1977b) Teaching about floating and sinking: further studies toward closing the gap between cognitive psychology and classroom practice, *Science Education,* 61(4), 527-540.

ROWELL, J.A., DAWSON, C.J. (1979) Skill integration, Piaget and education, *Studies in Science Education,* 6, 45-68.

ROZIN, P. (1976) The evolution of intelligence and access to the cognitive unconscious *in* Sprague, J.M., Epstein, A.A. (Eds.), *Progress in psychobiology and physiological psychology,* New York, Academic Press.

RUMELHART, D.E., NORMAN, D.A. (1976) *Accretion, tuning and restructuring: three modes of learning,* University of California, San Diego, Dept. of Psychology, Center for Human Information Processing. Technical Report No.63.

RUSSELL, H.H. (1962) The measurement of reasoning ability in adolescents, *Ontario Journal of Educational Research,* 5, 33-40.

SATTERLEY, D.J., TELFER, I.G., *Cognitive style and advance organizers in learning and retention,* Research report, to be published.

SCARDAMALIA, M. (1977) Information processing capacity and the problem of horizontal decalage: a demonstration using combinational reasoning tasks, *Child Development,* 48, 28-37.

SCHAEFFER, B., EGGLESTON, N., SCOTT, J.L. (1974) Number development in young children, *Cognitive Psychology,* 6, 357-379.

SCHAEFER, G. (1972) *Kybernetik und Biologie,* Stuttgart, Metzler.

SCHAEFER, G. (1973) *Kybernetische Zeichensprache als Hilfsmittel zur Strukturierung eines integrierten Curriculum Naturwissenschaft,* Kiel, IPN.

SCHAEFER, G. (1975) *Ökologie - Lehrfach oder Unterrichtsprinzip?* in Müller, P. (Ed.), *Verhandl.d.Ges.f.Ökologie,* 269-274, den Haag, Junk.

SCHAEFER, G. (1978a) *Inklusives Denken - Leitlinie für den Unterricht* in Trommer, G., Wenk, K. (Eds.), *Leben in Ökosystemen,* Köln, Aulis.

SCHAEFER, G. (1978b) *Kybernetik im Biologieunterricht* in Schaefer, G. (Ed.), *Biokybernetik. Unterricht Biologie Heft,* 21, 2-10.

SCHAEFER, G. (1979) Concept formation in biology: the concept of growth, *European Journal of Science Education,* 1(1), 87-101.

SCHANK, R.C. (1976) The role of memory in language processing in Cofer, C.N. (Ed.), *The structure of human memory,* San Francisco W.H. Freeman and Co.

SCHILDKAMP-KÜNDIGER, E. (1974) *Frauenrolle und Mathematikleistung,* Düsseldorf, Schwann.

SCHILDKAMP-KÜNDIGER, E. (1979) Einstellungen, Anwendungsbezug, Leistungen in Volk, D. (Ed.), *Kritische Stichwörter zum Mathematikunterricht,* München, Fink.

SCHUTZ, A., LUCKMANN, T., (1974) *The structures of the life-world,* London, Heinemann.

SCHWAB, J.J. (1971) The practical: arts of eclectic, *School Review,* 79(4), 493 - 542.

SCIENCE TEACHER EDUCATION PROJECT (1974), London, McGraw Hill Book Company (UK) Limited.

SHAVELSON, R. (1972) Some aspects of the correspondence between content structure and cognitive structure in physics instruction, *Journal of Educational Psychology*, 63, 225-234.

SHAVELSON, R.J. (1974) Methods for examining representations of a subject-matter structure in a student's memory, *Journal of Research in Science Teaching*, 11(3), 231-249.

SHAVER, J.P. (1979) The productivity of educational research and the applied basic research distinction, *Educational Research*, 8(1), 3-9.

SHAYER, M. (1972) *Piaget's work and science teaching*, M.Ed. thesis, Leicester.

SHAYER, M., KÜCHEMANN, D.E., WYLAM, H. (1976) The distribution of Piagetian stages of thinking in British middle and secondary school children, *British Journal of Educational Psychology*, 46, 164-173.

SHAYER, M. (1976) Development in thinking of middle school and early secondary school pupils, *School Science Review*, 57, (200), 568-571.

SHAYER, M., WYLAM, H. (1978) The distribution of Piagetian stages of thinking in British middle and secondary school children. II: 14-16 year-olds and sex differentials. *British Journal of Educational Psychology*, 48, 62-70.

SHAYER, M. (1978a) *A test of the validity of Piaget's construct of formal operational thinking*, Ph.D. thesis, University of London.

SHAYER, M. (1978b) The analysis of science curricula for Piagetian level of demand, *Studies in Science Education*, 5, 115-130.

SHAYER, M. (1978c) Nuffield Combined Science: do the pupils understand it? *School Science Review*, 60 (211), 210-223.

SHAYER, M. (1979) *Has Piaget's construct of formal operational thinking any utility?* To be published.

SHAYER, M., ADEY, P., WYLAM, H. (1979) *Group tests of cognitive development: ideals and a realisation.* To be published.

SHEPARD, R.N. (1978) The mental image, *American Psychologist*, February, 125-137.

SHIMRON, J. (1975) *On learning maps,* Technical Report of Center for Human Information Processing, University of California, San Diego, La Jolla, California 92093.

SIEGLER, R.S. (1978) The origins of scientific reasoning in Siegler, R.S. (Ed.), *Children's thinking. What develops?* Hillsdale, N.J., Erlbaum.

SIGEL, I.E. (1967) *SCST manual - Instructions and scoring guide,* Princeton, N.J., Educational Testing Service.

SILLS, T.W., HERRON, J.D. (1976) Study of an electronic analog to the combination of chemical bodies Piagetian task in Modgil, S., Modgil, C. (Eds.), *Piagetian Research, Vol.4,* Slough, Berks, N.F.E.R.

SIMMONS, R., ROSENBERG, S., ROSENBERG, M. (1973) Disturbance in the self-image of adolescence, *American Sociological Review, 38,* 553-568.

SIMON, A., BOYER, G.E. (1970) *Mirrors for behaviour: an anthology of classroom observation instruments,* Research for better schools Inc., Philadelphia.

SIMON, D.P., SIMON, H.A. (1978) *Individual differences in solving physics problems* in Siegler, R.S. (Ed.), *Children's thinking. What develops?* Hillsdale, N.J., Erlbaum.

SINGER, E. (1975) *Een reflectie op de waarden die een rol spelen in het onderzoeken van common-sense denken/Een begripsmatige analyse van denken over opvoedend handelen,* Skoop-publicatie 1/2, Amsterdam-Kohnstamm-instituut.

SMEDSLUND, J. (1961-2) The acquisition of conservation of substance and weight in children, I - VI *Scandinavian Journal of Psychology, 2,* 11-20, 71-84, 85-87, 153-155, 156-160, 203, 210. VII *Scandinavian Journal of Psychology, 3,* 69-77.

SMEDSLUND, J. (1963) Patterns of experience and the acquisition of concrete transitivity of weight in eight year old children, *Scandinavian Journal of Psychology, 4,* 251-256.

SMEDSLUND, J. (1964) Concrete reasoning: a study of intellectual development, *Mon. Soc. Res. in Child Development, 29*(2), (serial No.93), 3-39.

SMEDSLUND, J. (1977) Practical and theoretical issues in Piagetian psychology: Piaget's psychology in practice, *British Journal of Educational Psychology, 47,* 1-6.

SMITH, K.U., SMITH, M.F. (1966) *Cybernetic principles of learning and educational design,* New York, Holt Rinehart and Winston.

SNOW, R.E. (1977) Individual differences and instructional theory, *Educational Researcher,* Nov.1977.

SNYDER, B. (1971) *The hidden curriculum,* New York, Knoff, M.I.T.

SPÄTH, H. (1977) *Cluster-Analyse-Algorithmus,* München.

STAKE, R.E., EASLEY, J.A. (1978) *Case studies in science education,* A project for the National Science Foundation conducted by CIRCE and CCC, 270 Education Building, University of Illinois at Urbana-Champaign, U.S.A.

STEINER, H.G. (1977) *Comments on Karl Frey's paper 'Methodology and main areas of research in science education'* in Frey, K. et al. (Eds.) (1977), *Research in science education in Europe,* Amsterdam, Swetz and Zeitlinger.

STEWART, J.H. (1978) *Assessing cognitive structure: cautions and suggestions,* Paper presented at National Association for Research in Science Teaching Annual Meeting, Toronto, Canada.

STEWART, J., VAN KIRK, J., ROWELL, R. (1979) Concept maps: a tool for use in biology teaching, *The American Biology Teacher,* 41(3), 171-175.

STRAUSS, S. (1977) *Educational implications of U-shaped behavioural growth,* A position paper for the Ford Foundation, Tel Aviv University, School of Education.

STUBBS, M. (1975) Teaching and talking: a sociolinguistic approach to classroom interaction in Chanon, G., Delamont, S. (Eds.), *Frontiers of classroom research,* Slough, N.F.E.R.

SUAN, M.Z. (1976) *Evaluation of A.S.E.P: a case study approach,* M.Ed. thesis, Melbourne, Monash University.

SUCHMAN, J.R. (1964) The Illinois studies in inquiry training, *Journal of Research in Science Teaching,* 2, 230-232.

SUPPES, P. (1966) Mathematical concept formation in children, *American Psychologist,* 21, 139-150.

TEN VOORDE, H.H. (1977) *Verwoorden en verstaan* (Verbalizing and understanding), Staatsutgeverij ('s-Gravenhage).

THOM, R. (1974) *Modèles mathématiques de la morphogenèse,* Paris, Union Générale d'Editions.

THOMAS, E.L., ROBINSON, H.A. (1972) *Improved reading in every class: a sourcebook for teachers,* Boston, Allyn and Bacon.

THORSLAND, M.N., NOVAK, J.D. (1974) The identification and significance of intuitive and analytic problem solving approaches among college physics students, *Science Education,* 58(2), 245-265.

TIBERGHIEN, A., GUESNE, E., DELACÔTE, G. (1978) Méthodes et résultats concernant l'analyse des conceptions des élèves dans différents domaines de la physique. Deux examples: les notions de chaleur et de lumière, *Revue Française de Pédagogie*, 45.

TIBERGHIEN, A., DELACÔTE, G. (1978) Résultats préliminaires sur la conception de la chaleur in Delacôte, G. (Ed.), *Physics teaching in schools*, London, Taylor and Francis. (Proceedings of the 5th Seminary of G.I.R.E.P., Montpellier, Sept. 1976.)

TIBERGHIEN, A. *Compte-rendu d'un apprentissage sur la chaleur à des élèves de 5e*, to be published.

TISHER, R.P. (1971) A Piagetian questionnaire applied to pupils in a secondary school, *Child Development*, 42, 1633-1636.

TÖRNEBOHM, H. (1976) Inquiring systems and paradigms, *Boston Studies in Philosophy of Science*, 39, Dordrecht-Holland.

TÖRNEBOHM, H. (1978) Vetenskapskritik (Science Criticism), *Reports from the department of theory of science and research*, University of Göteborg, No.102.

TÖRNEBOHM, H. (1978) Paradigmkritik (Paradigm Criticism), *Reports from the department of theory of science and research*, University of Göteborg, No.107.

TOULMIN, S. (1972)*The collective use and evolution of concepts, Human understanding, Vol.1*, Princeton, Princeton University Press.

TRABASSO, T. (1977) The role of memory as a system in making transitive inferences in Kail, R.V., Hagen, J.W. (Eds.), *Perspectives on the development of memory and cognition*, Hillsdale, N.J., Erlbaum.

TUDDENHAM, R. (1970) *On intelligence* in Dockrell, W.B. (1970), The Toronto Symposium on Intelligence, 1969, London, Methuen.

TULKIN, S.R., KONNER, M.J. (1973) Alternative concepts of intellectual functioning, *Human Development*, 16, 33-52.

TURNER, G.J. (1972) *Social class and children's language of control at age 5 and age 7,*in Bernstein, B. (Ed.) (1972), *Class, codes and control, Vol.2*, London, Routledge and Kegan Paul.

UZGIRIS, I.C. (1964) Situational generality of conservation, *Child Development*, 35(3), 831-841.

VANDENBERG, D. (1974) Phenomenology and educational research in Denton, D.E. (Ed.), *Existentialism and phenomenology in education*, Teachers College Press, Columbia University.

VEGTING, P. (1977) Luisteren naar leerlingen, I - Verdampen, II - Kracht, V - Warmte, *Faraday*, 46(1), 1-3; (3), 68-70.

VERGNAUD, G. et al. (1978) Acquisitions des 'structures multiplicatives' dans le premier cycle du second degré. Compte-rendu de fin d'étude de la recherche DGRST No.76-7-1093, Processus et Conditions de Travail de l'Elève.

VIENNOT, L. (1977) *Le raisonnement spontané en dynamique élémentaire*, Thesis, University of Paris VII.

VIENNOT, L. (1979) Spontaneous reasoning in elementary dynamics, *European Journal of Science Education*, 1(2), 205-221.

VOORDE, H.H. ten (1977) *Verwoorden en verstaan* I/II 's-Gravenhage, SVO, Staatsuitgeverij.

VYGOTSKY, L.S. (1962) *Thought and language*, Cambridge Mass., MIT PRESS.

WAERN, Y. (1972) Structure in similarity matrices, *Scandinavian Journal of Psychology*, 13, 5-16.

WAIN, G.T., WOODROW, D. (1979) Mathematics teacher education project (Section on children's thinking), Glasgow, Blackie.

WARD, J.E. (1973) *An investigation into the effect of task definition on observational attainment in Ordinary level chemistry*, M.Sc. Thesis, Norwich, University of East Anglia.

WARD, J.H. (1963) Hierarchical grouping to optimise an objective junction, *Journal of the American Statistical Association*, 58, 236.

WASON, P.C., JOHNSON-LAIRD, P.N. (1972) *Psychology of reasoning: structure and content*, London, Batsford.

WASON, P.C. (1977) The theory of formal operations: a critique in Geber, B.A. (Ed.), *Piaget and knowing*, Routledge & Kegan Paul.

WATSON, F.R. (1974) The pupil's thinking in Sutton, C.R., Haysom, J.T. (Eds.), *The art of the science teacher*, McGraw Hill.

WATSON, F.R. (1979) *Listening in to problem solving*, Proceedings of 3rd I.G.P.M.E. Conference, Warwick 1979.

WEBB, R.A. (1974) Concrete and formal operations in very bright 6 to 11 year-olds, *Human Development*, 17, 292-300.

WEINER, B., FRIEZE, I., KULKA, A., REED, L., REST, S., ROSENBAUM, R.M. (1971), *Perceiving the causes of success and failure*, New York, General Learning Press.

WEINER, B., HECKHAUSEN, H., MEYER, W.-U., COOK, R.E. (1972) Causal ascriptions and achievement behaviour: a conceptual analysis of efforts and reanalysis of locus of control, *Journal of Personality and Social Psychology*, 21, 239-248.

WEST, L.H.T., FENSHAM, P.J. (1974) Prior knowledge and the learning of science: a review of Ausubel's theory of this process, *Studies in Science Education*, 1, 61-81.

WEST, L.H.T., FENSHAM, P.J. (1976) Prior knowledge or advance organizers as effective variables in chemical learning, *Journal of Research in Science Teaching*, 13, 297-306.

WEST, L.H.T., KELLETT, N.C. (1979) *The meaningful learning of intellectual skills*. To be published.

WHORF, B.L. (1964) *Language thought and reality*, Cambridge, Mass., MIT Press.

WILKINS, M.C. (1928) The effect of changed material on ability to do formal syllogistic reasoning, *Archives of Psychology*, No.102.

WINER, B.J. (1971) *Statistical principles in experimental design*, 2nd ed., New York, McGraw-Hill.

WINKELMANN, W. (1974) Factorial analysis of children's conservation task performance, *Child Development*, 45, 843-848.

WINKELMANN, W. (1975) Die Invarianz der Substanz und der Zahl im kindlichen Denken II, Faktorenanalyse der Reaktionen auf verschiedene Invarianzaufgaben. (Conservation of substance and number in children's thinking II. Factor analysis of responses in different conservation situations.) in Modgil, S.,Modgil,C.(Eds.) (1976), *Piagetian research: compilation and commentary, Vol.4.*, Slough, Berks., N.F.E.R.

WINKELMANN, W. (1976a) Developmental test battery of cognitive operations. Piaget-oriented tests for children aged about 5 to 8 in Modgil, S., Modgil, C. (Eds.), *Piagetian Research, Vol.4*, Slough, Berks., N.F.E.R.

WINKELMANN, W. (1976b) Conservation of substance and number in children's thinking. I. Responses of five-to-eight year-old children in tests based on drawings and tests based on concrete materials in Modgil, S., Modgil, C. (Eds.), *Piagetian Research, Vol.4*, Slough, Berks., N.F.E.R.

WINKELMANN, W. (1976c) Conservation of substance and number in children's thinking. II. Factor analysis of responses in different conservation situations in Modgil, S., Modgil, C. (Eds.), *Piagetian Research, Vol.4*, Slough, Berks., N.F.E.R.

473

WITKIN, H.A., GOODENOUGH, D.R., KARP, S.A. (1967) Stability of cognitive style from childhood to young adulthood, *Journal of Personality and Social Psychology, 7*, 291-300.

WITKIN, H.A., OLTMAN, P.K., RASKIN, E., KARP, S.A. (1971) *A Manual for the embedded figures test,* Palo Alto, Consulting Psychologists Press.

WITKIN, H.A., DYK, R.B., FATERSON, H.F., GOODENOUGH, D.R., KARP, S.A. (1974), *Psychological differentiation,* Potomac, Maryland, Erlbaum.

WITKIN, H.A., MOORE, C.A., GOODENOUGH, D.R., COX, P.W. (1977) Field dependent and field independent cognitive styles and their educational implications, *Review of Educational Research, 47*, 1.

WITTGENSTEIN, L. (1973) *Philosophical investigations,* 2nd ed. Oxford, Blackwell.

WOLLMAN, W. (1977) Controlling variables: assessing levels of understanding, *Science Education, 61*(3), 371-383.

474

Cognitive Development Research in Developing Countries

REPORTER: PATRICK A. WHITTLE

A meeting was convened during the seminar to enable 24 members from, or associated with, research and teacher education in developing countries to discuss the particular problems relating to studies in science and mathematical cognitive development in the context of non-western cultures. In Africa, work of this nature was mentioned from Cameroon, Ghana, Kenya, Lesotho, Nigeria, Sierra Leone, South Africa, Swaziland and Zimbabwe. South-East Asia included Indonesia, Malaysia, the Philippines, Singapore and Thailand, while further work was described in Israel, Lebanon and the Caribbean, as well as cross-cultural studies in Britain.

A wide range of studies was reported, which included empirical investigations with Piagetian-based tasks by individual interview, small and large group testing, mainly at elementary school level, but several at the secondary school level, related to curriculum development goals. As well as cultural variations, the effect of mother-tongue and second-language upon response are under investigation, and other environmental factors that affect assimilation of scientific concepts. Of particular interest was the work of the Regional Centre for Science and Mathematics Education in Malaysia, which facilitates research conducted by local teachers in the mother-tongue; from information about cognitive growth and development new school science and mathematics curricula are being developed. Other studies mentioned included cognitive development of culturally deprived groups, and cross-cultural studies of animism. Doubt was expressed whether or not any culture-free cognitive test could be devised.

A new study of an overview of science and mathematics curricular materials which have been developed during the past twenty years was announced. An annotated bibliography of such materials, with respect to their cultural setting, is being compiled by Bryan Wilson and a request made for such materials from developing countries. They should be sent to: Cultural Contexts of Science and Mathematics Education Project, Centre for Studies in Science Education, University of Leeds, Leeds, LS2 9JT.

Discussion then centred upon the problems of exchange of information between researchers in the third world (sometimes even within countries, or regions) and the absence of appropriate journals, particularly in Africa, where it had been hoped that a research journal would have been developed as a consequence of the 1974 UNESCO conference on Conceptual Development. While S.E.P.A.* seemed an appropriate vehicle for such a journal, Nairobi was proposed as the most suitable centre for its production and distribution. Sources of funds for establishing and maintaining such a journal will be a problem, but some assistance may be available from international organisations. It was agreed as an interim measure to establish a 'Third World Cognitive Development Newsletter' which will be distributed among members of the present group, annually in March. Contributions will be requested by the first editor, Mr. Elwyn Thomas, University of London Institute of Education, Bedford Way, London W.C.1.

Opportunities for contact with other workers in the same field was another felt need, through regional seminars, or possibly training workshops. The universities of Leeds and Surrey were proposed as possible venues for the latter.

It was agreed that in addition to the process of interchanging research news, there is a separate problem of diffusion of information to, and among, the teachers in each country, to promote more effective teaching in science and mathematics. Academics have the responsibility of passing on appropriate advice through articles in teachers bulletins, but involvement of the teachers themselves at all stages of research, from identification of problems, to data collection, is also possible. It was pointed out that application of cognitive development research findings should begin during initial teacher education programmes and that teachers at the start of their careers should be made aware of the importance of on-going studies in this field.

In conclusion, it was agreed that cognitive development research has much to offer to the improvement of science and mathematics teaching and learning in the developing world, provided it is not approached from a western model, nor with over-sophisticated materials. The multiplier effect of circulating information will be of assistance to the small number of workers in the field, but the exercise will be ineffective unless the mathematics and science teachers are sufficiently involved and informed to implement the findings.

---

*Science Education Project in Africa

List of Participants

Acuña-Gavino, J., Dr.,
  Science Education Centre, Pardo de Tavera, Vidal Town Hall,
  University of the Philippines,
  Diliman, Quezon City, Philippines

Adey, P., Dr.,
  Chelsea College Centre for Science Education,
  90 Lillie Road,
  London S.W.6., United Kingdom

Andelfinger, B., Dr.,
  Bezirksseminar für das Lehramt am Gymnasium Mönchengladbach,
  Karl-Barthold-Weg,
  4050 Mönchengladbach, Federal Republic of Germany

Andersson, B., Dr.,
  University of Göteborg, Department of Educational Research,
  Ekna-Project, Fack,
  S-43120 Mölndal, Sweden

Archenhold, W.F.,
  School of Education,
  University of Leeds,
  Leeds, LS2 9JT, United Kingdom

Bell, A.W., Dr.,
  The Shell Centre for Mathematical Education,
  University of Nottingham, University Park,
  Nottingham, NG7 2RD, United Kingdom

Black, P.J., Professor,
  Centre for Science Education,
  Chelsea College,
  Bridges Place,
  London, SW6 4HR, United Kingdom

Brookes, W.M.,
  Department of Education,
  University of Southampton,
  Southampton, SO9 5NH, United Kingdom

477

Brown, M.L., Mrs.,
  Chelsea College,
  University of London,
  Bridges Place,
  London, SW6 4HR, United Kingdom

Brown, S.A., Dr.,
  Department of Education,
  University of Stirling,
  Stirling, FK9 4LA, United Kingdom

Carter, D.C.,
  School of Education,
  University of Leeds,
  Leeds, LS2 9JT, United Kingdom

Cochaud, G.A.M.,
  Department of Educational Studies,
  University of Oxford,
  15 Norham Gardens,
  Oxford, United Kingdom

Davies, J.K.,
  Department of Education,
  University of Stirling,
  Stirling, FK9 4LA, United Kingdom

Delacôte, G., Professor,
  Laboratoire interuniversitaire de recherche sur l'enseignement
  des sciences physiques et de la technologie,
  Université Paris VII,
  2 place Jussieu,
  75221 Paris CEDEX 05, France

Derrick, J.,
  School of Mathematics,
  University of Leeds,
  Leeds, LS2 9JT, United Kingdom

Driver, R., Dr.,
  School of Education,
  University of Leeds,
  Leeds, LS2 9JT, United Kingdom

Gilbert, J.K., Dr.,
  Institute for Educational Technology,
  University of Surrey,
  Guildford, Surrey, United Kingdom

Gosden, M.S., Dr.,
    School of Education,
    University of Leeds,
    Leeds, LS2 9JT, United Kingdom

Griffiths, K., Dr.,
    Westhill College of Education,
    Selly Oak,
    Birmingham, 29, United Kingdom

Guesne, E., Mrs.,
    Laboratoire interuniversitaire de recherche sur l'enseignement
    des sciences physiques et de la technologie,
    Université Paris VII,
    2 place Jussieu,
    75221 Paris CEDEX 05, France

Haggis, S.M., Mrs.,
    Division of Science, Technical and Vocational Education,
    UNESCO,
    7 place de Fontenoy,
    75700 Paris, France

Hamlyn, D.R., Ms.,
    Science Education Project, Centre for Continuing Education,
    University of the Witwatersrand,
    1 Jan Smuts Avenue,
    Johannesburg, South Africa 2001

Harlen, W., Dr.,
    Centre for Science Education,
    Chelsea College,
    University of London,
    Pulton Place,
    London, SW6 5PR, United Kingdom

Hart, K., Dr.,
    Chelsea College, C.S.M.S.,
    88-90 Lillie Road,
    London S.W.6., United Kingdom

Hartley, J.R.,
    Computer Based Learning Project,
    University of Leeds,
    Leeds, LS2 9JT, United Kingdom

Head, J.,
    Chelsea College, C.S.M.S.,
    88-90 Lillie Road,
    London S.W.6., United Kingdom

Hughes, E.R.,
    School of Education,
    University College of North Wales,
    Bangor, United Kingdom

Hull, R.A.,
    School of Education,
    University of Nottingham, University Park,
    Nottingham, NG7 2RD, United Kingdom

Jungwirth, E., Professor,
    Hebrew University of Jerusalem,
    Faculty of Agriculture,
    P.O. Box 12, Rehovot, Israel

Kamara, A.I., Dr.,
    University of Njala, PMB,
    Freetown, Sierra Leone

Kelly, P.J., Professor,
    Department of Education,
    University of Southampton,
    Southampton, S09 5NH, United Kingdom

Kempa, R., Professor,
    Department of Education,
    University of Keele,
    Keele, Staffordshire,ST5 5BG, United Kingdom

Küchemann, D.E.
    Chelsea College,
    Centre for Science Education,
    90 Lillie Road,
    London, SW6 7SR, United Kingdom

Lovell, K., Professor,
    School of Education,
    University of Leeds,
    Leeds, LS2 9JT, United Kingdom

Lowenthal, F., Professor,
    Université de l'Etat à Mons,
    Rue des Dominicains 24,
    B 7000 Mons, Belgium

Lybeck, L., Dr.,
    Institute of Education,
    University of Göteborg,
    Fack, S-431 20 Mölndal, Sweden

Maskill, R., Dr.,
School of Chemical Sciences,
University of East Anglia, University Plain,
Norwich, Norfolk, United Kingdom

McRobbie, C.J.,
Department of Science,
Mount Gravatt College of Advanced Education,
Mount Gravatt, Queensland, Australia

Novak, J. Professor,
Cornell University,
Department of Education, 103 Stone Hall,
Ithaca, New York 14853, U.S.A.

Nussbaum, J., Dr.,
Israel Science Teaching Centre,
The Hebrew University of Jerusalem,
Jerusalem, Israel

Ogborn, J.M.,
Chelsea College,
Centre for Science Education,
Bridges Place,
London, SW6 4HR, United Kingdom

Okeke, E.A.C., Dr.,
Department of Education,
University of Nigeria,
Nsukka, Nigeria

Orton, A.,
School of Education,
University of Leeds,
Leeds, LS2 9JT, United Kingdom

Otaala, B., Professor,
Kenyatta University College,
P.O. Box 43844,
Nairobi, Kenya

Pearson, R., Dr.,
Department of Science Education,
University of Cape Coast,
Cape Coast, Ghana

Reynolds, C.,
School of Education,
University of Leeds,
Leeds, LS2 9JT, United Kingdom

Russell, T.,
SEAMEO - Regional Centre for Science and Mathematics,
Glugor, Penang, Malaysia

Schaefer, G., Professor,
Institute for Science Education,
University of Kiel,
Olshausenstrasse 40-60,
D-2300 Kiel 1, Federal Republic of Germany

Schildkamp-Kundiger, E., Asst.Professor Dr.,
Universität des Saarlandes,
Erziehungswissenschaft,
66 Saarbrücken,
Fachr. 6.1, Federal Republic of Germany

Shayer, M., Dr.,
Chelsea College,
90 Lillie Road,
London, S.W.6., United Kingdom

Shipstone, D.M., Dr.,
School of Education,
University of Nottingham, University Park,
Nottingham, United Kingdom

Sjøberg, S.,
Institute of Physics,
Oslo University,
P.O. Box 1048,
Blindern, Oslo 3, Norway

Sutton, C.R., Dr.,
School of Education,
University of Leicester, University Road,
Leicester,LE1 7RH, United Kingdom

Tait, K.,
Computer Based Learning Project,
University of Leeds,
Leeds, LS2 9JT, United Kingdom

Tamir, P., Professor,
Israel Science Teaching Centre,
Hebrew University of Jerusalem,
Jerusalem, Israel

Ten Voorde, H., Dr.,
University of Amsterdam,
Van't Hoff Instituut, Nieuwe Achtergracht 166,
Amsterdam, The Netherlands

Theobald, J.H., Dr.,
    Faculty of Education,
    Monash University,
    Clayton, Victoria, Australia 3168

Thomas, E.,
    University of London Institute of Education,
    Bedford Way,
    London, W.C.1., United Kingdom

Tiberghien, A., Mrs.
    Laboratoire interuniversitaire de recherche sur l'enseignement
    des sciences physiques et de la technologie,
    Université Paris VII,
    2 place Jussieu,
    75221 Paris CEDEX 05, France

Van Aalst, H.F., Drs.,
    Physics Curriculum Development Project,
    State University of Utrecht,
    PLON, Lab.Vaste Stof,
    Princetonplein 1,
    Postbus 80,008,
    3508 TA Utrecht,
    The Netherlands

Vegting, P., Dr.,
    Department of Chemistry,
    University of Groningen,
    Nyenborgh 16 - Paddepoel, 9747 AG,
    Groningen, The Netherlands

Vergnaud, G.,
    Centre National de la Recherche Scientifique,
    École des Hautes Études en Sciences Sociales,
    Centre étude des processus cognitifs et due langage,
    54 boulevard Raspail,
    75006 Paris, France

Viennot, L., Dr.,
    Université Paris VII,
    G.P.S. Tour 23,
    2 place Jussieu,
    75221 Paris CEDEX 05, France

Wain, G.T.,
    School of Education,
    University of Leeds,
    Leeds, LS2 9JT, United Kingdom

Watson, F.R.,
 University of Keele,
 Keele, Staffordshire, ST5 5BG, United Kingdom

West, L.H.T., Dr.,
 Higher Education Advisory & Research Unit,
 Monash University,
 Clayton, Victoria, Australia 3168

Whittle, P.A.,
 Faculty of Education,
 National University of Lesotho,
 P.O. Roma 180
 Lesotho, Southern Africa

Wierstra, R.F.A., Drs.,
 Physics Curriculum Development Project,
 State University of Utrecht,
 PLON, Lab. Vaste Stof,
 Princetonplein 1,
 Postbus 80,008,
 3508 TA Utrecht, The Netherlands

Wilson, J.M.,
 College of Education,
 Hilton Place,
 Aberdeen, AB9 1FA, United Kingdom

Wood-Robinson, C.,
 School of Education,
 University of Leeds,
 Leeds, LS2 9JT, United Kingdom

Wylam, H.E.,
 Chelsea College, C.S.M.S.,
 90 Lillie Road,
 London, SW6 7SR, United Kingdom

Z'Arour, G., Dr.,
 Science & Mathematics Education Centre,
 American University of Beirut,
 Beirut, Lebanon